Pedagogy and the Shaping of Consciousness

Open Linguistics Series

Series Editor
Robin F. Fawcett, Cardiff University

The *Open Linguistics Series*, to which this book makes a significant contribution, is 'open' in two senses. First, it provides an open forum for works associated with any school of linguistics or with none. Linguistics has now emerged from a period in which many (but never all) of the most lively minds in the subject seemed to assume that transformational-generative grammar – or at least something fairly closely derived from it – would provide the main theoretical framework for linguistics for the foreseeable future. In Kuhn's terms, linguistics had appeared to some to have reached the 'paradigm' stage. Reality today is very different. More and more scholars are working to improve and expand theories that were formerly scorned for not accepting as central the particular set of concerns highlighted in the Chomskyan approach – such as Halliday's systemic theory (as exemplified in this book), Lamb's stratificational model and Pike's tagmemics – while others are developing new theories. The series is open to all approaches, then – including work in the generativist-formalist tradition.

The second sense in which the series is 'open' is that it encourages works that open out 'core' linguistics in various ways: to encompass discourse and the description of natural texts; to explore the relationship between linguistics and its neighbouring disciplines such as psychology, sociology, philosophy, artificial intelligence and cultural and literary studies; and to apply it in fields such as education and language pathology.

Relations between the fields of linguistics and artificial intelligence are covered in a sister series, Communication in Artificial Intelligence. Studies that are primarily descriptive are published in a new series, Functional Descriptions of Language.

Recent titles in this series

Pedagogy and the Shaping of Consciousness

Linguistic and Social Processes

Edited by
Frances Christie

CONTINUUM

London and New York

Continuum
Wellington House, 125 Strand, London WC2R 0BB
370 Lexington Avenue, New York, NY 10017-6503

First published by Cassell in 1999. Reprinted in paperback in 2000.

British Library Cataloguing-in-Publication Data
A catalogue record for this book is available from the British Library.

ISBN 0-304-70228-5 (hardback)
  0-8264-4747-3 (paperback)

Library of Congress Cataloging-in-Publication Data
  Pedagogy and the shaping of consciousness : linguistic and social
  processes / edited by Frances Christie.
      p. cm. — (Open linguistics series)
    Includes bibliographical references and index.
      ISBN 0-304-70228-5 (hardback) — 0-8264-4747-3 (paperback)
      1. Educational sociology. 2. Sociolinguistics. 3. Literacy —
  Social aspects. 4. Teaching — Social aspects. I. Christie,
  Frances. II. Series.
  LC191.P37   1998
  306.43—dc21
                                                      97-32854
                                                        CIP

Typeset by Textype Typesetters, Cambridge
Printed and bound in Great Britain by Bookcraft Ltd, Midsomer Norton, Avon

Contents

Contributors

Basil Bernstein is Professor Emeritus of Sociology of Education, University of London. He is the Karl Mannheim Professor of the Sociology of Education.

Frances Christie is Foundation Professor of Language and Literacy Education at the University of Melbourne. In 1991 she led a research team which produced a report to Government titled *Teaching English Literacy: A Project of National Significance on the Preservice Preparation of Teachers for Teaching English Literacy*. She has currently co-edited with J. R. Martin *Genre and Institutions: Social Processes in the Workplace and School* (Cassell, 1997).

Carmel Cloran is currently teaching in the Department of English Language and Literature at the National University of Singapore. Her research interests include context and language, language and socialization, language and cognitive development, discourse semantics, and lexis as delicate grammar. Among her recent publications are *Rhetorical Units and Decontextualisation: An Enquiry into Some Relations of Grammar, Meaning and Context*, (1994); and 'Defining and relating text segments: subject and theme in discourse' (in *On Subject and Theme: A Discourse Functional Perspective*, edited by Ruqaiya Hasan and Peter Fries, Benjamins, 1995).

Ruqaiya Hasan retired as Emeritus Professor of Linguistics in 1994 from Macquarie University, where she taught semantics, grammar, discourse and sociolinguistics, and directed a federally funded research on semantic variation. Her publications cover many of the areas of her interest, the most recent being 'The conception of context in text', in *Discourse in Society*, edited by Peter Fries and Michael Gregory (Ablex, 1995); *On Subject and Theme: From a Discourse Functional Perspective*, edited with Peter Fries (Benjamins, 1995); *Functional Descriptions: Theory in Practice*, edited with Carmel Cloran and David Butt (Benjamins, 1996); *Literacy in Society*, edited with Geoff Williams (Longman, 1996); and *Ways of Saying, Ways of Meaning: Selected Papers of Ruqaiya Hasan*, edited by Carmel Cloran, David Butt and Geoff Williams (Cassell, 1996).

J. R. Martin is currently Associate Professor of Linguistics at the University of Sydney. His research interests include systemic theory, functional grammar, discourse semantics, register, genre and critical discourse analysis, focusing on English and Tagalog, with special reference to the transdisciplinary fields of educational linguistics and social semiotics. Publications include Harcourt Brace Jovanovich's *Language: a resource for meaning* programme (co-authored with Frances Christie, Brian and Pam Gray, Mary Macken and Joan Rothery) (1990, 1992); *English Text: System and Structure* (Benjamins, 1992); *Writing Science: Literacy and Discursive Power* (with M.A.K. Halliday) (Falmer, 1993); *Working with Functional Grammar* (with C. Matthiessen and C. Painter), (Edward Arnold, 1997).

Clare Painter is currently lecturing in social semiotics at the School of English at the University of New South Wales. Her teaching and research interests are child language, systemic functional linguistics and English language and literacy education. She is the author of *Into the Mother Tongue* (Pinter 1984), *Learning the Mother Tongue* (Deakin University Press, 1985, 1990) and co-author, with J.R. Martin and C. Matthiessen of *Working with Functional Grammar* (Arnold, 1997)

David Rose has worked for many years in indigenous education and community development in various regions of Australia. He is currently teaching educational linguistics at the University of Adelaide, as well as training teachers in literacy strategies for indigenous learners, and researching the language of Australia's Western Desert from a systemic functional perspective.

William Tyler taught in high schools in Australia and Canada before taking up a lecturing position in the sociology of education in England. He returned to Australia in 1985 to the Northern Territory University in Darwin, where he is Associate Professor in Sociology and Director of the Centre for Social Research.

Robert Veel works as a lecturer in language education at the University of Sydney and as a private consultant. His research interests include the specific language demands of school disciplines and literacy education for disadvantaged students. He has published on the literacy demands of school science, eco-science and mathematics, critical literacy, and literacy issues for Aboriginal students.

Geoff Williams is Senior Lecturer in English at the University of Sydney, where he teaches courses in systemic functional linguistics and child language and literacy development. He has recently co-edited, with Ruqaiya Hasan, *Literacy in Society* (Longman, 1996).

Introduction

Frances Christie

Basil Bernstein's early work as a sociologist grew out of his experience as a teacher in London schools in the 1950s, and his profound concern for the many students of working-class background who failed in schools. He wanted to find an explanation for the apparent differences in school performance of students of different social classes. His efforts to explain why middle-class children were more successful in schools caused him to focus on aspects of language use. He thus cast about for some linguistic theories to assist him. The explanations he was to propose would lead him in time to mount a major sociological theory, addressing questions of social structure, power relations, the differential ways in which power and knowledge are distributed to various social groups, and the mechanisms by which such distribution occurs.

Bernstein's early endeavours led him to test a number of language theories, including for example, those of Goldman-Eisler on hesitation phenomena, while he also briefly considered the work of Chomsky. He was, however, much more attracted to functional linguistic theories of the kind represented by Sapir, Whorf and Firth, for example, and he was familiar with Malinowski. Bernstein's endeavours brought him into contact with Michael Halliday and his colleagues including Ruqaiya Hasan, who in the late 1950s and the early 1960s were developing their first formulations of what would in time become known as systemic functional (SF) linguistic theory. Bernstein directed the Sociological Research Unit at the University of London in the 1960s, and Halliday moved in 1963 to the same university, where he became Head of the Communication Research Centre, which was later absorbed into the Department of Linguistics, of which Halliday became the Head. Hasan was one of the group working for a time with Bernstein. Mary Douglas, Professor of Social Anthropology at the University of London, was another significant colleague, interested in and supportive of the sociology Bernstein and his colleagues were developing. By a series of happy convergences, the sociological theories Bernstein was formulating in the 1960s were brought into fruitful dialogue with the linguistic theories Halliday and his colleagues were developing.

To a linguist such as Halliday, one of the most distinctive of Bernstein's early contributions was his insistence that a theory of language must have an important role in a theory of sociology. Halliday has said of Bernstein that he was 'the first sociologist to give a place to language in his chain of explanations; and by doing so he offers an explanation of how culture is transmitted' (Halliday 1988: 6). While Bernstein was working at early formulations of his proposals to do with language and the social positionings of different social class groups, Halliday and others were pursuing a model of discourse and of social practice. This drew from the work of the linguist Firth and his notions of context of situation, as taken from Malinowski. Malinowski (1923) had suggested that language use is always a condition of the context of situation in which it is found. Halliday and his colleagues sought to find a means of explaining systematically the ways in which language changed depending on context of situation. Their early formulations of register theory (see Halliday *et al.* 1964) identified the three factors of *field of discourse* (to do with what was going on), *mode of discourse* (to do with the medium or mode of the language activity), and *style of discourse* (to do with the relations of the participants in the field of activity). All three, it was argued, accounted for changes in register. A major theoretical issue Halliday and others wanted to address was how to bring together their emerging functional interpretation of grammar on the one hand and their sense of the social, as theorized in the notion of register.

Halliday was in time to propose that we think in terms of a 'lexicogrammar'. The term was chosen to suggest that, contrary to structural theories of language, a functional theory sees no clearcut distinction between grammar on the one hand, and lexis or vocabulary on the other. The lexis represents the most delicate expression of the grammar. Choices in the grammar (the term normally used, though it is always to be understood as involving the lexis as well) lead to the production of text – any meaningful stretch of language. For the SF linguist, it is the text, not the isolated utterance or sentence, which is the fundamental unit of analysis.

Early work on the grammar led Halliday and others to begin to demonstrate systematic ways in which choices in the language system realized meanings in texts (see e.g. Halliday 1976). The notion of system was always important in the emerging account of language. A language offers sets of choices or interrelated options for making meanings, drawn from the various systems within the language, be they choices with respect to Tense, for example, Mood, Person and so on. Sets of linguistic choices, it seemed, were made in selective and non-arbitrary ways to make particular kinds of meanings. The choices tended to cluster in particular ways. These observations led in turn to the theory of three metafunctions in language – that is, three functional components of any natural language fundamentally involved in building different aspects of meaning. The theory states that the three metafunctions are 'basic to the evolution of the semantic system' of every natural language (Halliday, in Halliday and Hasan 1985: 17). The three metafunctions identified are the ideational, the interpersonal and the textual. The ideational metafunction itself embraces two metafunctions, the experiential and the logical. The experiential, having to do with the nature of the experience represented in language, is realized most fundamentally in English in the Transitivity system and associated resources for naming, such as the nominal group structure. The logical metafunction, having to do with the logical relations between clauses, are realized in the different clause relationships of parataxis and hypotaxis. The interpersonal metafunction, having to do with the ways relationship is constructed, is realized in the systems of Mood, Modality and Person. The textual metafunction, having to do with the ways the discourse is put together as a message, is realized in the systems of Theme and Information, as well as the various resources for building cohesion.

With the development of the theory of the metafunctions, Halliday and others had begun to find answers to the question alluded to above of how to explain in functional terms the relationship of choices made in the linguistic system and the context of situation in which language was used. Choices with respect to the three metafunctions were said to be realized simultaneously, and together they were said to parallel the three aspects of register in a context of situation.

While Halliday, Hasan and their colleagues were working on early formulations of SF theory, Bernstein was pursuing his research. Focusing on what he termed 'modes of language use', he early proposed (e.g. Bernstein 1971) a distinction between a 'public' language, associated with lower-working-class children, and 'formal' language, which was associated with middle-class children. Public language, he argued, arose out of communalized social relationships where much could be taken for granted, and as a consequence meanings were implicit, and the meanings tended to narrative. In such a language, there was a reduced pressure to elaborate explanations and principles, or to individualize the verbalization of feeling. 'Formal' language involved, among other things, uses of language which encouraged individual responses and expression of feelings, as well as elaboration of explanations. Bernstein argued that working-class families tended to use only public language, while middle-class families used both public and formal language. Each type of language, once internalized, built particular perceptions of experience and predisposed children to interact with others in particular ways. Schooling, it was suggested, especially rewarded the formal language, and so middle-class children tended to perform better in school than working-class children.

By the mid-1960s the social class analysis was refined and the forms of language use received different modalities of realization, depending upon the orientation of the family to 'positional' or 'personal' types. This class specialization of communication was mediated through types of families. The latter was a point often lost on the critics.

A finer formulation of the notions of different language uses led to the notion of the restricted and elaborated codes. A code was a 'regulative principle which controlled the form of the linguistic realisation' of speakers in different socializing contexts. (Bernstein 1971: 15) A later formulation of code developed in the late 1970s and 1980s and quoted by

Bernstein (1981), read,

> a code is a regulative principle, tacitly acquired, which selects and integrates relevant meanings, forms of realisations, and evoking contexts.

With the formulation of the theory of the two codes, Bernstein had already moved on from his concerns with educational failure (though he has never lost interest in this issue) to developing a larger theory to do with the question of cultural transmission. As early as 1971 (124), Bernstein wrote:

> As the child learns his speech or, in the terms used here, learns specific codes which regulate his verbal acts, he learns the requirements of the social structure.

About the relative values of the two codes Bernstein (1971: 135) was always clear:

> Clearly one code is not better than another; each possesses its own aesthetic, its own possibilities. Society, however, may place different values on the orders of experience elicited, maintained and progressively strengthened through the different coding systems.

Despite the very careful and measured observations Bernstein made about the two codes, he was frequently misrepresented by other writers, some of whom included linguists (e.g. Stubbs 1976, Labov 1972 *passim*)[1], while others were educational theorists (e.g. Rosen 1973). Such writers only served to cloud and confuse the issues, rather than enlighten. In more recent years, other writers have offered more thoughtful and intelligent assessments of Bernstein's work. (See, for example, Atkinson 1985 and the collection of papers edited by Sadovnik 1995.)

An important paper, demonstrating how useful could be the dialogue between Bernstein's sociology and SF theory, was that by Hasan (1973) discussing 'Code, register and social dialect'. Dialects represented varieties in language depending on the language community. A dialect could reflect geographical location, social class, or even temporal location, and it was at best a descriptive category. A register, much as outlined above, was distinguished according to use. A code, unlike either dialects or registers, was described in terms of 'its semantic properties' (Hasan 1973: 258). Hasan noted in this connecton that while Bernstein's early formulations of public and formal language had used notions of syntax, lexis and sometimes phonology, he had in fact always been interested not in such linguistic features, but rather in characterizing 'the varieties of code by reference to the differences at the level of meaning' (290–1).

Hasan's discussion threw light on an important problem that Bernstein's work had been addressing for some time: how to explain the fact that people draw upon the one grammar, yet exploit its meaning potential in very different ways. Of Bernstein's contribution in this regard, Halliday (1993: 14) wrote:

> What Bernstein understood was that, given a single grammar, the potential of that grammar can be taken up in consistently different ways by different groups of people, selecting with different probabilities in the same system and so in effect construing different forms of social relationships and different models of experience.

In Bernstein's theory, class relations are fundamental to the regulation of the distribution of power. Certain principles apply by which such power is generated, reproduced and legitimated, so that relationships within and between social groups are regulated, and forms of consciousness are produced. The notion of codes is quite crucial to the theory, for codes are directly involved in the formation of consciousness. For Bernstein, principles of order and their potential disorder are intrinsic to code acquisition. Thus reproduction and change are both possibilities of code theory.

Code theory was used to illuminate how the specializations of pedagogic communication acted selectively on the processes of acquisition, and Bernstein went on to pursue these matters in the late 1970s and the 1980s. Code theory provided a conceptual language which could generate a range of modalities of pedagogic communication, and so different forms of the institutionalizing of elaborated codes. Thus the realizations of elaborated codes were regulated by their classification and framing values (e.g. Bernstein 1975, 1990, 1996 for discussions). It was then possible to analyse those modalities which led to selective acquisition. A crucial paper, entitled 'Code modalities and the process of reproduction: a model' (Bernstein 1981) formalized the early work on transmission, acquisition and their vicissitudes, and opened the way to developing a theory towards the explanation and description of the production of discourse (see Chapter 4 and Chapter 10 of this volume). The analysis of this involved development of the notion of a pedagogic device which provided the 'intrinsic grammar' controlling the operation of a pedagogic discourse. The production of pedagogic discourses according to Bernstein, was regulated by three hierachically related rules: distributive, recontextualizing, and evaluative (see Chapter 4 and Chapter 6). Briefly, the recontextualizing rule or principle was responsible for what discourses were delocated from their original site of enactment, relocated, refocused and related to other delocations, in order to form a particular pedagogic discourse. Bernstein distinguished two fields which regulated the process of recontextualizing: an Official Field controlled and constituted by the state, and a Pedogogic Field, consisting of members and positions drawn from agencies of education, together with specialized journals and media, and private funding agencies.

While Bernstein was addressing questions of pedagogic relations and pedagogic discourse in the 1970s and 1980s, SF theory was also developing. Halliday's account of the functional grammar appeared in 1985, and this was to some extent revised in the edition that appeared in 1994. Martin produced his *English Text: System and Structure* in 1992, a work that was intended to complement from a discourse perspective the account of the functional grammar Halliday had provided. Matthiessen produced his *Lexicogrammatical Cartography: English Systems* in 1995. The latter discussion provides the systemic account which Halliday had left out of his functional discussion of the grammar. Other versions of SF grammar have been provided, including for example that of Fawcett and his colleagues at the University of Wales, Cardiff (Fawcett 1980). Various formulations of register theory also appeared (e.g. Gregory and Carroll 1978, Benson and Greaves 1973, Halliday and Hasan 1985). Martin (1992) and his colleagues developed an associated model of register and genre, whose effect is to provide a rather different account of register from that of Halliday and Hasan (1985). (See Hasan 1995 for a critique of Martin's model.)

While the work of developing accounts of the functional grammar was proceeding, Hasan undertook her major study of mother–child interactions. In a study of the talk between mothers and their three- and four-year-old children, Hasan was able to show systematic evidence of semantic variation in the ways mothers talked to their children. Two factors, she has shown, are involved: the sex of the child and the social class of the family (see Hasan 1989, 1991, 1992). The work Hasan and her colleagues (see Chapter 2 and Chapter 4) have done on semantic variation provides powerful support for Bernstein's formulations with respect to coding orientations.

In his introduction to *The Handbook of Sociolinguistics*, Coulmas (1997: 5) has noted how rarely social theories have usefully brought together insights from sociology and linguistic studies, though he identifes Bernstein, Cicourel and Grimshaw as theorists who have used 'actual speech data' to develop their social theories. Coulmas suggests there is an important need to bring together sociological and linguistic theories in order to extend and enhance the body of social theory generally.

It is in the latter sense that this book aims to make a contribution. Specifically it aims to bring together a range of papers using SF linguistic theory and Bernstein's sociology. The dialogue between the two traditions that commenced in the late 1950s and 1960s is thus renewed. Hasan's paper makes a fitting opening contribution by addressing the question of how the linguistic and the sociological can engage in meta-dialogue. She draws a distinction between theories that are endotropic, that is centred on their object of study, and exotropic theories, which are not confined to the bounds of their own area of study, but which rather engage with their 'central problematic in a context'. Bernstein's theory, she argues, is exotropic, and she goes on to illustrate the point by considering the ways his theory of code and the concept of language in SF linguistic theory are 'highly compatible'.

Subsequent papers by Cloran, Painter and Williams address questions of the early language experience of young children, the kinds of meaning orientations that are established in their early years, and the predispositions for living and for school learning that are established. Martin reports on work done with Rothery and others on the development of a pedagogical theory which draws both on Bernstein's theories with respect to pedagogic practice, and on theories of genre and register, developed with use of the SF grammar. Taking Bernstein's work in particular on the notion of the pedagogic device and its associated discourse, Christie seeks to demonstrate both how the pedagogic discourse operates in secondary school English and how the pedagogic subject position is constructed in this discourse. Veel draws upon Bernstein's theories and SF theory to address issues of how mathematical knowledge is constructed and transmitted. Linguistic and sociological theories alike have made few inroads into discussions of mathematics education, and Veel seeks to demonstrate how the two sets of theory can make a useful contribution. Rose, drawing on the experience of dealing with the education of Australian Aboriginal children, opens up broader questions to do with the educational opportunities of underprivileged children more generally. He uses a recent discussion of Bernstein (1996: 54–81) in which he considers the use of 'competence' and 'performance' models in social theorizing, and their pedagogical consequences.

In contrast to the linguistic deliberations of the earlier chapters, Bernstein and Tyler take the discussions in different, if essentially related directions. Bernstein's chapter is concerned with the politics of the Official Recontextualizing Field referred to above, which as we have noted, is itself part of the larger theoretical model he has developed over the years, deriving from his original work on code theory. In Chapter 9 Bernstein constructs a model showing the oppositions among the recontexualizing positions in this field or arena. He shows that Official Pedagogic Discourse arises out of a struggle for dominance among those positions. Bernstein sees this struggle for the production of pedagogic discourse as a means whereby the state can create pedagogic identities whose motivations, aspirations, values and practices are in accordance with the state's management of contemporary economic and cultural change. Tyler, enjoying the last word in Chapter 10, engages with Bernstein's model from a postmodern perspective.

I am grateful to all the contributors to this volume for the care and thoroughness with which they put their chapters together. In particular I am grateful to Basil Bernstein for the support and encouragement he gave to the whole enterprise.

Note

1 It is notable that Labov's observations on Bernstein, while certainly critical, amounted to no more than passing references in his book. No real engagement with Bernstein's work was provided. Yet Labov was afterwards often credited with

mounting a major critique of Bernstein. The evidence for this is actually very hard to find!

References

Atkinson, P. (1985) *Language, Structure and Reproduction: An Introduction to the Sociology of Basil Bernstein.* London: Methuen.
Benson, J.D. and Greaves, W.S. (1973) *The Language People Really Use.* Agincourt: Book Society of Canada.
Bernstein, B. (1971) *Class, Codes and Control. Vol. 1. Theoretical Studies towards a Sociology of Language.* London: Routledge and Kegan Paul.
Bernstein, B. (ed.) (1973) *Class, Codes and Control. Vol. 2. Applied Studies towards a Sociology of Language.* London: Routledge and Kegan Paul.
Bernstein, B. (1975) *Class, Codes and Control. Vol. 3. Towards a Theory of Educational Transmission.* London: Routledge and Kegan Paul.
Bernstein, B. (1981) 'Code modalities and the process of reproduction: a model', *Language and Society,* 10, 327–63.
Bernstein, B. (1990) *Class, Codes and Control. Vol. 4. The Structuring of Pedagogic Discourse.* London: Routledge.
Bernstein, B. (1996) *Pedagogy, Symbolic Control and Identity: Theory, Research, Critique.* London: Taylor and Francis.
Coulmas, F. (1997) (ed.) *The Handbook of Sociolinguistics.* Oxford: Blackwell.
Fawcett, R. (1980) *Cognitive Linguistics and Social Interaction.* Heidelberg: Julius Groos.
Gregory, M. and Caroll, S. (1978) *Language and Situation: Language Varieties and their Social Contexts.* London: Routledge and Kegan Paul.
Halliday, M.A.K. (1976) *Halliday: System and Function in Language.* (ed. G.R Kress) London: Oxford University Press.
Halliday. M.A.K. (1988) 'Language and socialisation: home and school'. In L. Gerot, J. Oldenburg and T. Van Leeuwen (eds), *Language and Socialisation: Home and School.* Proceedings of the Working Conference on Language in Education, Macquarie University, Sydney, 17–21 November 1986, 1–14.
Halliday, M.A.K. (1993) 'New ways of meaning: a challenge to applied linguistics'. In M.A.K. Halliday, *Language in a Changing World.* Occasional Paper 13. Applied Linguistics Association of Australia, 1–41. (This paper was originally given at the opening session of the Ninth World Congress of Applied Linguistics, Thessaloniki, Greece, April 1990.)
Halliday, M.A.K. (1994) *Introduction to Functional Grammar* (2nd edn). London: Arnold.
Halliday, M.A.K. and Hasan, R. (1985) *Language, Context and Text: Aspects of Language in a Social-Semiotic Perspective.* Geelong: Deakin University Press.
Halliday, M.A.K., McIntosh, A. and Strevens, P. (1964) *The Linguistic Sciences and Language Teaching.* London: Longman.
Hasan, R. (1973) 'Code, register and social dialect'. In B. Bernstein (ed.), *Class, Codes and Control. Vol. 2. Applied Studies towards a Sociology of Language.* Routledge and Kegan Paul, London, 253–92.
Hasan, R. (1989) 'Semantic variation and sociolinguistics', *Australian Journal of Linguistics,* 9,(2), 221–75.
Hasan R. (1991) 'Questions as a mode of learning in everday talk'. In Thao Le and M. McCausland (eds), *Language Education: Interaction and Development.*

Proceedings of the International Conference, Vietnam. University of Tasmania, Launceston, 70–119.

Hasan, R. (1992) 'Meaning in sociolinguistic theory'. In K. Bolton and H. Kwok (eds), *Sociolinguistics Today: International Perspectives*. London: Routledge.

Hasan, R. (1995) 'The conception of context in text'. In P. Fries and M. Gregory (eds), *Discourse in Society: Systemic Functional Perspectives*. Norwood, NJ: Ablex, 183–283.

Labov, W. (1972) *Language in the Inner City: Studies in the Black English Vernacular*. Oxford: Blackwell.

Malinowski, B. (1923) 'The problem of meaning in primitive languages'. Supplement 1, in C.K. Ogden and I.A. Richards (eds), *The Meaning of Meaning*. London: Kegan Paul, 296–336.

Martin, J.R. (1992) *English Text: System and Structure*. Benjamins. Amsterdam:

Matthiessen, C. (1995) *Lexicogrammatical Cartography: English Systems*. Tokyo: International Language Sciences Publishers.

Rosen, H. (1973) *Language and Class: A Critical Look at the Theories of Basil Bernstein*. Bristol: Falling Wall Press.

Sadovnik, A. (ed.) (1995) *Knowledge and Pedagogy. The Sociology of Basil Bernstein*. Norwood NJ: Ablex.

Stubbs, M. (1976) *Language, Schools and Classrooms*. London: Methuen.

1   Society, language and the mind: the meta-dialogism of Basil Bernstein's theory[1]

Ruqaiya Hasan

Introduction

How right was Hjelmslev to point to the invisibility of language! One is surrounded in life by language games of one kind or another, any one of which is capable of exciting a multitude of questions but in actual practice they hardly get asked seriously. Take for example one such simple game in my trade of linguistics, that of plucking from thin air any number of imaginary examples of saying. It is amazing how many questions can arise from reflection on it. To begin with: if what language does is to correspond to reality, as common wisdom has it, then what sort of reality is it to which language corresponds in such sayings? What are the words and vocables of our language to the world we live in and to the worlds we imagine? Why can we use language to construe imaginary situations and how do these relate to the real ones – questions I explored early in my apprenticeship (Hasan 1964), little suspecting the depths of their complexity (Hasan 1985, 1995a). Then again, if the imaginable and the sayable hold to each other so closely, one has to ask: what kind of resource is language (Hasan 1984) that it can match the flights of human imagination? To do so successfully, its potential must be infinite, which in turn raises another question: if speakers have control over this inexhaustible potential – if they can say anything they like, whenever they like – on what basis do they decide to say one thing rather than another on specific occasions? The practice of producing imaginary examples is in agreement with the belief that speakers are free to say *anything* – and by the same token, *nothing*: after all, we know that unlike animal communication, human use of language is not reflex action. But while granting speakers such freedom of choice in speech shows due respect for their autonomy – for their power as unique individuals to engage dynamically in unpredictable linguistic acts – it is nonetheless a view challenged by the experience of real language use in everyday life. For in real life, more often than not, our sayings merge unremarked into the living of life: they do not draw attention to themselves, simply because, conforming largely to our expectations, they fail to surprise – which is surely one of the prime causes for the invisibility of language. So we need to ask how these shared expectations come about?

Who are the sharers, what is the extent of their sharing? How do we specify the limits of our expectations about the sayable, especially when hardly any use of language is identical *word for word* to any other? Then, apart from these questions which arise simply from the practice of giving imaginary examples, there are the examples themselves, most of which in the earlier days of linguistics invoked the names of John and Mary, names whose popularity has declined only recently by the arrival of (corporate) corpora. Back in the exciting 1960s, though, one met John and Mary on a daily basis, both perpetually engaged in some process or other. So John was in London; or Mary in trouble; they ran, and they laughed; they broke the window; opened the door; kissed and killed. And yet, despite this frenetic engagement in so many processes, surprisingly they had no *being*, such as, for example the imaginary Mr Pickwick has or even Mr Percival, the pelican, in Colin Thiele's *Storm Boy*. Could it be that if *almost anything* can be ascribed to a category, if a category has total freedom in being, saying and doing, then paradoxically such enjoyment of unhampered freedom would dissolve the category itself, deny it identity? Are categories of human agents identified by the nature of their practices, including discursive ones? If so, what are the principles for the distribution of classes of discursive practices to categories of social agents? What has language to do with this distribution, and what has such distribution to do with the nature of language?

I am sure that at least some of these questions must have engaged some linguists in the early 1960s, but I must admit in honesty that for my part I did not enter the field of linguistics burning with a desire to pursue them: much worse, like most other speakers, I was in fact oblivious of most. It was my good fortune and my privilege to be present in London during the mid to late 1960s when the dialogue took place between Basil Bernstein's Sociolinguistic Research Unit and Michael Halliday's Communication Research Centre.[2] Thanks to the sociological and linguistic insights provided by these seminal scholars, the nature of language – its potential and its power – began to be relatively more visible to me; questions began to take shape, perhaps got better defined over the years. A general problem fascinated me as I witnessed the meta-dialogue between the disciplines of sociology and linguistics: What does it take for theories to engage in dialogue? Could any linguistic theory dialogue with Bernstein's sociology? Could any sociology dialogue with Halliday's linguistics? If not, how do we explain this selectivity? This paper is intended as a continuation of reflection on this general problem. I want to ask first: what makes it possible for theories to engage in meta-dialogue? I will then highlight those design features of Bernstein's theory of the social which create a space for theories of language and of mind to take a dialogic turn with his theory of the social. But obviously, the continuation of a dialogue requires more than the granting of a turn. So a second question to be raised is that of compatibility. To explore this issue, I will draw attention briefly to a compatible theory of the mind (for discussion, see Hasan 1995b, Painter 1996, Halliday 1995, Matthiessen 1998). This will prepare the ground for examining what features of the systemic functional linguistic theory enable it to *maintain* a dialogue with Bernstein's theory of the social.

So first, what is meta-dialogue?

On meta-dialogue

By meta-dialogue I do not mean to refer to the processes that characterize the iterative cycle of a theory's trial and modification, even though this typically does bring different theories in contact; this is after all the normal mode for the development of a theory still in operation, i.e. not defunct. All living knowledge changes, and theories as instances of such knowledge do so too. The use of the middle voice (Halliday 1994) here to describe this state of affairs might appear to bestow autonomy on knowledge and theory. So I add immediately that whatever the potential of existing knowledge to guide its own development as in Popper's (1979) views on World 3, the ultimate active agency for the development of knowledge is indisputably always human. This has implications: for example, the processes of a theory's trial and modification must occur in a human – i.e. social – environment, and this invariably means in the context of other (like-)discourses. It so happens, then, that in the process of the modification/development of a theory, its proponents can and often do insert into it concepts that have become familiar to them from other (like-)theories.[3] This simple conceptual adaptation, not to call it appropriation, is as necessary for the life of a theory as breathing for the human organism. In this sense, there are no *absolutely original* theories; rather, absolute originality and human practice are antithetical concepts.

The partial interpenetration of one theory by another in the above manner – call it intertextuality if you like – is, then, not what I mean by meta-dialogue. A meta-dialogue, much like an object dialogue, presupposes reciprocity[4] of a positive kind and a necessary condition for theories to engage in dialogue is a reciprocity of concern. To my mind, this does not reside in simply sharing the same problematic, otherwise all linguistic theories would be in dialogue, which is patently not the case. What I mean by this expression is that one theory's mode of addressing its problematic – the conceptual syntax (Bernstein 1996) in terms of which its theoretical goal is interpreted – complements the conceptual syntax of the other reciprocating theories.[5] I suggest that for this to come about, a theory must conceptualize its object of study as something that in Bernstein's terms is 'weakly classified' – that is to say, the central problematic is not something enclosed within a sharply defined, impermeable boundary which keeps the impurities and dangers of the outside world at bay; rather, the object of study is open to external phenomena, which though different in kind from it, still form the context for its existence and act as a resource for its subsistence. Seen thus, theories appear to approximate to two general kinds: **endotropic** and **exotropic**. Let me elaborate on these terms.

Endotropic theories are centred onto their own object of study, isolating it from all else. The phenomena they attempt to describe are viewed as if they were self-generating, self-fertilizing, self-renewing; they are, thus, autogamous with respect to their central problematic. An example would be the conceptualization of language in Chomskian linguistics, where language as a mental organ is simply a variety of biological phenomena having no connection with anything else, not even biological evolution (Pinker 1994). This type of strong classification appears to give the object of study an autonomy, which is sometimes interpreted as the source of a theory's strength. Due to its autogenetic conceptualization of its object of study, the theory can – perhaps, rather shortsightedly – congratulate itself on being free from the intellectual imperialism of other universes of experience explored by other theories, other disciplines: in the eyes of the theory, these have nothing to contribute to the understandings it seeks. However, viewing the central problematic from the perspective of its relevance to human life, this isolation is an impoverishment, not a strength. It is not surprising that the central problematic in endotropic theories appears static and accounts of its history pose problems.

By contrast, an exotropic theory is not confined within the bounds of its object of study. Rather, it is cosmoramic, typically embedding its central problematic in a context where the processes of its maintenance and change originate in its interaction with other universes of experience. From this point of view, the object of study in an exotropic theory is a component of what Lemke (1984, 1993) calls a 'dynamic open system', changing and being changed by its reciprocal engagement with the other components of the larger system. History is clearly not a problem for such theories: the genesis, fertilization and change in the object of study are accounted for to a large extent by reference to its relation with the different components of the dynamic open system. As a consequence of this constant exchange, the object of study in exotropic theories appears to be always on the move, presenting a different facet with every change in the observer's vantage point. This apparent absence of a still centre is sometimes misinterpreted as absence of order. Such theories are likely to be viewed with suspicion where there is a low tolerance for attending to a number of simultaneously operating forces which interact with each other. However, it is quite obviously this type of theory that has a greater potential for engaging in meta-dialogue. I say 'quite obviously' because the gaze of the exotropic theory is relational: its problematic is at the centre of different kinds of processes, and there thus exists a greater chance for reciprocal engagement amongst them.

It is not that the exotropic theory is a theory of everything; rather, it places its object of study in relation to phenomena which though relevant are by definition *different in kind*. Thus if the object of study is, say, human consciousness, then from the point of view of an exotropic theory the relevant phenomena could be human biology, including both evolution and development, which would implicate interaction with the environment thus leading to consideration of semiotic exchange, which in turn would implicate social relations among interactants,[6] and so on. It would be a mistake to think of such a theory of human consciousness as a theory of human evolution, of semiotic interaction or of social positioning,[7] and the rest. Rather, it is simply *open* to, i.e. allows dialogue with, theories of these phenomena provided their mode of engaging with their problematic is not in contradiction to its own. At the same time, it has to be emphasized that precisely because it reaches out into so many different domains, the threat of chaos for an exotropic theory is very real and at least two conditions must be met if the theory is to avoid confusion. First, to contain the potential for chaos, the theory's languages of description (see Bernstein 1996: 134ff on languages of description and the relations among them) need to be well-developed; and secondly, because it connects with phenomena of different kinds, its conceptual syntax must not only be able to distinguish among the different kinds of phenomena it invokes by way of description/explanation but it must also be able to specify the relations between them. I suggest that of these two conditions the first is necessary but not sufficient to enable a theory to engage in meta-dialogue: we do know endotropic theories with highly developed languages of description, which by definition possess no potential for meta-dialogism. Hjelmslev's (1961) elaborate and elegant linguistic theory comes to mind as a possible example.[8] The necessary and sufficient condition for an exotropic theory's potential for meta-dialogism is met when its conceptual syntax is so developed that not only does the theory distinguish the different orders of relevant phenomena but it is also able to specify the nature of this relevance. I suggest that it is in specifying this relevance that the theory actually creates locations, interstices, openings – call them what you will – which form the logical points for the theory to address the other components of the dynamic open system.

Hopefully this brief discussion has outlined at least in general terms the conditions for meta-dialogism in a theory. In the next section, I examine the instantiation of these general principles in Bernstein's theory, pointing out its exotropism and identifying the points where it reaches out to other relevant phenomena.

Coding orientation: an exotropic theory of the social

For my purposes, it is not necessary to present in detail Bernstein's theory of coding orientation. An account of the elements of the theory and of the stages of its development can be found in Bernstein's own writings (see especially 1971, 1977, 1990, 1996), together with comments, critiques and interpretations by others (e.g. Bernstein 1973, Atkinson 1985, Sadovnik 1995). Let me begin then with Figure 1.1.

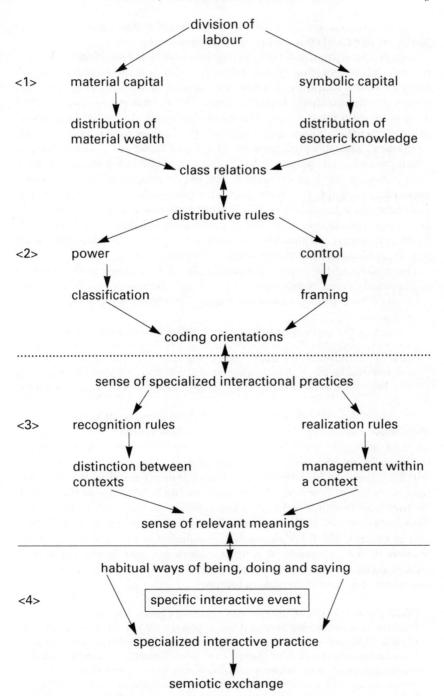

Figure 1.1 Class, codes and communication: an interpretation

Figure 1.1 relies heavily on Bernstein[9] and is offered as a representation of just those aspects of code theory which I consider relevant to the present discourse. As the margin indicates, the figure consists of four identifiable components, each consisting of a number of terms and their relations, which together sketch formulaically some specific area of human experience (discussed shortly) which are brought together by Bernstein's exotropic theory. To achieve this end, obviously, the theory has a well developed language of description which allows it to 'translate' the entities and relations of one component into those of another. The elements in each component, of which the first three are presented in the shape of a hexagon, and those at their interstices are logically related. The logical relation at the interstices is important not simply for what it stands for but also because it implies a general claim: the relation between the four components is not one of collection as between members of a list, but of integration as between elements made significant by virtue of the theory's conceptual syntax: this is how the theory sees its problematic in interaction with its environment.

The nucleus of the coding orientation theory is captured in the relations within and between components <2> and <3>. Bernstein (1990: 13) introduces the central problematic of the theory – its 'enduring focus' – as follows:

> In terms of the particular problems of the relationship between class and the processes of its cultural reproduction, . . . what has to be shown is how class regulation of the distribution of power and of principles of control generates, distributes, reproduces, and legitimates dominant and dominated principles regulating the relationships within and between social groups and so forms of consciousness.

Note that the term constituting the highest element in hexagon <2> is **distributive rules**. This is itself related to **class relations**, the lowest element of hexagon <1>. The relation between distributive rules and class relations is that of manifestation: the latter – class relations – are manifested as, come to be known via, the distributive rules: this is partly how class is 'done' in practice. The vertical double-headed arrow thus stands for the 'manifestation' relation. Class relations manifested as distributive rules/principles underlie both the **distribution of power** and the **principles of control**, which are themselves manifested in the practices of **classification** of the categories of human experience and in the **framing** of human social practices, respectively. A brief characterization of these four important elements of the theory follows:

> power always operates on the relations *between* categories. The focus of power . . . is on the relations *between* and, in this way, power establishes legitimate relations of order. Control, on the other hand, . . . establishes legitimate forms of communication appropriate to different categories. Control carries the boundary relations of power and socializes individuals into these relationships . . . To summarize . . . control establishes legitimate communications, and power establishes legitimate relations between categories. (Bernstein 1996: 19)

Classification refers to the degree of insulation between categories of discourse, agents, practices, contexts, and provides recognition rules for both transmitters and acquirers for the degree of specialisation of their texts.

Framing refers to the controls on selection, sequencing, pacing, and criterial rules of the ... pedagogic communicative relationship between transmitter/acquirer(s) and provides the realisation rules for the production of their text. (Bernstein 1990: 24)

It is the specific modalities of classification and framing that underlie the different **coding orientations**. The diverging slanting arrows thus indicate '*x* underlies *both a and b*' e.g. distributive rules underlie both (the distribution of) power and (the principles of) control; the converging slanting arrows indicate '*a and b both* underlie *c*', e.g. classification and control both underlie coding orientations. This, then, is the abstract syntax within component <2>, not its semantics (for which see below). <2> is itself related to <3> by the *manifested as* relation: thus the lowest term of the hexagon <2> – coding orientations – is manifested as the social subject's **sense of specialized interactional practices**. It is this sense of specialized interactional practices (**SSIP**) that underlie the **recognition** and **realization rules** that constitute the immediate resources for the subject's participation in semiotic exchange.

Recognition rules create the means of distinguishing between and so recognizing the speciality that constitutes a context, and realization rules regulate the creation and production of specialized relationships internal to that context. (Bernstein 1990: 15)

The specificity of a context – its value and identity – is not given by its own internal structure; rather, it is a function of relations between contexts.[10] *Recognition rules* thus refers to one's sense of what defines possible contexts. How one acts, the specialized practices pertinent to a specific context, constitute the *realization rules*: this is how the subject's sense of the context is realized. Thus component <3> shows that recognition rules are manifested as the subject's ability to make **distinction between contexts** and realization rules are manifested as the subject's **management (of relevant SIP) within a context**. The subject's **sense of relevant meanings** 'is' in fact her/his relation to contexts in these terms. This contextually generated sense of relevant meanings is manifested in the subject's **habitual ways of being, doing and saying** over the total range of semiotic exchange. This is the first element of the last component (discussed below).

Note the dotted line separating <2> and <3>: this symbolizes a qualitative relation between the two components. Bernstein (1990: 17, Fig. 1.3) refers to the area covered by <2> as that which analyses 'inter-subject (class) relations' and of <3> as that which concerns the 'intra-subject (class) relations'. Because of the logical relation of manifestation between coding orientations and SSIP, the concept of coding orientation faces in two directions: a coding orientation manifested as SSIP is an intra-subjective phenomenon, but its etiology is not entirely intra-subjective. Coding orientations have

value only within the environment of inter-subjective class relations which
regulate the practices of power and control, manifested by the various
modalities of classification and framing. Coding orientation is thus a complex concept, having both a social and a psychological dimension. This is
reminiscent of Vygotsky when he describes the essential nature of the
development of higher mental functions (1978: 57):

> Every function in the child's cultural development appears twice: first, on the social
> level, and later, on the individual level; first *between* people (*interpsychologically*), and
> then *inside* the child (*intrapsychologically*). . . . All the higher functions originate as
> actual relations between human individuals. (emphases in original)

So it is at this theoretical juncture between coding orientations as
socially engendered, socially maintained, socially altered phenomena and
SSIP as individual psychological predisposition or orientation to certain
practices of meaning that Bernstein's theory opens up the possibility of
dialogue with, offers a dialogic turn to, a compatible theory of human
consciousness. Such a theory would be one that – like Vygotsky's, and
more recently Edelman's (1992) and Dennett's (1991) – recognizes the
participation of culture in the processes of consciousness:

> The underlying neural architecture is far from being a *tabula rasa* or a blank
> slate at birth, . . . but it is nevertheless a medium in which structures get built as
> a function of the brain's interactions with the world. And it is these built struc-
> tures . . . that explain cognitive functioning. (Dennett 1991: 259)

Unlike Gazzaniga (1993), these scholars do not see consciousness as entirely
'hard wired' – the work of nature alone. Dennett (1991), for example, bor-
rows Dawkins's (1982) concept of 'meme' as significant cultural ideas,
describing the mind as a nest for memes, or as a meme making machine. But
in this account, the relation of individuals to memes as cultural forces is both
accidental and unproblematic: memes appear to free-float in the atmosphere
and individuals somehow happen to incorporate them. To think of 'interaction with the world' in such general terms is one thing, and recognizing the
specific role of social interaction in the fashioning of individual consciousness is another. Vygotsky took a decisive step in accepting the importance of
the *biogenetic* foundation, and at the same time making a more specific claim
about the *sociogenesis* of the human mind by introducing the notion of semiotic mediation. It is Vygotsky's concept of semiotically mediated minds that
brings his theory close to the 'theoretical question of classical sociology: how
does the outside become the inside, and how does the inside reveal itself and
shape the outside?' that has engaged Bernstein (1987: 563) throughout his
scholarly career. The acceptance of the view that the cultural reappears in
the individual creates a common ground for dialogue between the two theories. However, by ignoring systematic variation in semiotic mediation, Vygotsky tells a simple story. For Bernstein the story is more complex: the varying
social relations of class through the varied functioning of their distributive

rules ultimately become differentiated internal realities of the differently positioned subjects, shaping differently their notions of the significant and the relevant. *The child* is no longer generic: differently positioned children become the concern; the adult agent of semiotic mediation is no longer culturally neutral: s/he is the voice of a distinct ideology (Hasan 1989, 1992b, 1992c, 1993; Hasan and Cloran 1990; Cloran 1994, Chapter 2, this volume; Williams 1995, Chapter 4, this volume). Focusing simultaneously on local and official pedagogic practices, Bernstein's theorization of '*the social construction of pedagogic discourse*' (1990: 165–218) problematizes the modifier *higher* in Vygotsky's 'higher mental processes': the essentially hierarchic nature of all knowledge, the positive and high valuation of official knowledge and the logical relations between local and official knowledge, all invite us to question the treatment of the latter as the reference point for measuring the attainment of higher mental functions (consider in this light Luria's explanation (1976) of the logical abilities of the Uzbeks). If between language and its use lies social structure, as code theory maintains, then semiotic mediation is not a neutral and innocent process; it is socio-logically sensitive to social phenomena and creates socially differentiated individual minds (Hasan 1992a, 1995b).

Although Vygotsky's theory of the mind ignores social variation as a significant feature of its central explanatory concept, I believe it is still compatible with Bernstein's framework: unlike others such as Popper (1979) or Gazzaniga (1993) it does not deny the importance of the social; quite the contrary – from the point of view of code theory, it simply does not go far enough. Equally, from the psychologist's point of view, Bernstein's interests bypass the biological altogether; but while the role of the bio-genetic in the making of human consciousness does not attract his attention, there is no reason to imagine that such exploration would be incompatible with his theory. It seems important to emphasize that neither theory is a theory of every phenomenon it needs to invoke; instead, the depth of the analysis of such phenomena is governed strictly by the need to explain the central problematic. Both theories have however proved productive because they are open: they allow meta-dialogue.

I have claimed that the relations within and between the terms of components <2> and <3> form the nucleus of Bernstein's coding orientation theory, because it is here that society and the individual are brought in a dialectical relation through the workings of semiotic exchanges which are themselves sensitive to and which sensitize the interactants to the social foundations of their own social positioning:

> What we are asking . . . is how the distribution of power and the principles of control are transformed, at the level of the subject, into different, invidiously related, organizing principles, in such a way as both to position subjects and to create the possibility of change in such positioning. The broad answer given by this thesis is that class relations generate, distribute, reproduce, and legitimate distinctive forms of communication, which transmit dominant and dominated codes, and that subjects are differentially positioned by these codes in the process of acquiring them. 'Positioning' is used here to refer to the establishing of a specific rela-

tion to other subjects and to the creating of specific relationships within subjects
... from this point of view, codes are culturally determined positioning devices
... Ideology is constituted through and in such positioning ... ideology inheres
in and regulates *modes of relation* (emphasis in original). Ideology is not so much a
content as a mode of relation for the realizing of contents. (Bernstein 1990: 13)

Let me turn now very briefly to component <1>, which I see as representing the basis of class relations in capitalist societies. The primary consideration here is the mode of the **division of labour** (Scase 1992, Marshall *et al.*
1988, Marx 1975, Poulantzas 1975, Wright 1985). It is this that underlies
the access to **material** and **symbolic capital** which is manifested as control on
the means for the production and distribution of **material wealth**, and **esoteric knowledge**, with the two representing instruments of control for both
physical and human environment. It is the consequences of the differential
access to and control of these resources that underlies social **class relations**
in societies as we know them today. The globalization of the division of
labour does not alter the essentials of the relations expressed in the terms of
this hexagon: the exercise of power and control simply shifts its boundaries,
implicating other locations, other agents. In this sense, I see Bernstein's
notion of class firmly based in an analysis of the politico-economic, thus
linking modes of communication logically with social division of labour:

> the most primitive conditions for the location of coding orientations is given by
> the location of agents in the social division of labour. Different locations gener-
> ate different interactional practices which realize different relations to the
> material base and so different coding orientations. (Bernstein 1990: 20)

The relation between <1> and <2> is that between the material 'outside' and
the principles governing the sociogenesis of the 'inside'. And at the interstices
of these two components, there exists a space for dialogue with politico-economic theories. The *internal relations of <3> in interaction with the other components* provide a schematic account of what the inside consists in. Let me turn
now to the relations between <3> and <4>, as these, particularly the latter, are
central to any description of semiotic exchanges. I see this component as
closely related to the theory of discourse, and this in turn implies relation to
the theory of language. The following section focuses, then, on these points.

A linguistic theory for meta-dialogue

The basis of communication according to Bernstein is in the intra-subject
class relations represented in component <3>; but these are themselves a
manifestation of coding orientations, which are in the final analysis regulated by social class as the relations of <2> show. Bernstein (1990, see especially Figure 1.3, p. 17) has called this part – i.e. components <2-3> – of the
communicative apparatus 'invisible', and that represented in component
<4>, 'visible'. The solid line between components <1-3> and <4> thus repre-
sents the relation of system to instance: if the *specialized interactive practice* is

what is produced in the specific interactive event, then the abstract syntax which generates it is in components <2–3> whose material base is represented in component <1>. Component <4> is, then, the area where actual semiotic exchanges occur; it is here that we come face to face with instances of coding orientations. In Bernstein's theory, the term *semiotic exchange* – and even *text* – refers to *all* social practices, not *just* the linguistic ones. However, in the following discussion I shall restrict myself simply to the linguistic modality alone,[11] for reasons which will hopefully become obvious.

One way or another language features in most instances of semiotic exchanges, and any theory that invokes the concept of semiotic exchange in the resolution of its central problematic creates a space where a compatible linguistic theory might dialogue with it. Code theory creates an explicit location at this point between <3> and <4> where the social and the linguistic can engage with each other. Further, if it is in the context of semiotic exchange that Bernstein's theory makes explicit contact with language, then it logically encounters language as instance. This is important for at least three reasons. First, because of the dialectic relation between system and instance (Halliday 1993), the discourse of instance will carry implications for what specific properties must be conceptualized as inherent to the system, the details of which will depend on what the theory expects the instances to achieve. This in turn furnishes a principle of selectivity whereby only certain linguistic theories may prove capable of maintaining a dialogue with Bernstein's theory of the social. Second, instances of semiotic exchange and social context are inseparable: a compatible linguistic theory will need to specify systematic, non-*ad hoc* means for relating the linguistic instance to its social context in such a way that it does not negate the relevant elements of the code theory. Finally, since underlying the specialized interactive practices is the subject's sense of relevant meanings, and since it is from the point of view of the relevant meanings that the instances have to be examined, then a linguistic theory will need to have a view of semantics that goes beyond meaning as the representation of 'real reality': real reality is by definition socially invariable and coding orientations are inherently claims about socially significant variation. I will discuss these closely inter-related issues, but first a comment on the explicit point of contact between code theory and language.

It may be true to say that the code theory comes in contact with language explicitly in component <4> where it finds language mediating as the 'final' act of realization with a long social history behind it; but if so, the significance of the explicit and the implicit in this context needs to be taken into account. If it is supposed that this is the only location for a theory of language to take its turn in its meta-dialogue with Bernstein's theory of the social, this would be tantamount to putting the world before the word: it would be claiming that the specifically human construal of the social is capable of manifesting itself without language. In my view, this is a misrecognition of the situation.[12] Consider for example components <1–3> in Figure 1.1. If the claim is correct that access to knowledge is a form of capital – symbolic or intellectual capital – then the basis of class relations is already 'coloured' by language: a certain way of examining reality, explaining its parameters, and using it as a resource for the exploitation of labour is associated with a group of persons who are socially positioned thus and thus and who by their activities perpetuate the 'invidious' class relations.[13] Intentionality or absence of it is beside the point: in fact the less the intention counts, the more potent the ideology. Further, it is well-nigh impossible to think of classification and/or framing without implicating language;[14] in this sense, Vygotsky certainly had a point: the internalization of the external requires semiotic mediation, and in this semiotic mediation he was right to draw attention to the abstract tool of language as the most pervasive one for manipulating the internalization of the external. If this is true, then language is already there from the very beginning. I conclude that code theory and semiotic theory – especially linguistic theory – are closely intertwined: code theory attempts to explain the social; the social is inherently (also) linguistic just as the linguistic is itself grounded in the social. We know no language outside human community and we know no human community without language: the Trappist monks are able to give value to absence of language – to silence – precisely because language has presence in the affairs of humans.[15] So then the explicitness of contact between language and society at the conjunction of component <3> and <4> notwithstanding, one must conclude that code theory implicitly brings in language from the very beginning precisely because its explanation of its central problematic invokes semiotic exchange as a crucial concept, and the linguistic aspects of interaction are a variety of semiosis. Further, what the code theory requires of the instances of semiotic exchange is un-doable without the complicity of language. Moreover, in order for anyone to maintain that instances of language use can achieve what the theory suggests, one must have a particular conception of what the system of language is like. At this point, we have returned full circle to the issues that arise from encountering language as instance, which in my view call for deducing the properties of the system from the characteristics assigned to the instance.

First then, what is language as instance expected to achieve in the code theory? To quote Bernstein (1971: 144):

> the particular forms of social relation act selectively upon what is said, when it is said, and how it is said . . . [they] can generate very different speech systems or codes . . . [which] create for their speakers different orders of relevance and relation. The experience of the speakers may then be transformed by what is made significant and relevant by different speech systems. As the child . . . learns specific speech codes which regulate his verbal acts, he learns the requirement of his social structure. The experience of the child is transformed by the learning generated by his own, apparently, voluntary acts of speech . . . From this point of view, every time the child speaks or listens, the social structure is reinforced in him and his social identity shaped. The social structure becomes the child's psychological reality through the shapings of his acts of speech.

The experience of participating in exchanges regulated by specific coding orientations translates itself into the subject's psychological reality: the experience of the instance creates the subject's system for linguistic interaction. Codes thus acquire the status of 'culturally determined positioning devices'. 'Ideology is constituted through and in such positioning'; from this perspective, 'ideology is not so much a content as a mode of relation for the realising of contents' (Bernstein 1990: 13–14). If we adopt the position of the systemic functional linguist, a language instance makes sense by its relation to language system (Halliday 1993, 1996, Hasan 1995a; Matthiessen 1995). This is not to claim that the system is a constraint or fully predicts all features of the performance; it is simply to claim that no matter what the feature of performance, its interpretation invokes the listener's sense of a system. The system is the reference point both for interpreting features that are predicted by the system and for those that are not; as Firth remarked, novelty implies departure from the expected. That an instance of language is related in this way to language system is significant: what the instance is capable of doing must in large part be what the system has built into it as its design features. If instance is able to contribute to the construal of ideology, then this is largely because the system acts as the resource for this. So what does this say about the conceptualization of language as system for a theory of language which is compatible with code theory?

Elsewhere (Hasan 1996), I have drawn attention to the fact that protolanguage is innocent of ideology. This is because, having no level of lexicogrammar, it is a simple pairing of meaning and sound – a relation that comes very close to meaning by naming or by correspondence to external phenomena. I suggest that (Hasan 1996: 104–5):

> what makes it possible for human languages to be ideologically saturated is the plasticity of relations between the levels of content and expression . . . this plasticity of relations appears impossible where meaning is simply a function of 'correspondence' between a signifier and some 'bit' of extralinguistic reality . . . To be complicit in the creation and maintenance of ideology . . . the system of language . . . must on the one hand have some resource for construing meanings, and, on the other, . . . the meanings construed by language must relate to an extralinguistic reality capable of being contested in some respect or other. In other words there has to exist the possibility of variation in how people use the lexicogrammatical resources of their language to construe meanings and there has to exist the possibility of variation in using the semantic potential of language to construe contexts.

Not only does language have to be a multiple coding system where meaning is realized as wording and wording by sound, but at the same time the social context itself is realizationally implicated. It is important to appreciate both the elements of necessity and of freedom in these statements. A subject's linguistic meanings are necessarily construed by the resources of the lexicogrammatical system, but within lexicogrammar itself there is no necessity for the use of this resource rather than some other; such necessity is activated by the meanings to be meant (Hasan 1995a), and this implies meanings relevant to some occasion of talk. When we claim that speakers can say anything anywhere they like, all we mean is that the resources of the system of wording are not inaccessible to them. However, the orders of meaning that a subject is predisposed to – the semantic aspects of his linguistic *habitus* (Bourdieu 1992) – are not specified by the grammar: they are code regulated, and it is these meanings in the context of that person's positioning that activate the speaker's use of wordings:

> if code selects and integrates relevant meanings, then code presupposes a concept of irrelevant and illegitimate meanings; . . . if code selects forms of realization, then code presupposes a concept of inappropriate or illegitimate forms of realization; . . . if code regulates evoking contexts then again this implies a concept of inappropriate, illegitimate contexts. (Bernstein 1990: 14)

The necessity is in the relation *between* levels, not *within* a specific level. Speakers' meanings do not pour out independent of their context; their grammar does not unroll independent of their meanings, notwithstanding unexpected occurrences and dynamic moves befitting our unique (dare I say middle-class) individualities. This suggests a systematic relation between these levels – in SF this relation is known as realization (Halliday 1992, 1996; Hasan 1995a, in press; Matthiessen 1995). I believe that the realizational relation between these three strata of linguistic description is a dialectic: thus, for example, context activates meanings and meanings construe context; meanings activate grammar and grammar construes meanings – a principle necessary for showing that 'decontextualized' language is language encapsulating its context, not language independent of social context (see Cloran 1994, this volume Chapter 2). The realization relation between phonology and these three strata is criterially different: the relation here is of conventional association, what Saussure described as the arbitrary bond between the signifier and the signified. Clearly Saussure's notion of language was not presented as multi-stratal.

If we are to account for how the instance is able to achieve what it is hypothesized to achieve in code theory, it becomes obvious that linguistic theory must be conceptualized as comprising not just the three traditionally recognized strata – semantics, grammar and phonology – but also the stratum of context. Without this, the predisposition towards certain orders of meaning would remain a mystery; and parole would appear wilful and disorderly as it did to Saussure. This requirement itself acts as a principle of selectivity on the possibility of meta-dialogue: to dialogue with Bernstein's theory of the social, the theory of language must extend to and include the concept of social context. Not only this, but it would appear that we have to go further.

A theory for which context is simply a feature of the instance, having no relation to the system itself, poses a serious problem: how/why does a displaced instance of language use construe its own context, to the extent that it does? SF theory answers this by postulating the principle of meta-functionality: according to Halliday's famous remark, the structure of language is as it is because of the functions language is made to serve in the life of communities. The metafunctional principle resonates through the levels of context to that of wording, as shown in Figure 1.2. Language in

Metafunction	Contextual Variable	Meaning system	Wording system	Wording structure
interpersonal	social relation (=*tenor*)	role exchange; assessment of probability, obligation	mood system (e.g. declarative v. interrogative . . .); systems of modality, modulation	prosodic
experiential	social action (=*field*) →	states of affairs; classification of phenomena	transitivity system (e.g. material v. verbal . . .); lexical systems . . .	segmental
logical	social action (=*field*) →	relations of states of affairs; relations of phenomena	expansion, projection systems; modification . . .	iterative
textual	semiotic management (=*mode*)	point of departure; news focus; points of identity, similarity	thematic, information systems; cohesive connections	periodic

Figure 1.2 Functionality in Language Use and Language System

use is able to construe certain by now well known aspects of social context.

It is interesting to compare the SF notion of context of situation with the account of the social underlying Bernstein's view of semiotic exchange as represented in Figure 1.1. Would a compatible theory of language need to develop its view of context so as to encompass the social phenomena as code theory sees it? This is not a question that can be answered within the scope of this chapter, but it is certainly one that SF linguists might devote attention to. On the one hand in SF theory today at least two rather different views of context are to be found – that proposed by Martin (1985, 1992) and that proposed by Halliday *et al.* and Halliday (1991, and elsewhere). Neither of these fully captures the perspective on context found in code theory. On the other hand, there is a view abroad that a social semiotic theory of language such as SF must necessarily be a theory of culture. I am not convinced that this is a tenable position.

Returning to context and language use, I am tempted to comment that different coding orientations 'fragment' what from some points of view may be seen as the same register; an example is the register of joint book reading by mothers and children, which is fragmented by systematic variation in coding orientation (Williams this volume Chapter 4). The variation that Williams is able to demonstrate, which in its broad outlines agrees with the findings of Hasan, Hasan and Cloran, and Cloran (see references above), are variations in coding orientations. This detailed analysis of semantic variation has been made possible by the development of semantic networks as a tool, which is itself a natural extension of the model. There still remains the question whether semantic variation tells the whole story of variation in coding orientations. As Figure 1.1 shows, codes regulate relevant meanings and their organization within the context of specialized interactive practices relevant to distinct contexts. This implies that a full scale linguistic study of variation in coding orientation must analyse not simply the elements of messages but also the deployment of messages in texts, probing into variation in textual organization. Cloran's (1994) development of the notion of rhetorical unit is significant in this respect as it moves from the message to larger constituents of text structure.

Although SF linguistics needs to develop in specific respects – this as I remarked above is a condition of a living theory – what appears important here is the fact that the concept of language put forward by it is highly compatible with that of code theory. If a theory is known by the descriptions it can generate (Bernstein 1996), then certainly SF is a theory, which by virtue of its conceptualization of the relations of context, meaning, and grammar can be interpreted as a social semiotic theory of language.

Notes

1 My thanks are due to Michael Halliday with whom I have discussed issues included in this paper. The responsibility for the views expressed is entirely mine.

2 Later subsumed in the Department of Linguistics, with Halliday as its first Chair and Head.

3 In doing this, they may use the same labels or different ones, they may

acknowledge their debt to the other theory or not. All permutations are generously exemplified in the practices of the field of linguistics.

4 Reciprocity does not entail consensus at every point (see discussion of Vygotsky's theory below) — simply a readiness to grant an opening to a potential interactant. Thus a fight, as opposed to indifference towards a potential interactant, is reciprocal; and although non-consensual, a fight is a dialogue, unlike silence. Nor does reciprocity demand identity of attitude from the interactants. In *agreeing to disagree*, the conflictual reciprocal activity of disagreeing necessarily implies opposing perspectives, which are themselves embedded within the consensual activity of agreeing. This explains perhaps why *agreeing to disagree* is fraught with tension.

5 This relation of complementation between theories is of course variable, occupying a region of delicate tension between, at one end, the appropriation of the concerns of other related disciplines, and at the other, a complete indifference to their existence. The former ceases to be complementation; it turns into domination. The latter invites solipsism where the concerns of other disciplines cease to exist. A dialogue simply on terms of one interactant is in fact a monologue: it has complete unity of perspective.

6 Vygotsky provides a good example of an exotropic theory of human consciousness; though he does not relate it to the social variable (Hasan 1992a; 1995b), there is no element in the theory to the best of my knowledge which would prevent the consideration of this variable in the context of his approach to mental development. See comments below.

7 If the theory of human consciousness attempted to be a theory of genetics, of evolution, of development, of exchange and of social relation, it would cease to be an exotropic theory, whose nature it is to occupy the ambiguous ground between appropriation and indifference (see Note 5). A theory that claims to explain/describe everything is simply an appropriating, dominating discourse, which treats all else as subservient to its own central problematic. In short, it represents a failure of imagination.

8 The arguments for this claim are lengthy (for some hints see Hasan 1995a). Very briefly, although Hjelmslev attempts to reach out to phenomena other than language by invoking the notions of purport and connotative semiotic, the relation between language and other phenomena is far from reciprocal in his theory. Rather for Hjelmslev everything is subjugated to language. Thus language does not enter here in a dialectic with the social conditions of human existence, changing and being changed by it; language simply construes our sense of the social. This may in large measure be true: most human beings come to know their world the way they do mainly through the processes of language, but this emphatically does not mean that the social can be reduced simply to the linguistic any more than it is true (cf. Bourdieu 1992; Atkinson 1985) that the linguistic can be reduced simply to the social (see Hasan in press).

9 I have naturally drawn on my understanding of Bernstein's writing to an extent that specific acknowledgment is problematic. However, see in particular Bernstein 1990: *13–62*; 165–218 and 1996: 17–34 and 91–144. I see my Figure 1.1 as directly derived from some of Bernstein's own e.g. his Figures 1.1 and 1.3 (see 1990: 13 and 17 respectively). However, it is important to emphasize that I alone am responsible for the interpretation of the theory and of the figures, without any implication of Bernstein's concurrence with my reading.

10 This is reminiscent of the paradigmatic principle of description favoured by Saussure and developed by Hjelmslev (1961), Firth (1957) and Halliday (1996).

11 Even if I were able to talk sensibly of all semiotic modalities, the constraint of space engineered by the publishing trade is severe. My position is that linguistics is *not* semiotics. The theory of language is not a theory of everything one

can mean in any semiotic modality; it is simply a theory of language as meaning potential: that is complex enough. I would prefer the theory to be exotropic; this means making connections with the relevant environment with the specific purpose of providing insightful descriptions of language as meaning potential. Being exotropic, it would enable a principled invoking of other elements of the dynamic open system, and their description to the extent that they are criterial for throwing light on the nature of language as meaning potential. I would argue that if a linguistic theory tries to be a theory of everything, it will be a theory of nothing! From this point of view the fervour of many colleagues to describe the entire culture through linguistics appears misplaced. All socially sensitive linguistics can do is to make explicit the part played by language in the creation, maintenance and change of (certain aspects) of culture, and this again is complex enough to keep linguists occupied for decades.

12 See my critique of Bourdieu on language in the affairs of humanity (Hasan 1992). A similar view, presumably historically traceable to Marx's entirely untenable theory of language as superstructure, is taken by Atkinson (1985) when he declares that language is simply an epiphenomenon.

13 The discourse of class is so unwelcome perhaps because, as Halliday (1993) points out, at some level of consciousness we know that we are all implicated in its creation and its maintenance; perhaps it needs to be pointed out that by the same logic we are also implicated in change. Our reflections and actions 'can have a crucial role in creating tomorrow's optimism in the context of today's pessimism' (Bernstein 1996: 5).

14 I am not concerned here with the arbitrary valuation of certain categories of language (see debate in Hasan in press). If arbitrary is in opposition to 'logical', I question the possibility of arriving at a logic that is in the end not socio-logical. But this socio-logic is not arbitrary where material and intellectual capital is conscripted in the exploitation of labour: it becomes 'the' logical way of maintaining control. Language is not cosmetics; it is lethal. If you use it to maintain hegemony, you destroy the other; if you use it to destroy hegemony, you become self-critical.

15 This implies that sociology without an understanding of language tells an incoherent story while linguistics without an understanding of the social is built on sand.

References

Atkinson, P. (1985) *Language, Structure and Reproduction: An Introduction to the Sociology of Basil Bernstein*. London: Methuen.

Bernstein, Basil (1971) *Class, Codes and Control, Vol. 1: Theoretical Studies towards a Sociology of Language*. London: Routledge.

Bernstein, Basil (1973) *Class, Codes and Control, Vol. 2: Applied Studies towards a Sociology of Language*. London: Routledge.

Bernstein, Basil (1977) *Class, Codes and Control, Vol. 3: Towards a Theory of Educational Transmission* (2nd rev. edn). London: Routledge.

Bernstein, Basil (1987) 'Elaborated and restricted codes: an overview 1958–1985'. In U. Ammon, N. Dittmar and K. J. Mattheier (eds), *Sociolinguistics/Soziolinguistik: An International Handbook, Vol 1*. Berlin: Walter de Gruyter.

Bernstein, Basil (1990) *Class, Codes and Control, Vol. 4: The Structuring of Pedagogic Discourse*. London: Routledge.

Bernstein, Basil (1996) *Pedagogy, Symbolic Control and Ideology: Theory Research Critique*. London: Taylor & Francis.

Bourdieu, Pierre (1992) *Language and Symbolic Power*. (trans. by G. Raymond and M. Adamson, ed. by J.B. Thompson) Cambridge: Polity Press.

Cloran, C. (1994) *Rhetorical Units and Decontextualisation: An Enquiry into Some Relations of Context, Meaning and Grammar.* Monographs in Systemic Linguistics, 6. Nottingham University: Nottingham School of English Studies.

Cloran, C. Butt, D. and Williams, G. (eds) (1996) *Ways of Saying: Ways of Meaning: Selected Papers of Ruqaiya Hasan.* London: Cassell.

Dawkins, Richard (1982) *The Extended Phenotype.* New York: Oxford University Press.

Dennett, Daniel C. (1991) *Consciousness Explained.* London: Penguin.

Edelman, Gerald M. (1992) *Bright Air, Brilliant Fire: On the Matter of the Mind.* New York: Basic Books.

Firth, J.R. (1957) *Papers in Linguistics 1934–1951.* London: Oxford University Press.

Gazzaniga, M.S. (1993) *Nature's Mind.* London: Penguin.

Halliday, M.A.K. (1977) 'Text as semantic choice in social context'. In T.A. van Dijk and J.S. Petofi (eds), *Grammars and Descriptions.* Berlin: Mouton de Gruyter.

Halliday, M.A.K. (1991) 'The notion of "context" in language education'. In Thao Le and Mike McCausland (eds), *Language Education: Interaction and Development. Proceedings of the international conference, Ho Chi Minh City, Vietnam 30 March – 1 April 1991,* Launceston: University of Tasmania.

Halliday, M.A.K. (1992) 'How do you mean?' In M. Davies and L. Ravelli (eds), *Recent Advances in Systemic Linguistics: Theory and Practice.* London: Pinter.

Halliday, M.A.K. (1993) 'The act of meaning'. In J.E. Alatis (ed.), *Georgetown University Round Table: Language Communication and Social Meaning 1992.* Washington, DC: Georgetown University Press. (Repr. in Halliday, *Language in a Changing World,* Occasional Papers Number 13. Applied Linguistics Association of Australia).

Halliday, M.A.K. (1994) *Introduction to Functional Grammar.* (2nd edn) London: Arnold.

Halliday, M.A.K. (1995) 'On language in relation to the evolution of human consciousness'. In Sture Allén (ed.), *Of Thoughts and Words: The Relation between Language and Mind, Proceedings of Nobel Symposium 92.* London: Imperial College Press.

Halliday, M.A.K. (1996) 'On grammar and grammatics'. In Ruqaiya Hasan, Carmel Cloran and David Butt (eds), *Functional Descriptions: Theory in Practice.* Amsterdam: Benjamins.

Halliday, M.A.K., McIntosh, A. and Stevens, P. (1965) *The Linguistics Sciences and Language Teaching.* London: Longmans.

Hasan, Ruqaiya (1964) *A linguistic study of contrasting features in the style of two contemporary English prose writers.* Unpublished PhD dissertation, University of Edinburgh.

Hasan, Ruqaiya (1984) 'What kind of resource is language', *Australian Review of Applied Linguistics,* 7(1), 57–85. (Repr. in Carmel Cloran *et al.* 1996).

Hasan, Ruqaiya (1985) *Linguistics, Language and Verbal Art.* Geelong, Vic.: Deakin University Press.

Hasan, Ruqaiya (1989) 'Semantic variation and sociolinguistics', *Australian Journal of Linguistics,* 9(2), 221–76.

Hasan, Ruqaiya (1992a) 'Speech genre, semiotic mediation and the development of higher mental functions'. *Language Sciences. Special Issue: Current Research in Functional Grammar, Discourse and Computational Linguistics with a Foundation in Systemic Theory,* M.A.K. Halliday and F.C.C. Peng (eds), 14(4), 489–528.

Hasan, Ruqaiya (1992b) 'Rationality in everyday talk: from process to system'. In J. Svartvik (ed.) *Directions in Corpus Linguistics: Proceedings of Nobel Symposium 82,* Stockholm 4–8 August 1991. Berlin: Mouton de Gruyter.

Hasan, Ruqaiya (1992c) 'Meaning in sociolinguistic theory'. In K. Bolton and H. Kwok (eds), *Sociolinguistics Today: International Perspectives.* London: Routledge.

Hasan, Ruqaiya (1993) 'Contexts for meaning'. In J.E. Alatis (ed.), *Georgetown University Round Table: Language Communication and Social Meaning 1992.* Washington, DC: Georgetown University Press.

Hasan, Ruqaiya (1995a) 'The conception of context in text'. In Peter H. Fries and

Michael Gregory (eds), *Discourse in Society: Systemic Functional Perspectives: Meaning and Choice in Language: Studies for Michael Halliday*. Norwood NJ: Ablex.

Hasan, Ruqaiya (1995b) 'On social conditions for semiotic mediation: the genesis of mind in society'. In Alan R. Sadovnik (ed), *Knowledge and Pedagogy: The Sociology of Basil Bernstein*. Norwood NJ: Ablex.

Hasan, Ruqaiya (in press). 'The dispowerment game: Bourdieu and language in literacy', *Linguistics and Education*.

Hasan, Ruqaiya and Cloran, Carmel (1990) 'A sociolinguistic interpretation of everyday talk between mothers and children'. In M.A.K. Halliday, J. Gibbons and H. Nicholas (eds), *Learning, Keeping and Using Language: Selected Papers from the 8th World Congress of Applied Linguistics*, Sydney 16–21 August 1987. Amsterdam: Benjamins.

Hjelmslev, L. (1961) *Prolegomena to a Theory of Language*. (trans. by F.J. Whitfield). Madison: University of Wisconsin Press.

Lemke, J.L. (1984) *Semiotics and Education*. Toronto: Victoria College/Toronto Semiotic Circle Monographs.

Lemke, J.L. (1993) 'Discourse, dynamics and social change'. *Language as Cultural Dynamic*, M.A.K. Halliday (guest editor), *Special Issue*, 6(1–2), 243–75.

Luria, A.R. (1976) *Cognitive Development: Its Cultural and Social Foundations* (trans. by M. Lopez-Morillas and L. Solotaroff, ed. by M. Cole). Cambridge, MA: Harvard University Press.

Martin, J.R. (1985) 'Process and text: two aspects of human semiosis'. In J.D. Benson and W.S. Greaves, (eds), *Systemic Perspectives on Discourse, Vol. 1*. Norwood, NJ: Ablex.

Martin, J.R. (1992) *English Text: System and Structure*. Amsterdam: Benjamins.

Marshall, G., Newby, H., Rose, R. and Vogler, C. (1988) *Social Class in Modern Britain*. London: Hutchinson.

Marx, Karl (1975) 'Preface to a contribution to the critique of political economy'. In *Karl Marx: Early Writings*. Harmondsworth: Penguin.

Matthiessen, Christian (1993) 'The object of study in cognitive science in relation to its construal and enactment in language', *Language as Cultural Dynamic*, M.A.K. Halliday (guest editor), *Special Issue*, 6(1–2), 187–242.

Matthiessen, Christian (1995) *Lexicogrammatical Cartography: English Systems*. Tokyo: International Language Sciences Publishers.

Matthiessen, Christian (1998) 'Construing processes of consciousness: from the commonsense model to the uncommonsense model of cognitive science'. In J.R. Martin and Robert Veel (eds), *Reading Science: Critical and Functional Perspectives on Discourse of Science*. London: Routledge, pp. 327–56.

Painter, Clare (1996) 'The development of language as a resource for thinking: a linguistic view of learning'. In Ruqaiya Hasan and Geoff Williams (eds), *Literacy in Society*. London: Addison-Wesley Longman.

Pinker, Steven (1994) *The Language Instinct*. New York: Morrow.

Popper, K.R. (1979) *Objective Knowledge: An Evolutionary Approach*. (rev. edn). Oxford: Clarendon Press.

Poulantzas, N. (1975) *Classes in Contemporary Capitalism*. London: New Left Books.

Sadovnik, Alan R. (ed.) (1995) *Knowledge and Pedagogy: The Sociology of Basil Bernstein*. Norwood, NJ: Ablex.

Scase, Richard (1992) *Class*. Buckingham: Open University Press.

Vygotsky, Lev S. (1978) *Mind in Society: The Development of Higher Psychological Processes* (ed. M. Cole, V. John-Steiner, S. Scribner and E. Souberman). Cambridge MA: Harvard University Press.

Williams, Geoff. (1995). *Joint book-reading and literacy pedagogy: a socio-semantic interpretation, CORE*, vol. 1, 19(3); vol. 2, 20(1).

Wright, E. O. (1985) *Classes*. London: Verso.

2 Contexts for learning

Carmel Cloran

Introduction

The co-occurrence of the lexical items 'context' and 'learning' in the title of this chapter suggests a connotation of learning in the environment of the school – the institutional learning context. When the home and neighbourhood are viewed as kinds of learning environments they are generally considered to be qualitatively different from the school environment not just in terms of the fact of their non-institutional or local nature but also in terms of the kind of learning that goes on there. Yet these sites – home/neighbourhood and school – are critical learning contexts in the life history of the individual and, furthermore, there is an important association between them. The nature of the association, however, is likely to be different in the experience of different sectors of society. One of the factors influencing – indeed, construing – the differences concerns the nature of the discourse.

In the following I will examine an important characteristic of the type of discourse that occurs in the school environment, namely expository instructional discourse. The examination will entail the description of a particular way of analysing discourse – rhetorical unit analysis. This analysis will be presented after a discussion of a characterizing feature of instructional discourse, i.e. decontextualization. I then present a small indicative empirical study of the use of decontextualized (and, by implication, contextualized) varieties of discourse in the home environment. The discussion then leads to an examination of the kinds of contexts within the home environment which tend to promote the use of particular types of discourse. These contexts are conceptualized in terms of the four generalized critical contexts of primary socialization identified by Bernstein – the regulative, the instructional, the interpersonal and the imaginative. From the systemic functional (SF) perspective, these contexts may be considered to be construed by interactional practices which are specific to the process of socialization. The examination of interactional practices of mothers with their preschool children will bring us to a consideration of the defining principles of coding orientation, i.e. strength of classification and framing. In Bernstein's conceptualization, a code is considered to be restricted or elaborated depending on the strength of the classification of these contexts and of the framing within them. In other words, coding orientation is inferred by the strength of classification and framing principles. These concepts will be discussed and exemplified. (For related discussions see Painter, Chapter 3, and Williams, Chapter 4, in this volume.)

Characterizing instructional discourse

What is instructional discourse? How do we recognize it? We all participate in it from the perspective of the instructed – the receiver – and from the perspective of the instructor – the transmitter. In addition, we may also participate, as researchers, in the construction of the knowledge to be transmitted – the 'what' of this kind of discourse. In other words, we generally have no trouble recognizing when the process of instruction is occurring.

The question, from the linguist's point of view is: what are the characteristics of such discourse that distinguish it from other types of discourse? Indeed, does instructional discourse have such distinguishing characteristics?

According to Bernstein, instructional discourse is a component of pedagogic discourse; it is an embedded component which transmits specific skills and their relations to each other (1996: 104). The other component of pedagogic discourse, in this conceptualization, is regulative discourse in which are transmitted the rules of the moral order and their various supports. The relation between the two types of discourse is one of embedding: instructional discourse is embedded in regulative discourse.

A characteristic feature of pedagogic discourse in Bernstein's view is the use of decontextualized language. Much has been written in the last twenty years about 'decontextualized' language, principally in discussions of cognitive development, in comparisons of spoken and written language, and in accounts of the development of literacy. The reason for the location of these discussions is that 'decontextualized' language is viewed as a feature of literate language (Scinto 1986: 56), or a prerequisite for its development (Snow 1983). Given the importance of the concept, it would seem to be appropriate to review the literature. It should be noted however that consensus among scholars concerning the adequacy or, indeed, the accuracy of the terms 'contextualized' and 'decontextualized' language is generally lacking.

Current definitions and terminology

Decontextualized language is language that is not 'rooted in an immediate context of time, space or situation' (D'Anglejan and Masny 1987) but is context-independent (Bernstein 1971), autonomous (Olson 1977) or disembedded (Donaldson 1987). The process of decontextualization is that 'whereby the meaning of signs become less and less dependent on the unique spatio-temporal context in which they are used' (Wertsch 1985: 33).

The terms context-independent, autonomous and disembedded appear, from their usage in the literature, to be synonymous; they are the antonyms of the terms context-dependent, non-autonomous and embedded. These three terms and their opposites are used largely by sociolinguists, literacy theorists, and cognitive psychologists respectively though there are cross-linkages. In this chapter I will use, wherever appropriate, only one member of the antonymous pair, i.e. context-independent, autonomous or disembedded. It is hoped that the antonymous relation will permit the interpretation of the other term in each pair, i.e. context-dependent, non-autonomous or embedded.

Decontextualization in sociolinguistic theory

Bernstein's use of the terms context-dependent and context-independent seems to have developed from his earlier linguistic description of socio-linguistic codes as involving language that is tied to or free from its context of use. Bruner (1970: 15,) drawing on the work of Bernstein, expressly refers to context-independent language as decontextualized language, noting that middle class children learn

> to use language without dependence upon shared percepts or actions, with sole reliance on the linguistic self-sufficiency of the message. Decontextualization permits information to be conceived as independent of the speaker's vantage point, it permits communications with those who do not share one's daily experience or actions, and in fact does . . . allow one to transcend restrictions of locale and affiliation.

The terms context-dependent and context-independent are also used by Greenfield (1972) but the definition and linguistic characterization of the concepts remained largely global until Hasan's 1973 publication of the distinction between codes, registers and social dialects. Hasan defined context-independent language as language that encapsulates explicitly all the features of the **relevant immediate situation** in which the verbal interaction is embedded. Since the relevant features of the situation are encapsulated in the language, the text may be interpreted without the need to invoke any prior knowledge of the situation. In this sense such language is context-independent.

The distinction between **relevant** immediate situation and **material** immediate situation is crucial in Hasan's definition. She describes relevant immediate situation as that subset of material immediate situation to which reference is made implicitly (in the case of context-dependent language) or explicitly (in the case of context-independent language) by the forms of the message. She points out that

> The implicitness of the context dependent language implies that the correct decoding of the verbal message would be dependent upon the awareness of the relevant immediate situation, which awareness would be derived from sources

other than the verbal message under focus. That is to say, in order to have access to the meanings of the verbal message, the decoder has to utilise other sources of information than just the language of the text under focus. (1973: 284)

The explicitness of context-independent language, by contrast, implies that 'the correct decoding of the message is a simple function of one's understanding of the language, requiring no extra-linguistic sources of knowledge'. It is clear then that Hasan distinguishes between context and material situation. Indeed, it would appear that the term situation-independent may more accurately identify the concept of context-independent language as defined by Hasan.

Decontextualization, literacy and written language

The expression 'situation-independent' is used by Smith (1984: 147) and Simons and Murphy (1986). The latter point out that the term 'context' is used to refer to an utterance's situational as well as verbal context. Seeing the need to distinguish these two 'contexts', Simons and Murphy adopt the terms 'situation-dependent' and 'text-dependent'. Situation-dependent language refers 'to language that relies on situational cues' (Simons and Murphy 1986: 187) and text-dependent language refers 'to language that can be interpreted without reference to the immediate situational context'. Decontextualized language, for Simons and Murphy, then, is language that 'minimises situation related cues' and this definition is reminiscent of Hasan's context-independent language.

Tannen (1982: 15) adopts the term autonomous to refer to written language and argues that

In the autonomous or literate-based mode, the content or verbal channel are elaborated, while the oral-based strategy elaborates paralinguistic channels and emotional or interpersonal dynamics. (Tannen 1982: 15)

The so-called doctrine of autonomous text is most clearly enunciated by Olson (1977). According to Olson, written texts, unlike speech, must be able to function apart from the context of their production – to be fully explicit in order to be 'acontextual' or autonomous.

Decontextualization and cognitive development

Donaldson (1987: 103) uses the terms embedded and disembedded to refer to the distinction between 'a situation which you are actually in' and that from which you are remote in time and space. In the former thinking arises spontaneously and is wholly embedded within 'a context of action, direct perception, purpose and feeling'.

Donaldson is concerned with the cognitive demands of disembedded thinking which, she suggests, is typical of the educational context. However, she acknowledges that the difficulties presented by disembedded problems 'have a great deal to do with the handling of language' (104) though, she warns, they cannot be reduced to linguistic knowledge:

> In our ordinary embedded thinking and language-using we do not normally even attempt to make sense of words in isolation. We interpret what people say with the help of what they do – their gestures, their movements – and with the help of the entire setting within which the speech occurs. We use all the clues we can get to arrive at what the speaker means. But when we are given a disembedded problem we have the task of figuring out what the words mean: the words on their own. This is an austere and difficult enterprise for the human mind. (104)

In other words, the cognitive demands of embedded language are reduced because the physical setting (i.e. Hasan's material situational setting) provides the clues necessary for interpretation – to make sense of what is said, to locate the sign's signification in linguistic terms. Disembedded language or thought, on the other hand, requires that the hearers supply their own 'cognitive contributions' (Donaldson 1987: 105) in order to make sense, since the extra-linguistic reality by which a sign's signification is established is not perceptually accessible.

Decontextualization and language development

Olson (1977) argues that there is a cultural and developmental transition from oral language to written language and that 'this transition can be described as one of increasing explicitness, with language increasingly able to stand as an unambiguous or autonomous representation of meaning' (Olson 1977: 258).

In support of his position Olson cites de Laguna's oft-quoted discussion of the evolution of language:

> The evolution of language is characterized by a progressive freeing of speech from dependence upon the perceived conditions under which it is uttered and heard, and from the behaviour that accompanies it. The extreme limit of this freedom is reached in language which is written (or printed) and read. For example, it is quite indifferent to the reader of these words under what physical conditions they have been penned or typed. This represents, we repeat, the extreme limit of the process by which language comes to be increasingly independent of the conditions of its use. (De Laguna 1927/70: 107)

The Soviet psychologist Lev Vygotsky, writing about the function and development of speech, gives an account of the early stages in the development of language that is disembedded or context-independent or autonomous. In his discussion of the development of (word) meaning Vygotsky (1981: 219–20) postulates two primary functions: in the early stages of development, words serve an indicative or indexical function, i.e. to direct a child's attention to an object. This is one of the ways in which, in Saussurean terms, a sign's signification is established. Later, speech serves a symbolic function where words serve to categorize objects and events in terms of generalized categories. This symbolic function leads to the formation of relationships among the categories it creates. In Saussurean terms this is how the value of signs develops for the individual and the development of this symbolic function may be viewed as the first stage in the development of decontextualized language.

James Wertsch (1985: 98–9), one of the foremost Western interpreters of Vygotsky's work, poses the question:

> If the original function of speech in Vygotsky's account is the indicative (that is, indexical) function, how is it related to the symbolic function? This is part of the larger question of how the decontextualization of mediational means occurs. On the one hand, one finds sign functioning that reflects the context-bound aspect of linguistic organization; it is concerned with the relationship between sign vehicles and the context in which they occur. On the other hand, one finds sign functioning that reflects the decontextualized aspect of linguistic organization; it is concerned with the notion that certain aspects of language organization can operate independently of the context in which sign vehicles occur. Both aspects are latent potentials in human language. The task of genetic analysis is to account for the transition from a level where semiotic functioning is always contextualized to a level where decontextualized functioning is also possible.

Wertsch, then, is interested in the means whereby the use of decontextualized language develops. Vygotsky (1978: 97) seems to hint at the answer in his discussion of the role of play in the child's development. He writes: 'In play, thought is separated from objects and action arises from ideas rather than from things: a piece of wood begins to be a doll and a stick becomes a horse.' Vygotsky (99) goes on to say that

> The creation of an imaginary situation is not a fortuitous fact in a child's life, but is rather the first manifestation of the child's emancipation from situational constraints.

For Vygotsky, then, play creates an imaginary situation so that an object, e.g. a stick, used in such play becomes a signifier for something else, e.g. a horse, the substitute object (stick) functioning as a pivot through which children detach themselves from immediate sensory experience.

The role of language in the social process

Is there any common thread in the definition of decontextualized language in the literature reviewed above? It would seem that the terms contextualized and decontextualized are used in a relatively non-metaphorical sense as applying to the way in which language is or is not tied to any specific material base within the context of an interaction. In non-technical terms, what the scholars cited above are referring to by the terms embedded, context-dependent or contextualized language use is that kind of language use in which the entities spoken about are present in the material situational setting (MSS) (e.g. Hasan 1973) of the interaction, and the event spoken about is occurring concurrently with the moment of speaking or will occur immediately as a result of the talk. In the case of decontextualized language use, by contrast, entities spoken about are generalized or class-exhaustive and the events are habitual. These two characterizations – co-present versus generalized entities and concurrent versus habitual events – represent the extremes, i.e. most contextualized and the most decontextualized uses of language. This characterization suggests (as, indeed, do the original terms) that (de)contextualization involves just two varieties of language use. In fact, by focusing on the nature of the entities and the events spoken about, degrees of (de)contextualized language use may be identified. Decontextualization may thus be represented as a cline or continuum as shown in Figure 2.1. Here, ten 'degrees' are named, from the most 'contextualized' to the most 'decontextualized' language use.

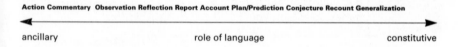

Action Commentary Observation Reflection Report Account Plan/Prediction Conjecture Recount Generalization

ancillary   role of language   constitutive

Figure 2.1 Continuum of the role of language in the social process

These varieties of language use are termed rhetorical activities or rhetorical units.[1] They occur in all types of discourse from the most mundane everyday discourse to academic written discourse; furthermore, the messages which constitute them tend to be chunked together. In other words, any text is describable in terms of its constituent rhetorical units (RUs). This formulation implies a theory of text structure based in constituency relations between identified units. Indeed such a theory is implicit in Hasan's (1989) description of the message as the basic constituent unit of text. The concept of rhetorical unit takes Hasan's message semantics as its point of departure; the RU is viewed as an intermediate unit of text, being constituted by one or more messages and constituting – either alone or in combination with other such units – a text. The RUs which make up a text do not occur in isolation in the text; rather, they are related to each other in various ways, these ways being determined by the concept of function in context (Firth 1935) and this concept itself being realized by patterns of cohesion.

Consider Extract 1[2] which has been segmented in accordance with the location of entities and events with respect to the occasion of the speech event itself, i.e. into its constituent rhetorical units. The extract[3] is a fragment of an interaction between a mother and her preschool child, Stephen, and occurs while the mother is cleaning the oven.[4]

Extract 1

		Observation
196 C	What is that stuff?	
197 M	Oven cleaner	
198 C	What is it called?	
199 M	Hi-Speed Oven Cleaner	
200 C	Oh (LAUGHS) .. Hi-Speed Oven Cleaner!	

		//Action//
204	Don't stick your nose in the oven	
		.1 Commentary
205	It's too smelly, darling	
206 C	Oh yuk!	
216 M	Oops! Stand back a bit, I think	
217	because this is splashing	.2 Commentary
	It's a chemical	2.1 Observation
	and chemicals burn you	2.1.1 Generalization
	if they splash on you	

		//Account//
218	In the new house that we're going to there's an oven that cleans itself	
219 C	Oh!	
220 M	It's a very fancy new kind of oven..	.1 Report
221	and it also turns itself on	
222 C	Oh! (LAUGHS)	
		.2 Prediction
223 M	We'll be able to set it	
224	to turn itself on	
225	so that when we come home from wherever we are	
226	the dinner'll be cooked	
227 C	Aha!	
230 M	And we've got a washing-up machine	.3 Reflection
231 C	Does the - does the oven door open by itself?	
232 M	No	
233 C	Oh	

		//Recount//
251 M	I've never heard of an oven that opens itself	
		.1 Conjecture
252	It wouldn't be much use	
253	because who would get the things out of the oven	
254	if no one was there?	
255 C	The oven	
256 M	Oh. Would the oven eat the dinner?	
257 C	No!	
258	I would eat the dinner	

The extract begins with a sequence of messages which constitute the RU Observation, i.e. the talk is about an inherent characteristic of a co-present object, the cleaning agent being used by the mother. Apparently the child comes closer to investigate the process, for the mother issues an injunction in the form of the Action RU and follows this with a Commentary RU. The Commentary is considered to be embedded in the Action since it functions within this context as a reason for the Action. This analysis is supported lexicogrammatically by the location of the componential cohesive device *It* (=*the oven*) in the Theme of the message initiating the Commentary. Note that the Action RU is not analysed as embedded within the previous Observation since it has no function in the context of that RU. However, it is analysed as being related to the Observation (as indicated by the dotted horizontal line). Again the analysis is supported by the location of the componential cohesive device *the oven* not in Theme (which would indicate an embedding relation) but in the Theme of the initial message of the Action RU.

The Action RU continues with another injunction (message 216). This is again followed by an embedded Commentary which functions as a reason for the injunction, this function being explicitly indicated by the organic cohesive conjunction *because*. Two RUs follow – an Observation concerning an inherent characteristic of the co-present object (the cleaning agent) and a Generalization concerning an inherent characteristic of the whole class *chemicals*. Both these RUs are embedded, i.e. they serve some function in the context of the previous RU, the Observation within the context of the Commentary and the Generalization within the context of the Observation. The analysis is again supported by the patterns of cohesion: the componential cohesive device *It*(=*this*) located in the Theme of the message constituting the Observation and the organic cohesive device *and* in the initial message of the Generalization.

The Account beginning at message 218 and describing an inherent characteristic of a situationally absent object is related to the previous RU with its embeddings but is not considered to be embedded since it does not seem to serve any function within the context of the previous matrix and/or embedded RUs. The non-thematic componential cohesion –*oven* – supports the analysis. The Report constituted by message 220, however, is

embedded within the Account in the context of which it is considered to
serve an elaborative function, further specifying the item under discussion
in terms of its non-inherent characteristic. The thematic componential
cohesion – *It* (=*oven*) – supports the interpretation. At message 223 the
mother makes a Prediction. Note that this RU is analysed as embedded
within the Account. This analysis is not, however, supported lexicogrammatically by thematic componential or organic cohesion. There is nevertheless a covert (unexpressed) consequential relation between the initial
message of the Prediction and the prior messages constituting the
Account. In other words, the fact that such a relation can be inferred
(note the plausibility of the insertion of the conjunction *so* at the beginning of message 223) is sufficient grounds for the analysis of the Prediction as serving an enhancing function within the context of the Account.

The Reflection occurring at message 230 serves to extend the Account.
The child, however, remains focused on the Account and so the Reflection is discontinued. At message 251 the mother initiates a Recount and
follows this up with a Conjecture where possible actions and states of
affairs which might occur under certain conditions are considered.

The most superficial reading of the above analysis will indicate that a
particular entity in each message is being singled out as the entity whose
semantic features are central to the identification of classes of RU. A close
reading will reveal that the relevant entity in each message is considered
to be, typically, that entity which manifests the lexicogrammatical role of
Subject in the clause realizing the message. Table 2.1 presents in summary
form the semantic features of the central entity (CE) and event orientation (EO) that are relevant in the identification of the classes of RU.[5]

These RU classes are considered to be realizationally related to an
aspect of the contextual variable mode of discourse known as the role of
language in the social process. This fact is implied by the values of the
semantic features by which they are identified, i.e. the specificity and location of the spoken-about entity; and the location in time-and-reality of the
event spoken about. In any social process language may be ancillary to the
task in hand serving merely to facilitate the non-linguistic goings-on. This
is the case when people are co-operatively involved in some non-linguistic
task such as moving furniture, and use language simply to give directions
to each other and to co-ordinate their actions. Alternatively some social
processes are actually constituted by language and simply could not occur
in the absence of language. The relationship between RU types and the
contextual feature is shown in Figure 2.1.

In sum, then, it may be said that in examining the use of contextualized
and decontextualized language we are examining those occasions of talk
in which language is ancillary to – or constitutive of – the goings-on in an
interaction. Occasions of interaction may contain any number of such
uses of language. It is to an examination of such occasions in the everyday
talk of mothers in interaction with their preschool children in the routine
activities of everyday life that I now turn.

Table 2.1 Values of CE and EO in the identification of classes of RU

EVENT ORIENTATION / CENTRAL ENTITY	PRIOR	CONCURRENT		FUTURE		
		non-habitual	**habitual**	**goods/services exchange**	**information exchange**	**hypothetical** (possible-conditional)
Within material situational setting (MSS)						
• interactant	Recount	Commentary	Reflection	Action	Plan/ Prediction	
• other person/object	Recount	Commentary	Observation	Action	Prediction	Conjecture
Not within MSS						
• person/object		Report	Account	Prediction		
Class			Generalization			

Language in context

If decontextualized language use is a characteristic of the instructional discourse of the school then it would seem that those children who habitually participate in such language use before they enter school would be at
a distinct advantage in the school environment. The question to be
addressed then is: Is there any variation in the extent to which children
from different social groups participate in the kind of discourse characteristic of the school environment? This question may be addressed by investigating the frequency of occurrence of the use of classes of RU in the talk
of mothers and children. Such an investigation was carried out on a small
scale: the discursive practices of only eight dyads were investigated. Consequently, the study cannot be regarded as anything but suggestive.

Analysing decontextualized language: the subjects

The subjects upon whose interaction this indicative study was based form a
subset of Hasan's set of 24 mother–child dyads. These 24 mothers and
their preschool children were drawn from two social groups – middle and
lower class – and the children were evenly represented by sex. Hasan (e.g.
1989) defined social class in terms of the degree of autonomy that the
occupation of the family breadwinner permitted. High-autonomy professionals (HAP) were those whose occupation permitted a high degree of
autonomy in decision-making, affecting not only their own working life
and practices but also that of others. Bank and business managers, doc-
tors, teachers, etc. represented the HAP families in Hasan's study. Lower-
autonomy professionals, by contrast, work in occupations in which they
have little control over their work practices and none over that of others
in the workplace. Such LAP families in Hasan's study included a council
truck driver, a paint mixer, as well as single mothers whose sole source of
income was the supporting mothers' benefit. Hasan (1992a) gives a rationale for her operationalization of social class (see Williams, this volume
Chapter 4).

In terms of Bernstein's theory, HAP occupations are those in which the
individual has a non-specific relation to the material base of his/her work
so that the relation between meanings and this material base is indirect,
giving rise to an elaborated coding orientation. In the LAP occupations,
by contrast, the individual is likely to have a specific and local relation to
the material base of his/her work so that the relation between meanings
and the material base will be more direct, generating a restricted orientation to meaning.

For purposes of the present study the eight dyads chosen from among
the 24 comprised four HAP and four LAP dyads, with two girls and two
boys in each social group.

The texts

Extracts of texts produced by the eight mother–child dyads within a similar interactional frame were analysed. This similar interactional frame was that of meal-time. The frame was chosen because it was expected that it would give rise to the use of situated language – the categories of less constitutive language use – but would not preclude the more constitutive categories. This frame, then, was expected to give rise to at least a varied if not full range of variants of 'situated' and 'non-situated' language. The RUs identified in fact arose from a consideration of this interactional frame.

The extracts were, on average, about four hundred messages in length representing 20 to 30 minutes of interaction. The analysis of the extracts began where the talk first introduces the meal-time activity and ended when the mother turned off the tape.

The analysis

Each message of the talk of the eight dyads was analysed and messages having the feature [**progressive**] (see e.g., Hasan 1989) were identified as belonging to one of the ten classes of RU. In the analysis, the following types of messages were excluded: i) those having the feature [**punctuative**] (Hasan 1989): ii) unintelligible messages; and iii) those in which the retrieval of ellipsis was problematic. These types of messages are shown in Extract 2.

Extract 2

156	Mother	You'll slip down in a minute with a strap around your bottom
157	Karen	With what strap?
158	Mother	I've got a strap
159	Karen	What?
160	Mother	For naughty girls
161	Karen	[?]
162	Mother	Mm
163	Karen	Eh?
164	Mother	I've got a strap for naughty girls

In Extract 2 the messages that were not coded as constituting (part of) any particular kind of RU are messages 159, 161–3. (It should be noted here that this illustrative extract was chosen because of the density of these types of messages; such density is not typical in the extracts). Message 159 is a [**punctuative**] type of message; message 161 is unintelligible and so, consequently, is message 162; finally message 163 is also a [**punctuative**] message.

Results

The exclusion of messages having the feature [**punctuative**] and those which were unintelligible and/or problematic reduced the total number of messages assigned to one RU type or other. The final number of messages involved in RUs is given for each dyad (identified by initials) in Table 2.2. In this table, the number of messages involved in a particular RU type is given as a percentage of the total number of messages involved in the construal of RUs. Each category of RU was subjected to the Mann-Whitney test for equal averages, a non-parametric test which is based on the sum of ranks of the data points (Book 1977: 409ff). For each RU the hypothesis tested was that there is no difference between HAP and LAP speakers in the average frequency with which they used each type of RU. The results of this test for each of the RU types is given in the final column where the value of the Mann-Whitney statistic – T – is given at a probability level of 0.05.

Table 2.2 shows that the hypothesis that there is no significant difference between HAP and LAP speakers in the average frequency with which they use each type of RU is rejected for three of the RU types: Action, Generalization and Conjecture. In the sample studied, the HAP speakers are likely to use the Action RU less often than the LAP speakers ($p < .05$) but are likely to use the Generalization and Conjecture RUs more often ($p < .05$) than the LAP speakers. Testing for sex differences revealed no significant differences between dyads in which the child was male and those in which the child was female.

Discussion of the results

It was suggested earlier that Action and Generalization are located at the opposite ends of the continuum representing the role of language in social processes. Action is located at the most ancillary end representing therefore the most 'contextualized' language – language that is directly related to a specific material base, this base being the speech event itself. Generalization is located at the constitutive end representing the most decontextualized language – language that is related only indirectly to a material base. In the RU Action, the spoken-about entity is an interactant and the temporal orientation of the event is to the immediate future – 'what you or I will do in the now of our speaking time'. A Generalization, by contrast, is most removed from the interactants' here-and-now. The spoken-about entity is categorical and this gives the concurrent temporal reference of the event a timeless or habitual value. The results show that, in the overall talk, LAP speakers more often than HAP speakers use the RU Action – an RU type that is most directly related to the material base of the speech event. By contrast, HAP speakers more often than LAP speakers use the RU Generalization – an RU that is not directly related to any specific material base.

Table 2.2 Proportion of messages involved in each type of RU

| RU \ Dyad | HAP | | | | LAP | | | | Mann-Whitney $T_{4,4}\ 11-25$ $p < .05$ |
| | MALE | | FEMALE | | MALE | | FEMALE | | |
	HS	HC	MK	GD	MJ	DC	JK	SR	
Action	8.0	10.0	14.0	9.0	15.0	21.0	17.0	30.0	$T_{HAP} = 10.0*$
Commentary	8.0	25.0	12.0	6.0	26.0	19.0	14.0	21.0	$T_{HAP} = 13.0$
Observation	8.0	4.0	6.0	7.0	9.5	4.0	3.0	6.0	$T_{HAP} = 20.0$
Reflection	3.0	10.0	14.5	11.0	16.0	18.0	23.5	12.0	$T_{HAP} = 14.0$
Report	4.0	0.0	1.5	2.0	0.0	1.5	0.0	1.0	$T_{HAP} = 13.5$
Account	13.0	4.0	11.0	7.0	10.0	5.0	3.0	3.0	$T_{HAP} = 23.0$
Generalization	20.0	17.0	9.0	5.0	4.5	3.5	2.0	0.0	$T_{HAP} = 26.0*$
Plan/Prediction	14.0	16.0	13.0	20.0	9.0	20.0	15.0	19.0	$T_{HAP} = 17.5$
Conjecture	3.0	1.0	1.0	2.0	0.5	0.0	0.0	0.5	$T_{HAP} = 26.0*$
Recount	19.0	13.0	18.0	31.0	9.5	18.0	22.5	7.5	$T_{HAP} = 21.5$
%	100	100	100	100	100	100	100	100	
No. of messages	362	365	393	433	397	361	288	416	

(* = significant at p <.05)

HAP and LAP speakers also vary in the frequency with which they use the RU identified as Conjecture, as Table 2.2 shows. Conjecture involves speculating about possible outcomes under certain conditions; its criterial linguistic features reside within event orientation: hypotheticality together with possibility. Hypotheticality is realized by a secondary conditional clause and probability by modality in the primary clause. Hasan's investigations (e.g. Hasan 1987,1989) have shown that such conjecture is a feature of pedagogic discourse even in the first year of school.

Bernstein (1990) examines pedagogic discourse which he characterizes as involving meanings which are not directly related to a specific material base but are applicable to a range of situations. In terms of the notion of RU introduced in this study, the RU Generalization, for example, would constitute a significant proportion of the instructional discourse of the school. Clearly, then, where meanings which are not directly related to a specific material base form a significant proportion of the discursive practices of the home, where children are encouraged to speculate about what might be, then children from such homes are at an advantage in the classroom. Bernstein (1975: 194) notes that such children are likely to be middle class, for it is children from this stratum of society who are sensitized to and

> incorporate as crucially relevant, principles which construct texts that are related only indirectly to a specific material base. Further, they become sensitive to the social relationships which induce, regulate and call for such realisations, codings or texts, either in the family or the school.

The RU analysis of the texts from the eight dyads summarized in Table 2.2 clearly supports this statement. However, differences in the overall usage of the types of RU reported in Table 2.2 say nothing about the function of RUs such as Generalization or Conjecture in the contexts of everyday life, particularly the critical socializing contexts identified by Bernstein. It is to this issue that I now turn.

Contexts of instruction

What are the contexts in the home that promote this type of language use? To investigate this issue it might be useful to examine 'contextualized' and 'decontextualized' language use in its role in construing Bernstein's critical generalized socialization contexts – the regulative, the instructional, the interpersonal and the imaginative.

The regulative context

The regulative context is construed by those specialized interactional practices which make the child aware of the rules of the moral order and their various supports through the enactment of authority relationships

(Bernstein 1971). One might expect, within this context, to find certain kinds of language use – a command, perhaps, prescribing or prohibiting certain behaviour(s) supported by an assertion expressing the rationale for the prescription or prohibition. One might predict, then, that the regulative context might be realized by the RU Action with/without, for example, a Prediction, Generalization or Conjecture. Extracts 3 and 4 represent topically similar regulative contexts. These extracts (as well as those following) are analysed in terms of their constituent RUs and the kind of context construed. The boundaries of the RUs are indicated by fine lines; the boundaries of contexts by thick lines. Thus in Extract 3, the mother's messages 300–1 constitute the RU Action and construe the regulative context. The child's response in message 302 constitutes a Commentary and construes an imaginative context.

Extract 3: JK

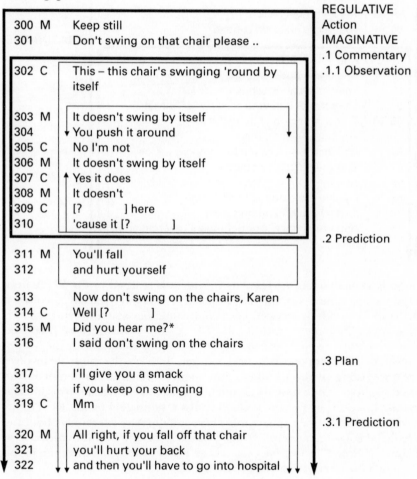

			REGULATIVE
300	M	Keep still	Action
301		Don't swing on that chair please ..	IMAGINATIVE
			.1 Commentary
302	C	This – this chair's swinging 'round by itself	.1.1 Observation
303	M	It doesn't swing by itself	
304		You push it around	
305	C	No I'm not	
306	M	It doesn't swing by itself	
307	C	Yes it does	
308	M	It doesn't	
309	C	[?] here	
310		'cause it [?]	
			.2 Prediction
311	M	You'll fall	
312		and hurt yourself	
313		Now don't swing on the chairs, Karen	
314	C	Well [?]	
315	M	Did you hear me?*	
316		I said don't swing on the chairs	
			.3 Plan
317		I'll give you a smack	
318		if you keep on swinging	
319	C	Mm	
			.3.1 Prediction
320	M	All right, if you fall off that chair	
321		you'll hurt your back	
322		and then you'll have to go into hospital	

Note that the mother does not encourage the construal of the imaginative context here and the child eventually abandons it. This contrasts with Extract 4 where the mother actively participates in the construal of the imaginative context:

Extract 4: HS

REGULATIVE
Action

| 52 | M | You won't tip that chair, will you? |

.1 Conjecture

53		Because you might fall over
54		If you do
55	C	Mm and spill my tea
56	M	Yes ..
57		And crack your head
58	C	Yes - no!
59	M	Yes if you fall back
60		you might crack your head ..

IMAGINATIVE

61	C	And [? kick] [?]
62		And crash down into the tea (LAUGHING) ...
63		Then catch an octopus
64		Then throw it in your face (LAUGHING)
65	M	Throw an octopus in my face!
		You horrible little boy!
66	C	And kick the - kick the ball into your face
67		And then catch a octopus
68		And then put it in your eyes (LAUGHING)
69	M	I'd give the octopus back to you
70		And it would hang on to you
71		And put all its sticking things all around your neck

In both these extracts the regulative context is realized by the RU Action. This was predicted on the basis that this context typically involves a demand for goods or services, i.e. a command; messages involving a goods or services exchange constitute the RU Action. It was further predicted that the regulative context may also contain some rationale for the action. In fact, this element occurs in both extracts. In both, the rationale involves the forecasting of the possible consequences which are inherent in the child's actions. The rationale is couched in slightly different terms in each extract however: in Extract 3, the forecast is construed by the RU Prediction, in Extract 4 by a Conjecture. There is a degree of certainty about the predicted consequences in Extract 3 which is lacking in the Conjecture of Extract 4. Note that Extract 3 contains a further rationale, this time in the form of a threat construed by the RU Plan.

These two extracts, in addition to their topical similarity, share another feature: they both develop into the imaginative context. The introduction – by the child – of the imaginative context is the extent of this similarity however; the development of a context is obviously dependent on the cooperation of the interactional partner; in other words, it involves what is often referred to as context negotiation. In Extract 3, the mother does not encourage the child's fantasy which is perhaps interpreted as defiance since it implies non-compliance. In Extract 4 the mother actively participates in the development of the imaginative context.

Is the regulative context always realized by the Action RU? Consider Extract 5.

Extract 5: HS

311	M	Oh .. Did you like flying in an aeroplane?
312	C	Yes
313	M	We might go on an aeroplane again one day
314	C	To where? ..

			REGULATIVE
315	M	I don't think Nanna wants her blind cord chewed	Report
			.1 Commentary
316		It's filthy, darling	
317		Very dirty	
318		All that dirt's going into your mouth and down into your tummy	
			.1.1 Generalization
319		It's really best not to fill your tummy with dirt	
			.1.1.1 Action
320		Would you like some mandarin to put in your tummy instead?	
321	C	Yes	
322	M	There you are ...	
323		How many pieces can you eat?	
324	C	A hundred	
325	M	Oh a hundred! ... four	
326		Here, you can have four pieces	

The demand for goods and services here (message 315) is not realized by the Action RU; rather, this message involves a giving of information. In this respect it is indistinguishable from the prior and following messages. In other words, in terms of primary speech function, there is no boundary between this and the previous messages. What is happening here? By expressing message 315 as the RU Report, Stephen's mother achieves two rhetorical purposes – telling Stephen what he should not do and why. Hasan (1992b: 105) points out that

> In demanding goods and services, speakers usually ground their demands in some assertion which is presented to the addressee as the motivation for complying with the demand.

An assertion can, in other words, act as a reason. Stephen's mother, in Extract 5 gives reasons why he shouldn't act in a certain way without actually expressing this demand. Stephen must infer, therefore, that he must desist. Thus, when an assertion is given instead of a command, the hearer must arrive at the implication of the assertion – the prescription or prohibition – through acts of reasoning. With reference to Extract 5, Stephen arrives at the injunction on his behaviour via a path of reasoning such as: 'Why is mummy telling me that Nana doesn't like her blind-cord being chewed? She must want me not to chew it.' Note that in this extract, Stephen's mother, by presenting a number of reasons, ensures that the correct inference is picked up.

If the social process being achieved in the regulative context is the regulation of someone's action or conduct, then clearly the RU Action, perhaps having embedded within it a Plan or Prediction, is a congruent rhetorical device for bringing this about. However, as Extract 5 shows, speakers need not use this RU; there are more indirect, tangential means of achieving the same ends, for example, by simply stating a reason. The use of an RU other than Action for achieving the social process of regulation would seem to be an example of the non-congruent or metaphorical use of RUs for the construal of the regulative context. Such non-congruent realization of the regulative context occurs repeatedly in certain dyads and may be interpreted as illustrating the concept of weakening of principles of classification of contexts resulting in weakening of the boundaries between contexts. This notion will be taken up later in the chapter.

The imaginative context

The interactional practices of the imaginative context encourage the child to experiment and re-create his world on his own terms and in his own way (Bernstein 1971). This process of re-creation is considered by a number of scholars (e.g. Vygotsky 1978) to have far-reaching consequences. It is also a process which seems to be almost universally construed by preschool children at mealtimes. In Extract 6 Julian initiates this context and in Extract 7 Stephen does.

The impetus – or pivot in Vygotsky's (1978) terms – for the construal of the imaginative context in Extracts 6 and 7 seems to be an object in the immediate environment. It is clearly a cup in Extract 6 but the actual identity of the object in Extract 7 is not so obvious. What is certain however, is that neither object is what it is claimed to be – 'a driving cup' and 'a boat that flies.' Given that the immediate situational setting provides the impetus for the development of the imaginative context, it is no surprise that the RU Observation and/or Commentary should be the means of its construal.

Extract 6: MJ

497 M   Did you know Maree is your cousin?
498 C   Yeah
499 M   Mm

IMAGINATIVE
Observation

501 C	He's got a driving licence
502 M	Oh it has not
503	It's only a cup
504 C	No
505	He's a driving cup
506	Just pretending [?] (MAKES ENGINE NOISES)
507	That jumps higher
508 M	Mm, it does, doesn't it?
509 C	Yeah ..
510	'Cause watch, I do that [?], don't I?
512	[?]

REGULATIVE
.1 Action

| 513 M | All right, don't play with the forks |
| 514 C | Why? |

1.1 Commentary

| 515 M | 'Cause they're dirty |

Extract 7: HS

207 M   Oh, it's nice sitting here in the sun...

IMAGINATIVE
Observation

208 C	This is a boat that flies
209 M	A boat that flies!
210 C	Yeah ..
211 M	Is it a hydroplane?
212 C	Yes

INSTRUCTION
.1 Generalization

| 213 M | A hydroplane is a plane that can land on the water |
| 214 C | Yes |

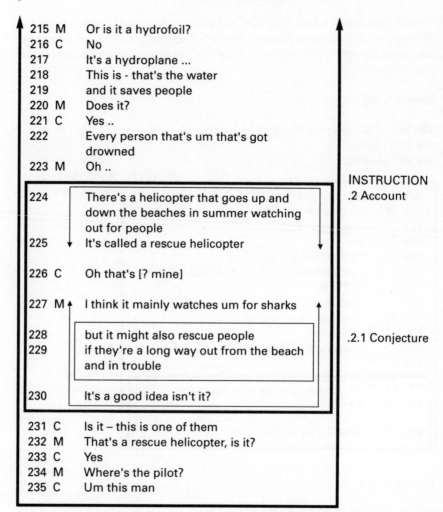

215 M	Or is it a hydrofoil?	
216 C	No	
217	It's a hydroplane ...	
218	This is - that's the water	
219	and it saves people	
220 M	Does it?	
221 C	Yes ..	
222	Every person that's um that's got drowned	
223 M	Oh ..	

INSTRUCTION
.2 Account

224	There's a helicopter that goes up and down the beaches in summer watching out for people
225	It's called a rescue helicopter
226 C	Oh that's [? mine]
227 M	I think it mainly watches um for sharks

.2.1 Conjecture

228	but it might also rescue people
229	if they're a long way out from the beach and in trouble
230	It's a good idea isn't it?

231 C	Is it – this is one of them
232 M	That's a rescue helicopter, is it?
233 C	Yes
234 M	Where's the pilot?
235 C	Um this man

In Extract 6 the mother, like the mother in Extract 3, discourages the construal of the imaginative context at mealtime. In Extract 7 the interactants are those already met in Extract 4. In that extract as in the present extract, this mother actively encourages the child's re-creation of his world by participating in it. In addition, however, she takes the opportunity to instruct the child in 'real world' matters so that the imaginative context evolves into an instructional context. The mother in this dyad belongs to the HAP social group and, like other members of this group, seems to avail herself of every opportunity to teach the child about the objective nature of objects and persons.

It seems that the imaginative context is somewhat fragile, in that many mothers seem to discourage its embedding within any context where more immediate matters are the concern – getting the child fed, bathed, dressed, etc. Other mothers actively encourage imaginative play and participate in it, often transforming it into an instructional context. It would seem that the imaginative context is one which actually promotes the use of Conjecture. In such contexts the child (and mother) recontextualize some object assigning them attributes and roles which belong to the imagined rather than to the actual. This activity entails the exploration of 'what might be' under the given (imaginative) condition.

What is the significance in the life of the individual of the imaginative context? The most persuasive answer to this question is to be found in Vygotsky's (1978) discussion of the role of play in the development of the child. According to Vygotsky, it is through play that the child's relationship to reality is crucially changed 'because the structure of his perceptions changes' (1978: 98). Through the use of a pivot the child transfers meaning from the real object to the imaginary object; in this way, meaning is detached from object. An object *is* whatever the child wants it to be simply by virtue of the process of saying. The construal of the imaginative context represents, then, an intermediate stage in the development of thought from the situationally constrained stage characteristic of early childhood to the situationally unconstrained stage characteristic of adult thought.

The interpersonal context

An interpersonal context is one in which the child is made aware of affective states, both his own and others. Such a context may provide a point of departure for the construal of an instructional context as Extract 8 shows.

Extract 8: HC

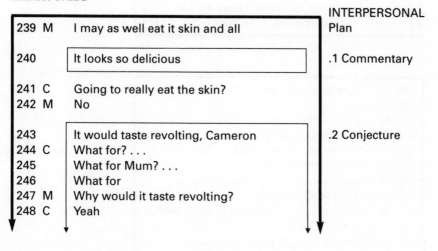

			INTERPERSONAL
239	M	I may as well eat it skin and all	Plan
240		It looks so delicious	.1 Commentary
241	C	Going to really eat the skin?	
242	M	No	
243		It would taste revolting, Cameron	.2 Conjecture
244	C	What for? . . .	
245		What for Mum? . . .	
246		What for	
247	M	Why would it taste revolting?	
248	C	Yeah	

INSTRUCTIONAL
.2.1 Observation

.2.1.1 Generalization

249	M	Because it's not food
250	C	Oh
251	M	it's the packet (C LAUGHS)
252		Isn't it?

253		Some food comes in packets
254		and some food comes with skins on
255	C	Mm ..
256	M	And the skin is the mandarin's packet,
257		keeping it nice
258		until somebody's ready to eat it
259	C	Oh
260	M	And then if nobody eats it
261		and it falls on the ground
262		well the skin keeps the mandarin seeds safe
263		until they're ready to grow
264		and then they can grow
265		This protects them
266		It protects the mandarin seeds
267	C	Yeah
268	M	And then, when the mandarin seeds are ready to grow
269		this breaks
270		and the mandarin seeds start to grow into little mandarin trees

Extract 9:JK

INTERPERSONAL
Prediction

179		School tomorrow
180	C	Eh?
181	M	School tomorrow
182	C	Mmhm (NEGATIVE)
183	M	Mmhm (AFFIRMATIVE)
184	C	Mhmh (NEGATIVE)
185	M	Yes
186	C	But it will be raining
187	M	Well? . . . you've still got to go to school . . . don't you?
188		School, school, school for Karen
189	C	School, school, school for Julie – my mummy

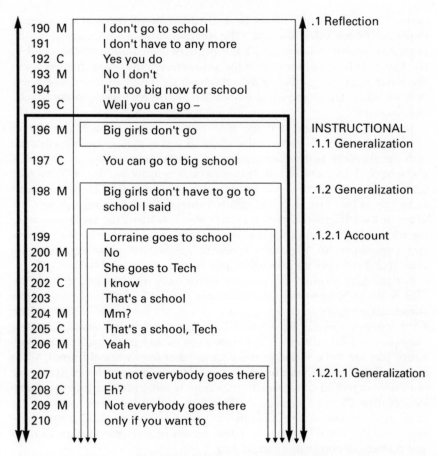

190 M	I don't go to school	.1 Reflection
191	I don't have to any more	
192 C	Yes you do	
193 M	No I don't	
194	I'm too big now for school	
195 C	Well you can go –	
196 M	Big girls don't go	INSTRUCTIONAL .1.1 Generalization
197 C	You can go to big school	
198 M	Big girls don't have to go to school I said	.1.2 Generalization
199	Lorraine goes to school	.1.2.1 Account
200 M	No	
201	She goes to Tech	
202 C	I know	
203	That's a school	
204 M	Mm?	
205 C	That's a school, Tech	
206 M	Yeah	
207	but not everybody goes there	.1.2.1.1 Generalization
208 C	Eh?	
209 M	Not everybody goes there	
210	only if you want to	

Extract 8 is from a HAP dyad; however, instruction often evolves out of an interpersonal context in LAP dyads also as Extract 9 shows.

Extracts 8 and 9 are good illustrations of what might be termed the prototypical instructional context, i.e. that process of teaching about the objective nature of persons and objects in which the specific (*the mandarin* in Extract 8; *I* (=the mother) in Extract 9) and the general (*food with skin* in Extract 8; *big girls* in Extract 9) are related so that instruction departs from the known and proceeds to the unknown – from the specific to the general. These two extracts also represent the extent of the occurrence of the prototypical instructional RU – Generalization – in HAP and LAP dyads: in the HC (HAP) interaction (Extract 8), the Generalization constitutes a substantial proportion of the text, and contrasts with the JK (LAP) interaction (Extract 9) in this respect. Thus these two extracts serve to render some of the statistics (Table 2.2) meaningful.

In Extracts 8 and 9, the interpersonal context develops into the instructional. In fact, of the four generalized socializing contexts identified by Bernstein, it is the instructional context which is unlikely to be 'disembedded'. Rather it will always be embedded in (or take as its point of departure) some other context – the interpersonal, the imaginative or the regulative within the context of the primary socialization of the child in the family. It is in this sense that the instructional discourse that occurs in the home differs from that of the school where it is likely to be 'disembedded' or, more strictly speaking, embedded almost exclusively in the regulative discourse.

In summary, it seems that the HAP mother in the extracts given takes every opportunity to instruct the child in terms that are commensurate with the forms of instruction favoured in the official pedagogic context – the school. This form of talk seems to be a priority for the HAP mother who also encourages the child in his/her imaginative play. These two facets – the use of the most decontextualized categories of RU and the development of the imaginative context – are not unrelated; the latter promotes the former by enabling the child to free him-/herself from immediate sensory experience, in Vygotsky's terms to emancipate meanings from the objects and actions with which they had been directly fused before.

For the LAP mother, the priority seems to be the immediate concern. This is not to suggest the generalization that LAP children's imaginative construals are not encouraged; that would be missing the point altogether. Furthermore, it would be a totally inaccurate conclusion, since countless examples of LAP mothers' encouragement of and participation in imaginative play are to be found in the data **in other interactional frames**. What is clear is that **in the interactional frame investigated**, such construals are not encouraged; in other words, mealtime is not considered an appropriate occasion for such construals. This fact, and indeed, the fact that the HAP mothers encourage imaginative play – is unremarkable, even predicted by Bernstein's theory – if the notion of strength of classification and framing of contexts is considered.

Classification and framing of contexts

The analysis I have given so far identifies a particular type of RU as construing a part of the regulative context – that part of the context which involves the prescription or prohibition of the child's behaviour. This element of the regulative context is typically realized by the RU Action. Given that this is typically, or congruently, the case, the possibility is raised of the non-congruent realization of this context. The reason for considering such a possibility is that it is via such means that we may be able to identify variation among the dyads in the strength of classification and framing and therefore variation in modalities of code.

The concepts of classification and framing were introduced by Bernstein in order to integrate the macro and micro levels of analysis (Bernstein 1990: 21ff). Classification refers to the relation between categories, to the extent to which they are insulated from each other. Depending on the strength or weakness of the classification principle, categories are strongly or weakly insulated. Framing refers to communication, in particular 'to variations of the modalities of control' (Bernstein and Diaz 1984: 23), i.e. to the way in which interactional practices within a category are realized. The strength of the framing principle regulates the interactional practices within a category such that a strong framing principle is realized in what Bernstein terms positional and imperative forms of control. The principle of classification is itself the manifestation of power relations, and the framing principle realizes the form of control.

At the micro level of analysis (the level with which we are concerned in this chapter), power relations are transformed into principles of communication and it is by means of these principles or codes that subjects are positioned and interactions regulated. Codes control the production of meanings which construe contexts that are strongly or weakly insulated from each other depending on the principle of classification; the framing principle determines the kinds of meanings that are considered legitimate within the contexts that are recognized.

At the linguistic level, the concept which enables these issues to be investigated would seem to be that of congruent and non-congruent realizations. This is a concept introduced by Halliday and, in very simple terms, refers to the typical versus atypical form of the lexicogrammatical realization of some semantic feature. For example, and considering for present purposes only realizations of interpersonal meanings, a command is prototypically realized by the imperative clause, a statement by a declarative clause, and a question by an interrogative. Therefore, if a command is realized by a declarative or interrogative clause then such a realization is said to be non-congruent or metaphorical.

The concept of non-congruent realization is a factor that accounts for the non-one-to-one relationship between form and meaning. However, to say that a command is a command whether it be realized by an imperative, declarative or interrogative form seems to deny the fact that differences in form express differences in meaning. One way of reconciling these two fundamental postulates of the systemic functional model is to consider a third fundamental concept, the notion of delicacy. Thus, we may say that **at the most primary degree of delicacy** a command is a command whether it is realized by an imperative (*Shut the door*), declarative (*You must shut the door*) or interrogative (*Would you shut the door?*) form. At further degrees of delicacy, however, each of these forms expresses some semantic feature not found in the others. The interrogative form, for example, implies a degree of discretion with regard to the performance of the action that is not present in the other two forms. And this is precisely what Hasan's semantic networks capture.

Variation in strength of framing

What is the relevance of all this to classification and framing? It is suggested that variation in strength of framing is manifested in the mother–child talk by the type of selections made from the range of choices available to express a particular primary meaning. Strong framing is manifested by the selection of congruent forms; weak framing by the selection of non-congruent forms. Thus, in the regulative context, for example, the element which prescribes or prohibits behaviour – the command – may:

a) select i) the feature [**exhortative**][6] realized by an imperative clause, or ii) the feature [**assertive; addressee-oriented**] realized by a declarative clause with second person pronoun at Subject and high-value modal at Finite;

b) select i) the feature [**consultative**] realized by an interrogative clause, or the feature [**assertive; speaker-oriented**] realized by a declarative clause with first person singular pronoun at Subject.

Each of these options construes messages which constitute the RU Action which is the congruent RU for construing commands. However, there are two further choices available, i.e. the element command

c) may be expressed within an RU that is constituted by messages selecting the semantic features [**give; information**] (as opposed to [**demand; goods/services**]) as in Extract 10 below;

d) may not be expressed at all. This was seen in Extract 5 where the mother presented a number of reasons why the child should not 'chew the blind cord'.

Where the regulative context is realized by the options suggested in c) and d) then it is suggested that these constitute non-congruent realizations of this context.

Extract 10: MJ

```
125 C    Fish . . . chips . . . dim-sim . . . four (M LAUGHS)
126      Dim-sim . . . chips . . . four [?    ]
127 M    All right . . .
```

128 C	This chair must be [?able to] move around		IMAGINATIVE Observation
129 M	Beg your pardon?		
130 C	This chair must be [?able to] move around		
131 M	No		.1 Commentary
132	It's because Julian's pushing it under the table with his feet		
133		and he'll get smacked	REGULATIVE .1.1 Prediction
134		if he doesn't stop . . .	

In this extract Julian's mother does not demand that he stop pushing the chair around with his feet. This demand must rather be inferred from the fact that she threatens to punish him. A further non-congruent feature of this extract is the fact that the mother talks to him as if she is talking about a third person. One can probe the 'stratal tension' (Martin, 1997) arising from the non-congruent construal in Extract 10. Thus, instead of responding appropriately to the implied meaning – *Stop pushing the chair with your feet* – Julian might facetiously respond to the 'form' – the fact that information appears to be the commodity involved in the exchange, e.g. 135 C *And what will happen to him if he does stop?*

Extracts 11 and 12 present two topically similar but congruently opposite construals of the regulative context.

Extract 11: HS

251 C	[?] (UNINTELLIGIBLE)	REGULATIVE Recount	
252 M	I can't hear what you said		
253	because you filled your mouth full of peanut butter sandwich		
254	It's hard talking to you	.1 Observation	
255	when you've got your mouth full, isn't it?		
256	It's a bit rough, I think		

In Extract 11, messages 252–6 assert reasons why Stephen should discontinue a particular behaviour, i.e. talking with his mouth full. The mother does not explicitly demand that he discontinue this behaviour. In fact, if Stephen is to satisfy his mother he must infer this command from the fact that the mother has made these statements.

In Extract 12, messages 163–5, Lisa's mother, like Stephen's mother, is concerned with the problems caused by eating and speaking at the same time.

Extract 12: LL

159 M	Are you enjoying that? . .	INTERPER-SONAL Commentary
160	Are you enjoying that?	
161 C	Yes Mama	
162 M	Good, darling	
163	Don't talk with food in your mouth, all right?	REGULATIVE Action
164	You can talk	
165	when you've finished . . .	

Extract 12 contrasts sharply with Extract 11 in that the behaviour considered desirable is specified via the RU Action (messages 163–5) though no reason is given.

Variation in the meanings which realize contexts such as the regulative context illustrated in these extracts requires that interactants be able to recognize from the meanings expressed that a context is a context of a particular type; conversely, that in order to construe a particular context, particular kinds of meanings should be expressed. In Bernstein's terms, coding orientation provides recognition and realization rules which provide the means for distinguishing between contexts and so recognizing a context as such. In this way, coding orientation determines what can legitimately and relevantly be meant in the recognized context. Hopefully, the extracts presented clarify how it is that such recognition and realization rules are acquired by individuals within these critical socializing contexts within the family.

The realization of the regulative context by meanings which involve the exchange of information weakens the boundary between this context and another context in which the exchange of information is a genuine one, requiring no non-verbal action on the part of the child. In a 'genuine' exchange of information, it is up to the hearer to act on information received. When an information exchange realizes a regulative context, such discretion is only apparent; in fact, the hearer is **required** to act as a result of the information received. The regulation is thus made 'invisible' (Bernstein 1975, Hasan 1992a).

If weak framing is manifested by the selection of non-congruent forms to realize contexts then Extracts 5, 10 and 11 manifest weakness of framing in the regulative context. Extract 12, by contrast, manifests strong framing as does the regulative context in Extract 3 and that embedded in the imaginative context of Extract 6. Regulation in these latter extracts is highly visible.

Variation in strength of classification

Weakness in the framing of a context such as is exemplified above can lead to a weakening of boundaries between contexts resulting in a weakening of classification. This can be seen in Extracts 5 and 10 where the mothers' giving of information makes the regulative context indistinguishable from a genuine information exchange context. In Extract 12, however, the boundary between the regulative and interpersonal contexts would seem to be clearly demarcated.

A further manifestation – perhaps the most obvious – of variation in the strength of the boundaries insulating contexts from one another is represented by the tolerance of interactants for the construal of particular contexts within particular interactional frames. Weak classification would be said to occur where contexts are unrestricted so that they seem to interweave, one providing the context for the construal of another. Strong classification, by contrast, occurs where the development of a particular type of context is discouraged. Thus in the extracts presented here, the way in which mothers permit or do not permit the construal of the imaginative context within the meal time interactional frame would seem to be a manifestation of the strength of classification. It is suggested that classification of contexts is strong in the LAP dyads represented here and weak in the HAP dyads.

According to Bernstein, classification and framing strengths vary independently. If these are taken as two independently varying vectors then four possible combinations arise: strong (+) versus weak (−) classification and framing. The analysis presented allows us to speculate about the location of individual dyads with respect to these two dimensions of coding orientation. Figure 2.2 locates three of the dyads whose interaction has been represented in the extracts presented in this chapter – JK (Extracts 2, 3 and 9), HS (Extracts 4, 5 and 7), and MJ (Extracts 6 and 10). In the figure, the horizontal axis represents the strength of classification and the vertical axis the framing strength, the poles on each axis representing the extremes of strength of the dimensions.

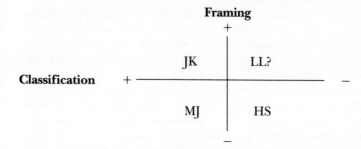

Figure 2.2 Dyads representing modalities of code

The dyads MJ and HS are located in the modalities of code represented by −F−C (HS) and −F+C (MJ). In other words, the mothers in these two dyads have in common a tendency to express their messages in a non-congruent way resulting in the non-congruent realization of the regulative context. In the HS dyad there is a weakening of the boundaries between contexts as evidenced by the mother's tolerance for the construal of the imaginative context within the mealtime interactional frame (Extracts 4 and 7). By this measure, the MJ dyad, on the other hand, seems to strongly classify contexts as manifested by the mother's intolerance for the construal of the imaginative context in Extracts 6 and 10.

The JK dyad is clearly +F+C (cf. Extract 3): realizations of messages and contexts are unambiguous and the mother clearly considers that flights of fancy are incompatible with the goings-on of the mealtime interactional frame. Which dyad is represented by the modality +F−C? It seems that the LL dyad (Extract 12) may be located here though it is difficult to demonstrate the weakness of the boundaries between contexts without extended extracts.

Conclusion

In this chapter, I have tried linguistically to characterize and theoretically locate instances of the kind of discourse that is said to be a feature of the instructional discourse of the school and, indeed, a prerequisite for school success, i.e. decontextualized language use. It was suggested that such language use actually entails a number of varieties which, in the systemic functional model, are realizationally related to the contextual variable – the role of language in the social process. An indicative study was presented showing that the use of certain 'decontextualized' varieties – Conjecture and Generalization – by preschool children in interaction with their mothers varied systematically according to social class membership. Instances of the use of such decontextualized varieties were presented in order to throw light on the functions of such language use in the mundane activities of the everyday life of preschool children in interaction with their mothers. It was concluded that, depending on social class membership, the imaginative context which is the context that promotes one such variety – Conjecture – may or may not be tolerated within a particular interactional frame. It was further suggested that such tolerance is relatable to Bernstein's concept of the strength of principles of classification.

Code is defined by Bernstein (1990: 14) as a tacitly acquired regulative principle which selects and integrates relevant meanings, forms of their realization, and evoking contexts. For the systemic linguist this formulation, bringing together contexts, meanings and wordings, is a familiar one: contexts are construed by meanings which are, in turn, construed by wordings. In this chapter I have attempted to elucidate the way in which the tacit acquisition of code occurs within the contexts of the primary socialization of the child in the family.

In light of the present undertaking, two issues present themselves. The first is practical but urgent and refers to the need to verify the findings of the indicative study. The data on which the study reported here was based, being but a subset of the total data set, was limited and the remarks presented here should be read with that fact in mind. However, given the importance indicated in the literature of the use of (varieties of) decontextualized language, the findings point to the need to examine the full data set from the perspective of the use of decontextualized varieties of language and the functions of such varieties in the routine everyday activities of the preschool child's life.

The second issue is a theoretical one and concerns the status of a notion used in the investigation – that of 'interactional frame'. This notion was used in a pre-theoretical way. However, evidence for the inclusion of this notion in the category *context* may be adduced from two sources within the current discussion: the concept of context embedding; and the fact that certain practices were considered by some mothers to be inappropriate within the particular 'interactional frame' considered here. These two considerations would seem to suggest that the notion could be theorized as a kind of context. If the concept of what Hasan terms material situational setting (MSS) and the concept of context were brought into relation, and contexts conceptualized as being materially near or not near (with the implied degrees in between) to MSS, then 'interactional frame' could be considered a context located at the 'near' end of such a continuum. Indeed, such a conceptualization is implied in Hasan's 1973 discussion. It would seem that, indeed, the concept of context needs to be conceptualized in this way.

Notes

1 For a detailed description of the lexicogrammatical realizations of rhetorical units see Cloran (1994).
2 Extract 1 is a modified fragment of mother–child interaction in which is represented nearly all the identified RUs and the various relations into which they may enter. Modifications have been made by: inserting an RU not present in the original text for the sole purpose of exemplification of that RU in context; and for the sake of brevity, omitting messages which constitute RUs already represented in the extract. The location of the inserted RU is shown by the absence of identifying numbers next to constituent messages and that of omissions by discontinuities in numbering of messages.
3 I am deeply indebted to Professor Ruqaiya Hasan, not least for access to this data.
4 *Transcription Conventions*

Speaker, e.g. Mother = M; Child = C; unintelligible item = [?];

uncertain transcription of item = [? item]

pause in conversation = ..; more dots = lengthier pause;

transcription commentary = (IN CAPITALS)

Speaker does not allow time for hearer to answer a question = ?*

Interrupted or discontinued speech = - ;

elaborating message interrupting primary message = <17>

e.g. 16   M   It gives you a pain <17> doesn't it?
     17   when it's going down
5 Table 1.1 presents those RUs identified in the mother–child interaction; there is no suggestion here that those presented exhaust the possibilities.
6 This and the other semantic features of commands together with their lexicogrammatical realizations are taken from Hasan 1992a.

64 CARMEL CLORAN

References

Berstein, B. (1971) *Class, Codes and Control, Vol. 1: Theoretical Studies towards a Scoiology of Language.* London: Routledge.

Bernstein, B. (1973) *Class, Codes and Control, Vol. 2: Applied Studies towards a Sociology of Language.* London: Routledge.

Bernstein, B. (1975) *Class, Codes and Control, Vol. 3: Towards a Theory of Educational Transmission.* London: Routledge.

Bernstein, B. (1990) *Class, Codes and Control, Vol. 4: The Structuring of Pedagogic Discourse.* London: Routledge.

Bernstein, B. and Diaz, M. (1984) 'Towards a theory of pedagogic discourse', *CORE*, 8(3), 1–212.

Book, S. (1977) *Statistics.* New York: McGraw-Hill.

Bruner, J. (1970) *Poverty and Childhood.* Detroit: Merril-Palmer.

Cloran, C. (1994) *Rhetorical Unit and Decontextualisation: An Enquiry into some Relations of Context, Meaning and Grammar.* Monographs in Systemic Linguistic Linguistics, No. 6. Nottingham: Department of English Studies, University of Nottingham.

Cloran, C. (1995) 'Defining and relating text segments'. In R. Hasan and P. Fries (eds) *On Subject and Theme: From a Discourse Functional Perspective.* Amsterdam: Benjamins.

D'Anglejan, A. and Masny, D. (1987) 'Determinants socioculturels de l'apprentissage du discours decontextualise en milieu scolaire: vers un cadre theorique integre', *Revue Quebecoise de Linguistique* 16(2), 145–62.

De Laguna, G. (1927/70) *Speech: Its Function and Development.* College Park: McGrath (originally published 1927 by Yale University Press).

Donaldson, M. (1987) 'The origins of inference'. In J. Bruner and H. Haste (eds), *Making Sense: The Child's Construction of the World.* London: Methuen, 97–107.

Firth, J.R. (1935) 'The technique of semantics'. In *Transactions of the Philological Society.* Reprinted in Firth, J.R. (1957) *Papers in Linguistics 1934–1951.* London: Oxford University Press, 7–33.

Greenfield, P. (1972) 'Oral or written language: the consequences for cognitive development in Africa, the United States and England', *Language and Speech* 15, 169–77.

Halliday, M.A.K. (1994) *Introduction to Functional Grammar* (2nd edn) London: Edward Arnold.

Hasan, R. (1973) 'Codes, register and social dialect'. In B. Bernstein (ed.), *Class, Codes and Control, Vol. 2.* London: Routledge.

Hasan, R. ((1987) 'Reading picture reading: invisible instruction at home and in school'. In *Proceedings from the 13th Conference of the Australian Reading Association,* Sydney, July 1987.

Hasan, R. (1989) 'Semantic variation and socio-linguistics', *Australian Journal of Linguistics*, 9, 221–75.

Hasan, R. (1991) 'Questions as a mode of learning in everyday talk'. In T. Lee and M. McCausland (eds), *Language Education: Interaction and Development.* Launceston: University of Tasmania Press, 70–119.

Hasan, R. (1992a) 'Meaning in sociolinguistic theory'. In K. Bolton and H. Kwok (eds), *Sociolinguistics Today: International Perspectives.* London: Routledge, 80–119.

Hasan, R. (1992b) 'Rationality in everyday talk: from process to system'. In J. Svartvik (ed.), *Directions in Corpus Linguistics.* Berlin: de Gruyter, 257–307.

Martin, J.R. (1997) 'Analysing genre: functional parameters'. In F. Christie and

J. Martin (eds), *Genre and Institutions: Social Processes in the Workplace and School.* London: Cassell, 3–39.

Olson, D. (1977) 'From utterance to text: the bias of speech and writing', *Harvard Educational Review,* 47(4), 257–81.

Scinto, L. (1986) *Written Language and Psychological Development.* Orlando: Academic Press.

Simons, H. and Murphy, S. (1986) 'Spoken language strategies and reading acquisition'. In J. Cook-Gumperz (ed.), *The Social Construction of Literacy.* London: Cambridge University Press, 185–206.

Smith, F. (1984) 'The creative achievement of literacy'. In C. Goelman, J. Oberg and F. Smith (eds), *Awakening to Literacy.* London: Heinemann Educational Books, 143–53.

Snow, C. (1983) 'Literacy and language: relationships during the preschool years', *Harvard Educational Review,* 53(3), 165–89.

Tannen, D. (1982) 'The oral/literate continuum in discourse'. In D. Tannen (ed.), *Spoken and Written Language: Exploring Orality and Literacy.* Norwood, NJ: Ablex.

Vygotsky, L. (1978) *Mind in Society.* Cambridge, MA: Harvard University Press.

Vygotsky, L. (1981) 'The development of higher forms of attention in childhood'. In J. Wertsch, (ed.), *The Concept of Activity in Soviet Psychology.* New York: Sharpe, 191–240.

Wertsch, J. (1985) *Vygotsky and the Social Formation of Mind.* Cambridge, MA: Harvard University Press.

3 Preparing for school: developing a semantic style for educational knowledge

Clare Painter

Introduction

The question of why educational success should be so firmly linked to socio-economic class is one which Basil Bernstein long ago recognized as requiring an explanation which gives a central place to the role of language. He has argued that a child's semiotic interactions within the family – the site of primary socialization – will take subtly different forms depending on the social positioning of the speakers. One facet of this theory is the claim that, in families of higher socioeconomic status, patterns of parent–child linguistic interaction will, from the earliest years, sensitize the child to the kinds of meanings relevant for later school learning – for dealing with what has been termed 'educational knowledge' (Bernstein 1971 and elsewhere). For such a view to make sense, linguistic interaction needs to be seen in its semantic aspect (Bernstein 1990: 14), and language development as a process of 'learning how to mean' (Halliday 1975), rather than as the mastery of a formal system of structural rules. This chapter will use case study data to illustrate this position, interpreting aspects of one child's language development as an apprenticeship into ways of meaning relevant for learning educational knowledge.

Although there is a considerable body of literature on adult–child speech in early language development, it has most often been concerned simply with whether and how adult talk facilitates the child's linguistic progress (e.g. Snow and Ferguson 1979, Gallaway and Richards 1994). During the 1980s, however, there were several naturalistic studies of child language that considered the question of how English-speaking children's early language experience relates to their future schooling. Heath's (1983) celebrated ethnographic study, for example, links an account of language and literacy practices in two rural, working-class communities in the Southern USA with the children's experiences moving from home to school learning. However, although a comparison is made with a 'mainstream' community, the description of family interactions here is much less detailed and without textual exemplification. Wells' (1987) longitudinal research in Britain, on the other hand, provides many examples of parent–child interactions, but the discussion turns chiefly on issues such as the adult's propensity to take an interest in what interests the child, answer questions and justify commands, features which he specifically argues do not distinguish families from different social classes. Hasan's cross-sectional study, however, (reported in Hasan 1989, 1991, 1992, Hasan and Cloran 1990, Cloran, this volume Chapter 2) and that of Williams (1995, this volume Chapter 4) have demonstrated that when a close linguistic analysis is made of mother–child talk, quantifiable differences emerge, in terms of the semantic choices made by mothers and children of the same age from different social classes. Such differences were also suggested, though less clearly demonstrated, in an earlier, less linguistically sophisticated study by Tizard and Hughes (1984). In addition, the work of the Scollons, exploring features of their daughter's language development up to the age of three, illustrates nicely how Rachel 'was in most ways literate before she learned to read . . . because of the literate orientation that we had given her' (Scollon and Scollon 1981: 61). The present paper will complement Hasan's work on semantic variation by taking a developmental perspective on one semantic style; it will complement the Scollons' account of Rachel's language by using data from a slightly older child. The aim will be to document more fully how, for a middle-class child, language develops in use over time in such a way as to constitute a semiotic preparation for formal learning and educational knowledge.

The data on which the descriptions are based were collected from my son, Stephen, during the course of his everyday life at home over a period of two and a half years, up to the age of five (Painter, forthcoming). On two or three occasions during most weeks, a small tape recorder was switched on in the house or car and then disregarded. Stephen was kept unaware of the recording function on the machine so as to facilitate the aim of obtaining recordings of talk as uninfluenced as possible by the fact and process of data collection. In interpreting the data, I will take the view of language necessarily implied by Bernstein's theory of cultural transmission, which is that language is not simply a 'neutral' means for expressing a pre-existing structure of thought or of material reality, but that it shapes our consciousness. This is a view explicitly articulated by Halliday in his writings on linguistic theory and also presented in some form in ethnographic cross-cultural accounts of child language, such as those of the Scollon and Scollon (1981), Heath (1983), Ochs and Schieffelin (1984) and Ochs (1990). In brief, the perspective here is that children learn their first language in contexts of use, initially within the family setting, and in the process of learning the words and structures of their mother tongue they are invisibly learning the ways of being, doing and interpreting that are the ways of their particular community. In this chapter I will illustrate something of what this means by showing how Stephen's interactive experience guided him towards a particular 'semantic style' (Hasan 1996: 192) that is consonant with that of the school.

Commonsense vs educational knowledge

Learning within the family is a matter of building up what Bernstein (1975: 99) has characterized as 'commonsense' knowledge. He contrasts this with the more specialized educational knowledge learned in school and tertiary institutions. The question to be explored then, is how the child's experience in learning commonsense knowledge in the years before school may take such a form as to resonate with and facilitate the later learning of educational knowledge. To explore this, the characteristics of commonsense knowledge will be considered and contrasted with those of educational knowledge and then a number of features of Stephen's language use will be documented to show how he was implicitly being prepared for learning in school. For economy, the focus will be restricted to occasions where information exchange is the focus, rather than joint action or contexts of control.

I take the term 'commonsense knowledge' to mean knowledge that appertains to the visible material world, that is functional for the routine living of daily life, that is non-specialized, shared by all members of the culture/community and realized through everyday forms of talk. It is in the process of building commonsense knowledge that language is first learned and it is in the process of learning language that everyday understandings are first construed by the child. The learning of commonsense knowledge is informal and gradual, an incidental part of participating in the routines of everyday life. In Wells' (1987: 67) words, 'such learning is ... spontaneous and unplanned ... sporadic and, for the most part, unsystematic'.

These points can be illustrated from Text 1 below, taking it as typical of an interaction in which commonsense understandings are being realized, enacted and developed:[1]

Text 1: 2; 7; 1

    [M and S settling down on couch to read bedtime books]

M: ... Oh they [=your feet] are not very warm actually. Do you want to go and get the little blanket off your bed?

S: Mm.

M: You go and get that and we'll put it around us.

S: All right. Put it round me, [running to door] I'm going to put it round me.

[S wrestles with door trying to get out of the room]

M: Turn the handle first. [S does so] That's it. Ooh, mind your toes.

[S goes to bedroom, fetches blanket and returns. Some talk omitted here]

M: ... There; all cosy now? [having tucked blanket over their laps, leaving books alongside]

S: Mm.

M: Right. Okay.

S: [reaches over and puts books in his lap] I like it on, I like it on my knee.
M: Do you darling?
S: Mm.
M: Going to have this one first?
S: Mm.
M: [pointing to picture on cover] Do you know what the name of this tiger is? [brief pause] He's called, [growly voice] Growl.
S: Mm, [mimicking M's voice] Growl.
[M's reading of story omitted]
M: [reading] '. . . your shadow,' chuckled Trumpet. [Turns to S] Do you know what a shadow is?
S: Mm.
M: [holds hand between light and book] You see my shadow, here on the book? See that? See my hand? See the shadow of my hand? (?Shadow); [wiggles fingers] fingers moving; see the fingers moving.
[further murmured talk about story, then M resumes reading]
' . . . oh Growl, you really are the timidest tiger in the world!'
S: What's that? [pointing at character from the back cover]
M: That's Snap the crocodile.
S: Looks like a clown.
M: Yes. [then reconsiders] Why's he like a clown? [brief pause] Because he's got big eyes?
S: Mm. He hasn't got big eyes, he got big teeth.
M: Ah yeah he has.
S: Mm.

In important respects this text exemplifies clearly the construal of commonsense knowledge. For one thing, the kinds of things named and referred to are physical entities of the domestic environment (blanket, bed, toes, book), together with other entities (e.g. clown, tiger, crocodile) familiar from entertainment sources available at home and within the wider community, which are equally tangible and visible in nature. Second, the text is typical in that the give and take of dialogue allows the child not only to express his own intentions and preferences, but to access new understandings through language closely tied to the immediate context of situation in which he is participating. He does this by seeking information (*what's that?*) and by receiving instruction, both to enable action (*turn the handle, mind your toes*) and to facilitate understanding (*see my shadow, here on the book?*), learning new meanings by relating names deictically to the observable referents in the immediate context (*what's **that**?, turn **the** handle, mind **your** toes, see **my** shadow **here**, on **the** book*).

The meanings construed are thus commonsense in nature in being concrete and everyday, while the mode of learning is typical of the construction of commonsense knowledge in being oriented via dialogue to 'you and me' and what we can see and do in the immediate context of situation. In addition, the dialogic learning is unplanned and unsequenced in terms of its content, (the need to open the door, understand the word *shadow* or identify a particular image just happening to arise on this occasion and bearing no particular relation to each other). The interaction is controlled to some degree by the child learner, who, for example, makes the choice of book and later asks a question unrelated to the previous turn. Thus, in Bernstein's terms (1975: 88–9), there is relatively weak 'framing' (i.e. there is little regulation of 'the selection, organization, pacing and timing of the knowledge transmitted and received in the pedagogical relationship'), as well as weak 'classification' (i.e. a low 'degree of boundary maintenance between contents').

Educational knowledge, on the other hand, has been referred to by Bernstein (1975: 99) as 'uncommonsense' in nature, since 'the school is necessarily concerned with the transmission and development of universalistic orders of meaning' (1971: 197), which 'go beyond local space, time, context' (1990: 182), rather than meanings appertaining to the specifics of a local situational context. Educational knowledge will be concerned with concepts which are both more specialized and more abstract than those of commonsense knowledge. It is also, as Halliday (1988a: 11) has observed, typically embodied in written monologic discourse, abstracted from any situational context shared with the interlocutor. And because of its specialized and abstract nature, it is inaccessible to incidental, observational learning and is likely to be accessed through conscious teaching and learning undertaken in a particular sequential order.

Almost any paragraph from a reference book, even one aimed at young children, will illustrate these tendencies. For example:

Text 2 [original text accompanied by large colour diagrams]

Inside the earth
The earth is a ball of very hot rock which measures over 12,700 kilometres in diameter. Scientists study the shock waves from earthquakes and nuclear explosions to find out what the inside of the earth is like.
The earth has a thin outer 'shell' which is cooler and more rigid than the rocks below. The shell rests on a layer of rock that is partly molten, like hot toffee. Only the very thin top layer of the earth's shell is called the 'crust'.
Below these surface layers lie about 2,900 kilometres of white-hot, solid rock that slowly churns around. This is called the 'mantle'. At the earth's centre is the 'core' which is largely made up of iron. The outer core is liquid rock. Only the inner core is solid.

The outer layers
The slow churning of the rock in the earth's mantle causes molten rock to rise up to the surface where it cools to form new crust. The crust and

the solid top layer of mantle together make up the earth's shell . . . (Mercer 1980: 15-16)

Here, concepts are carefully defined, introduced in a logical order and assigned technical terms in quick succession. Abstract things and generic groupings are referred to (e.g. *diameter, scientists*), and while there is some linkage to the commonsense world (e.g. *like hot toffee*), the knowledge stands outside any local context shared by the author and reader, who remain invisible in the text. Information must be taken on board immediately to be built on in following parts of the text; for example the 'crust' and the 'mantle' are defined in paragraph one and then themselves become part of a new definition of the 'shell' in paragraph two. As well, *that slowly churns* in the first paragraph is referred to as *the slow churning* in the second and constitutes an example of what Halliday (1994: 340*ff*) refers to as 'grammatical metaphor,' in that the meaning does not match the typical linguistic form for that meaning. That is, the expression *the slow churning* construes a process, but uses a nominalized form to do so, giving the event a kind of dual meaning as process and yet thing. (See Halliday and Martin 1993, Martin 1993, 1995, Olson 1989 for more detailed discussion of the linguistic demands of educational knowledge.)

Differences between commonsense and educational knowledge can be summarized as in table 3.1:

Table 3.1 Contrasts between commonsense and educational knowledge

Commonsense knowledge	Educational knowledge
Relevant to a specific context	Universalistic in orientation
Based on personal/shared experience	Distant from personal experience
Based on language mediated observation and participation	Based on semiotic representation
Concrete nontechnical meanings	Abstract and technical meanings
Negotiated in spoken language	Constituted in written language
Built up unconsciously	Built up consciously
Built up slowly and gradually	Built up rapidly
Pace of learning at discretion of learner	Pace of learning at discretion of instructor
Built up in a piecemeal, fragmented way	Systematically presented, logically sequenced within a topic
Lack of insulation between topics	Disciplinary boundaries may be maintained

Characteristics of a meaning style relevant for educational knowledge

In Text 1, I have given a typical example of how a middle-class mother and her two-year-old child interact on an occasion chiefly concerned with information exchange. Since this text exhibits features of commonsense learning, we need to understand what else there is in such a text, and/or in subsequent discourse developments, that might facilitate the middle-class child's transition into literacy and formal schooling. I will argue that, if Stephen's case is typical, the important developments of the preschool years involve the child being guided towards a linguistic learning style in which the process, products and nature of the meaning system itself are brought to consciousness to become accessible to reflection. In what follows I will exemplify this general point and discuss its significance as a preparation for school education.

By the time he was five, Stephen had been inducted into a meaning style with an orientation to five features:

1. Learning from definitions.
2. Attending to principles underlying categories
3. Specifying contextual information in language.
4. Privileging textual (over perceptual) information and inferencing.
5. Construing information exchange as a means of learning.

I will discuss the development in use of each of these aspects of semantic style in turn, although in the child's experience they were developed simultaneously rather than sequentially.

An orientation to learning from definitions

We have already seen in Text 1 how an older speaker can demonstrate the meaning of an unfamiliar word (such as *shadow*) by pointing out an instance of what the word refers to. At about this time, however, Stephen began to be introduced to a new way of learning names, as exemplified in Text 3.

    Text 3: 2; 8; 18

        [S has been singing *Mary had a little lamb*]
    S: Fleece, not feece, no; not teece; not teece. [laughing]
    M: No, not teeth.
    F: [sings] Teeth were as white as snow.
    S: No, not teeth, fleece.
    M: Yes, fleece; fleece is the wool on the lamb. All the lamb's soft wool is called the fleece.

Here the meaning of *fleece* is explained by relating it to another meaning, *the wool on the lamb*, rather than by pointing physically to what it refers to.

This constitutes an alternative strategy for learning vocabulary, one which Stephen certainly found difficult to handle at first, as shown in the following example, where he was evidently not satisfied with his mother's definitional response.

Text 4: 2;11;5

[M and S's older brother talking; they mention the word 'pet']
S: What's a pet?
M: A pet is an animal who lives in your house; Katy's our pet.
[some time elapses]
S: What's a pet called?

However, once established, explaining through definitions became a typical adult instructional form, and half a year onward it was favoured by Stephen himself as a way of trying out his own understandings, in utterances such as *Drown is go down to the bottom and be dead* (3;7;5) or *Speeding means fast* (3;7;17). The importance of this development lies first in the fact that it is the means for learning new meanings 'detached' from the immediate situational context – no observational example is necessary to clarify the meaning. And this will necessarily be the case with the generalized, technical or abstract meanings of educational knowledge. (Having instances of viruses, electorates or inflationary spirals pointed out on the model of *see my shadow* is hardly a feasible means to developing such concepts.) Second, the use by the child of this kind of defining clause provides occasions for detaching linguistic form and function. Thus in the above examples we have verbs (e.g. *drown, speeding*), an adverb (*fast*) and even a pair of coordinated clauses (*go down to the bottom and be dead*) functioning as Subject or Complement, where a noun would be a more typical and 'congruent' choice. This unhinging of grammatical class and function is the first step towards grammatical metaphor, a central tool for creating the technical and abstract terms of uncommonsense taxonomies and for creating coherent written discourse. (See Painter 1996a for a more detailed discussion.) Third, to develop language by relating one piece of language to another is to have a technique for learning at a potentially much greater speed than is possible from observing the repeated use of words in local contexts. It also allows for a more conscious and deliberate teaching–learning strategy. Overall, the effect of habitually learning by relating linguistic items to one another, often in the absence of any instance of the category being learned, is to have attention directed to the meaning system and its relations of synonymy and hyponymy, rather than to remain focused on specific observed instances of categories.

Attending to principles underlying categories

A closely related development observable in Stephen's language was the specification of criteria for category membership. Even as early as 2;8 we can see from Text 1 how Stephen was oriented in this direction by the parent. The final section of this example is repeated below with the relevant utterance in bold:

Text 1: 2; 7; 1

S: . . . What's that? [pointing at character from the back cover]
M: That's Snap the crocodile.
S: Looks like a clown.
M: Yes. [reconsidering] **Why's he like a clown?** [pause] **Because he's got big eyes?**
S: Mm. Not got a big eyes, he got a big teeth.
M: Ah yeah he has.
S: Mm.

Here Stephen is first challenged to provide the basis for identifying the picture as of a clown and then when he is unable to do so, a possible criterion is modelled for him (*because he's got big eyes*). Whether or not Stephen's comment about big teeth should be taken as his explanation for classifying the picture as of a clown or simply a comment about what was big is unclear. But the fact of being pressed in this way as a two-year-old was surely a factor in the considerable attention Stephen gave to explicating the grounds for categorizations in the following year. By age three and a half he was likely to be the one doing the challenging:

Text 5a: 3; 5; 7

[M teases that the zoo bears fancy some 'juicy boys' to eat]
S: We're not juicy boys, cause we haven't got juice in.

Text 5b: 3; 9; 0

[M refers to an airship as a 'spaceship balloon']
S: Not a spaceship – an airship – cause a spaceship has bits like this [gestures] to stand it up.

He would also produce utterances in which it was clearly the criterion for classification rather than the category itself that he was interested in exploring, as when he suggested: *Our cat is an animal because it's got fur* (3;11;15).

The kind of causal relation involved in these examples has been referred to as 'internal' to the text (Halliday and Hasan 1976), because the link is not between events, feelings or states in the world, but between a statement (such as a categorization) and the grounds for it. The (*be*)*cause* explains 'why I say', rather than 'why something happens'. When used by the child in conjunction with categorization, such internal explanations become a significant strategy for reflecting upon the basis for naming things. And doing this amounts to deploying a new ability to treat language – the meaning system – as an 'object' of reflection.

In Stephen's case, reflecting more consciously on linguistic categorizing also motivated the use of a dependent clause to clarify possible contexts for appropriate naming. For example:

Text 6: 3; 4; 5

[S has been served spaghetti bolognaise – a favourite]
S: So this is bolognaise. [pause] So that's bolognaise [poking it]. **When you eat it**, it's bolognaise, isn't it? It's still bolognaise when you eat it, isn't it?
M: (puzzled) Yes.
S: Yeah, but we call it meat, don't we? We call it meat, don't we?
M: You make bolognaise with meat . . .

In puzzling over the semantic relations between the linguistically realized categories of 'meat' and 'bolognaise', Stephen uses the *when* clause to specify a generalized situation[2] which he thinks might be relevant as a criterion for changing the category from one to the other. Such occasions, exploring what things are called, in fact constituted one of the first situations in which Stephen used the conjunction *when* in its conditional or generic sense, rather than for temporal sequencing. A major functional motivation for this new development appears to have been the child's growing interest in probing the bases of classifications.

The focus on categories, rather than things, encouraged Stephen to repeatedly ask questions about general classes and non specific instances: *Are seals dolphins?* (3;8;14), *Is a platypus an animal?* (3;8;7), as well as to offer justifications for his own classifications. In doing all of this he was maintaining an orientation to the meaning system (rather than the material instance of the category), and so adopting a cognitive stance that would be essential for the later learning of categories of the uncommonsense world, which can only be determined through linguistic specification. In fact, by the end of his fourth year, Stephen was able to receive instruction in elementary matters of educational knowledge in this way, as shown in the following fragment of talk, where the focus is entirely on generalized categories and their relationships:

Text 7: 3; 10

[S complains to his brother that there is no picture of a seal in his book about fish]
Bro: Seals aren't fish, that's why.
S: Are seals mammals?
Bro: Yes, cause they don't lay eggs; they have babies.

One further result of this new reflectiveness about categories was that Stephen became so oriented to the 'general' that he would sometimes construe even specific present or past personal experience as a generalization removed from his personal experience of it. For example, on recalling, but not mentioning, how a melamine plate had shattered the previous day, he said *You know plastic plates can break, can't they?* (3;8;22). And his comment on a particular lion observed at the zoo jumping onto a raised shelf to feed was: *Lions could jump up their things to eat* (3;8;25). This tendency to 'global statements' was also remarked on by the Scollons as a feature of Rachel's speech, which they refer to as showing 'an interest in viewing the world in terms of categories rather than individuals', an aspect of Rachel's literate orientation. (Scollon and Scollon 1981: 91).

Construing contexts beyond personal experience

In the process of developing the conceptual system through definitions and explicated classifications, the language is necessarily moved into a 'context independent' style, and this began to pervade other aspects of Stephen's talk. Previous studies have already observed an orientation to this style of speech in middle-class dyads with respect to the creation of dialogic recounts and anecdotes of personal experience. (See, e.g., Ochs and Schieffelin 1984, Painter 1986, 1989, Scollon and Scollon 1981). Young children, even before their second birthday are 'scaffolded' to provide texts which do not depend on shared experience for their interpretation, even when the interlocutor actually does share the knowledge being constructed. The following example from Halliday's (1984) data exemplifies the use of adult prompts (in bold) leading the child to greater explicitness.

Text 8: 1; 10; 14

C: Auntie Joan cook quackquack for you.
F: Auntie Joan cooked quackquack for you, did she?
C: Auntie Joan cook greenpea.
F: And green peas.
C: Began shout.
M: **Who began to shout?**
C: Nila began shout.
M: Did you? **What did you shout?**
C: 'Greenpea'.

Clearly this is important for teaching children to interpret the relaying of personal experience as a context where shared meanings are not assumed, fitting them from birth to interact in a world where the self will be presented to others with whom shared backgrounds and assumptions are unlikely. More immediately, it has been observed that this verbal explicitness also orients the child towards storying in the written mode, where interlocutors have no personal contact. In fact, Scollon and Scollon's (1981) account of Rachel's early orientation to literacy focuses on her transformation of personal experience into stories in which shared experience is verbalized and distanced through a third person representation.

Stephen's route to disembedded talk did not involve third person storying of this kind, but centred instead on the exchange of factual information. We have already seen, in Text 6, how the linguistic construal of a context for appropriate naming might be used to assist categorization. In addition, at about the same time, Stephen began to use dependent conditional clauses to construe explicitly the necessary contexts for a variety of propositions. The data suggest that he had long been guided in this direction by the adult talk addressed to him. As a two-year-old, Stephen did not himself use conditional *when* or *if* clauses, but was regularly addressed with adult utterances which modified a command. Significantly, these were not simply here-and-now directives, such as *Go outside if you want to play with the ball*, but were often used where the instruction was relevant only to a purely hypothetical, non-current situation. For example:

Text 9: 2; 8; 24

[M & S looking at picture of a large snake]
S: That's two snakes?
M: No it's only one. He's wound round and round the branch (tracing outline with her finger). It's a big snake.
S: (touches snake's mouth)
M: You have to be careful of snakes. **If you see one, you don't touch it** because they're dangerous.
S: Mm. This is a picture of a snake.

Once Stephen had begun to deal in generalizations himself – talking about general classes as described in the previous section, using generalized *you* (as M does above) and talking about what *could* happen – he found that adults increasingly modified their own factual statements with linguistically construed conditions, and he began to adopt the same strategy.[3]

Text 10: 3; 6; 5

S: Mum, could you cry; could you cry or not?
M: Yes, I could cry.
S: How?
M: What do you mean? **If I hurt myself**, I might cry, same as you.
S: **If you fell down bump really, really hard**.
M: Yes.

The habitual use of dependent clauses to construct contexts beyond the child's lived experience is important not simply because it expands the child's knowledge by offering additional 'situations,' since after all viewing television also does this.4 The importance of the linguistic creation of context is that it involves the child in construing contexts which have never been observed, whether at first hand or via images, so that the learning is entirely disengaged from any particular past or present situational context. In Donaldson's (1978) well-known expression it gives rise to 'disembedded thinking'.

After several months of this kind of interactive experience, where the behaviour of the dialogue partners was explored through conditionals, and personal observations were generalized, Stephen was able to follow more distanced information of this kind. That is, he could participate in talk relating entirely to the world of third parties, in which contextual information was elaborated through dependent *when* and *if* clauses, as in the following example:

Text 11: 4; 10; 3

[Looking at a book about birds a few days after a dead bird was found in the garden]
S: How could birds die?
M: How could birds die?
S: Yes.
M: Well, the same way as anybody else – people or animals, when they get very old – Oh you mean like the one in the garden.
S: Yes.
M: . . . are you thinking of? Well sometimes birds die just when they get very old, or maybe they got sick because they [pause] got some disease, or maybe a cat (?got it). Baby birds sometimes die when they fall out the nest, or in the winter, if you were in a cold place, birds might die because they can't get enough food.
S: Yeah, but what happens if one bird falls out and then – and then – and when it's just about at the ground, it flies.
M: Yes, well if it's big enough to fly, it'll be all right.

In his last utterance we see Stephen trying to reconcile the newly received information that falling may be fatal for birds with the longstanding knowledge that birds can fly. There is no question, then, of his learned ability to take up 'on the run' information relating to scenarios which are beyond his personal experience, but which have been presented linguistically by means of multi-clause sentences. It took considerable time and linguistic experience to reach this point, but once a child is able to participate in these ways of using language, much more rapid and conscious 'instruction' becomes possible from the adult, as will of course be the norm when learning in the more formal context of school.

The privileging of textual information and inferencing

One fundamental aspect of the middle-class English discourse style which has been foregrounded by ethnographic studies of children's language use is the way physical learning is so typically mediated through language. This is evident in Text 1, where the parent neither opens the door for the child, enabling him to learn from observation, nor leaves him to learn from trial and error, but provides a verbal commentary to facilitate the physical task. The significance of this – as a habitual experience – is that it orients the child to learning through text rather than relying on observational or physical experience. This can be compared with an alternative semantic style described in Heath (1983) and Harris (1980, cited in Christie 1985), where children are encouraged in the opposite strategy.

In the later preschool years, this privileging of linguistically presented information over observational experience may be evident quite outside the context of physical learning, as Text 12 exemplifies.

Text 12: 3; 7

[F & S have noticed a sports car in the traffic and begin talking about sports cars]
F: And they go fast, because they've got a big engine.
S: But that doesn't go faster than us. See? We will go faster.
F: He's not trying; if he was really trying, he could go much faster than us.
S: If he goes very fast, he can – if he goes very fast, he can beat us.

In the course of the conversation, the observable situation in which 'that one' doesn't go fast is discounted by the adult in favour of a linguistically construed context in which it would. And the fact that Stephen reformulates his father's conditional statement into one of his own shows that he accepts this implicit devaluing of the more immediate perceptual information. (cf. Text 9, where he seemed to find the adult's comment somewhat puzzling given the actual situation). The most important thing Stephen was learning on such occasions, then, was not the particular fact about sports cars or whatever else was the topic, but that a factual proposition following from a 'situation' created through language may have more validity than one formed from observation of a specific actual situation.

With this experience, he soon practised drawing his own conclusions from linguistic premises, as in Texts 13a, b.

Text 13a: 3; 11; 10

[At service station]
F: [Tells S that he is putting air in the tyres]
S: Why?

F: Otherwise the tyre might go flat.
S: [pause] If all of the tyres be flat, the car will walk!

Text 13b: 4; 0; 20

S: Trees can grow and grow, can't they?
M: Yes, they certainly can.
S: They can grow and grow and grow.
M: Mm.
S: If they grow and grow, they will (?) right up, right up in the sky.

By the time he was four, then, Stephen could use a syllogistic rhetoric to
work out new facts for himself on the basis of information just received or
validated in language. And this style of reasoning from textual information was evident on other occasions where the steps in reasoning were not
explicated overtly in the form 'if p, then q', as in Texts 14a, b.

Text 14a: 4; 7; 23

S: I wonder where you get tiger food.
Bro: Tigers eat meat.
M: [teasingly] Give it a little boy.
S: [pause] Is a boy meat?

Text 14b: 4; 4; 10

M: A creature is anything that's alive.
S: [sounding astonished] Are we creatures?

The more experience Stephen gained in learning by following the logic of
the text, the more likely his dialogue partners were to expect him to draw
inferences from linguistically presented information. The need to do this,
rather than to rely on personal experience, when dealing with educational
knowledge can be seen in Text 15 where Stephen raises an uncommonsense topic.

Text 15: 4; 11; 16

S: I keep thinking that the earth goes round the sun instead of the
        sun goes round the earth.
M: The earth does go round the sun!
S: [pleased] Oh! How come you can't feel it go round?
M: Yeah, it's funny that you can't feel it . . . [further talk omitted
        here]
S: Are the houses going round?
M: **They're on the earth so they have to go round,** don't they?

Here, rather than simply being given an affirmative reply, Stephen's attention is directed to the fact that his proposition is linked to a previous, just negotiated one (*the earth does go round the sun*), providing a premise that allows for only one conclusion. Unconsciously, the adult foregrounds this learning point above the specific bit of knowledge at issue.

Construing information exchange as a means of learning.

One final characteristic of the semantic style into which Stephen was inducted which seems relevant here is the use of language to reflect on the self as a learner and on the texts of others as sources of information. This is another feature which is evident in Text 1, despite the context-embedded, commonsense nature of most of what was being learned on that occasion. In that conversation, Stephen is asked *Do you know what a shadow is?* as a preface to having the meaning demonstrated to him, and such a remark was a very typical feature of the adult talk. *Do you know* could be recognized by the child as a formula to signal that instructional information-giving was to follow, and this doubtless alerted him to the need to attend particularly to the adult's next move. But the literal meaning is also relevant, in that it constructs the piece of information to be attended to (e.g. what a shadow is) as a piece of knowledge, and the child as one coming to know (through talk).[5] In this incidental way then, Stephen was 'tuned in' to recognizing instructional situations and encouraged to become more overtly conscious of the learning process he was engaged in.

Adults were also likely to challenge Stephen when he repeated 'new knowledge' picked up in one dialogue as his own propositions in another. For example when he repeated at home information previously asserted by his friends at the child-care centre, such as: *Frank's got a strong one [=car], when it crashes into another car, it doesn't break* (3;11;17), he might be faced with a sceptical response. The effect of such experience was evident in a new tendency after age four, to attribute to its source any unsubstantiated new knowledge gained outside the family, as in: **Graham says** *if you look at the sun, you go blind* (5;0;6).[6] The knowledge at stake in such a case is presented linguistically as at one remove, enabling it more readily to become an object of contemplation, rather than to be unreflectingly adopted into the child's own system. The habit of constructing information as a report of what someone says is also important in facilitating the understanding that meaning is accessible from other semiotic sources which 'say' things to us, such as books. (See Painter 1996b for a more detailed examination of this area.)

A related aspect of the adult talk was the tendency to question the child directly about the source of his knowledge if it concerned the realm of the uncommonsense.[7] This led Stephen, as a four-year-old, to talk explicitly about himself as learning from others' talk, as in Text 16.

Text 16: 4; 7; 28

S: That's not very long; it's only eight sleeps.
M: That's right!
S: I know, cause Hal told me.

As well, he began to reflect on the adult's sources of knowledge for the first time, asking *How do you know?* or *Have you seen one?* in relation to information he was receiving.

Given that educational knowledge cannot be 'picked up' unconsciously in the way so much of everyday knowledge is, all these developments are important. That is, being made aware of instructional situations and the process of learning, being consciously aware that knowledge is accessed from authoritative sources (including books), and being in the habit of holding constructions of information at a distance until they have been 'attended to' reflectively, will all contribute to habits of meaning that will be drawn on in the new learning context of the school.

Conclusion

To learn one's first language is to engage in a process of symbolic exchanges with other persons on all the apparently trivial occasions that make up the living of daily life. Language is neither witnessed nor engaged in as a neutral, formal system untainted by what particular speakers are using it to achieve, and so a child learning the mother tongue is always learning more than linguistic forms. The process necessarily involves also learning through language the ways of interacting and ways of reflecting that are taken for granted by those with whom meanings are exchanged. I have argued here that the ways in which Stephen was engaged in conversation within his family led him to develop particular semantic habits, and that it is these habits, rather than the forms per se (e.g. relational clauses, conjunctions, conditional and reporting clauses, etc.), which will be significant in his later learning.

The features of Stephen's language described here were developed and deployed in interrelated ways, so that, taken collectively, they form what Whorf (1956: 158) referred to as a 'fashion of speaking'. The definitional mode of learning new concepts involves the overt identification of one linguistic construal with another, allowing the speaker to attend to the meaning rather than the referent. (Compare *a pet is an animal who lives in your house* with *that's a pet*.) Using definitions also has a potential as a means of learning abstract and/or technical concepts, where no concrete referent is observable, and gives the child some experience related to the phenomenon of grammatical metaphor, so pervasive in written language. As well, it allows for more overt and speedy forms of tuition and provides a basis for making logical inferences to learn new facts. To deploy a definitional style as a habitual means of learning in turn depends on being ready to articulate and attend to criteria for class inclusion, which itself involves being verbally explicit about meaning and focusing on the generic rather than the specific, observable actual. All of this facilitates learning from text where hypothetical situations outside personal experience are construed, and enables the tracking of more monologic text (multi-clause in the first instance). At the same time, the orientation to verbal explicitness, text-based learning and multi-clause construals also facilitates a syllogistic style of reasoning in which personal and shared experience need not intrude. All these features represent a way of using language that entails being consciously attentive to the linguistic meaning system and to its realizations in text (at least those texts that have the potential to expand or change the system), making it both desirable and possible for the child to reflect on the sources of information being received and their relative status as authoritative. Overall, then, the developments described have a clear functional and semantic interrelation, producing a fashion of speaking in which language is turned back on itself to enable reflection on meaning.

Of course, this characterization of a semantic style being developed by Stephen by the time he was five years old does not encompass every aspect of his discourse, since such matters as his handling of interpersonal relations have not been addressed here. What I have described is Stephen's fashion of speaking for learning, a 'learning style,' which was not an innate endowment, but the result of an apprenticeship in ways of meaning that serve his particular speech community. If we now consider the characteristics of educational knowledge outlined in Table 3.1, it is not difficult to see how this is an apprenticeship into an orientation highly relevant for schooling. Table 3.2 summarizes the relevance of Stephen's pre-school linguistic experience to the features of educational knowledge.

From the description of Stephen's language use given here, it should not be assumed that he was invariably linguistically explicit, spoke primarily in generalizations and learned exclusively through definitions, text-based inferencing and so on. This was certainly not the case. But during the period of the study he was guided to develop these additional new ways of using his language to build his knowledge and to reflect upon that process while doing so. Since everything that he was learning in this regard was interrelated, we can fairly say that even when construing the mundane – what causes birds to die, that he once broke a plate, that we put air in car tyres, that some cars go faster than others – he was repeatedly gaining experience in deploying a learning style well suited to the learning of less everyday facts. As with all of us, much of his daily speech was context-embedded and unreflective, and he was not yet able to read, but by age five he was prepared with linguistic tools that could be adapted to rapid and conscious instruction in matters more abstract and technical than was typical in the home environment, including those associated with literacy.

Table 3.2 Stephen's linguistic preparation for learning educational knowledge

Educational knowledge	Linguistic preparation
Universalistic in orientation.	Experience with generalizations in contexts of information exchange.
Distant from personal experience.	Orientation to linguistic explicitness, hypothetical and generalized meaning, attending to text
Based on semiotic representation.	Orientation to learning and reasoning from text.
Abstract and technical meanings.	Familiarity with construing definitions and criteria for categories.
Constituted in written language.	Some experience with grammatical metaphor. Experience with 'disembedded' language. Some experience with more monologic segments of spoken text (as well as read-aloud written texts). Some experience inferring meaning from text. Awareness of written texts as information sources.
Built up consciously.	Experience in reflecting on meanings. Awareness of self as learner, building knowledge from various sources.
Built up rapidly; paced at discretion of instructor.	Experience with definitions, inferences.
Systematically presented, logically sequenced.	Familiarity with definitions, criteria for classifications, reflecting on meaning.
Disciplinary boundaries may be maintained	(No obvious relevant experience in spoken language)

A fundamental point to draw from this account is that learning is centrally a matter of building and using language, and that teaching therefore 'means intervening in what are indisputably linguistic processes' (Halliday 1988b: 2). This is as true of learning science or history as of learning to read and write. The specialized bodies of knowledge of formal education are constituted as systems of meanings, with their own metalanguages and their own forms of discourse. Accessing and engaging with them is in the end a linguistic enterprise. Secondly, given that there are acknowledged differences between everyday and educational knowledge, a child is advantaged if he or she arrives in school with a linguistic learning style which is well suited to school demands, though even these children will need to adapt to different degrees of framing and classification and the one-to-many situation of teacher–child discourse. Children whose speech community has a different semantic style will inevitably face a greater discontinuity upon entering school. It remains an issue how best to address that fact: the pedagogical relationship, the nature of the knowledge and the learner's orientation towards using language as a tool for reflection are all features of the situation that are potentially open to change.

Notes

1 Throughout, the age of the child will be given in years, months and days – e.g. 2;5;16 – and uncertain transcription will be indicated by placing text in parentheses with a preceding question mark. Other notes are in square brackets.
2 Note that *you* has a generalized meaning here, rather than referring to the addressee.
3 Stephen's initial use of conditional clauses was chiefly for information exchange, as here, in contrast with the subjects of the McCabe *et al.* (1983) study where the most frequent use was for bribes or threats. The difference may be due to the fact that these latter data were of siblings at play rather than adult–child talk.
4 Television viewing, however, offers information about situations in a way less tied to the child's ongoing and affectively charged concerns.
5 In fact Stephen, after age three, often constructed himself and others in the same way, prefacing announcements of interesting information with *I know . . . you didn't know . . .* or *did you know . . .?*
6 'Reported speech' develops much earlier than this, but in Stephen's case, it was chiefly used to recall dialogue in the context of recounting personal experience. After age four, it was also used to introduce a potentially problematic utterance into a new context.
7 Asking the child *how do you know?* was one of the features of adult talk specifically associated with middle-class homes in the Tizard and Hughes study (1984: 145).

References

Bernstein, Basil (ed.) (1973) *Class, Codes and Control, Vol. 2: Applied Studies towards a Sociology of Language.* London: Routledge & Kegan Paul.
Bernstein, Basil (1975) *Class, Codes and Control, Vol. 3: Towards a Theory of Educational Transmissions.* London: Routledge & Kegan Paul.
Bernstein, Basil (1987) 'Social class, codes and communication'. In U. Ammon, K. Matthier and N. Dittmar (eds), *Sociolinguistics/Soziolinguistik.* Berlin: W. de Gruyter.
Bernstein, Basil (1990) *Class, Codes and Control. Vol. 4: The Structuring of Pedagogic Discourse.* London: Routledge.
Christie, Michael J. (1985) *Aboriginal Perspectives on Experience and Learning: The Role of Language in Aboriginal Education.* Deakin: Deakin University Press.

Donaldson, Margaret (1978) *Children's Minds*. London: Fontana/Croom Helm.

Gallaway, Clare and Richards, Brian J. (eds) (1994) *Input and Interaction in Language Acquisition*. Cambridge: Cambridge University Press.

Halliday, M.A.K. (1975) *Learning How to Mean*. London: Edward Arnold.

Halliday, M.A.K. (1978) *Language as Social Semiotic: The Social Interpretation of Language and Meaning*. London: Edward Arnold.

Halliday, M.A.K. (1984) Listening to Nigel: Conversations with a Very Small Child. Sydney: University of Sydney, mimeo.

Halliday, M.A.K. (1988a) 'Language and socialisation: home and school'. In L. Gerot, J. Oldenburg, T. van Leeuwen (eds), *Language and Socialisation: Home and School: Proceedings from the Working Conference on Language in Education*, Macquarie University 17–21 November 1986. Sydney: Macquarie University.

Halliday, M.A.K. (1988b) 'Language and the enhancement of learning'. Unpublished talk given at the Language in Learning Symposium held at Brisbane C.A.E.

Halliday, M.A.K. (1994) *Introduction to Functional Grammar* (2nd edn). London: Arnold.

Halliday, M.A.K. and Hasan, Ruqaiya (1976) *Cohesion in English*. London: Longman.

Halliday, M.A.K. and Martin, J.R. (1993) *Writing Science: Literacy and Discursive Power*. London: Falmer.

Harris, S.G. (1980) *Culture and Learning: Tradition and Education in NE Arnhem Land*. Darwin: Northern Territory Dept of Education.

Hasan, Ruqaiya (1989) 'Semantic variation and sociolinguistics', *Australian Journal of Linguistics*, 9(2), 221–76.

Hasan, Ruqaiya (1991) 'Questions as a mode of learning in everyday talk'. In T. Le and M. McCausland (eds), *Language Education: Interaction and Development*. Launceston: University of Tasmania Press, 70–119.

Hasan, Ruqaiya (1992) 'Rationality in everyday talk: from process to system'. In J. Svartvik (ed.), *Directions In Corpus Linguistics: Proceedings of Nobel Symposium 82*, Stockholm 4–8 August 1991. Berlin: de Gruyter.

Hasan, Ruqaiya and Cloran, Carmel (1990) 'A sociolinguistic interpretation of everyday talk between mothers and children'. In M.A.K. Halliday, J. Gibbons and H. Nicholas (eds), *Learning, Keeping and Using Language Vol. 1: Selected Papers from the 8th World Congress of Applied Linguistics*. Amsterdam: Benjamins, 67–100.

Hasan, R. (1996) 'Ways of saying: ways of meaning', in C. Cloran, D. Butt and G. Williams (eds) *Ways of Saying: Ways of Meaning: Selection Papers of Ruqaiya Hasan*. London: Cassell, pp. 191–242

Heath, Shirley Brice (1983) *Ways with Words: Language, Life, and Work in Communities and Classrooms*. Cambridge: Cambridge University Press.

McCabe, A., Evely, D., Abramovitch, R., Corter, C. and Pepler, D. (1983) 'Conditional statements in young children's spontaneous speech', *Journal of Child Language* 10, 253–8.

Martin, J.R. (1986) 'Intervening in the process of writing development', in C. Painter and J.R. Martin (eds), *Writing to Mean: Teaching Genres Across the Curriculum*, Applied Linguistics Association of Australia (Occasional Papers no. 9), 11–43.

Martin, J.R. (1993) 'Secret English: discourse technology in a junior secondary school'. In B. Cope and M. Kalantzis (eds), *Genre Approaches to Literacy: Theories and Practices* (Papers from the 1991 LERN Conference, UTS) Sydney: Common

Ground, 43–76. Originally published in L. Gerot, J. Oldenberg and T. van Leeuven (eds), *Language and Socialisation: Home and School* (Report of the 1986 Working Conference on Language in Education). Sydney: Macquarie University, 1988: 143–73.

Martin, J.R. (1995) 'Waves of abstraction: organizing exposition'. In T. Miller (ed.), *Functional Approaches to Written Text: Classroom Applications*. Paris: TESOL France & USA.

Mercer, Ian (1980) *The Changing Earth*. London: Macmillan Children's Books.

Ochs, Elinor (1990) 'Indexicality and socialisation'. In J.W. Stigler, R.A. Shweder and G. Herdt (eds), *Cultural Psychology: Essays on Comparative Human Development*. New York: Cambridge University Press.

Ochs, Elinor and Schieffelin, B.B. (1984) 'Language acquisition and socialization: three developmental stories and their implications'. In R.A. Shweder and R.A. LeVine (eds), *Essays on Mind, Self, and Emotion*. Cambridge: Cambridge University Press, 276–320.

Olson, David R. (1989) 'On the language and authority of textbooks'. In S. de Castell, A. Luke and C. Luke (eds), *Language, Authority and Criticism*. London: Falmer Press, 233–44.

Painter, Clare (1986) 'The role of interaction in learning to speak and learning to write'. In C. Painter and J.R. Martin (eds), *Writing to Mean: Teaching Genres Across the Curriculum*. Applied Linguistics Association of Australia (Occasional Papers no. 9).

Painter, Clare (1989) 'Learning language: a functional view of language development'. In R. Hasan and J.R. Martin (eds), *Language Development: Learning Language: Learning Culture*. (Advances in Discourse Processes, vol. 27). Norwood, NJ: Ablex, 18–65.

Painter, Clare (1991) *Learning the Mother Tongue* (2nd edn). Geelong: Deakin University Press.

Painter, Clare (1996a) 'The development of language as a resource for thinking: a linguistic view of learning'. In R. Hasan and G. Williams (eds), *Literacy in Society*. London: Longman, 50–85.

Painter, Clare (1996b) 'Learning about learning: construing semiosis in the pre-school years', *Functions of Language*, 3(1), 95–125.

Painter, Clare (forthcoming, 1999) *Learning Through Language: In Early Childhood*. London: Pinter.

Scollon, Ron and Scollon, Suzanne B.K. (1981) *Narrative, Literacy and Face in Interethnic Communication*. Norwood, NJ: Ablex.

Snow, Catherine E. and Ferguson, C.A. (eds) (1979) *Talking to Children: Language Input and Acquisition*. Cambridge: Cambridge University Press.

Tizard, Barbara and Hughes, Martin (1984) *Young Children Learning*. Cambridge, MA: Harvard University Press.

Wells, Gordon (1987) *The Meaning Makers: Children Learning Language and Using Language to Learn*. London: Hodder & Stoughton.

Whorf, Benjamin Lee (1956) *Language, Thought and Reality: Selected Essays*, J.B. Carroll (ed.). Cambridge, MA: MIT Press.

Williams, Geoff (1995) 'Joint book-reading and literacy pedagogy: a socio-semantic examination', *CORE*, vol. 1, 19(3), Fiche 2 BO1–Fiche 6 BO1.

4 The pedagogic device and the production of pedagogic discourse: a case example in early literacy education

Geoff Williams

Introduction

The point of departure for this discussion is a common domestic activity: caregivers reading books with children and talking to them. It is often one of the more relaxed aspects of domestic life, and at first glance perhaps not a likely site for intensive linguistic and sociological analysis. What makes the activity of more than passing interest is the fact that, recontextualized into schooling, it has become a key element in a pedagogic discourse of early school literacy. Today it is usual in most English-speaking countries to see joint book-reading as a significant part of children's early literacy education. Additionally, there have been many advisory handbooks for parents[1] which promote specific aspects of interaction during joint book-reading as appropriate family practice to ensure children's success in school literacy (NSW Department of School Education [nd]).

The research basis for this development in early literacy education is work describing relations between reading in the home and early pedagogic success. The most influential research was carried out by Durkin (1966), Clark (1976), Clay (1967), and Wells (1985, 1987), but there is also a large amount of lesser known case study data, typically produced by academics in faculties of education who have studied their own children's literacy development (e.g. Snow 1983). So persuasive has this discourse been that it is now a matter of commonsense that joint book-reading is a key aspect of a necessary *partnership* between home and school (Cairney and Munsie 1992, Dwyer 1989).

My interest here, however, is not in the efficacy of the activity. Rather, it is in the ways in which joint-book reading is recontextualized into school literacy practices from its origins in domestic life. I am particularly interested in the possibility of different variants of joint book-reading occurring in families in different social locations, and how these variants are positioned in relation to pedagogic discourses of early literacy development. Since the antithesis of partnership is preclusion, some important pedagogical questions derive from uses of the partnership metaphor: in particular, who may enter the desirable partnership to prepare children for school literacy success, and on what terms?

There is a strong basis in existing research literature for suspecting that variation in interaction during 'literacy events' (Heath 1983) will occur between fractions of families in different social locations. Variation has, of course, been a major focus of literacy research for many years, in fields as diverse as the history of literacies (Cressy 1980, Graf 1987); literacy, culture and cognition (Cook-Gumperz 1986, Goody 1987, Heath 1983, Street 1984, 1993), feminism and literacies (Christian-Smith 1993, Cranny-Francis 1992, Gilbert 1990, 1992) and in critiques of relations between ideology, discourses and educational practices (Bourdieu and Passeron 1990, Kress 1985, 1987, Gee 1990).

More specifically, in joint book-reading research there has been a good deal of interesting work on variation. The problem in thinking about the pedagogic consequences is not that variation is unresearched to this point. For example, it is a significant strand in Heath's ethnographic study of 'ways with words' in three south-eastern US communities. Heath found interaction during joint book-reading in the working-class families of Roadville to be markedly different from practices among the families of her teacher informants in Gateway. Additionally, there is Wells' report of variation in the time-sampled interactions he observed in the Bristol study (e.g. Moon and Wells 1979). Teale (1986) and Tizard and Hughes (1984) also discuss variation in interaction in association with speakers' social location. This is by no means an exhaustive list.

However, a real problem is that in none of the work of which I am aware has there been any detailed linguistic analysis of 'intact' sessions of joint book-reading, which explicates what variant practices there are, with what social features of speakers they correlate, why these relations might have arisen, and how the variant practices are positioned in relation to school pedagogic discourses. Nor has any study considered how research about precocious reading development, often regarded as an outcome of extensive joint book-reading, is projected into pedagogic discourses of the early years of schooling. Much of this research either celebrates or regrets difference without reference to any privileging text or the social structuring conditions through which it is produced.[2]

An enquiry which attempts to overcome these problems and develop a more fully theorized account of variation in relation to speakers' social locations requires two strategies. First, the research must give a detailed account of linguistic interaction during joint book-reading as a basis for observing whether or not significant semantic variation occurs across families in contrasted social formations (Hasan 1996), and then compare these accounts with typical school practices. The detailed linguistic analysis is necessary because it is *talk* around object texts, which typically pervades joint book-reading activity, not shared reading to children per se, which has been the focus of pedagogic interest. Wells (1985: 253) provides a succinct statement of a widely-held position:

it is not the reading of stories on its own that leads children towards the reflec-
tive, disembedded thinking that is so necessary for success in school, but the
total interaction in which the story is embedded. At first they need a competent
adult to mediate, as reader and writer, between themselves and the text; but
even when they can perform the decoding and encoding for themselves, they
continue to need help in interpreting the stories they hear and read and in
shaping those that they create for themselves.

The manner in which the adult – first parent and later teacher – fulfils this
latter role is almost as important as the story itself.

First, then, I will report on some aspects of a detailed exploration of
interactive language across families in contrasted social locations, using a
linguistic analytic framework developed by Hasan (1983, 1996) in which
each clause of each utterance is analysed from a range of semantic perspectives. Second, some account is needed, based on sociological theory,
of the social processes through which joint book-readings are selectively
recontextualized into the pedagogic discourse of the first years of schooling. In interpreting the results of the linguistic analysis, the chapter
explores the potential of a theoretical resource in Bernstein's work: the
pedagogic device.

In his writing over the last decade or so Bernstein (1986, 1990) has
drawn attention to the importance of two types of analysis of pedagogic
discourse. In one type, analyses consider the differential effects of what is
relayed, the content of pedagogic discourse and its differential effects on
various categories of learner. Here the object of analysis is to reveal a
'double distortion' in communication: first, a privileging of the communication of principles of order and relation, and of specific content and
skills associated with dominant social groups; and second, misrepresentation of the cultural practices of the dominated group in pedagogic
discourse (Bernstein 1990: 171).

However, in the other neglected type of analysis the issue is pedagogic
discourse as a relay. Such an account is required, Bernstein argues, in
order to interpret the sets of relations into which a specific form of pedagogic discourse enters and the processes through which it is constructed
out of other discourses. His account, given as a highly original description
of the pedagogic device, is an important extension of analyses of the ways
in which formal schooling participates in the cultural transmission of
dominant social principles of order and relation. Here I will attempt to
consider how one might approach research into ways in which the pedagogic device produces a particular form of pedagogic discourse in relation
to typical linguistic interaction in families in different social locations.

More generally, the research addresses specific aspects of relations
between symbolic structures and social structures. Bernstein has recently
commented on a tendency in contemporary uses of 'discourse' as the
centre of gravity for social analysis for the 'social' to be re-written by non-
sociologists and taken over by sociologists, with the consequence that

The privileging of discourse . . . tends to abstract the analysis of discourse from the detailed empirical analysis of its basis in social structure. The relationships between symbolic structures *and* social structures are in danger of being severed (1996: 13).

The research approach

There were three phases of data-gathering in the research project: a preliminary survey of joint book-reading to map the distributions of the activity in a large number of families in different social locations; gathering samples of interactive language between mothers and four-year-old children in a smaller number of families, contrasted carefully on specific social features; and gathering samples of interactive language in kindergarten classes in the suburbs in which these families lived. The K samples were obtained during the first month or so of schooling.

The first rather straightforward task for the research was to establish whether or not joint book-reading was a widely-practised activity in families with pre-school children in different socio-geographical regions of Sydney. The results of a questionnaire survey suggested that it was. The regions were contrasted on the general criterion of how early childhood services were provided.[3] In the one, the state was largely responsible for this provision as a form of early educational intervention, in response to the region's many perceived educational disadvantages. Early Childhood Education centres (hereafter ECE centres) were built in the grounds of local primary schools. In the other, provision was through privately operated ECE centres, to which the families paid a daily fee for services. From an initial list of 603, 427 families, each of which had a child of approximately four years of age enrolled at one of the ECE centres, responded to the survey. Of these, there were 240 responses from among the state-funded ECE group, and 187 from the privately funded ECE group. Proportions of responses from the two regions were equal. From the responses it was evident that a large majority of families in both regions did read regularly to their pre-school children, and typically it was the mother who did so. From responses to many of the questionnaire items, such as those which asked about purposes for the activity and the types of text typically read, there were also strong informal grounds for hypothesizing that variation in interaction was likely.

In their responses many mothers in both regions indicated willingness to record interaction during joint book-reading. Since this was to be a study of intra-cultural variation a first selection was made of those families in which both parents had been born in Australia, used English as their mother tongue, and had attended school in Australia. The ensuing problem was to select from among the volunteers in such a way as to be able eventually to provide a theoretically explicit account of relations between social features of speakers and any finding of semantically variant forms of interaction common among members of social groups. This has been a key difficulty with previous work describing joint book-reading interaction.

The strategy adopted for this research derives from Bernstein's concepts of classification, framing and field, and largely follows the approach developed by Hasan in her investigations of semantic variation in casual conversations in the home (Bernstein 1975, Hasan 1989). The concepts classification and framing provide a means for theorizing relations between, and relations within, categories in the social division of labour. Under conditions of strong classification and framing, categories of labour acquire distinctive meanings, and distinctive forms of communication tend to become associated with them because they are differentially distributed on dimensions of power. The variable possibility of an agent within a labour category exercising choice in effecting meanings associated with the category is a crucial distinguishing feature of categories. Variable degrees of choice can exist for both the meanings and the communicative practices within categories of labour. Using this perspective, the criterion specified by Hasan for selecting participants to form contrasted social class groups was *the relative autonomy of an agent to exercise power in the workplace* (e.g. 1989). With minor elaborations it was the criterion used in this study.

Professional autonomy is a relative rather than a fixed feature of an occupation. The feature gives a cline of relations between labour categories rather than sets of discrete levels of occupations. For example, a district manager in a government bureaucracy may have considerable autonomy from one perspective, as in making local budget decisions, but from another perspective, as in determining policy on staffing levels, the same worker has virtually no autonomy. Nevertheless it can reasonably be hypothesized that a social security clerk would *generally* have more workplace autonomy than a building labourer in making and transmitting decisions, but considerably less than a district manager in a government bureaucracy.[4]

The occupations of parents[5] in what I will now call the Lower Autonomy Professional (LAP) group, again following Hasan, are displayed in Table 4.1, and those of the Higher Autonomy Professional (HAP) group in Table 4.2.

Since the preliminary survey indicated that it was mothers who most frequently read to children, the study focused on their interaction. The key problem was to obtain audio-recordings of data with minimal intrusion into the usual family practices. Certain strategies used in previous research were excluded. The presence of an observer at pre-arranged times was considered to be too intrusive, and potentially to limit the spontaneity of occasions of reading and talk (Heath 1983, Teale 1986). For this reason, too, videorecording was considered not to be feasible, as it would have made unacceptable demands on the mothers (cf. Tizard and Hughes 1984). Remote recording devices were excluded because time-sampling was not appropriate in a project investigating the *whole* of the linguistic interaction in a session of joint book-reading (cf. Wells with Bridges *et al.* 1981). More positively, it has been shown in previous research in the semantic variation field that clear, natural data can be obtained from audio recordings made by participants (Hasan, 1989).

Table 4.1 Lower-Autonomy Professional group: parents' occupations

Child	Mother in current paid employment	Mother's occupation	Father's occupation
Philip	yes	packer	paint batcher
Dennis	no	clerk	loader driver
Janet	yes	child-minder	carpenter
Rhonda	yes	word processor	soldier
Angela	yes	clerk	drainer
Anthony	no	factory assistant	accounts clerk
Paul	no	shop assistant	boilermaker
Ashley	yes	waitress	blacksmith/welder
Robin	no	cleaner	(no father in this family)
Wayne	yes	barmaid	labourer

Table 4.2 Higher-Autonomy Professional group: parents' occupations

Child	Mother in current paid employment	Mother's occupation	Father's occupation
Simon	yes	librarian	engineer
Stephen	yes	teacher	engineer
Rachel	yes	company secretary	sales manager
Benjamin	yes	teacher	civil engineer
James	no	occupational therapist	financial consultant
John	no	secretary	engineer
Andrew	no	office manager	managing director
Glenn	no	dental assistant	investment planner
Emily	yes	teacher	barrister
Michael	yes	medical specialist	medical specialist

Participants were therefore provided with small, powerful audio recorders and tapes, and asked to record eight occasions of joint book-reading. They were invited to destroy recordings of sessions which they felt were 'unnatural', or which contained material they wished to keep private. All data from the family recordings were transcribed, and from this four occasions per family were selected for intensive analysis. For the LAP group these sessions were those with the largest number of interactive messages (an analytic unit which will be formally defined in the following section). For the HAP group the four sessions were those which most closely approximated the mean number of interactive messages.

It was also possible to gather samples of kindergarten classroom discourse for comparison with the family discourse. Teachers of kindergarten classes in the schools in which the children would ordinarily enrol in the subsequent year made eight recordings of joint book-reading sessions during the first month or so of the school year. This gave a total sample of 160 recordings. Approximately 50 per cent of these were transcribed, and random selections made from the first two recordings within each class. A check ensured that the selected session was not atypical of other recorded lessons.

So far as is possible under any recording constraint, the sessions appear to be essentially natural occasions of linguistic interaction. Unself-conscious use of language is evident throughout the recording when family matters are discussed, children and mothers joke together, and mothers yawn and comment ruefully on their domestic work. There is no evidence that the readings were rehearsed, or that the children were constrained by the presence of the tape recorder in what topics they could talk about. In fact, the children sometimes asked at the end of a recording session when recording would begin. All of the transcript data which was subsequently analysed is reproduced in Williams (1995).

Linguistic analysis of joint book-reading interaction

The lack of studies which consider linguistic interaction *during intact sessions* of joint book-reading is one of the difficulties besetting the modelling of pedagogic discourse of early literacy development. There are some case studies in which scholars have analysed samples of language from single sessions, for example Snow (1983) and Dombey (1983), and in the Bristol study Wells looked at fragments of many family sessions, fragments determined by time-interval recording techniques. Though Heath's *Ways with Words* (1983) is a very detailed ethnographic study, the discussion of interactive language is largely in terms of broad types of questions used in the different social locations she describes. Obviously, it is necessary to overcome some rather large methodological hurdles in order to be able to describe variation in linguistically explicit ways through analyses of whole texts.

The linguistic analyses used in this study were made possible by Hasan's development of a theory of semantic variation, including the methodologically crucial resource of a contextually open analytic framework (Hasan 1983, 1989, 1996). Hasan's work extends suggestions initially made by Halliday (1973) for the mapping of meaning resources available to speakers within a particular situation type as this is defined within systemic functional linguistic theory. I will briefly outline key aspects of Hasan's approach, introduce two fragments of her semantic network and then present the results of the analyses for these data based on the framework.

The unit which is the point of origin for analysis in semantic networks is message, glossed as 'the smallest semantic unit that is *capable of realizing an element in the structure of texts* (Hasan 1995: 227). Message is typically realized at the lexicogrammatical stratum as clause. At a primary level of delicacy message is the entry point in the semantic stratum to the system of options [**progressive**] versus [**punctuative**]. For each semantic feature there is a statement specifying its lexicogrammatical realization. For example, for the feature [**progressive**] the lexicogrammatical realization statement is:

1. preselect option *major* at clause rank;
2. insert element *Predicator* in clause;
3. preselect an instance of verbal group at Predicator (Hasan, 1992: 91)

Progressive messages are described through sets of related options.[6] These are given as:

i.   systems of interpersonal meanings, for example options in message function (questioning, informing, commanding . . .), options in personal evaluation, point of view, etc.;
ii. systems of experiential meaning, for example the ascription of actional, evaluational roles, identification, definition; construction of time, etc.;
iii. systems of logical meaning, for example cause, condition, and meta-textual relations, etc.;
iv   systems of textual meanings, for example options in topic maintenance, topic change, etc. (Hasan, 1989: 244).

As a result it is possible for a researcher to model potential variation in terms of differential and differentiating patterns of selection of the semantic options available to speakers. The lexicogrammatical realization statements function virtually as recognition criteria for semantic features.

Punctuative messages are realized by clauses which do not select for Predicator, typically minor clauses. Some informal examples of punctuative messages are formulaic greetings, address, and reactive expressions such as 'gosh'.

For this research the range of analyses of semantic features was determined on the following criteria:

i.   features which, described in some reasonably comparable form, have been the focus of major interest in previous research;
ii. sets of relevant features selected from those which Hasan and her colleagues established (Hasan 1989, 1991, 1992; Hasan and Cloran 1990);
iii. those features which have not been widely discussed in previous research but which are of particular theoretical interest in joint book-reading as a context for literacy learning.

Illustration from the range of analyses, rather than comprehensive discussion, is obviously necessary here for reasons of space. However, it does create a difficulty in interpretation, which is that the realization of semantic variants may appear to be given only by configurations of the semantic features discussed. Such is not the case. The features are presented as illustrations only from the full range of analyses on which the general claims rest. These are available in Williams (1995).

The obvious place to begin the enquiry is with questions, or, more precisely, demands for information, since these have been central to researchers interest in children's early literacy development. Each question asked by mothers and children was analysed through the framework of Hasan's semantic network. Figure 4.1 presents the relevant fragment of the network, and it is followed by some brief examples of analysis procedures.

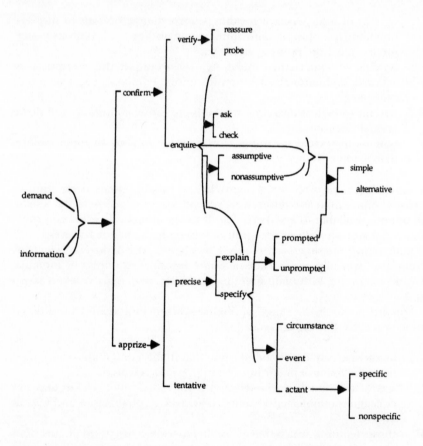

Figure 4.1 Hasan's network of choices in making demands for information

Reading the network from left to right, which is to say from the primary features to more delicate systems dependent on these features, produces selection expressions such as [**demand; information: confirm: verify: reassure**]. An example of a message selecting these features is: 'She's going to the beach, isn't she?' The lexicogrammatical realization statement for this option is [major: indic: declarative: tagged: reversed]. In contrast, a message selecting [**demand; information: confirm: verify: probe**], exemplified by 'She's going to the beach, is she?' is realized lexicogrammatically by [major: indic: declarative: tagged: constant]. To recapitulate, the analysis of each demand for information through the framework of the semantic network is based on an analysis of the lexicogrammar. So, when a child asks a question, 'Why is that there?', the semantic analysis of this message from the perspective of its interpersonal function as a demand for information is: [**demand; information: apprise: precise: explain**]. The ground for this claim is the lexicogrammatical realization [major: indicative: interrogative: nonpolar: wh conflated with Adjunct and Circumstance of cause why^F^S^P].[7]

Prefacing of messages was also of particular interest because it has been shown to contribute importantly to semantic variation in Hasan's research. Selection from the preface system plays an important part in the construal of 'point of view' (Cloran 1994) and has been shown to contribute to differences in extent of individuation (Hasan 1989, 1991).

In order to consider the nature of this resource it is necessary to slightly refine the earlier comment that a message is typically realized by a clause. The refinement has to do with the contribution of projecting clauses to messages. These are clauses such as '<u>They all thought</u> that was such a funny idea'. Projecting clauses realize the feature [**prefaced**] rather than a separate message. Informally speaking, they realize the meaning that the message is a metarepresentation. For example, the clause complex 'I think that we can have a holiday in Port Douglas' realizes a single message, and this message selects the feature [**prefaced**], which is realized by the projecting clause 'I think'. This semantic feature is itself the entry condition to several further dependent systems which describe more delicate meaning options in 'metarepresenting', realized through further lexicogrammatical options selected by the projecting clause. The difference in lexicogrammar, for example, between '<u>I said</u> that they could visit Port Douglas', where the projecting clause selects a Verbal Process and '<u>I think</u> that they could visit Port Douglas', where a Mental Process is selected. In Hasan's description of [**prefaced**] messages, the first message is a metarepresentation of a locution, and selects the features [**prefaced: experiential: saying**]. The second message is a metarepresentation of an idea, but with the interesting further grammatical characteristic of the projecting clause acting as a form of interpersonal grammatical metaphor of modality (Halliday 1994: 354ff). This message selects the features [**prefaced: interpersonal: nonattitudinal: modal**].

There is also a potential for the experience of different figures to be projected through the grammatical resources of Subject in the projecting clause, as exemplified in the following extract.

Example 1

Mh: **'Toad steals a motor car'. Toad eagerly scrambled into the seat vacated by the driver**
> 01   Remember he was dressed up like an old woman
> 02   and the car came along
> 03   and they offered he offered him a lift?
> 04   Remember that?

Cd: 05   Mm.
Mh: 06   And then he said that he would like to have a go at the driving?
> 07   And they all thought that was such a funny idea.

Message 1 '(Do you) remember he was dressed up like an old woman' is of course addressed to the child. It selects the feature [**prefaced: subjective: other: addressee: child**]. In contrast Messages 6 and 7, which concern some aspects of the experience of the fictive characters, select [**prefaced: subjective: other: third party: object text figure**], Toad and his friends. One interesting question about variation in these data is the frequency with which families and teachers make the subjective experience of the child the focus of enquiry, as in Messages 1 and 4 in Example 1. I will return to this question shortly.[8]

Describing semantic variation in joint book-reading

In all, 15,337 interactive messages were analysed: 8276 from the family data and 7061 from the K class data. Statistical comparisons[9] of the selection of semantic features in the two family data sets and in the two classroom discourse data sets were made. However, comparisons between the family and school data sets were not possible since the general constraints on the frequency of occurrence of semantic features could not be assumed, for statistical purposes, to be the same in the two environments. This restriction did not, though, prevent comparisons of *tendencies* to select sets of semantic features between the two family groups and the school groups. The central question for these comparisons was: if x semantic features, or constellation of features, appear to be implicated in variation in linguistic interaction between the two family social groups, is there any evidence that x (constellation of) features achieves prominence in linguistic interaction in joint book-reading in kindergarten classroom discourse?

For economy in the subsequent discussion it is useful to give the general finding that no significant differences were found between the sets of classroom discourse data in the two social locations. There appears to be no statistically significant difference which is associated with the social area location of the schools on features relevant to this discussion. Further, this finding parallels those in Hasan's project, 'The role of everyday talk between mothers and children in establishing ways of learning, Phases 1 and 2'. It has therefore been most productive to collapse the two sets of classroom discourse data and describe median frequencies of features in the interactive talk for the whole set, thus providing twenty examples of classroom discourse across which comparisons with the family data could be made.

The first issue to be addressed in the family data analyses was the basic one of the extent of object text reading. The total number of object text messages read by mothers was very similar, though mothers were not constrained by the project instructions to choose any particular length or type of text. This finding is perhaps not very surprising given the age of the children and the conventions of publishing, which determine fairly standard lengths of text for this age group. Some mothers did, of course, read more than one text per session, but those who did so tended to be distributed evenly between the two social groups. Table 4.3 presents the totals of object text messages read during the four joint book-reading sessions for each mother-child dyad.

Table 4.3 Total number of object text messages read by mother–child dyads in four joint book-reading sessions

LAP group		HAP group	
Child	**Total**	**Child**	**Total**
Anthony	117	John	231
Philip	189	Simon	288
Wayne	281	Stephen	304
Angela	459	Ben	346
Paul	456	Glenn	220
Ashley	562	Michael	354
Rhonda	652	Emily	552
Dennis	763	Rachel	568
Janet	764	Andrew	692
Robin	796	James	1261
Total	5039		4816

The mean number of object text messages read is similar in the two social groups: for the LAP group it is 503.9 and for the HAP 481.6. The difference between medians is greater, with the LAP frequency of 510.5 a good deal higher than the HAP of 350.0. However this difference is not statistically significant (p<.6563). The HAP frequencies are distributed across a larger range, from 231 to 1261, in comparison with the LAP range from 117 to 796. For both groups, the dyad with the highest frequency of object text messages is not that with the highest number of interactive text messages. Neither is the dyad with lowest object text message frequency the same as that with the lowest interactive text frequency. Clearly the extent of talk around a text is not directly related to the amount of object text read in a session. Therefore, any differences between median frequencies for the selection of semantic features cannot be explained as a function of the *extent* of object text reading.

A comparison of the total number of interactive linguistic messages exchanged in joint book-reading sessions is of great interest. Table 4.4 presents the results of this analysis for totals of punctuative and progressive messages, and Table 4.5 the medians of the distributions for the two social groups.

There is a statistically significant difference between the median scores for total interactive messages and for progressive messages (p<.0230 in each case). The difference between the median scores for punctuative messages is not significant (p<.1789). Despite the similarity of extent of object text reading the total number of interactive messages exchanged by the HAP group is more than 300 per cent greater than for the LAP group. This

Table 4.4 Total mother–child interactive messages

LAP group				HAP group			
Child	Punct.	Prog.	Total	Child	Punct.	Prog.	Total
Philip	2	3	5	Glen	20	133	153
Angela	12	35	47	John	49	125	174
Dennis	7	47	54	Andrew	126	243	369
Anthony	36	28	64	Ben	72	335	407
Paul	40	162	202	Simon	61	374	435
Ashley	59	188	247	Michael	98	593	691
Robin	65	198	263	James	84	649	733
Wayne	62	214	276	Stephen	93	663	756
Rhonda	96	281	377	Emily	102	791	893
Janet	58	425	483	Rachel	318	1329	1647
Totals	437	1581	2018	Totals	1023	5235	6258

Table 4.5 Median frequencies of mother–child interactive messages

Social group	Punctuative median	Progressive median	Total median
LAP	49.0	175.0	224.5
HAP	88.5	483.0	563.0

percentage difference also holds for the total number of progressive messages exchanged. The median scores for total interactive messages differ by approximately 250 per cent, and for the progressive messages by approximately 275 per cent. Underscoring this difference is the fact that the HAP dyad transcripts selected for intensive analysis were those which approximated the mean number of interactive messages for each dyad, whereas for the LAP social group it was the four transcripts with the highest number of interactive messages.

It is important to emphasize, however, that although there is a large difference between the social groups, extensive linguistic interaction does nevertheless occur in the LAP social group around object text for most dyads. The results do not imply some general lack of linguistic interaction since, typically, mothers and children in this group exchange about 50 messages per joint book-reading session.

Were the LAP children relatively passive in talking about the books they read, as is a common pedagogic stereotype of children from lower working-class backgrounds? Given the difference in extent of interaction it might appear that the LAP children are relatively less interested in the object texts, or even perhaps that they demonstrate much less initiative in linguistic interaction about the meanings of books. The frequency with which children initiated interaction during joint book-reading is a useful indicator of the degree of their active involvement in the sessions. The median frequency is 15 for each of the two social groups, so the suggestion of a relative passivity of the LAP group children can be rejected with confidence. Figure 4.2 presents a graph of the frequencies of selection of the semantic feature [initiate] by individual children in the two social groups. (The realization of this feature is the first primary clause in a stretch of interactive text.)

Though the HAP children did tend to initiate interaction specifically by making a demand for information somewhat more frequently than the LAP children, the result was not significantly different. The median frequency for selection of [initiate; demand; information] was 2.00 for the LAP children, and 6.00 for the HAP group (p<.1789).

Since the pioneering research of Ninio and Bruner (1978) on changes in a mother's questioning as the child's understanding of literacy developed, questions during interaction have been central to previous research in this field. They have assumed particular importance in descriptions of differences in literate practice within different social formations, as well as more generally in studies of variation in mother–child interaction.

Almost all mothers asked questions of their children during the interactions. No significant difference between the social groups was found in the total number of demands for information made by mothers. However, when the selection of more delicate options was examined, significant differences were found in some options dependent on [apprise], and for one option dependent on [confirm]. Table 4.6 presents median frequencies and levels of significance for these features.

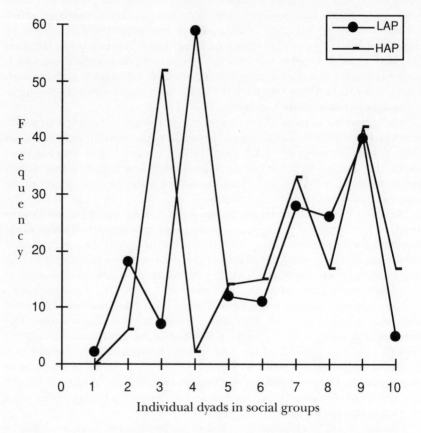

Figure 4.2 Frequency of selection of [**initiate**] in the two family groups

The option [**explain**] was selected significantly more frequently by the HAP mothers (p<.023). Selection of this feature is exemplified in a question James' mother asked him while they were reading *The Magic Pudding:* 'Why do you think Bill got in such a rage?' In the LAP group only Janet's and Rhonda's mothers select the feature, while in the HAP group eight of the ten mothers select it at least once.

The option [**circumstance**] is also selected significantly more frequently by the HAP mothers (p<.0055). In this data the type of demand frequently required the child to specify information about the location of a character or feature of the setting in a visual image, as when Emily's mother asked 'Where's Hannah?', and Emily replied 'Hannah? She's the big girl, isn't she?' The type of question is interesting in that, though in a sense it is closely related to questions which require the child to label object text features, it is somewhat more complex in that it assumes prior knowledge of the visual representation and requires the child to locate a

Table 4.6 Median frequencies of selection of some types of demands for information in the two social groups

Semantic option	Social group		Probability
	LAP	HAP	
[demand; information: confirm:]			
[check]	0.5	5.5	0.0055
[reassure]	3.5	26.5	0.6563
[probe]	–	–	1.0
[ask]	10.5	28.0	0.1789
[demand; information: apprize:]			
[explain]	–	4.5	0.023
[circumstance]	–	5.0	0.0055
[event]	1.5	6.0	0.1789
[actant: specific]	2.5	5.5	0.6563
[actant: nonspecific]	6.0	16.0	0.0198

narrative figure in *relation to* other figures in the image. Consistent with this finding, [**non-specific actant**] was also selected significantly more often by the HAP group (p<. 0198). However, the difference for [**specific actant**] was not statistically significant, nor was the difference for [**event**].

The option [**check**] is the one feature of those dependent on [**confirm**] to emerge as significantly different (p<. 0055). Only half of the LAP mothers select the option at all during the four occasions of reading, but in the HAP group all except Glenn's mother do so. A discussion between Michael and his mother about some troubles at the ECE centre provides a typical example.

Example 2

Mh:	01	Did you cry at kindy
	02	when you hurt your foot?
Cd:	03	No.
Mh:	04	So it was a bit sore
	05	but it wasn't quite sore enough to make you cry?
Cd:	06	No.
Mh:	07	Dear me.

Message 05 exemplifies the selection of [**demand; information: confirm: enquire: check**]. The difference between the social groups appears to be associated with a broader characteristic of the HAP group, that of requiring children to expand on a comment, either about an object text feature or about some aspect of individual experience.

The medians for the classroom data show that all of the options included in Table 4.6 make some contribution to classroom discourse. Comparisons of the family and school medians are reported as a graph in Figure 4.3.

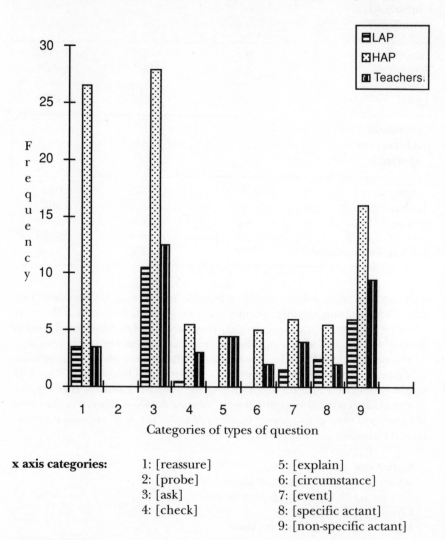

Categories of types of question

x axis categories:

1: [reassure]	5: [explain]
2: [probe]	6: [circumstance]
3: [ask]	7: [event]
4: [check]	8: [specific actant]
	9: [non-specific actant]

Figure 4.3 Median frequency of mothers' and teachers' selection of some types of questions

The sharpest contrast appears to be on the feature [**explain**], where the median frequency per individual lesson is 4.5, a prominence which is not typical of the LAP families. Recalling that the school median frequency is for an individual lesson, [**non-specific actant**] appears also to be comparatively more similar to the HAP practice.

Though the median scores for [**reassure**] appear to be very different, there is considerable variance in individual dyad scores for both the LAP and the HAP groups, resulting in the statistically non-significant findings. (The median for all the family data on this option is 15.) The extent of variance for the frequencies of [**ask**] in the two groups also accounts for the non-significant finding, though it can be seen from Figure 4.3 that this option did play an important, if not clearly contrastive, part in classroom discourse.

One specific function of mothers' questions is to expand children's responses in some way, to extend beyond a first specific comment. In the terms of the descriptive framework, they do so by selecting the feature [**develop**]. The option is dependent on simultaneous prior selection of the features [**demand; information**] and [**follow: maintain topic**]. In Example 3, Michael's mother selects the option in Messages 04 and 06.

Example 3
Mh:		**So he got ready to go to camp. He packed his**
	01	What would you pack . . .
	02	if you were going away to camp?
Cd:	03	Lots of toys.
Mh:	04	And what *else?
Cd:	05	*And that's all.
Mh:	06	What would you wear?

On this feature there was a marked contrast between the social groups. For the LAP group the median frequency was 7.00, and for the HAP group 58.50 (p<.023). For the school data the median frequency was 24.50 per individual lesson, so the school practice is again much more closely approximated by the typical HAP practice.

The result is interesting theoretically since it suggests that the HAP mothers and the teachers both seek to extend children's talk beyond the local and specific instance of the object text to develop a form of literate practice in which explicit linguistic reasoning about written text is valued. The reasoning does not necessarily take the form of an explanation – it can sometimes simply be a comment on a further aspect of the object text instance. Nevertheless the interaction, because of the semantic function of the question following the child's initial response, is always extended beyond the first, specific observation.

Children's questions have also been a major focus of research interest in the emergent literacy field, and in studies of social class differences in language use. In pedagogical literature children are almost stereotypically represented as actively enquiring about characters and events in narrative text in particular. These data were examined, first, to ascertain whether there were significant differences between the median frequencies of children's questions.

All except two children asked questions at some point during the sessions, but there was a clear difference between the medians for the two groups. For the LAP group the median frequency was 5.00, and for the HAP group 18.00 (p<.0011). As a consequence the data was probed to a further level of delicacy, in order to examine the medians for children's selection of the features [**confirm**] and [**apprise**].

For [**confirm**] there was, again, a significant difference: the LAP group median was 1.50 and the HAP 10.50 (p<.023). Though the median figures are quite small it is notable from the raw frequency data, presented in graph form in Figure 4.4, that the difference tends to be sustained across individual dyads.

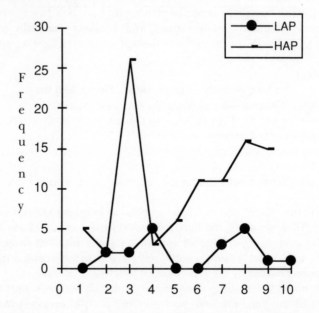

Figure 4.4 Frequencies of children's selection of [**confirm**] in the two social groups

There was also a significant difference for [**apprise**], where the LAP median frequency was 3.00 and the HAP 8.50 (p<.0011). The raw frequency difference is consistent across the dyads, with only one HAP dyad falling within the LAP range, though in this case there is much more variation in the frequency for the LAP children. Figure 4.5 presents a graph of this raw frequency data.

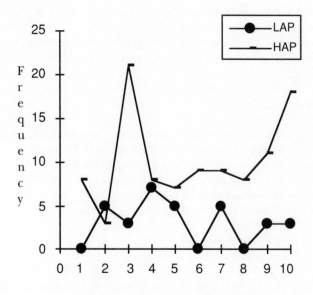

Individual dyads in social groups

Figure 4.5 Frequencies of [**apprise**] in children's questions

Though it was technically possible to pursue differences to a greater level of delicacy by examining children's selection from systems dependent on [**confirm**] and [**apprise**], the very low frequencies for selection of these more delicate features in the LAP group made this comparison fruitless.

In the classroom discourse there were few questions asked by children, consistent with results in the work of previous scholars. The median frequency for both types of questions was 2.00, and for both [**confirm**] and [**apprize**] it was 1.00. If children in the two social groups enter school with variable experiences in asking questions in joint book-reading, it is not likely to impact directly on initial school literacy learning. However, Heath's finding (1983) that some effects of difference in home and school literate traditions between Roadville and Gateway did not appear until much later in a child's school experience may be apposite to these results, since it is in the more advanced stages of schooling such experience would be particularly relevant.

I move now to consider the prefacing of messages. A range of perspectives will be taken on the selection of the feature [**prefaced**] and its dependent sub-systems, considering differences in the deployment of various features by the two social groups. Additionally, the simultaneous selection of [**prefaced**] and demands for information will be examined since in the contexts of everyday talk between mothers and children studied by

Hasan and her colleagues the prefacing of questions was implicated in the observed variance between the social groups (Hasan 1991). The simultaneous selection of [**prefaced**] with [**demand; information**] is exemplified in Example 4. James and his mother were discussing an event in *The Magic Pudding.*

Example 4

Mh:		**For you was both singing out 'Yoo heave ho' for half an hour and him trying to hold on to Bill's beard.**
	01	Who do you think's got the right story?
	02	The pudding reckons they pushed him off.
	03	They think that he fell off.
	04	Who do you think's got the right story?
Cd:	05	Pudding.
Mh:		(LAUGHS)
	06	I think you might be right.

All the interactive messages in this stretch select [**prefaced**]. (In 05 it is very likely to be taken as an ellipsed element.) Here, also, we can observe the simultaneous selection of prefacing with demands for information. Messages 01 and 04 are prefaced demands for information.

From an initial comparison of total prefaced messages, selected by both speakers, it was clear that there was likely to be variation in this semantic region for more delicate options. On this very general contrast there was a significant difference between the medians: for the LAP group the median frequency was 7.00, and for the HAP group it was 51.00 ($p < .023$). In the classroom discourse data the feature was selected at some point by all except one teacher, and the median frequency per lesson was 35.00.

The extent of the difference in total justified further probing of the more specific means through which individual points of view were constructed. There is a variety of resources available for this purpose. One particularly interesting resource for this project is that through which mothers implicated some aspect of the child's subjective state of consciousness in their talk. Formally, this is the feature [**prefaced: subjective: other: child**], selected by the mother. In Example 4, Message 01 is an example of this choice: 'Who do you think's got the right story?' Among the LAP group seven of the ten mothers selected this feature on some occasion, and in the HAP group nine of the ten, so its use was widely distributed in both social groups. However, despite this overall scope of use there was a significant difference between the median frequencies. The median for the LAP group was 2.50 and for the HAP group 14.50 ($p < .023$). Analysis of the classroom discourse again shows that this was a resource teachers frequently selected, despite some diversity across individual K groups. The median frequency per lesson was 9.50.

The frequencies of a related feature, children's selection of [**prefaced: self: exclusive**] were also compared. Informally these are messages in which the children construct a representation of their own subjective states of consciousness. When Emily and her mother were reading *The Great Wungle-Bungle Aerial Expedition*, for example, the mother commented 'He's playing a didgeridoo' and Emily replied, selecting this feature, '<u>I</u> <u>wish</u> I had a didgeridoo'. For this feature the medians for the LAP and HAP groups were 2.00 and 9.50 respectively, but the results were not significant at the .025 criterion level.

From the resources for [**prefaced**] the discussion here focuses on one feature, [**prefaced: interpersonal: nonattitudinal: modal**]. The selection of this feature is exemplified by a message such as a mother's comment, '<u>I</u> <u>think he's using it as a paintbrush</u>'.

Taking first a comparison of the frequencies of selection of [**prefaced: interpersonal: nonattitudinal: modal**] by either mother or child, there was a significant difference. The LAP median was 0.50 and the HAP 21.00 (p<.023). The feature was also quite extensively implicated in classroom discourse, where the median frequency of selection by either category of speaker was 10.00 per lesson. More specifically with respect to the mothers' speech, the selection of this feature was again significantly different between the two social groups. For the LAP group the median frequency was 0.50 and the HAP 18.00 (p<.023). In classroom discourse the feature was prominent in the teachers' speech, where the median frequency was 7.00.

In the children's speech the feature was not selected so frequently but nevertheless there was again a significant difference between the medians for the two social groups. No LAP child selected the feature, but the median for the HAP group was 1.5 (p<.023). Six of the ten HAP children selected the feature at some point in the interaction. In the classroom discourse the median frequency of selection was 2.00 occasions per lesson.

So far the discussion has treated selection of options in prefacing and in demanding information separately. However, the analytic framework enables the researcher to test simultaneous selection of features from these two meaning resources. For example, a speaker may ask a question such as 'Do you think he's using it as a paintbrush?', which simultaneously selects the features [**prefaced: interpersonal: nonattitudinal: modal**] and [**demand; information: confirm: ask**]. In Example 4 the mother's question 'Who do you think's got the right story?' simultaneously selects [**prefaced: interpersonal: nonattitudinal: modal**] and [**demand; information: apprise: specify: actant: specific: unprompted**].

Initially the frequency of prefacing for all types of demands for information by mothers was tested and, since the results were significant, further analyses were completed on the more delicate options [**confirm**] and [**apprise**]. Table 4.7 presents the details of these data. (A comparison of selection of this feature in the children's speech was not made since no child selected it.)

Table 4.7 Median frequencies for mothers' selection of [prefaced: interpersonal: nonattitudinal: modal; demand; information] with the options [**confirm**] and [**apprise**]

Social group	Median frequencies		
	Total	[confirm]	[apprise]
LAP	0.50	0.00	0.00
HAP	7.00	4.00	4.50
probability	0.023	0.0698	0.0198

For the total of both types of demands for information and for [**apprise**] there is a significant difference between the median frequencies. In classroom discourse the configuration of features did appear to play some role, even for children in their first school term. The median frequency for prefacing of all types of demands for information was 4.50, and for [**confirm**] 2.5 and [**apprise**] 1.5. The highest total for both types of questions for a K class was 39, and in seven of the twenty classes the configuration of features is selected on more than ten occasions in the one lesson. Conversely, there were six classes in which the frequency was either one or zero.

In summary, the data are consistent with Hasan's findings with respect to distributions of the selection of prefaced messages within the two social groups. Additionally, the statistical procedure adopted for this study enabled exploration of the selection of configurations of more delicate features dependent on [**prefaced**]. Perhaps the most striking finding has been the extensive use of prefacing to create modalities of possibility specifically with respect to individual states of consciousness.

These then are some illustrations of results from the analyses of interactive language. Together with findings from analyses of other features across all four metafunctions which are reported in Williams (1995), they provide a strong basis for claiming that there is significant variation between the sets of semantic features typically selected within the two social groups, and that one of these sets is strongly associated with typical practice in the first few weeks of schooling.

At this point in the research what one seeks is a set of integrative principles through which to make sense of the pattern of results of the semantic analyses. One of the problems most strikingly evident in previous joint book-reading research has been a cleft between analyses of social formations and their relations, and the analyses of linguistic interaction in families. Bernstein's theory of cultural transmission provides two sets of resources relevant to overcoming these problems. It presents, first, a theory of the development of coding orientations, which includes resources for modelling relations between family social positioning and typical interactive practices. Second, it presents a model of the pedagogic device, the discursive means through which pedagogic discourse is produced.

Since in the space available it is only possible to take up one of these, I will make the pedagogic device the focus in the remainder of the chapter. This will oblige me to assume, from the perspective of Bernstein's theory, an interpretation of relations between the social locations of the families and the communicative practices they adopt. However, it will enable me specifically to explore the structuring principles through which joint book-reading as a domestic activity is recontextualized into a pedagogic discourse of early literacy education.

The pedagogic device

It may be useful to begin the interpretation by taking a few moments to outline some basic features of the pedagogic device. The focus of interest in Bernstein's analysis is the means through which any particular form of pedagogic discourse becomes 'a symbolic ruler of consciousness' (Bernstein 1990: 180, Christie this volume Chapter 6, re the pedagogic device). The account of the pedagogic device is developed through a metaphor of a 'grammar', constituted by three types of rules which are hierarchically related: distributive rules, recontextualizing rules and rules of evaluation. As with the grammar of a language, the small number of rules is argued to be capable of producing an enormous variety of specific instances of pedagogic discourse. In the hierarchy, distributive rules regulate the recontextualizing rules, which regulate the rules of evaluation.

Distribution rules regulate who may have access to what knowledge, and therefore who may have access to discursive power. To develop this point Bernstein uses a distinction between mundane and esoteric knowledge, the 'thinkable' and the 'unthinkable'. In contemporary Western society access to, and control of, the 'unthinkable' tend to lie in the upper levels of the education system which, par excellence, require the use of an elaborated coding orientation. Since children from families in different locations in the social division of labour have differential access to this coding orientation, the pedagogic device is centrally implicated in distributing access to knowledge which is 'unthinkable' or esoteric.

Recontextualization rules provide a means for understanding the embedding of discourses which are produced in sites outside formal schooling within pedagogic discourse itself. To begin informally, consider the production of new knowledge in the culture about, say, the HIV virus. A significant question for cultural production and reproduction is: in what form should this knowledge be reproduced in pedagogic discourse? The move from the original site of discursive production to reproduction in pedagogic discourse requires selection and ordering of the content according to some set of principles, perhaps implicitly held. Recontextualizing rules are, in part, the rules which regulate the movement of discursive content from its initial production into pedagogic contexts.

The account of discourse embedding is extended to consider a more general aspect of cultural reproduction: relations between discourses of social order, called regulative discourse, and those of educational knowledge, termed instructional discourse. The focus is, again, on general relations constituting the pedagogic device, not on any specific relations between content and specific discourses of order. Bernstein's argument is, pursuing the metaphor of grammar one step further, that the general structure of the pedagogic device is to embed instructional discourse in regulative discourse. That is to say, rules of social order selectively transmit contents and skills because pedagogic discourse is not formed independently in relation to a particular content to be relayed.

By the term regulative Bernstein does not mean simply the local regulative practices of management of learners as a function of the moral code, though these are relevant. The larger sense of order is the social regulation of discourse determined by those principles which themselves determine the principles of the social division of labour within a social formation. The general embedding relation between regulative and instructional discourse is derivable, that is, from the fact that distribution of power between categories is the primary determinant of the social order. The regulative must therefore necessarily embed the instructional. The argument is obvious with respect to the moral order, as Bernstein himself points out, but perhaps rather less obvious with respect to the ways in which 'order, relation and identity' are created in instructional discourse (Bernstein 1990: 184). The latter relation is crucial because it is the specific means through which specialized competencies are created for, and distributed to, specific categories of learners.

From the nature of this relationship it also follows that specific forms of pedagogic discourse will *always* be created through the recontextualization of other discourses. This is a much more radical form of the earlier illustrative outline. It is not just a matter of 'controversial' topics being subject to particular scrutiny, regulation and recontextualization. In its most general form the argument is that:

> Pedagogic discourse is a principle for appropriating other discourses and bringing them into a special relation with each other for the purposes of their selective transmission and acquisition. (*ibid.*, 183–4)

The third set of rules for producing pedagogic discourse are evaluative. These derive from actual pedagogic practice and are the analytic means for interpreting specializations of variables such as time, space, context and age. I will pass over a detailed description of these in order to be able to develop the discussion of aspects of recontextualization which are relevant to joint book-reading research and pedagogic practice. To do so it is economical to present Bernstein's model of the general form of the pedagogic device. It is included as Figure 4.6. Attention will be drawn particularly to the following three features: recontextualizing field, the pedagogic recontextualizing field, and the primary contextualizing context.

The primary contextualizing context is that of the family and local community, including peer group relations. In its function of providing primary contextualization the family uses a local pedagogic discourse (see the last lines of Figure 4.6), which may of course be in some conflict with local school practices, as well as with official pedagogic discourse. This difference can arise for many reasons, but particularly because of differential access within families to knowledge of how and why schools adopt certain practices. As an aside, it is interesting that joint book-reading is often raised by some families as a specific example of local school pedagogic discursive practice which causes perplexity.

In fact, Bernstein (1990: 179) suggests it is possible to distinguish between families 'with respect to the extent to which the "local pedagogic practice" is embedded in an "official pedagogic practice" '. Where local pedagogic discourse dominates the family, where there may even be a complete absence of official pedagogic discourse, then learners will be disadvantageously positioned with respect to privileging texts. The inverse relation is where official pedagogic discourse dominates the family, with a close fit, as it were, between the privileging text and family practice. This effectively gives the condition for two sites of access of discourse.

Relations between family joint book-reading practices and the pedagogy of literacy development in kindergarten are particularly interesting with respect to these relations. The question is: how is this relationship constructed? The model enables a critical re-reading of this relationship, particularly through the further concepts noted above: the recontextualizing field and the pedagogic recontextualizing field.

The general recontextualizing field can be considered briefly, given the preceding discussion. It is represented in the figure by the broken line and is the field in which the forms of content and the means of their transmission are determined: for example, both the 'what' and the 'how' of curricula. For the current purpose it is particularly important to note that discourse produced in the primary contextualizing context must be recontextualized to enter the pedagogic recontextualizing field.

The pedagogic recontextualizing field is broad, and includes a range of agencies specializing in normative judgements about 'best practice' in pedagogy, to use the phrase these agencies currently employ in the Australian state of New South Wales. The pedagogic recontextualizing field is defined by Bernstein (1990: 192) in the following way:

1. This will include university and polytechnic departments of education, colleges of education together with their research, and private foundations.
2. It will include specialized media of education, weeklies, journals, etc., and publishing houses together with their readers and advisers.
3. It may extend to fields not specialized in educational discourse and its practices, but which are able to exert influence both on the State and its various arrangements and/or upon special sites, agents and practices within education.

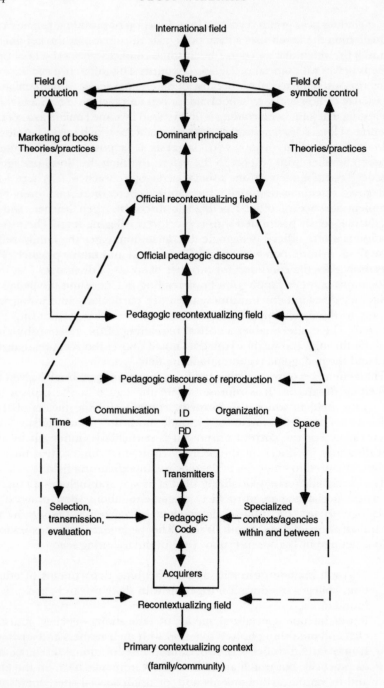

Figure 4.6 A model of relations of pedagogic discourse (from Bernstein, 1990:197)

From the model it can be seen that the pedagogic recontextualizing field is distinguished from official pedagogic discourse through a more direct relationship with the fields of production and symbolic control. This is a double relationship, in which these fields exercise both a direct influence on the discourses to be transmitted, and also more indirectly through the specific requirements of agents who will eventually participate in the primary fields. Various forms of teacher education are an obvious example.

Specific forms of literacy will be one set of those demands, though there may well be considerable internal difference with respect to those demands, given the different ideological orientations of the two fields of primary discursive production (Luke 1993). So the model would predict that work in the pedagogic recontextualizing field would select, integrate and re-identify discourse 'about' literacy (in the sense of specific knowledge and competencies). This work may well be accomplished to *some limited extent* independently of official pedagogic discourse: my understanding is that Bernstein's concept of relative autonomy predicts this potential difference. Under these conditions it is virtually certain that discursive re-shaping will be considerable.

But there will be other important influences on this process as well. One complex issue is the relation between the originating field of pedagogic interest in joint book-reading and primary contexts for joint book-reading discourse. The originating field is the pedagogic recontextualizing field though even here there are multiple discursive bases. On the one hand analyses of precocity in reading development and, on the other, interest in specific forms of semiotic mediation in child language development both contributed to the development of emergent literacy discourse. As predicted by the model, selected aspects of local pedagogic practice were (and are) recontextualized more or less directly into the pedagogic recontextualizing field.

Selection occurs in many ways, but primarily through two means. First, much of the research discourse is produced by specific agents in the pedagogic recontextualizing field (usually university staff in schools of education), who have studied their own practices or those of colleagues (e.g. Snow 1983). There is an unusual circularity here, but it is important to note that it is not a circularity purely internal to the pedagogic recontextualizing field. The research data about instructional practice in the primary contextualizing context of the family, which in these cases is already very likely to be dominated by official pedagogic discourse, is itself *recontextualized,* leading to the creation of the imaginary subjects in pedagogic discourse.

The problem here is not that previous joint book-reading research is fundamentally flawed as research discourse. Rather, the problem is that the process of recontextualization of research discourse is very likely to produce imaginary subjects in a pedagogic discourse of reproduction who are considerably removed from interactional practices of lower working-class families. Second, where variable local pedagogic discourse has been the research issue, including research on social class variation in joint book-reading practices itself, various agencies in the pedagogic recontextualizing field have (implicitly) selected from and re-ordered the descriptions of local practice, thus privileging certain of them.

To reiterate, the crucial point in this argument is that 'recontextualize' does not mean simply to 'summarize' or 'restate' or even 'treat reductively'. Rather the process of reproducing research texts into a description of valued pedagogic practice reshapes them in relation to dominant and dominating principles of social interaction, principles which are common to only one fraction of the population. (Here the central vertical dimension in Figure 6 is crucial.) The process is likely to involve eliding of elements of research texts, reformulation of these texts in relation to other texts, and reorganization particularly with respect to desired rate of acquisition of skills and competencies.

In the case of joint book-reading the effect of this general feature of recontextualization in the pedagogic device is intensified by specific features of the content to be relayed. The intensification occurs because of the unusual circularity of the relations between specific agents of the pedagogic recontextualizing field and a dominating form of local pedagogic discourse in families derived from one fraction of the field of symbolic control. The intensity of the relations here create conditions approximating the ideal for the development of different forms of consciousness in young children as they commence school.

A model of pedagogic relations for joint book-reading in a pedagogic discourse of early school literacy development

To summarize, Figure 4.7 models some important aspects of relations between descriptions of joint book-reading practices in the two social locations, position of the family in social class relations and schooled literacy practice.

The most significant contrasts are in the relations described on the left of Figure 4.7. Beginning from the left, the model describes the primary condition for the development of variant forms of joint book-reading as principles regulating the social division of labour. Different coding orientations, deriving from speakers' locations in the social division of labour and the communicative practices associated with them, give the primary condition for the development of variant forms of interaction in joint book-reading.

These features of the model are a key aspect of the interpretation of the findings of this study. They represent a quite different claim about the antecedents of intracultural variation in joint book-reading from previous work.

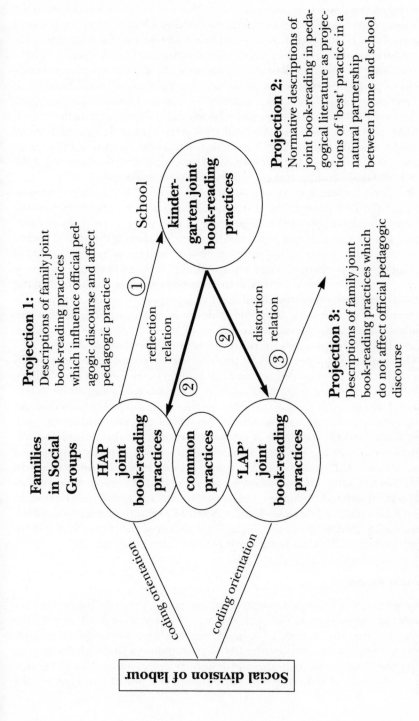

Figure 4.7 A model of pedagogic relations in joint book-reading

Variant practices in the two social groups are also shown as related through a region of common practices. This is an important condition for the development of misrecognition. Its inclusion is supported by many of the findings of this study such as, to cite just one specific example, children's frequent initiation of interaction during joint book-reading. Three projections of joint book-reading practices are critical for the development of pedagogic discourse: projections of 'HAP' practices, labelled (1); projections of 'LAP' practices, labelled (3); and normalizing projections of literacy pedagogy deriving from educational institutions, labelled (2). It is HAP practices which are forcefully projected through the medium of research and pedagogic text into school K practice, and it is these practices which are projected back as regulating discourse to both the HAP and LAP family groups in the discourse of literacy pedagogy.

A 'mirror' relation is created for the HAP group, but a distortion relation for the LAP group. The distortion is not just one of isolated specific aspects of interaction such as frequency of questions, even types of questions, nor of the tenor of relations between mother and child. It rather concerns a difference in the development of literate subjectivities within the social groups through joint book-reading. Where interactive language plays a reasonably prominent part in joint book-reading in the home, the activity appears to be a very similar set of interpretive practices when it is recontextualized in schooling. The evidence of this study suggests that this 'mirror' relation only holds for members of the HAP group. For members of the LAP group the basis for misrecognition is effectively laid.

One interesting aspect of HAP practice is that it appears to be an exaggerated version of school practice. HAP mothers generally foreground the individuation of consciousness through joint book-reading more intensively than do the K teachers. In this specific respect the findings contrast with results in Hasan's study, where the school practice was an exaggerated form of HAP practice. A plausible reading of the reason for this difference is that the idealized subjects of pedagogic discourse, projected back to the HAP group, act to magnify crucial aspects of interaction in joint book-reading in this social location. The HAP group appropriates features of official pedagogic discourse to inform family interaction in joint book-reading, but in so doing it is actually re-adopting features which were earlier derived from this region of social class practices for use in literacy pedagogy. This is a particularly intense form of partnership.

Final comment

The analyses of the pedagogic relations made possible by Bernstein's model of the pedagogic device and Hasan's semantic network as a framework for the interaction of talk in families and kindergarten classes seriously bring into question the use of metaphors of 'naturalness' and of a 'partnership' between home and school practices in emergent literacy. Certainly there is some form of partnership, but not of the kind usually used in the discourse of literacy pedagogy. The sense of 'natural' is, of course, already seriously challenged by Vygotsky's theory of semiotic mediation, but the analysis made possible by the model of the pedagogic device implicates a much wider set of social relations in the construction of specific forms of pedagogic discourse.

The metaphor of pedagogic partnership is one which deserves close interrogation since it is very likely to be productive, however inadvertently, of pedagogic preclusion as young children enter school.

Notes

1 One of the starker examples is the following.
   Ten Commandments for Parents
   1. I will read to my child daily.
   2. I will help my child start a word collection of at least one unknown word daily.
   3. I will listen to my child read daily.
   4. I will take dictation (talk written down) of the stories, poems and sayings my child creates.
   5. I will help my child pursue an interest and find five books to read on the topic.
   6. I will praise my child for at least one success daily.
   7. I will arrange for my child to use the library and visit bookstores or counters to select his or her own books.
   8. I will help my child find a listener to read to (another child, grandparent or friend.)
   9. I will allow my child to buy books and educational games.
   10. I will listen to my child daily about his or her school reading of stories and progress in learning to read (quoted in Goldfield and Snow, 1984: 204-5).

   The text is quoted by Goldfield and Snow (1984) from a publication of the Parent Committee of the Michigan Reading Association.
2 Interestingly, though research on variation is mentioned in pedagogic handbooks quite frequently, the consequences of it are invisible in the practices projected by these resources (see, for example, in the influential text by Holdaway, 1979).
3 The following discussion of important methodological issues is necessarily attenuated. Further details are available in Williams (1995).
4 There is obviously some inherent difficulty in using occupation as an indicator of relative positions in social class relations while explicitly avoiding the implication that the research utilizes a theory of discrete class categories or levels based on occupation. Connell *et al.* (1982: 212) put the methodological dilemma succinctly, referring to:

   an ambiguity about our method which arises because we could not think of a way of sampling relationships without first sampling people. We should make it very clear, then, that we do not take our sampling categories as defining classes. The object of our study was class relations and class processes; we wished to reach through the categories, which had to be used to get the research going, to the relations and processes behind them. We wished to make contact with situations where certain kinds of class processes could be expected to cluster thickly.

5 Details of the educational backgrounds of the participants, used to cross-check the occupational indicators of social class locations, are given in Williams (1995).
6 Hasan's description separates the experiential from the logical metafunctions, so that there is no internal grouping in an ideational metafunction as in Halliday's description.
7 The message further selects the features [nonassumptive: simple] in this region of interpersonal meanings. It would also, of course, be analysed from the perspective of experiential meanings, its role in turn-taking, topic maintenance and so on.
8 Further discussions of prefacing, including full presentations of Hasan's networks, together with realization statements, are to be found in Cloran (1994) and Williams (1995).
9 The statistical technique used to examine the results of the linguistic analyses was a test of significance of difference between median scores. Fisher's Exact Test was used, avoiding the requirement that the data be distributed in equal intervals, as is so for a commonly used test such as the Mann-Whitney. Given the relatively small number of cases, a significance level of $p < .025$ was set as the point below which results will be considered probably to be implicated in linguistically important variation.

References

Bernstein, B. (1975) *Class, Codes and Control. Vol. 3: Towards a Theory of Educational Transmissions.* London: Routledge and Kegan Paul.
Bernstein, B. (1986) 'On pedagogic discourse'. In J. G. Richardson (ed.), *Handbook of Theory and Research in the Sociology of Education.* New York: Greenwood Press.
Bernstein, B. (1990) *Class, Codes and Control. Vol. 4: The Structuring of Pedagogic Discourse.* London: Routledge and Kegan Paul.
Bernstein, B. (1996) *Pedagogy, Symbolic Control and Identity: Theory, Research, Critique.* London: Taylor and Francis.
Bourdieu, P. and Passeron, J.C. (1990) *Reproduction in Education, Society and Culture.* (2nd edn). London: Sage.
Cairney, T.H. and Munsie, L. (1992) *Beyond Tokenism: Parents as Partners in Literacy.* Carlton: Australian Reading Association.
Christian-Smith, L. (1993) *Texts of Desire: Essays on Fiction, Femininity and Schooling.* London: Falmer Press.
Clark, M.M. (1976) *Young, Fluent Readers: What Can They Teach Us?* London: Heinemann Educational Books.
Clay, M.M. (1967) 'The reading behaviour of five-year-old children: a research report', *New Zealand Journal of Education Studies*, 2(1), 11–31.
Cloran, C. (1994) *Rhetorical Units and Decontextualization: An Enquiry into Some Relations of Context, Meaning and Grammar.* Monographs in Systemic Linguistics, No. 6. Nottingham, Department of English Studies, University of Nottingham.
Connell, R.W., Ashenden, D.J., Kessler, S. and Dowsett, G.W. (1982) *Making the*

Difference: Schools, Families and Social Division. Sydney: Allen and Unwin.

Cook-Gumperz, J. (ed.) (1986) *The Social Construction of Literacy.* Cambridge: Cambridge University Press.

Cranny-Francis, A. (1992) *Engendered Fiction: Analysing Gender in the Production and Reception of Texts.* Kensington: University of NSW Press.

Cressy, D. (1980) *Literacy and the Social Order: Reading and Writing in Tudor and Stuart England.* Cambridge: Cambridge University Press.

Dombey, H. (1983) 'Learning the language of books'. In M. Meek (ed.), *Opening Moves: Work in Progress in the Study of Children's Language Development.* Bedford Way Papers No. 17. London: Institute of Education, University of London and Heinemann Educational Books.

Durkin, D. (1966) *Children Who Read Early: Two Longitudinal Studies.* New York: Teachers College Press.

Dwyer, B. (1989) *Parents, Teachers, Partners.* Rozelle: Primary English Teaching Association.

Gee, J.P. (1990) *Social Linguistics and Literacies: Ideologies in Discourses.* London: Falmer Press.

Gilbert, P. (1990) 'Authorizing disadvantage: authorship and creativity in the language classroom'. In F. Christie (ed.), *Literacy for a Changing World.* Hawthorn: Australian Council for Educational Research.

Gilbert, P. (1992) 'The story so far: gender, literacy and social regulation', *Gender and Education,* 4(3),185–99.

Goldfield, B.A. and Snow, C.E. (1984) 'Reading books with children: the mechanics of parental influence on children's reading achievement'. In J. Flood (ed.), *Promoting Reading Comprehension.* Newark: International Reading Association.

Goody, J. (1987) *The Interface Between the Written and the Oral.* Cambridge: Cambridge University Press.

Graf, H.J. (1987) *The Labyrinths of Literacy: Reflections on Literacy Past and Present.* London: Falmer Press.

Halliday, M.A.K. (1973) *Explorations in the Functions of Language.* London: Edward Arnold.

Halliday, M.A.K. (1994) *An Introduction to Functional Grammar* (2nd edn). London: Edward Arnold.

Hasan, R. (1983) A semantic network for the analysis of messages in everyday talk between mothers and their children. Mimeo.

Hasan, R. (1989) 'Semantic variation and sociolinguistics', *Australian Journal of Linguistics,* 9, 221–75.

Hasan, R. (1991) 'Questions as a mode of learning in everyday talk'. In T. Lee and M. McCausland (eds), *Language Education: Interaction and Development.* Proceedings of the International Conference held in Ho Chi Minh City, Vietnam, 30 March–1 April, 1991. Launceston: University of Tasmania.

Hasan, R. (1992) 'Meaning in sociolinguistic theory'. In K. Bolton and H. Kwok. (eds), *Sociolinguistics Today: International Perspectives.* London: Routledge.

Hasan, R. (1995) 'The conception of context in text'. In P.H. Fries and M. Gregory. (eds), *Discourse in Society: Functional Perspectives.* (Meaning and Choice in Language: Studies for Michael Halliday). Norwood, NJ: Ablex.

Hasan, R. (1996) *Ways of Saying: Ways of Meaning.* C. Cloran, D. Butt and G. Williams (eds), London: Cassell.

Hasan, R. and Cloran, C. (1990) 'A sociolinguistic interpretation of everyday talk between mothers and children'. In M.A.K. Halliday, J. Gibbons and H. Nicholas (eds), *Learning, Keeping and Using Language. Selected papers from the 8th World Congress of Applied Linguistics*, Sydney, 16–21 August 1987. Amsterdam: Benjamins.

Heath, S. B. (1983) *Ways with Words: Language, Life and Work in Communities and Classrooms.* Cambridge: Cambridge University Press.

Holdaway, D. (1979) *The Foundations of Literacy.* Sydney: Ashton Scholastic.

Kress, G. (1985) *Linguistic Processes in Sociocultural Practice.* Geelong: Deakin University Press.

Kress, G. (1987) 'Language as social practice'. In G. Kress (ed.), *Communication and Culture.* Sydney: University of NSW Press.

Labov, W. (1966) 'The linguistic variable as a structural unit', *Washington Linguistic Review*, 3, 4–22.

Luke, A. (1993) 'The social construction of literacy in the primary school'. In L. Unsworth (ed.), *Literacy Learning and Teaching: Language as Social Practice in the Primary School.* Melbourne: Macmillan.

Moon, B.C. and Wells, C.G. (1979) 'The influence of home on learning to read', *Journal of Research in Reading*, 2, 53–62.

New South Wales Department of School Education (nd) *Reading with Your Child at Home: Ideas for Parents of Young Children.* Sydney: The Department.

Ninio, A.Z. and Bruner, J.S. (1978) 'The achievements and antecedents of labelling', *Journal of Child Language*, 5, 1–15.

Snow, C.E. (1983) 'Literacy and language: relationships during the pre-school years', *Harvard Education Review*, 53, 165–89.

Street, B. (1984) *Literacy in Theory and Practice.* Cambridge: Cambridge University Press.

Street, B. (1993) *Cross-cultural Approaches to Literacy.* Cambridge: Cambridge University Press.

Teale, W.H. (1986) 'Home background and young children's literacy development'. In W.H. Teale and E. Sulzby (eds), *Emergent Literacy: Writing and Reading.* Norwood, NJ: Ablex.

Tizard, B. and Hughes, M. (1984) *Young Children Learning: Talking and Thinking at Home and at School.* London: Fontana Press.

Wells, C.G. (1985) 'Pre-school literacy-related activities and success in school'. In D.R. Olson, N. Torrance and A. Hildyard (eds), *Literacy, Language and Learning: The Nature and Consequences of Reading and Writing.* Cambridge: Cambridge University Press.

Wells, C.G. (1987) *The Meaning Makers: Children Learning Language and Using Language to Learn.* London: Hodder & Stoughton.

Wells, C.G. with Bridges, A., French, P., MacLure, M., Sinha, C., Walkerdine, V. and Woll, B. (1981) *Learning Through Interaction: The Study of Language Development.* Cambridge: Cambridge University Press.

Williams, G. (1995) 'Joint book-reading and literacy pedagogy: a socio-semantic interpretation'. Unpublished Phd dissertation, School of English, Linguistics and Media, Macquarie University. Also reproduced as: 'Joint book-reading and literacy pedagogy: a socio-semantic interpretation', Vol. 1, *CORE*, 19:3; Vol. 2, 20:1.

5   Mentoring semogenesis: 'genre-based' literacy pedagogy[1]

J. R. Martin

Inspiration

The literacy research which I shall be focusing on here began in 1979, a few months after Bernstein's first visit to Australia in 1978. At the time, writing instruction in Australia was shifting from traditional to progressive pedagogy (towards 'process writing' and whole language programmes). Addressing a group of language in education specialists in Canberra, Bernstein (1979: 300–1) warned of the dangers of this reorientation:

> As we move from the written word to the authentic word of the child, it is quite likely that the time dimension of the transmission is changing from the past to the present. If that is so, we must make very certain that the new pedagogy does not lock the child into the present – in his or her present tense. There is a danger that the new educational pull with its emphasis on the aural might well in fact do that unless we seek to understand systematically how to create a concept which can authenticate the child's experience and give him or her those powerful representations of thought that he or she is going to need in order to change the world outside.

In our research, however, we observed and documented that as far as progressive literacy teaching was concerned, children were indeed being locked into accounts of everyday personal experience (Rothery 1996; cf. Chouliarki 1997); and the less mainstream their background, the more locked in they had become – even more so, we felt, but could not document – than if they had received a traditional education. (Here and throughout the paper I am using *we* to refer to the critical mass of Hallidayan educational linguists in Australia whose work is cited continuously below.)

Our initial response to these developments is reviewed in Christie (1992) and Martin (1993). As far as my involvement has been concerned, the research has had three main phases of impetus – the Writing Project, beginning in the Department of Linguistics at the University of Sydney in 1979, and concerned with construing instructional discourse as genre; the Language and Social Power Project, beginning in the Metropolitan East Region of Sydney's Disadvantaged Schools Programme in 1986, and concerned with construing pedagogic discourse (both instructional and regulative) as genre; and the Write it Right Project,[2] beginning in the same DSP region in 1991, and concerned with construing secondary school and workplace discourse as genre and register.[3] Hasan and Williams (1996) survey a range of issues arising from this work, and Grabe and Kaplan (1996) contextualize the research from an international perspective. (See also Carter 1996, Hyon 1996, Richardson, 1994); for recent developments see Christie and Martin (1997), Martin and Veel (1998).

Challenging power

Our aim throughout this research was to open up access to genres, especially those controlled by mainstream groups – with the faith (considered naive by critics: cf. Luke 1996[4]) that this redistribution of discursive resources would involve recontextualizations by non-mainstream groups which would realign power. We did not attempt to prescribe the kind of social subject emerging from this programme (considered politically irresponsible by critics with a specific kind of post-colonial, post-patriarchal subject in mind: cf. Lee 1996). Bernstein (1990: 214) provides a grid, which I have adapted in Figure 5.1 to position the pedagogy we developed with respect to traditional, progressive and Freirean alternatives. As he outlines (1990: 213–14):[5]

> The vertical dimension would indicate whether the theory of instruction privileged relations internal to the individual, where the focus would be *intra-individual*, or . . . relations *between* social groups (inter-group). In the first case . . . the theory would be concerned to explain the conditions for changes within the individual, whereas in the second the theory would be concerned to explain the conditions for changes in the relation between social groups. The horizontal dimension would indicate whether the theory articulated a pedagogic practice emphasising a logic of acquisition or . . . a logic of transmission. In the case of a logic of acquisition the focus is upon the development of shared competences in which the acquirer is active in regulating an *implicit* facilitating practice. In the case of a logic of transmission the emphasis is upon *explicit* effective ordering of the discourse to be acquired by the transmitter.

As the grid implies, our approach has been a visible and interventionist one (Painter and Martin 1986, Hasan and Martin 1989, Cope and Kalantzis 1993), with a relatively strong focus on the transmission of identified discourse competences and on the empowerment of otherwise disenfranchized groups in relation to this transmission. In terms of semogenesis (see Halliday 1993a, b, Matthiessen 1995, Halliday and Matthiessen in press), we concerned ourselves with three dimensions of change:

- logogenesis   'instantiation of the text/process'   **unfolding**
- ontogenesis   'development of the individual'   **growth**
- phylogenesis   'expansion of the culture'   **evolution**

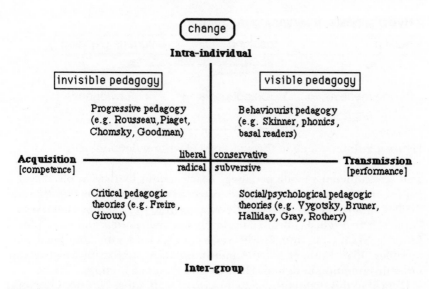

Figure 5.1 Types of pedagogy (after Bernstein 1990: 213)

Logogenesis is oriented to the unfolding of a text (e.g. Martin 1992, Christie this volume Chapter 6); ontogenesis to the development of an individual's meaning potential (e.g. Painter 1984, this volume Chapter 3, Halliday 1993a); and phylogenesis to the evolution of a culture (e.g. Halliday and Martin 1993). In Halliday and Matthiessen's terms, phylogenesis provides the environment for ontogenesis which in turn provides the environment for logogenesis; conversely, logogenesis provides the material for ontogenesis which in turn provides the material for phylogenesis.

With respect to this framework, intervention (which we might gloss hypergenesis) involves support during the logogenetic time frame (e.g. consultation with students with respect to revision; cf. Christie *et al.* 1992), explicit teaching as far as ontogenesis is concerned (e.g. scaffolding through models and joint construction; cf. Murray and Zammit 1992, Anderson and Nyholm 1996, Callow 1996) and language planning oriented to phylogenesis (e.g. revisions of state curricula and pedagogy to facilitate access to mainstream discourses; cf. Christie *et al.* 1991). An outline of this range of 'semocratic' initiatives is provided in Figure 5.2.

Control (reframing pedagogy)

> **the zone of proximal development** . . . is the distance between the actual development level as determined by independent problem solving and the level of potential development as determined through problem solving under adult guidance or in collaboration with more capable peers. (Vygotsky 1978: 86)

Hypergenesis: intervening in change

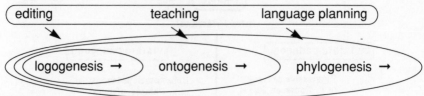

Figure 5.2 Intervening in the processes of writing development

The development of our pedagogy for teaching literacy involved a dialogue across approaches to guided instruction influenced by Vygotsky and
Bruner, and studies of language development undertaken by Halliday and
Painter. The Vygotsky/Bruner tradition was interpreted and exemplified
for us by Brian Gray, initially with respect to his work with Aboriginal communities; Joan Rothery led the metropolitan Sydney team which elaborated this tradition in light of Halliday and Painter's findings.

Critical to this dialogue was the notion of scaffolding (to adopt the term
introduced to us by Applebee and Langer 1983). Data such as the following, from spoken language development, were very influential (example
from Painter 1993).

Father:	This car can't go as fast as ours.
Child (4.8):	I thought – I thought all cars could – all cars could go the same – all cars could go the same (pause) fast . . .
Mother:	The same speed.
Child:	Yes, same speed.

Understandings about the guiding role played by care-givers in spoken
language development (see Painter, this volume Chapter 3) have been
built into the pedagogy as a Joint Construction stage in which students
and their teacher jointly construct written texts. The notion of **guidance
through interaction in the context of shared experience** has remained fundamental.

This 'guidance through interaction' principle gave rise to a number of
teaching models, which have been instantiated across a range of what
Christie (1989, this volume Chapter 6) has called curriculum genres. I will
consider just four of these models here. (See also Macken *et al.* 1989,
Derewianka 1991, Martin and Rothery 1991; the latter two packages
include video demonstrations for teacher training purposes.) The earliest
of the models is presented in Figure 5.3, from the first stages of the DSP
Language and Social Power Project. It comprises three main phases: Modelling, Joint Construction and Independent Construction. Modelling
involves introducing students to an example of the text type in focus, discussing the function of the genre, and examining its structure, including
relevant language features. Joint construction involves preparing for work

on another example of the genre, which will be jointly constructed by the teacher and students (with the teacher developing a text on the board, on large sheets of paper or on the overhead projector in response to suggestions from students). Independent construction involves students preparing for another instantiation of the genre, which they will write on their own; it explicitly encourages creative exploitation of the genre and its possibilities. The arrows pointing to the centre of the model and its circular design indicate that teaching can begin at any point, depending on the needs of the students. For example, some teachers found the Joint Construction stage unnecessary for some students, whereas for others, this stage needed to be worked through more than once before students were ready to write on their own.

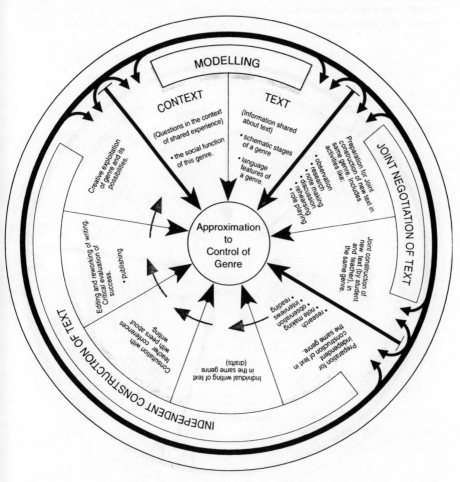

Figure 5.3 1989 DSP Primary Curriculum Model (Callaghan and Knapp 1989: 10)

Figure 5.4 is a later development of this model, and reflects the changing nature of the dialogue among Australian language and literacy educators at the time. Initial resistance to the pedagogy had tended to come from romantically inclined progressive educators concerned about its imagined debilitating effects on creativity. (Reid 1987 includes some representative contestation.) Our position was that creativity depends on control of the genre, and that without the relevant discursive capital, students cannot produce highly valued 'creative' texts – in narrative, or any other genre. Later, resistance to the pedagogy tended to come from critical theorists concerned about its imagined debilitating effects on non-mainstream discourses and the value placed on them by teachers and by students themselves (e.g. Freedman and Medway 1994, Lee 1996, Luke 1996, the New London Group 1996, Giblett and O'Carroll 1990 include some representative discussion). Our position was that students should

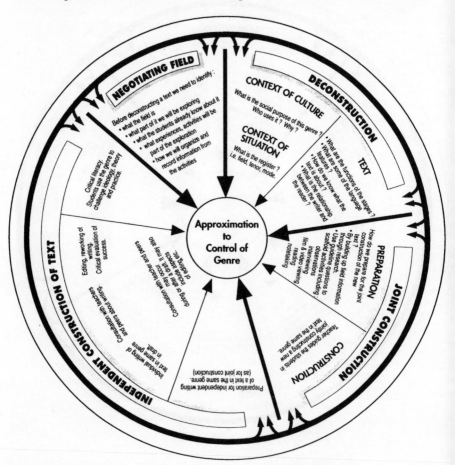

Figure 5.4 1992 DSP Primary Curriculum Model (Murray and Zammit, 1992: 7)

HOW THIS BOOK WORKS

This book begins with a detailed introductory section that explores the major understandings about the teaching and learning activities in this teaching program. The introduction is followed by specific teaching guidelines for each of the four Students Books accompanying this Teachers Book. You should eventually take time to read the introduction in full.

Getting ready to use this book

Before you read the detailed introductory section, however, we suggest that you turn to the Students Book appropriate to your particular group of students and their teaching program. Skim through the Students Book, and you will begin to see how the teaching program is intended to work. You will find that the headings in the Students Book relate closely to the teaching sequence proposed throughout the entire teaching program. There are three elements in the teaching sequence of particular importance: Deconstruction, Joint Construction and Independent Construction.

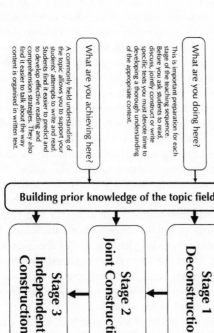

Building prior knowledge of the topic field

Stage 1 Deconstruction
Stage 2 Joint Construction
Stage 3 Independent Construction

What are you doing here?

This is important preparation for each stage of the teaching sequence.
Before you ask students to read, discuss, jointly construct or write specific texts you must devote time to developing a thorough understanding of the appropriate context.

What are you achieving here?

A commonly held understanding of the topic allows you to support your students' attempts to write and read. Students find it easier to predict and to develop effective reading and comprehension strategies. They also find it easier to talk about the way content is organised in written text.

What are you doing at Stage 1?

Here you are looking at models of the text to understand why/how they are organised to make effective meaning.

What are you achieving at Stage 1?

(1) You are developing your students' ability to read and comprehend the model text.
(2) You are extending their comprehension of the model text through the development of a commonly held 'language for talking about language'.

What are you doing at Stage 2?

Here you work with your students to jointly write a text. The negotiation process draws on:
(1) Commonly held understandings about the topic that the teacher has developed with the students.
(2) Commonly held understandings about the organisation of factual texts developed during Stage 1: Deconstruction.

What are you achieving at Stage 2?

You are enabling your students to participate in the construction of a successful written text of this genre.
The joint construction provides a scaffold that allows students to construct texts which are above their normal level of independent writing.

What are you doing at Stage 3?

Here you support your students to research and write their own texts in the genre.

What are you achieving at Stage 3?

Students who have worked with you during the previous two stages will have a clearer understanding of how to write texts appropriate to the genre in question. Students can draw on:
(1) a knowledge of how language is organised in the genre;
(2) experience of supported writing (joint construction) of a similar text;
(3) appropriate topic knowledge which you have helped them to organise and prepare.

Figure 5.5 1992 HBJ Primary Curriculum Model (Christie *et al.* 1992: 2)

indeed be given a critical orientation, and that this depends on control of both the discourse under critique and the discourses used to critique (Macken and Rothery 1991; Martin 1991). The modifications in Figure 5.4 were designed to encourage a critical stance. The Modelling stage was renamed Deconstruction, in part with reference to the relevant French masters; and the final wedge of the Independent Construction stage was explicitly oriented to critical literacy ('students use the genre to challenge ideology, theory and practice'). For practical suggestions about critical literacy in hands-on DSP materials for primary school teachers, see Murray and Zammit (1992: 39–40), Anderson and Nyholm (1996: 37–8) and Callow (1996: 13–4). Fairclough (1992) contains relevant material on critical language awareness from comparable contexts in Britain.

Figure 5.4 also foregrounds the importance of building up the social context of a genre, before beginning work on deconstruction. We found this to be critical in multicultural classrooms where shared mainstream understandings could not be assumed. Thus the Negotiating Field wedge, which encourages teachers to start with what students already know about the relevant institutions and guide them towards realms of experience with which they are not familiar. A related emphasis on building knowledge of the field to be considered is found in Figure 5.5, from the materials prepared for teachers by Christie *et al.* (1992). Detailed suggestions for using the model across a range of genres are also found in Macken and Rothery (1991), Christie *et al.* (1990a, 1990b), Derewianka (1991) and Martin and Rothery (1991).

The pedagogy under review here was adapted for secondary school during the DSP Write it Right Project (e.g. Rothery 1994), as outlined in Figure 5.6.[6] In this model, setting up the social context of the genre and building field knowledge are generalized across all stages of the model (Deconstruction, Joint Construction and Independent Construction). In addition, the goal of the model is explicitly oriented to both control of and a critical orientation to the discourse under consideration (for further development of the model in the direction of critical literacy see Callow 1996). Rothery's (1994) materials for secondary English include discussion of a range of responses to literature, including those based on Leavis, New Criticism and critical theory; the possibility of resistant readings of narrative in secondary school is discussed and explicitly modelled. For dialogue across the critical and functional linguistic perspectives inspiring this practice see Cranny-Francis (1993, 1996), Cranny-Francis and Martin (1993, 1994, 1995) and Martin (1995, 1996).

Alongside the distinctive types of scaffolding and interaction promoted by the pedagogy is a distinctive focus on the role of knowledge about language in literacy apprenticeship (cf. Carter 1990, 1996; Fairclough 1992). It was clear to us on the basis of ongoing research by Painter (1993, 1996, this volume Chapter 3; and see Halliday 1993a) that talk about language plays an important role in spoken language development. Accordingly, all stages in the pedagogy make use of explicit knowledge about different types of text (genres) and their stages, and as much information about the realization of stages as pre-service and in-service training afford; this

THE TEACHING-LEARNING MODEL

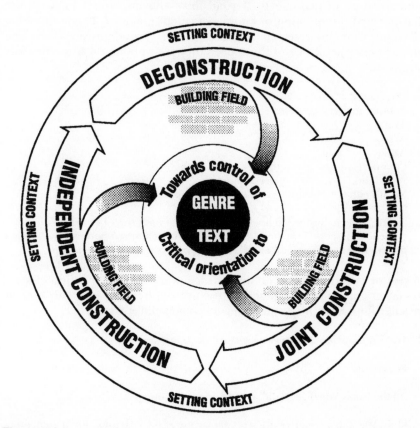

Figure 5.6 1994 DSP Secondary Curriculum Model (Rothery and Stenglin 1994: 8)

knowledge becomes part of the experience shared by teachers and students. Making this knowledge explicit and sharing it among members of the class helps put students on an equal footing as far as literacy development is concerned; it helps demystify the hidden curriculum of writing. Explicit shared knowledge also gives teachers and students a language for talking about texts during Joint Construction or consultation in the Independent Construction phase. This removes responses to writing from the realm of subjective reaction and places them within an objective framework in which students and teacher can work towards visible goals.

Ideally, to maximize the effectiveness of the pedagogy at issue here, teachers and students would share knowledge of both functional grammar and generic structure. We found in our in-service work with teachers of disadvantaged students that generic structure was a useful way to demonstrate the importance of knowledge about language, since it made connections with teachers' understandings of the beginning, middle and end structure of many texts. Beyond this, Williams (1995) in particular has pursued the question of knowledge about grammar. In the following dialogue from his research, a group of Year 7 students are discussing the process type of one of the clauses they are working on from the story *Piggybook*:7

> OK, 'hurry'.
> Another material process.
> 'Was'.
> 'Was'.
> 'Was'.
> I'm not really sure about that. I think it might be . . .
> Yes, I think it's another material process.
> No, it's either a relational . . . it could be a relational . . .
> OK.
> 'Inside', hold it. 'Inside the house was' means, I think it is . . . I can't think . . . it . . . existential process. That could be that. I'll write that down because 'was' means that his wife was there . . . it exists. [working on *Inside the house was his wife*]

A year or so earlier, the same students had worked on the relation of functional grammar to the generic structure of the same story with their teacher Ruth French (grammar terms from Halliday 1994):

> *What we learnt about the grammatical patterns of Piggybook.*
>
> Beginning.
>
> All the Goals Mrs Piggott did were to do with housework.
>
> Only Mrs Piggott had Goals. This shows she is the only one doing something TO something else.
>
> Mr Piggott and the boys only did things for themselves; they did not do work in the home. This is shown by the fact that they didn't have any Goals. They were the only characters that talked. They told Mrs P to hurry up.
>
> Resolution
>
> At the end, everyone did an action to something – to benefit the whole family, not just themselves. Everyone had Goals at the end.
>
> Now the Goals for Mrs Piggott included more than housework.
>
> [*She mended the car.* – imaged as Actor Process Goal]

The Goals had a big role in structuring the narrative. The pattern of Actors and Goals changes at the end. This makes the Resolution.

To date we have not gathered together the resources required for longitudinal studies which would fully explore the role that knowledge about language might play in our literacy programmes. Alongside its potential for demystifying the hidden curriculum of mainstream literacies, there is in addition the issue of making these literacies 'dangerous' for the mainstream children who at present learn them safely by osmosis – a sad waste of their possibilities as Bernstein (1990: 75–6) notes:

> Children who can meet the requirements of the sequencing rules will eventually have access to the principles of their own discourse. These children are more likely to be middle class and are more likely to come to understand that the heart of discourse is not order but disorder, not coherence but incoherence, not clarity but ambiguity, and that the heart of discourse is the possibility of new realities.
>
> We might ask ourselves, if this is the possibility of pedagogic discourse, why are the children of the dominant classes not demonstrating the possibilities of the discourses they have acquired? And the answer must be that the socialisation into a visible pedagogy tries, though not always successfully, to ensure that its discourse is safe rather than dangerous. In this way a visible pedagogy produces deformation of the children/students of both the dominant and the dominated social classes.

Negotiating text

In this section I would like to exemplify aspects of the pedagogy outlined above, and draw attention to selected issues. In particular I would like to discuss aspects of the register of the interactions between teacher and students with respect to tenor (the nature of guidance), field (moving into uncommon sense) and mode (modelling abstraction).

The students are in Year 6, in a working-class inner-city school with over 90 per cent of its students from non-English speaking backgrounds (a typical Disadvantaged Schools Programme school).[8] Excerpts from the Deconstruction stage, on a second cycle through the model for the exposition genre (Callaghan and Knapp 1989), are discussed below. In this stage the teacher is commenting on general problems arising from the expositions written by the class in the Independent Construction stage of the first cycle and then reviewing and consolidating the general points she has raised.

Tenor. Of special interest is the nature of guidance through interaction during this Deconstruction stage, as the teacher scaffolds a rehearsal of the understandings about the structure of exposition she wants to emphasize. Let's look at a few examples of this – first of all a point about the relationship of the Introduction to following Arguments (see Figure 5.7 for the expository structure the teacher is elaborating here):

T: O.K. So she's very clearly given her three Arguments. Can everyone see that? And the very interesting thing is that she lets you know in the Introduction what those three Arguments are going to be. She hasn't told you what they're going to be; she's just mentioned them.

The teacher then continues, in the same turn, with a warning about including too much detail in the Introduction – this time using the strategy of pausing before the information she wishes to reinforce (transcribed as . . . *giving the reasons for the Argument*):

Can you see the difference? Because people started in that Introduction going on to the Argument. You don't mention (sic) it there; you only mention it. You don't go into the . . . giving the reasons for the Argument. Can you see the difference?

She uses the same strategy in a subsequent turn:

T: The other thing is if you mention an Argument in your Introduction, or your Thesis, you have to make sure it's in your . . . Arguments.

Further on, she pauses and the students fill in the news, which she reinforces through an affirming repetition – so that what she initially modelled on her own is now jointly constructed in an exchange:

T: So whatever you mention in your Introduction, you have to make sure you mention in your . . .
Ss: . . . Arguments.
T: . . . in your Arguments.

Returning to the warning about including Arguments in the Introduction, she withholds the news in focus several times – involving students in a kind of silent dialogue she invites through tags (*hasn't she?*) and questions (*she may end up what?*):

T: She's actually expanded on her . . . Arguments. Remember, you don't have to expand on them in the . . . Intro . . . duction. You just have to . . . mention them. She's virtually given away her first Argument, hasn't she? She's told you already in the Introduction, so when we get down here, she may end up what? . . . repeating herself, saying the same thing again.

By the end of the review, the students are making the relevant points on their own, at the invitation of the teacher, but without her co-constructing the relevant knowledge about language:

T: O.K. So there's a few things to think about. What are some of the things I mentioned you are going to try to think about when we do this one today? Filippa?
Filippa: Not to, um, put an Argument into the Thesis.
T: Good. Right.

T: Something else, to think about. Yes.
Linh: The Argument that you're doing has to be like the topic or Thesis that you choose.
T: Right. So you make sure you mentioned all your Arguments in your Thesis. Good.

What these examples demonstrate is the way in which the notion of guidance through interaction in the context of shared experience shapes the structure of each phase of the pedagogy as well as the cycle as a whole. They also demonstrate the way in which linguistic choices are mobilized to enact movement through a zone of proximal development as scaffolding is provided, then gradually removed. The teacher first models the points at issue, and then constructs them interactively with the students – first by adjusting information flow inside the clause (technically by withholding the tonic syllable signalling new information (Halliday 1994)), then by reconstruing her message as an exchange (Martin 1992), with the students supplying the withheld tonic in a turn of their own. By the end of the stage, the students construct the relevant points on their own in response to relatively open trigger questions.

Field. Excerpts from the joint construction stage of the cycle (for discussion see Hunt 1994) are provided in Appendices 1 and 2. At this point the students are building up the information they will need for jointly constructing a further model exposition. They have worked together in

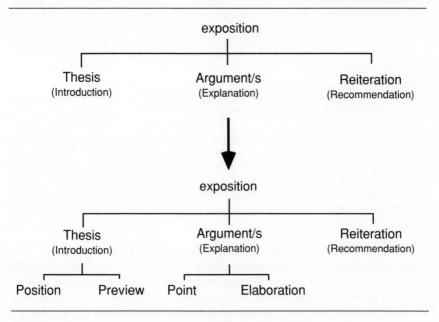

Figure 5.7 Expository structure discussed in Deconstruction phase

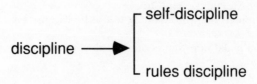

Figure 5.8 Types of discipline

small groups gathering ideas, and are now compiling these with their teacher. Of special interest here is the movement from common to uncommon sense as the information is organized. The teacher is moving the students from a collection of ideas towards a classification that can be used to arrange arguments in the exposition. As part of this process the teacher has distinguished two types of discipline (the relevant bit of taxonomizing is imaged in Figure 5.8).

> Nicole: Discipline.
> T: Discipline. O.K.
> . . .
> Filippa: Good ideas on how to behave.
> T: Right. Share with each other and in discipline. That can be what – self-discipline, so you can learn to look after yourself and control yourself and it can be discipline that other people enforce upon you – you have to learn to accept rules. So, it can be two sorts, can't it? Your self-discipline – that means you go home and do your homework at night, and you don't need someone to say, 'Hurry up; it's 4:30; it's time to do your homework.' You can just go in, do it yourself and look after yourself. And it can also mean discipline that's coming from . . . other . . . people – obeying the rules. If we have school rules, what do you have to do?
> Ss: Obey them.
> T: And you have to learn to follow them. When you leave school and go out and get a job, what will you have to do then?
> Ss: Obey the work rules.
> T: Obey the work rules. So you've got to learn to accept. If people ask you to do something usually there is a . . . a reason. Sometimes it mightn't be good and you might discuss that, but you have to learn to accept. If someone says that is what's going to happen, sometimes you just have to go a . . . along with it. You can, maybe discuss your way out of it, but sometimes you do have to do what they say. So I'll put *self* there, and I'll put *rules* there. Alright. So that means the two sorts of discipline. Right.

Finding general terms to operate as headings for their ideas can take quite a lot of work, and intervention by the teacher. But the generalizations at issue are critical to grouping ideas into paragraphs and referring forward to them in the introduction of an exposition. By the end of the phase, the students proffer relevant generalizations suggested earlier by the teacher (*So I have written down, 'Learn about a wide range of subjects.' These are just the notes*).

T: . . . Now, let's try and get these into an order . . . Who can see the main thing
that keeps coming through the whole way through? Lisa?
Lisa: Learn about a wide range of subjects.

Mode. One of the great advantages of joint construction is that it demonstrates for the children the differences between spoken and written language as their oral contributions are scribed and shifted towards written
mode by the teacher. In the excerpt below, the teacher is guiding the students towards a final sentence for the Preview section of the introduction
to the model exposition; specifically, she is encouraging them to preview
the ideas they have earlier collected under point 3 on the board. In spite
of her encouragement, and that of their ESL teacher who has joined the
session at this point, the students are stumped.

T: . . . 3, we haven't really mentioned, um, we really need to mention something
about socialising and, um, being a good place to be, friends and that. Can anyone give me a sentence just to finish that, so we can finish that Introduction?
Something . . . see where number 3s are, have a look at 3s and see if you can get
that into a sentence. Who can organise that in a sentence. Can someone get
that?

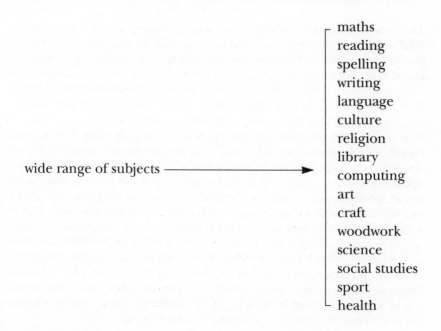

Figure 5.9 Kinds of subjects

Rana: Home?

T: No, we want a sentence, darling, just a sentence to sum up all of those things in 3: which we've got good ideas on how to behave, you have manners, sharing with each other, you learn to be responsible for your own things, you have discipline, um, it's fun, you play, socialise, all those sorts of things. Can we turn that into one sentence? Quick. Think about it. Come on!

ESL T: There's one word there you can put into a sentence that covers all of that. Learning to live with other people, work with other people.

Vu: Firstly . . .

T: No, we're not onto the firstlies, we just want to finish this. This is the Introduction and we just want to finish this last sentence so then we've concluded all things. Lisa. Come on, Nicole. Think. Quick. Look at the board and see if we can get that into a sentence. Right, yes?

Nicole: It, um, school also disciplines you.

T: It provides a social environment, doesn't it, where you learn all those social skills. Phalroth.

Phalroth: You learn to socialize and have fun with your friends.

T: O.K. So we can say [scribing] O.K. *Finally, it's a place where you learn to socialise and develop in a warm and friendly atmosphere.* Because, socialising means all those things: you're getting on with people, you can communicate, you can talk to them, you can understand what they're saying, and also, you develop a tolerance: you have to understand how somebody else feels and respond to them and they have to do the same for . . . you. O.K.

The reasons for their frustration have to do with grammatical metaphor (Halliday 1994, Halliday and Martin 1993, Rose, this volume, Christie, this volume), which Halliday has suggested (e.g. 1993a) is a resource which elaborates significantly as students of this age (12 to 13) move into a more abstract stage of literacy (symbolized in Western cultures by the shift from primary to secondary school). The teacher eventually rescues the children (*It provides a social environment, doesn't it, where you learn all those social skills*), introducing the heading socializing skills and scribing *Finally, it's a place where you learn to socialise and develop in a warm and friendly atmosphere.* At issue here is the question of what kind of 'thing' is the nominal group *socializing skills,* the point being that it is not really a thing at all, but an ability to act socially. In the students' spoken language, the meaning has to do with doing things – with acting in particular ways. But in writing, in order to sum up the points collected and to preview the arguments to come, doing is first reconstrued as a thing (*social skills*) and then worked as a verb (with the modifier *social* rendered as a process *socialize* by Phalroth, picking up the teacher's earlier *you play, socialise, all those sorts of things,* and then scribed by the teacher). Note the 'skills' cline from speaking to writing involved here: *you can do something, you are able to do something, you have the ability to do something, you have the skill.*

Here are some more examples of abstract written language, from later in the joint construction (relevant abstractions underlined):

So ultimately, this allows us to achieve a greater <u>understanding</u> of the world and increase our <u>knowledge</u>.

T: Alright. Now, secondly we really need to link that a little bit with the first paragraph. So what could we say? *Secondly, by achieving <u>this</u>,* what did we just achieve? Yes.

T & Ss: This <u>knowledge</u>.

T: We will be then what?

T & Ss: Be in a better position to . . . to get a job. And to pursue our . . . careers.
. . .

Nicole: *Secondly, after achieving this <u>knowledge</u>, it will then put all individuals who attend the school, in a better position to pursue their own career and job <u>prospects</u>.*

By the end of this second cycle of deconstruction and joint construction all students in the class were able to write an exposition presenting a range of arguments in support of a position on an issue. The following text exemplifies the control they have gained over the genre, addressing a local government concern.

Exposition for: Should an amphitheatre be built in Wiley Park? [Filippa]

I strongly believe that the amphitheatre in Wiley Park should be built for these following reasons, such as: it attracts more people to the area, shops and public transport will earn a larger profit, people will become more interested in Wiley Park, and it is suitable for all ages.

My first reason is that it will bring more people to our area because there are not many main attractions in our community and it can be something to remember our bi-centenary by in years to come.

Another point to mention is shops will earn more money, for example, the new restaurant which will be built with in the amphitheatre. And not to forget Public transport which will create more money for the government and will be more easier for the disabled to travel by if they wish to do so.

And last but not least it is not only for the grown ups but it is also suitable for children for example, there will be entertainment such as concerts, plays and shows. In my opinion from a child's point of view I think it's going to be fun and it's about time the council did something like this.

I hope I have convinced you that we should have a amphitheatre at Wiley Park.

This brings us to the issue of whether a pedagogy of this kind provides students with semiotic tools that can be adapted and redeployed in related contexts; or whether this kind of induction traps them in some kind of robotic posturing around a set of 'forms'. Consider then the following text, taken from a similar school, employing a similar pedagogy. The text is part of a unit of work focusing on local politics, with Jon Callow[9] acting as literacy consultant. The class involved has been studying the way in which politicians promote their causes and on the basis of this work these Year 6 students have attempted to intervene in a local community issue. Their local pool has been closed down, due to structural problems; the students launched a campaign for its replacement – including brochures to local residents[10] and letters such as the following to the mayor of the municipality.

Dulwich Hill Public School [letterhead]

Dear Mr Cotter,

Allow me to introduce myself, I am Luka Marsi & I am from the Aqua Party and a student from Dulwich Hill Public School, & my class have been discussing and investigating the matter & cost, closing down of Marrickville Pool. We are very anxious to see it renovated & reopened.

Here are some of the reasons why you should make the opening an important issue.

Firstly, after a long hot summer, Marrickville residents appear no closer to reclaiming their local Swimming Pool. Marrickville Pool was the most used facility in Marrickville.

Secondly only 25% of students surveyed in our school can swim. More people could drown & would blame local politicians.

Thirdly we also need a local pool to cool us down when it's hot (A pool is a solution for this hot hot HOT weather!) Families have a local, fun, and healthy place to go swimming together.

Finally a local pool would be useful for poorer people, – because some BIG families aren't able to afford public transport to travel so far.

So according to the survey responses, we need a local pool for more swimming lessons (I agree with this) Thank you for reading my letter, & taking your time. I hope you will help us by renovating the pool, be very careful with all those expenses!

    From a caring and concerned child
    Yours sincerely
    Luka M.

The expository structure outlined above is clearly visible in a text of this kind. But it has been recontextualized as a letter to a politician – including a self-introduction by the student writer, and a more personalized tenor than in the model jointly constructed above. Overall, although the municipality in question doesn't yet have a new pool, the students' campaign appears to have had some impact. The school's principal received complaints from local politicians about the inappropriateness of students involving themselves in local affairs along these lines – complaints that were strongly rebuffed by the school.

It has always seemed to my colleagues and me that this kind of generic recontextualization is the norm. Once guided into a genre students naturally rework the genre in light of their own subjectivity as new contextual pressures arise. It is the nature of semiotic systems, especially at this level of abstraction, to readily adapt themselves in this way. If the systems were more rigid, we would never be able to use them to renovate our society and get on with our lives. Lemke (e.g. 1995) provides a helpful discussion of the nature of dynamic open systems such as genre; for discussion of more and less categorical approaches to genre classification see Martin (1997).

Pedagogic discourse (towards a subversive modality . . .)

In his work on pedagogic discourse Bernstein (e.g. 1975, 1990) has developed the concepts of classification and framing as tools for situating modalities of pedagogic discourse with respect to one another:

> **Classification**, here, does not refer to *what* is classified, but to the *relationships* between contents. Classification refers to the nature of the differentiation between contents. Where classification is strong, contents are well insulated from each other by strong boundaries. Where classification is weak, there is reduced insulation between contents, for the boundaries between contents are weak or blurred. **Classification thus refers to the degree of boundary maintenance between contents**. Classification focuses our attention upon boundary strength as the critical distinguishing feature of the division of labour of educational knowledge. It gives us, as I hope to show, the basic structure of the message system, **curriculum**.
>
> The concept, **frame**, is used to determine the structure of the message system, **pedagogy**. Frame refers to the form of the *context* in which knowledge is transmitted and received. Frame refers to the specific pedagogical relationship of teacher and taught. In the same way as classification does not refer to contents, so frame does not refer to the contents of the pedagogy. Frame refers to the strength of the boundary between what may be transmitted and what may not be transmitted, in the pedagogical relationship. Where framing is strong, there is a sharp boundary, where framing is weak, a blurred boundary, between what may and may not be transmitted. **Frame refers to the range of options available to teacher and taught in the *control* of what is transmitted and received in the context of the pedagogical relationship**. Strong framing entails reduced options; weak framing entails a range of options. *Thus frame refers to the degree of control teacher and pupil possess over the selection, organisation, pacing and timing of the knowledge transmitted and received in the pedagogical relationship.* (1975: 88–9; italics original, bold added)

At a deeper level classification and framing are related to his deeper abstractions – power and control – as follows (including here the notions of internal and external classification and framing – indexed as [ie]):

> classification strength (Cie) is the means by which power relations are transformed into specialised discourses, and framing (F^{ie}) is the means whereby principles of control are transformed into specialised regulations of discursive practices (pedagogic relations) which attempt to relay a given distribution of power. (Bernstein 1996: 3)

From classification and framing Bernstein (1975: 116) derives his notions of visible and invisible pedagogy:

> In terms of the concepts of classification and frame, the [invisible – JRM] pedagogy is realised through weak classification and weak frames. Visible pedagogies are realised through strong classification and strong frames.

which he further unpacks (1975: 119–20) as follows:

> A visible pedagogy is created by:
> (1) explicit hierarchy
> (2) explicit sequencing rules
> (3) explicit and specific criteria.
> The underlying rule is: 'Things must be kept apart.'
>
> An invisible pedagogy is created by:
> (1) implicit hierarchy;
> (2) implicit sequencing rules;
> (3) implicit criteria.
> The underlying rule is: 'Things must be put together.'

As Joan Rothery and I asked in 1988, what would an authoritative and empowering pedagogy look like that got off the pendulum and drew on the strengths of both the visible and invisible regimes.

> How can we develop teachers who are authorities, without being authoritarian? How can we develop students who control the distinctive discourses of their culture, and at the same time are not simply co-opted by them but approach them critically with a view to renovation – to challenging the social order which the discourses they are learning sustain? . . . The major theoretical innovation of this paper is to try and begin to theorise a model of teaching and learning which uses explicit knowledge about language as the basis for double classification and double framing and to propose this as the basis for post-progressive developments in educational theory and practice. (Martin and Rothery 1988, first draft of this paper)

The strategy Joan and her colleagues adopted drew on a further dimension of Bernstein's work – the notion of pedagogic discourse as a rule for embedding discourses:

> I will define pedagogic discourse as a rule which embeds two discourses; a discourse of skills of various kinds and their relations to each other (= instructional discourse; JRM), and a discourse of social order (= regulative discourse; JRM) . . . the instructional discourse is embedded in the regulative discourse . . . to create one text . . . one discourse . . . the regulative discourse is the dominant discourse . . . produces the order in the instructional discourse . . . the purpose of the device is to produce a symbolic ruler for consciousness. (Bernstein 1996: 46–50)

From the perspective of functional linguistics, we would in fact prefer the term **projection** to embedding. Following Christie (e.g. 1995, this volume Chapter 6) we would say that one discourse gives voice to another much as a reporting verbal or mental process frames a locution or idea (*She said/thought he'd left*); thus the regulative discourse projects the instructional one (generally implicitly, except for irregular disruptions such as the one in bold face below from the curriculum genre under focus here).

> T: . . . So let's go first of all . . . who, Mohammed, would your group like to start? Now, what we're going to do is – if you have an idea that's the same, we won't repeat it, alright? So we'll go through any new ideas; we'll jot down but we won't repeat everyone's ideas. [**Sorry, Vu! Goodness!**] No, we'll just read through them first and we'll jot them down. If you've got them linked, can you give them to me linked, if you've got them already linked up. O.K. What's the first one?

In these terms, one of our main pedagogic renovations was to suggest that literacy pedagogy could be enhanced by adding a second instructional discourse derived from social semiotic theory, and using it to project instructional discourse. In simple terms this meant introducing explicit knowledge about text in social context that could be deployed throughout the pedagogic cycle. An example of this would be the use of explicit understandings of genre when working on scientific knowledge (e.g. Veel 1997). More radically, we might imagine using this social semiotic instructional discourse to project a pedagogic discourse as a whole (as I am doing here now) – in other words, to project the regulative discourse in turn projecting its instructional discourse. This would involve teachers and students using knowledge about text in social context to deconstruct their schooling, as well as its contents – a project in which numbers of critical theorists appear to have some political interest. An example of this would be the use of shared understandings about language development to inform negotiations between teacher and students about the best way to teach control of abstract language in secondary school. The drift of these renovations, from the one we generally practised, to the one some critics urge, is outlined in Figure 5.10.

For a discussion of the range of knowledges about text in social context at issue in interventions of this kind, see Martin (1997). For us, the critical value of adding a social semiotic instructional discourse in this way is its power to make as explicit as possible what it is that is expected to be learned, so that as many students as possible can recognize it – and then learn it or choose not to learn it as they will. As Bernstein (1996: 32) has remarked, 'Power is never more fundamental as far as communications are concerned than when it acts on the distribution of recognition rules.' We wanted to redistribute these rules.

Our other main pedagogic renovation was to introduce waves of weak and strong classification and framing as appropriate to different stages of our pedagogic cycle. These are outlined in Table 5.1 for substages of

ID	instructional discourse
SSID	social semiotic instructional discourse
RD	regulative discourse

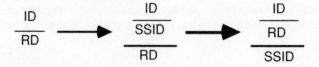

Figure 5.10 Deploying a social semiotic instructional discourse to project instructional discourse, or pedagogic discourse

Deconstruction, Joint Construction and Independent Construction. As inspired by Brian Gray's work with Aboriginal children in Traeger Park School in Alice Springs (see Gray 1985; cf. Rose, Chapter 8 this volume), the Deconstruction stage begins with weak classification and framing as teachers find ways of starting where students are at in order to open up the field and context of the genre. Framing and classification values strengthen when a model text is introduced, as the teacher authoritatively makes visible the structure and purpose of the text, including as much critical deconstruction as deemed appropriate. Joint Construction begins with weak classification and framing as students open up a new field, before strengthening these values as the teacher guides them into organizing the material; when jointly constructing text, the framing values split according to field (which the students control, proffering content) and

	Framing	Classification	[comments]
Deconstruction			
– setting context/field	−F	−C	starting where kids are at, including valuing their voice
– modelling	+F	+C	authoritative visibilizing, including critical literacy?
Joint construction			
– setting context/field	−F^+F	−C^+C	weaker for gathering ideas, then stronger for sorting
– negotiating text	+/−F	+C	kids controlling ID, teacher controlling SSID
Independent construction			
– setting context/field	−F	−C	return to kids' contexts, if possible beyond simulation
– writing	−F	+C...−C?	control/evaluation, public accountability... renovation?

Table 5.1 Waves of classification and framing in the pedagogic cycle

genre (which the teacher controls as guide). Independent Construction again opens with weak classification and framing as students open up another field, and with weak framing but relatively strong classification (since they are aiming for a specific genre) as they write a text on their own. The final stages of the cycle have always been designed to weaken this classification as students are encouraged to experiment creatively with the genre, or on the basis of deconstructing its politics to recontextualize it for alternative needs.

In our experience these waves of classification and framing, including double framing (both weak and strong) during joint construction, allow for both the incorporation and valuing of students' own voices during the negotiation and for critique where and when appropriate. We have not experienced the model as something that inherently devalues students' discourse and uncritically promotes mainstream discourses. Bernstein's comments on change in relation to his notion of pedagogic discourse are relevant to this issue:

> The potential for change is built into the model . . . there is always pressure to weaken the framing . . . because, in this formulation, pedagogic discourse and pedagogic practice construct always an arena, a struggle over the nature of symbolic control. And, at some point, the weakening of the framing is going to violate the classification . . . although classification translates power into the voice to be reproduced, we have seen that the contradictions, cleavages and dilemmas which inhere in the principles of classification are never entirely suppressed, either at the social or individual level . . . (1996: 30)

> not deterministic since in process of controlling the unthinkable it makes the possibility of the unthinkable available . . . and the distribution of power that speaks through the device creates potential sites of challenge and opposition . . . (1996: 52)

> text is not something which is mechanically reproduced. The text which is produced can feed back on the interactional practice. There can be a dynamic tension . . . The text itself, under certain conditions, can change the interactional practice . . . change in classification and framing values. Here the text has challenged the interactional practice and the classification and framing values upon which it is based. (1996: 32–3)

I'll close this section with three anecdotes in relation to the issue of students taking control of the genres they have been taught. Early in our work with the Disadvantaged Schools Programme Joan Rothery and I were unofficially banned from working with teachers in NSW schools during a state election campaign. The then Labor government was promoting a traditional 'back to basics' (including traditional grammar) approach to literacy teaching; at the same time its Department of Education released a Writing K–12 syllabus based completely on progressive models (process writing, whole language, poetry and narrative across the curriculum, grammar at point of need, if at all). Meanwhile we were having considerable success with our genre-based post-progressive pedagogy in several schools. The class of Year 6 students I worked with at Lakemba Public School took it on themselves to protest by writing expositions to the Minister of Education on why genre writing was a good thing (allowing for one anti-genre exposition, on the grounds that genre writing had been scheduled during that student's favourite part of the curriculum).

The next year these students moved to secondary school and were faced with new writing tasks for which they were given no explicit instruction. The Lakemba students took it on themselves to teach the genres they had learned to peers and returned on at least one occasion to their primary school to work with their former teacher on the structure of book reports, which they hadn't encountered before. With their teacher, they worked out the genre in a way that satisfied the needs of their new institutional environment.

I have already mentioned the Dulwich Hill Public School's campaign to get their municipal council to replace their local pool. Here is part of the six-page (folded A4) brochure they distributed to local residents to gain support for their proposals. It is based on their study of political discourse (with typed headings and handwritten text; images not included here) and formation of their Aqua party.

LOCAL GOVERNMENT SITS AROUND WHILE HUNDREDS OF KIDS MIGHT DROWN

WHAT'S THE PROBLEM?
● Marrickville pool has closed and we haven't got a pool.
● When summer comes! "WHERE'S THE POOL?!?!?!
● There's no pool SO! MORE PEOPLE DROWNING!!!
● Not enough people are learning to swim!!!

'... BUT I'M NOT AFFECTED!'
● When your kids whinge on a hot summer day ... Are you going to travel miles to a pool? Help us keep Marrickville pool open now or hear your kids whinge for LIFE!!!!

OUR CONCERNS
● We are very concerned about the idea of Marrickville pool closing down.
● Re-open the pool before IT'S TOO LATE!!!
● We are very concerned about ALL the kids who won't learn to swim during the closing of the pool.

ACTION – NOW!
(What we want to happen)
● We need parents and kids to help write letters for the local Government.
● We want you to talk to your friends, neighbours and anyone you know to make them involved in the issue.
● WE WANT THIS NOW:
● Make MP bigger, better and cheaper.

- Re-open MP (Renovated)
- Make it safer for everyone!!!!!!

WHO ARE WE?

We are kids from DHPS and we care and are very concerned about closing down MP so help us re-open it to make it better for our FUTURE!!!

SURVEY RESPONSE

- 80% of the people surveyed used Marrickville pool.
- If swimming lessons were free or cheaper 100% of students surveyed would learn to swim.
- Only 25% can swim who have surveyed.
- Most children learnt to swim at Marrickville pool.
- Marrickville pool is the most used facility in Marrickville.

[photo of three smiling campaigners]

michelle
D.O.B. 12/2/84
AGE: 11

gareth
D.O.B. 4/8/83
AGE: 11

hien
D.O.B. 20/11/83
AGE: 11

Please help us keep Marrickville pool open, just help by donating some MONEY!!!

These and numerous other encounters with teaching genre have convinced us that deploying a social semiotic instructional discourse in the pedagogic cycle outlined above gives students tools for acting on the world outside – tools that have been denied most working-class and migrant students in both traditional and progressive literacy regimes.

> Put your name and address on this form and send them in a letter to:
> RE-OPEN Marrickville pool trust-fund,
> Dulwich Hill P.S.
> Kintore st
> Initial Mr_.Mrs_ Ms_
> Name: _ _ _ _ _ _ _ _ _ _ _
> _ _ _ _ _ _ _ _ _ _ _ _ Address:
>
> _ _ _ _ _ _ _ _ _ _ _ _ _ _ _ _ _
> Suburb: _ _ _ _ _ _ _ _ _ _ _
> Donation Cash $_
> Cheque _ 5$_ 10$_
> Other: _

Democracy

Nothing has been more inspiring for us throughout our work than Bernstein's discourse on social class and education and the implications for social justice his words illuminate. And often, there has been nothing more moving.

> Biases in the form, content, access and opportunities of education have consequences not only for the economy; these biases can reach down to drain the very springs of affirmation, motivation and imagination. In this way such biases can become, and often are, an economic and cultural threat to democracy. (Bernstein 1996: 5)

We have unleashed some affirmation, motivation and imagination from school to school. To fill the springs we will have to become more dangerous still.

Appendix 1

Joint construction
 – development of a new field - in groups
  – **jointly on board**

T: Right. O.K. Now, let's try and get these into an order so we can organise how many paragraphs or how many new ideas we are going to introduce. Can someone sort of help me work that out? Can you just move back, Lisa, so I can get over to this side to put numbers next to things. O.K. Who can see the main thing that keeps coming through the whole way through? Lisa?
Lisa: Learn about a wide range of subjects.
T: Right. This seems to be one of the most important things, doesn't it? So we can put say a '1' next to it. Where else does it come up again?
Lisa: With the one [?]
T: Right. So we can put '1' against that – that could all be part of the same . . . paragraph, then, couldn't it? Somewhere else – the same sort of thing were we can link it together? Can you find any other links? Filippa?
Filippa: Use your education to get a good job.
T: Right. Now, would that be a new idea? Or is it the same, do you think? It all follows on; everything leads to help you to the next thing but you've got to try and organise it so you've got one complete. Remember that glue – trying to get that paragraph to stick together? We want to have a complete paragraph and then another complete paragraph. Do you think that one would work as a follow-up? After you've got your knowledge and you've applied all these skills, what are you going to be able to do there?
Safira: Support your family.
T: Support your family by what?
Safira: A job.
T: A job. So that would really be another paragraph, wouldn't it? That would be that paragraph, together, talking about that. Yes, Linh?
Linh: Good ideas on how to behave and how to live.

T: Um. Learn about a wide range of subjects and good ideas on how to behave. Yes, um, the only thing is, though, what's going to happen to this paragraph? It's going to be absolutely . . .

Ss. . . . long, huge.

T: Huge. So maybe we can almost have sub-paragraphs of the same thing. If we stick say all the education and learning in that paragraph, these are more socialising skills, aren't they? – getting friends, learning how to behave, following rules – they could all form one paragraph, couldn't they? So if we put good ideas, all friends, that could be all of 3. Instead of being bored at home – do you think that still relates there, or do you think that might go somewhere else? Have a think about that one. Where do you think it might go? Filippa?

Filippa: Number 1 . . . before *so you won't be bored at home and you can go to school to learn.*

T: So you're saying that would do well in your Introduction. So you're putting that as part of your Thesis. Alright, so we could maybe look at that part in our *intro*. Put *intro* there next to that, so we could think about that. Alright. Um. Something else now, that, um, what would link with that? Yes.

T & Ss: Parents don't have to look after you.

T: That might link with that one, wouldn't it, do you think? Would they link together?

Ss: Yes.

T: Alright. So we could maybe link those together, about the parents and not staying at home. So would you still like to see that in your Introduction.

Ss: Yes.

T: Then you are starting off your reasons for why children should come to school. Alright. O.K. We can keep that there. Now, is there anything we've missed out? Any area we haven't linked into something? . . .

Appendix 2

> Joint construction
> – negotiation of new text

T: . . . Filippa?

Filippa: I strongly believe that children should go to school for these main reasons . . . um, and I'm going to list them all.

T: Sorry, say that again.

Lisa: For these main reasons.

T: For these main reasons. Who can think of a different word other than *main*?

Ss: For the following reasons.

T: For the following reasons. Who can think of another word?

Loukia: Listed.

T: For these listed reasons, um. Who can think of another word?

Filippa: For these reasons shown here.

T: For these reasons written here. O.K. Who thinks main reasons. Hands up. Quick. A show of hands. *Main. These listed.* I've forgotten what the other ones were. [unison: *following*] O.K. Looks like *following.*

Ss & T: For the following reasons.

T: For the following reasons. Now, trying to think, um, before we go on, before we

list all of them, we want to include those things that you mentioned for that intro-duction, don't we? So how can we talk about that? Who can think? *I strongly believe children should go to school for the following reasons.* Filippa.
Filippa: You could, um, learn a wide range – a wide range of subjects and um reli-gions and um . . .
T: Right. Who can keep going from that?
. . .

T: We've got to get down to the main reasons as well; we're going to have thou-sands of them. *I strongly believe children should go to school for the following reasons: education is free, it can fulfil your time, parents can work and they don't have to worry about you while you're at school.*
Siraj: You're getting educated for free.
T: Right. How can we put that into a general thing? What's the big one there in that one? What's it all about? What are you actually going to gain?
Loukia: An education.
Lynette: Knowledge.
Ss: Knowledge.
T: You're going to what . . . gain knowledge, aren't you? So that might encompass [Sorry, Nicole, I don't know whether you're helping.] You actually, what do you actually achieve? You actually gain . . . [unison] knowledge, don't you?
So, how can we put that into the next little phrase? O.K. We've got – your parents won't be worrying about you, you're at school. Who can give it to me in a sen-tence? [Just ignore him please.] Lisa. Can you give it to me in a sentence? About gaining knowledge.
Lisa: Which one?
T: *I strongly believe children should go to school for the following reasons: education is free, it can fulfil your time, parents can work and they don't have to worry about you while you're at school.*
Lisa: You can learn a wide a wide range of subjects.
T: Right. [scribes]
Vu: Knowledge.
T: Right. Which will give you a tremendous amount of . . . knowledge . . . .

Notes

1 I am, as ever, deeply indebted to Joan Rothery, who worked with me on a previous version of this paper, and whose genius catalysed the pedagogy reviewed here.
2 Certainly not a title of my choosing, but used by DSP colleagues to secure funding for the research.
3 Tragically, as of 1997 the Disadvantaged Schools Program in New South Wales has lost its identity as an independent voice in the development of curriculum and pedagogy; long an embarrassment to state Departments of Education because of the enterprise and success of its various initiatives, the thorn has been removed.
4 For a penetrating deconstruction of the high moral ground assumed by critical theorists in educational debates see Hunter 1994.
5 He adds: 'It is a matter of interest that this top right-hand quadrant is regarded as conservative but has *often produced very innovative and radical acquirers.* The bottom right-hand quadrant shows a radical realization of an apparently conservative pedagogic practice . . . each theory will carry its own conditions of

contestation, "resistance", subversion.' (Bernstein 1990: 73)

6 It may seem that I am labouring the discussion of pedagogy here. However, as far as I am aware, as of 1996 extant critiques of the pedagogy (e.g. Freedman & Medway 1994, Luke 1996, Lee 1996) are based on *fears* about *imagined* implementations rather than consideration of the materials reviewed here – let alone classroom studies of the practice as it has evolved; this has tended to frustrate dialogue.

7 In this exchange the students undertake a successful collaborative analysis of a troublesome clause type – the existential clause with missing Subject *there*.

8 I am deeply indebted to Julie McCowage and the students of Lakemba Public School for their enthusiastic participation in the development of the teaching/learning cycle from which these texts arise.

9 Jon and I would like to thank the following teachers from Dulwich Hill Public School for their support in this project: Janthia Powditch, Lina Abeni, Annetta Tourta and Julie Ng.

10 The front page of the brochure reads: LOCAL GOVERNMENT SITS AROUND WHILE HUNDREDS OF KIDS MIGHT DROWN.

References

Anderson, L. and Nyholm, M. (1996) *The Action Pack: Technology (Activities for Teaching Factual Writing)*. Sydney: Metropolitan East DSP (Language and Social Power Project).

Applebee, A.M. and Langer, J. (1983) 'Instructional scaffolding: reading and writing as natural language activities', *Language Arts*, 60(2), 168–75.

Atkinson, P.A. (1985) *Language, Structure and Reproduction: An Introduction to the Sociology of Basil Bernstein*. London: Methuen.

Bernstein, B. (1971) *Class, Codes and Control, Vol. 1: Theoretical Studies towards a Sociology of Language*. London: Routledge & Kegan Paul.

Bernstein, B. (ed.) (1973) *Class, Codes and Control, Vol. 2: Applied Studies towards a Sociology of Language*. London, Routledge & Kegan Paul.

Bernstein, B. (1975) *Class, Codes and Control Vol. 3: Towards a Theory of Educational Transmissions*. London, Routledge & Kegan Paul.

Bernstein, B (1979) 'The new pedagogy: sequencing'. In J. Manning-Keepes and B.D. Keepes (eds), *Language in Education: the LDP Phase 1*. Canberra: Curriculum Development Centre, 293–302.

Bernstein, B. (1990) *Class, Codes and Control, vol. 4: The Structuring of Pedagogic Discourse*. London, Routledge.

Bernstein, B. (1996) *Pedagogy, Symbolic Control and Identity: Theory, Research, Critique*. London: Taylor & Francis.

Callaghan, M. and Knapp, P. (1989) *The Discussion Genre*. Sydney, Metropolitan East DSP (Language and Social Power Project).

Callow, J. (1996) *The Action Pack: Environment (Activities for Teaching Factual Writing)*. Sydney: Metropolitan East DSP (Language and Social Power Project).

Carter, R. (ed.) (1990) *Knowledge about Language and the Curriculum: The LINC Reader*. London: Hodder & Stoughton.

Carter, R. (1996) 'Politics and knowledge about language: the LINC project'. In R. Hasan, and G. Williams (eds), *Literacy in Society*. London: Longman, 1–28.

Cazden, C. (1995) 'Visible and invisible pedagogies in literacy education'. In P.A. Atkinson, B. Davies and S. Delamont (eds), *Discourse and Reproduction: Essays in Honor of Basil Bernstein*. Cresskill, NJ: Hampton Press, 159–72.

Chouliarki, L. (1997) 'Regulation in "Progressivist" pedagogic discourse: individualised teacher-pupil talk', in E.R. Pedro (ed.) Discourse Analysis: Proceedings of the First International Conference on Discourse Analysis, University of Libon, pp. 47–72.

Christie, F. (1989) 'Curriculum genres in early childhood education: a case study in writing development'. Unpublished Phd thesis, University of Sydney.

Christie, F. (1992) 'Literacy in Australia', *ARAL* 12, 142–55.

Christie, F. (1995) 'Pedagogic discourse in the primary school', *Linguistics and Education* 3(7), 221–42.

Christie, F., Devlin, B., Freebody, P., Luke, A., Martin, J.R., Threadgold, T. and Walton, C. (1991) *Teaching English Literacy: A Project of National Significance on the Preservice Preparation of Teachers for Teaching English Literacy*. Vols. 1–3. Canberra: Department of Employment, Education and Training; Darwin: Centre for Studies of Language in Education, Northern Territory University.

Christie, F., Gray, B., Gray, P., Macken, M., Martin, J.R. and Rothery, J. (1990a) *Exploring Reports: Teachers Book: Levels 1–4*. Sydney: Harcourt Brace Jovanovich.

Christie, F., Gray B., Gray, P., Macken, M., Martin, J.R. and Rothery, J. (1990b) *Exploring Procedures: Teachers Book: Levels 1–4* Sydney: Harcourt Brace Jovanovich.

Christie, F., Gray, B., Gray, P., Macken, M., Martin, J.R. and Rothery, J. (1992) *Exploring Explanations: Teachers Book (Levels 1–4)*. Sydney: Harcourt Brace Jovanovich.

Christie, F. and Martin, J.R. (1997) *Genre and Institutions: Social Processes in the Workplace and School*. London: Cassell.

Collerson, J. (ed.) (1988) *Writing for Life*. Sydney: Primary English Teaching Association.

Cranny-Francis, A. (1993) 'Gender and genre: feminist subversion of genre fiction and its implications for critical literacy'. In W. Cope and M. Kalantzis (eds), *The Powers of Literacy: A Genre Approach to Teaching Literacy*. London: Falmer, 90–115.

Cranny-Francis, A. (1996) 'Technology and/or weapon: the discipline of reading in the secondary English classroom'. In R. Hasan and G. Williams (eds) *Literacy in Society*. London: Longman, 172–90.

Cranny-Francis, A. and Martin, J.R. (1993) 'Making new meanings: literary and linguistic perspectives on the function of genre in textual practice', *English in Australia*, 105, 30–44.

Cranny-Francis, A. and Martin, J.R. (1994) 'In/visible education: class, gender and pedagogy in *Educating Rita* and *Dead Poets Society*', *Interpretations: Journal of the English Teachers' Association of Western Australia*, 27(1) 28–57.

Cranny-Francis, A. and Martin, J.R. (1995) 'Writings/readings: how to know a genre', *Interpretations: Journal of the English Teachers' Association of Western Australia*. 28(3) 1–32.

Derewianka, B. (1991) *Exploring How Texts Work* [video]. Sydney: Primary English Teaching Association.

Douglas, M. (1972) 'Speech, class and Basil Bernstein', *The Listener*, 9 March, 312.

Fairclough, N. (ed.) (1992) *Critical Language Awareness*. London: Longman.

Freedman, A. and Medway, P. (1994) *Genre and the New Rhetoric*. London: Taylor & Francis.

Giblett, R. and O'Carroll, J. (eds) (1990) *Discipline – Dialogue – Difference: Proceedings of the Language in Education Conference*, Murdoch University, December 1989. Perth: 4D Duration Publications, School of Humanities, Murdoch

University.

Grabe, W. and Kaplan, R. (1996) *Theory and Practice of Writing*. London: Longman.

Gray, B. (1985) 'Helping children to become language learners in the classroom'. In M. Christie (ed.), *Aboriginal Perspectives on Experience and Learning: The Role of Language in Aboriginal Education*. Geelong, Vic.: Deakin University Press, 87–104.

Gray, B. (1986) 'Aboriginal education: some implications of genre for literacy development'. In C. Painter and J.R. Martin, (eds), *Writing to Mean: Teaching Genres Across the Curriculum*. Applied Linguistics Association of Australia (Occasional Papers 9), 188–208.

Gray, B. (1987) 'How natural is "natural" language teaching: employing wholistic methodology in the classroom', *Australian Journal of Early Childhood*, 12(4) 3–19.

Gray, B. (1990) 'Natural language learning in Aboriginal classrooms: reflections on teaching and learning'. In C. Walton and W. Eggington (eds), *Language: Maintenance, Power and Education in Australian Aboriginal Contexts*. Darwin: Northern Territory University Press, 105–39.

Halliday, M.A.K. (1975) *Learning How to Mean: Explorations in the Development of Language*. London: Edward Arnold.

Halliday, M.A.K. (1978) 'Is learning a second language like learning a first language all over again'. In D.E. Ingram and T.J. Quinn (eds), *Language and Learning in Australian Society: Proceedings of the 1976 Congress of the Applied Linguistics Association of Australia*. Melbourne: Australian International Press & Publications, 3–19.

Halliday, M.A.K. (1993a) 'Towards a language-based theory of learning', *Linguistics and Education*, 5(2), 93–116.

Halliday, M.A.K. (1993b) *Language in a Changing World*. Canberra: Applied Linguistics Association of Australia (Occasional paper 13).

Halliday, M.A.K. (1994) *An Introduction to Functional Grammar* (2nd edn). London: Edward Arnold.

Halliday, M.A.K. (1995) 'Language and the theory of codes'. In Sadovnik, A. (ed.) (1995) *Knowledge and Pedagogy: The Sociology of Basil Bernstein*. Norwood, NJ: Ablex. 127–44.

Halliday, M.A.K. and Martin, J.R. (1993) *Writing Science: Literacy and Discursive Power*. London: Falmer.

Halliday, M.A.K. and Matthiessen, C.M.I.M. (in press) *Construing Experience Through Meaning: A Language-based Approach to Cognition*. London: Cassell.

Hammond, J. (1986) 'The effect of modelling reports and narratives on the writing of the Year 2 children from non-English-speaking backgrounds', *Australian Review of Applied Linguistics*, 9(2) 75–93.

Hasan, R. (1995) 'On social conditions for semiotic mediation: the genesis of mind in society'. In A. Sadovnik (ed.), *Knowledge and Pedagogy: The Sociology of Basil Bernstein*. Norwood, NJ: Ablex, 171–96.

Hasan, R. and Williams, S. (eds) (1996) *Literacy in Society*. London: Longman.

Hunt, I. (1994) *Joint construction*: PETA PEN. Sydney: Primary English Teaching Association.

Hunter, I. (1994) *Rethinking the School*. Sydney: Allen & Unwin.

Hyon, S. (1996) 'Genre in three traditions: implications for ESL', *TESOL Quarterly*, 30(4) 693–722.

Lee, A. (1996) *Gender, Literacy, Curriculum: Re-writing School Geography*. London: Taylor & Francis

Lemke, J.L. (1990) *Talking Science: Language, Learning and Values*. Norwood, N.J: Ablex.

Lemke, J.L. (1995) *Textual Politics: Discourse and Social Dynamics*. London: Taylor & Francis.

Littlefair, A. (1991) *Reading All Types of Writing: The Importance of Genre and Register for Reading Development*. Milton Keynes: Open University Press.

Luke, A. (1996) 'Genres of power? literacy education and the production of capital'. In R. Hasan and G. Williams (eds), *Literacy in Society*. London: Longman, 308–38.

Macken, M., Martin, J.R., Kress, G., Kalantzis, M., Rothery, J. and Cope W. (1989) *An Approach to Writing K-12: Vol. 1 Introduction, Vol. 4 The Theory and Practice of Genre-Based Writing*. Sydney: Literacy and Education Research Network & Directorate of Studies, NSW Department of Education.

Macken, M. and Rothery, J. (1991) *Developing Critical Literacy: A Model for Literacy in Subject Learning*. Sydney: Metropolitan East Disadvantaged Schools Programme (Write it Right Project).

Martin, J.R. (1991) 'Critical literacy: the role of a functional model of language', *Australian Journal of Reading*, 14(2), 117–32. (Focus Issue on Literacy Research in Australia edited by Peter Freebody and Bruce Shortland-Jones).

Martin, J.R. (1992) *English Text: System and Structure*. Amsterdam: Benjamins.

Martin, J.R. (1993) 'Genre and literacy: modelling context in educational linguistics', *ARAL*, 13, 141–72.

Martin, J.R. (1995) 'Reading positions/positioning readers: JUDGEMENT in English', *Prospect: A Journal of Australian TESOL*, 10(2), 27–37.

Martin, J.R. (1996) 'Evaluating disruption: symbolising theme in junior secondary narrative'. In R. Hasan and G. Williams, (eds), *Literacy in Society*. London: Longman, 124–71.

Martin, J.R. (1997) 'Analysing genre: functional parameters'. In F. Christie and J.R. Martin, *Genre and Institutions: Social Processes in the Workplace and School*. London: Cassell 3–39.

Martin, J.R. and Rothery, J. (1988) 'Classification and framing: double dealing in pedagogic discourse'. Paper presented at Post World Reading Congress Symposium on Language and Learning. Mr Gravatt College, Brisbane.

Martin, J.R. and Rothery, J. (1991) *Literacy for a Lifetime: Teachers' Notes*. Sydney: Film Australia.

Martin, J.R. and Veel, R. (1998) *Reading Science: Critical and Functional Perspectives on Discourses of Science*. London: Routledge.

Matthiessen, C.M.I.M. (1995) *Lexicogrammatical Cartography*. Tokyo: International Language Sciences Publishers.

Morgan, W. (1997) *Critical Literacy in the Classroom: The Art of the Possible*. London: Routledge.

Murray, N. and Zammit, K. (1992) *The Action Pack: Animals (Activities for Teaching Factual Writing)*. Sydney: Metropolitan East DSP (Language and Social Power Project).

New London Group (1996) 'A pedagogy of multiliteracies: designing social futures', *Harvard Educational Review*, 66(1), 60–92.

Painter, C. (1984) *Into the Mother Tongue: A Case Study of Early Language Development*. London: Pinter.

Painter, C. (1986) 'The role of interaction in learning to speak and learning to write'. In C. Painter and J.R. Martin (eds), *Writing to Mean: Teaching Genres Across the Curriculum*. Applied Linguistics Association of Australia (Occasional Papers 9), 62–97.

Painter, C. (1989) 'Learning language: a functional view of language development'. In R. Hasan and J.R. Martin (eds), *Language Development: Learning Language, Learning Culture*. Norwood, NJ: Ablex, 18–65.

Painter, C. (1991) *Learning the Mother Tongue* (2nd edn). Geelong, Vic.: Deakin University Press.

Painter, C. (1993) 'Learning through Language: a case study in the development of language as a resource for learning from 2½ to 5 years'. Unpublished PhD thesis, University of Sydney.

Painter, C. (1996) 'The development of language as a resource for thinking: a linguistic view of learning'. In R. Hasan and G. Williams (eds), *Literacy in Society*. London: Longman, 50–85.

Painter, C. (1999) *Learning through Language in Early Childhood*. London: Cassell.

Painter, C. and Martin, J.R. (eds) (1986) *Writing to Mean: Teaching Genres Across the Curriculum*. Applied Linguistics Association of Australia (Occasional Papers 9), 62–97.

Reid, I. (ed.) (1987) *The Place of Genre in Learning*. Geelong, Vic.: Centre for Studies in Literary Education, Deakin University.

Richardson, P.W. (1994) 'Language as personal resources and as social context: competing views of literacy pedagogy in Australia'. In A. Freedman and P. Medway (eds), *Learning and Teaching Genre*. Portsmouth NH: Boynton/Cook.

Rothery, J. (1986) 'Teaching genre in the primary school: a genre based approach to the development of writing abilities'. *Writing Project: Report 1986 (Working Papers in Linguistics* no. 4, Department of Linguistics, University of Sydney), 3–62.

Rothery, J. (1989) 'Learning about language'. In R. Hasan, and J.R. Martin (eds), *Language Development: Learning Language, Learning Culture*. Norwood, NJ: Ablex, 199–256.

Rothery, J. (1994) *Exploring Literacy in School English (Write It Right Resources for Literacy and Learning)*. Sydney: Metropolitan East Disadvantaged Schools Programme.

Rothery, J. (1996) 'Making changes: developing an educational linguistics'. In R. Hasan and G. Williams (eds), *Literacy in Society*. London: Longman, 86–123.

Rothery, J. and Stenglin, M. (1994) *Writing a Book Review: A Unit of Work for Junior Secondary English (Write It Right Resources for Literacy and Learning)*. Sydney: Metropolitan East Disadvantaged Schools Programme.

Veel, R. (1997) Learning how to mean – scientifically speaking: apprenticeship into scientific discourse in the secondary school. In F. Christie and J.R. Martin, *Genres and Institutions: Social Processes in the Workplace and School*. London: Cassell, 161–95.

Vygotsky, L.S. (1978) *Mind in Society: The Development of Higher Psychological Processes* (M. Cole, V. John Steiner, S. Scribner and E. Souberman (eds)). Cambridge, MA: Harvard University Press.

Walton, C. (1996) *Critical Social Literacies*. Darwin: Northern Territory University Press.

Williams, G. (1995) 'Grammar, children and learning'. Plenary address given at the 1995 Australian Systemic Functional Linguistics Conference at the University of Melbourne.

6 The pedagogic device and the teaching of English[1]

Frances Christie

Introduction

According to Bernstein (1996: 52), the pedagogic device

> acts as a symbolic regulator of consciousness; the question is, whose regulator, what consciousness and for whom? It is a condition for the production, reproduction and transformation of culture.

This chapter considers the operation of the pedagogic device in an educational discourse drawn from secondary school English teaching. While much of what will be argued of the manner in which the pedagogic device operates can be shown to hold true for educational discourse in the teaching of other school subjects (Christie 1991, 1995, 1997, 1998, provide discussions of the pedagogic discourse in some other subjects), the interest will be in exploring its significance in the teaching of the national language in an English-speaking community.

The teaching of the national language, at least in the Anglo-Australian tradition, has generated heated debate throughout this century. At no time has the debate been more heated, its political consequences more visible, than in the 1980s and 1990s (see Tyler this volume Chapter 10 re national curriculum movements). During this period both Britain and Australia have taken the unprecedented step of adopting national English curriculum statements, and they have also instituted national tests of English literacy. It is true that national curriculum statements for other subjects have also been developed, but it is very doubtful whether these have generated the heated arguments and, in particular, the frequent media attention that have accompanied the introduction of the English curriculum statements. The British experience has been perhaps the more remarkable in its political history and consequences. It involved initially the appointment of the Kingman Committee and its report (1988) on the English language. This was followed by the reports of the English Working Party chaired by Cox, the first of whose deliberations (1988),[2] on the programme of English for primary years, led to a request for more grammar on the part of the then Secretary of State for Education, Baker. Cox (1994: 27) argues that the request represented a hasty reaction by Baker, intended to placate conservative forces in Britain. He suggests it characterized a period of history in which strong conservative forces sought to control the education system.

Demands for more explicit teaching of grammar (normally conceived in Latinate, and hence dated terms), led to heated argument. Similarly, demands for the return to the English curriculum of pieces from the English literary past[3] rather than more recent works, including those from other cultures, led to debate. The debates over grammar and literature were symptomatic of the broader argument not only over what should be the content of the English curriculum, but who should control that content. More than one commentator (e.g. Cameron and Bourne 1988, Carter 1993, 1996, Cox 1994) has pointed out that the issues, in Britain at least, were often compounded by the apparent anxieties of those who wrote in defence either of traditional grammar or of the literary canon. For some, the learning of grammar was apparently seen as a palliative to the alleged tendencies towards self indulgence and indiscipline that they claimed were a feature of many contemporary youths. Achieving control of the English curriculum was, it seemed, for many people, part of achieving greater control of the whole population. Differences in dialect, like differences in language, were either denied, or given a diminished significance in the calls for an English curriculum that would unite by simplifying and standardizing what should be taught.

The history of events in Australia has not been the same as in Britain, though there are points of parallel. Discussions of the teaching of grammar have often been as heated as in Britain, and arguments over functional as opposed to traditional grammars have led to debate in several states over the grammar to be adopted in state-sponsored curriculum materials. Many curriculum resource materials using the functional grammar have enjoyed success and been extensively used by teachers. (See Martin this volume Chapter 5 re the functional grammar.) One of the claims that can be made for the teaching of a functional grammar is that it develops a critical capacity to interpret and challenge the ways language makes meanings. (Christie *et al.* 1991, discuss the pedagogic role of the functional grammar in developing critical capacities. See also Gerot and Wignell 1994, Lock 1996, Butt *et al.* 1995, Thompson 1996, Martin *et al.* 1997, for introductory discussions of the functional grammar.) Such a claim cannot be made for traditional Latinate grammar, whose concerns are not with meaning but with the syntax of the written sentence. Apart from arguments about grammar, there have also been arguments about the teaching of literacy, and arguments about appropriate literature for teaching purposes.

In universities in the English-speaking world, many departments of English have gone through often divisive debates as they have challenged the literary canon, and in the process developed new programmes under the general rubric of critical and/or cultural studies. (See Belsey 1980 for an early discussion.) Proposals for the teaching of literature in schools have opened up the English curriculum to include various media studies.

In addition, proposals have been made from time to time for the adoption in schools of critical perspectives on the teaching of literature (e.g. West 1994). Yet there is evidence to suggest, at least in Australia, that despite the apparent moves to widen the English curriculum, and despite the efforts of some to introduce more critical dimensions, the teaching of literature remains heavily influenced by ideologies drawn from the nineteenth-century preoccupations of Arnold, and in this century those of F.R. Leavis. Literature is used for the often uncritical development of various moral positions, while the wider, and potentially more provocative opportunities for the study of literary pieces and their language usages are often lost. Discussing this and related features of English teaching as that has emerged in Anglo-Australian traditions, Hunter (1994: 16) writes 'English should be understood not as the literary use of pedagogy but as a pedagogical use of literature.'

Some interesting issues are opened up. Who controls the national language curriculum? Why is its control so important, and why is the control an apparent source of continued debate, even conflict? What is its particular significance in the shaping of the national consciousness? Finally, whose interests are served by a pedagogy which, on the one hand, is ostensibly committed to development of abilities to communicate ideas in critical and independent ways, yet on the other hand, appears to deny its students the capacities in analysis of language necessary for the development of critical and independent action?

Bernstein's discussions of the pedagogic device (1990, 1996) will provide a framework in which to consider these questions, while use of a functional grammar (Halliday 1994) will allow some linguistic analysis and interpretation of the framework by reference to an instance of secondary literature teaching.

The pedagogic device and the pedagogic discourse[4]

Figure 6.1, drawn from Bernstein (1996: 52), summarizes the functioning of the pedagogic device. This device makes possible forms of pedagogic communication whose operation is determined by internal rules. (See Williams this volume Chapter 4 re the pedagogic device.) The device provides the 'intrinsic grammar' of a pedagogic discourse, and that grammar functions through three sets of interrelated rules: distributive, recontextualizing and evaluative. The distributive rules 'regulate the relationships between power, social groups, forms of consciousness and practice' (Bernstein 1996: 42). They produce specialized forms of knowledge, consciousness and practice, and are responsible for the distribution of these to different social groups. The recontextualizing rules 'regulate the formation of specific pedagogic discourse' (Bernstein 1996: 43), while the evaluative rules 'constitute any pedagogic practice' (Bernstein 1996: 43). It is pedagogic practice which produces 'a ruler for consciousness' (Bernstein 1996: 43).

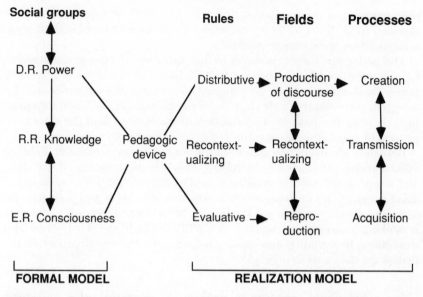

Figure 6.1 The pedagogic device (From B. Bernstein 1996: 52)

With respect to the distributive rules, Bernstein distinguishes between those forms of knowledge that are esoteric and mundane (1996: 43), or unthinkable and thinkable; the distinction between these is relative to a given period of history. Control of the unthinkable lies essentially but not exclusively in the 'upper reaches of the educational system' (1996: 43) while control of the thinkable lies in secondary and primary school systems. Power relations distribute the thinkable and the unthinkable, differentiating groups made possible by the distributive rules. The distributive rules create 'a specialized field of production of discourse' (1996: 45), and the state is increasingly assuming control of this.

The recontextualizing rules constitute particular pedagogic discourses, and, resting on the distributive rules that create specialized forms of communication, a pedagogic discourse 'selects and creates specialized pedagogic subjects through its contexts and contents' (1996: 46). A pedagogic discourse 'embeds rules which create skills of one kind or another and rules regulating their relationship to each other, and rules which create social order' (1996: 46). The discourse which creates skills and their relationships is termed the 'instructional discourse', while the moral discourse which creates order, relations and identity is the 'regulative discourse'. The instructional discourse is said to be embedded within the regulative discourse. The regulative discourse takes or appropriates discourses from sites beyond the school, and relocates these as instructional discourses for the specialized pedagogical purposes of schooling. In the process of relocation, the instructional discourse is transformed, and the manner of its introduction, pacing and sequencing, is determined by the operation of the regulative discourse. The recontextualizing principle involved in all this creates agents whose function is to recontextualize; in schools, these agents are teachers.

The pedagogic subject position in the pedagogic discourse is imaginary, for it is mediated by the procedure by which the discourse is relocated, rather than arising in an activity unmediated by any other practice. Finally, as noted, the evaluative rules transform the pedagogic discourse into practice, creating the field of reproduction of knowledge, and the associated process of acquisition. Evaluation is the key to pedagogic practice.

Bernstein identifies two manifestations of the recontextualizing field: an official recontextualizing field (ORF), which is the creation of the state; and a pedagogic recontextualizing field (PRF), which is the creation of those involved in educating, such as teachers in schools and colleges, and writers in specialist educational journals. According to Bernstein, the state is seeking currently to weaken the PRF through the ORF, thus also weakening the relative autonomy enjoyed over the construction of the pedagogic discourse (1996: 48).

Using a functional grammar to explore the operation of a pedagogic discourse

We will consider an instance of the teaching of literature to a class of Year 10 secondary students, aged about 16 years.[5] We will seek to identify how the pedagogic discourse functions, as well as the nature of the pedagogic subject position in construction. Consideration of these things will allow us to return to the questions about the role of English literature teaching with which we opened this chapter. Rather than using the notion of an instructional discourse embedded within a regulative discourse, I will propose the operation of two registers, regulative and instructional, and I shall argue that the former 'projects' the latter. The arguments in favour of this and other aspects of the model of the pedagogic discourse have been proposed elsewhere (Christie 1989, 1991), though a brief explanation will be offered.

To understand a pedagogic discourse, one must pursue teaching–learning activity throughout a sustained curriculum cycle. I have argued elsewhere (1989) that a lesson may be thought of as a curriculum genre – staged, purposeful and goal-oriented. (See Martin, this volume Chapter 5 for discussion of genres. Recent discussions using the register and genre theory proposed are found in Ventola 1987, Martin 1992, Eggins and Martin 1997, Christie and Martin 1997, Eggins and Slade 1997, Martin and Veel, 1998). A successful sequence of genres represents an instance of a curriculum macrogenre: a cycle of curriculum genres, all linked in relations that, metaphorically, reflect the relations of taxis or of dependency found in Halliday's (1994) account of clause complex relations. Operating throughout the unfolding of the curriculum macrogenre will be two registers, or sets of choices in language – the regulative and the instructional. As a general principle, the regulative register will be foregrounded at the start of a curriculum macrogenre, and it will remain foregrounded while the curriculum goals are being established and negotiated; this may absorb several genres within the overall macrogenre. At points where the regulative register is foregrounded, the instructional register may find no expression in the discourse, but in general as curriculum activity proceeds, the instructional register will also find expression, for the object will always be to pursue some pedagogical goals with respect to a 'content' of some kind. If the curriculum macrogenre succeeds, the regulative register eventually disappears, while the instructional register is foregrounded. In a manner consistent with Bernstein's proposals, while the instructional register comes to be foregrounded, the regulative register continues to operate tacitly. In fact, the success with which the instructional register comes to the fore is a measure of the continuing implicit operation of the regulative register.

The metaphor of projection rather than that of embedding is chosen to characterize the relationship of the two registers. This follows proposals of Halliday (1981, 1982) who argues that a text may be thought of metaphorically as operating like a clause. Hence, it is argued that the regulative register projects the instructional register, functioning rather as a clause of speech or of thinking does, when it projects another clause. (See Halliday, 1994, for a discussion of projection.) As the curriculum macrogenre unfolds, an ideal pedagogic subject position is constructed. Furthermore, the text's development is marked by a growth in logogenesis (Halliday in Halliday and Martin 1993): that process by which a text changes character, generating new meanings made possible by the cumulative building of the text and its emergent understandings.

An instance of a pedagogic discourse in a secondary English literature classroom

The unit of work involved the teaching of twenty 50-minute lessons, fifteen of which were recorded, enough to be able to identify a curriculum macrogenre. The recording commenced after several lessons in which the teacher, Mr Malcom, and his students[6] had been reading the American novel *To Kill a Mockingbird*, by Harper Lee. The first lesson recorded was one where the class and teacher finished their joint reading of the novel. The teacher suggested that recording start there, because it was there that the processes of discussing the novel began. Enough was gained from the first lesson recorded to judge the purposes of the opening genre, while the rest of the sequence was completely recorded. A macrogenre did apply, and there was unitary growth across the sequence of curriculum genres. Figure 6.2 provides an overview of the curriculum macrogenre.

The object of the Curriculum Initiation was to establish a shared reader position. Here there was a very strong requirement that students and teacher achieve consensus about the novel and its themes as a basis for proceeding further. The Curriculum Activity had a primary purpose, in the

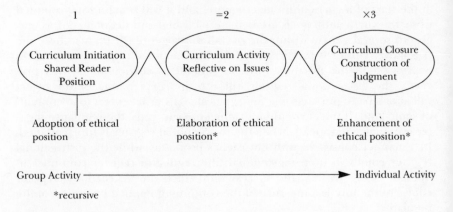

Figure 6.2 An English Literature macrogenre of the middle secondary school years: a Year 10 reading of *To Kill a Mockingbird*

words of the teacher, in developing *thinking about issues,* where the concern was to express opinion about the events of the novel and the characters. What the teacher termed important *issues* in the book were identified, first for some class discussion, and subsequently for some writing activities. While independence of opinion was ostensibly sought, as will be argued later, there was still a strong imperative at work to achieve consensus about ethical matters. The final curriculum genre, the Curriculum Closure, involved construction of judgement. Here students were required to *write formally* (to use the teacher's term), and the primary purpose was that they write an ethical judgement about life, extrapolated from the book's events.

Metaphorically at least, ideational, interpersonal and textual meanings are realized in the macrogenre. Thus, its experiential meanings are suggested in the functional names given in the Figure 6.2 to the three principal genres. They may be thought of as 'particulate'. Its logical meanings are a feature of the connectedness between the genres, where these meanings are associated with the notations used by Halliday (1994) for labelling the relations of taxis. The Curriculum Activity stands in a relation of elaboration (=) upon the Curriculum Initiation, in that it specifies in greater detail and/or exemplifies some of what is established in the first genre. The Curriculum Closure stands in a relation of enhancement (X) to the latter genre, in that it develops upon what is done earlier. The interpersonal meanings, functioning prosodically in a text, are suggested in the shift from Group Activity at the beginning of the macrogenre towards Individual Activity. Finally, the textual meanings, functioning like a wave (Halliday 1979), or like a 'pulse' (Matthiessen 1988, 1992) are suggested in the overall sense of sequence as the various genres unfold.

Curriculum Initiation: establishing the shared reader position

For those not familiar with *To Kill a Mockingbird*, the novel is set in the American state of Alabama in the 1930s. The story is told by a young girl, Scout, whose father Atticus Finch is the town lawyer. He becomes involved in the defence of a black man, Tom Robinson, wrongly accused of raping a young white woman. Robinson dies in a failed attempt to escape prison. The white man, Ewell, responsible for wrongly accusing him holds a grudge against Atticus, and he tries to injure Scout and her brother Jem, but they are saved by a pathetic recluse, 'Boo' (Arthur) Radley, who stabs Ewell to death. Atticus initially thinks Jem has killed Ewell. The sheriff, Heck Tate, concerned to protect Boo, and aware that Ewell was a corrupt person, insists that Ewell fell on his own knife.

We can cite only small fragments from the discourse, both in this and later genres. Portions of the discourse in the first recorded lesson are reproduced and some linguistic features are discussed below. Wherever the teacher reads directly from the novel, this is indicated in italics, although most of the novel's text is omitted, indicated with a row of dots. Where text is omitted, this is stated.

After establishing the relevant page in the book, the teacher goes on:

And I want you to, ah, look at the part where Atticus was sitting on the swing right in the middle of the page. OK.
Atticus was sitting on the swing and Mister Tate was sitting in the chair next (pause) *to him.*
And Nan (addressed because inattentive), I really want you to know what the next word is because, ah, this requires some clever attention. Atticus was sitting in the swing and Mister Tate was in the chair next to him, you got that?
The light went out in the living room windows. 'Heck, it's mighty kind of you and I know you're doin' it from that good heart of yours, but don't start anything like that.' Mr. Tate got up and went to the edge of the porch, spat into the shrubbery, then thrust his hands into his hip pockets and faced Atticus. 'Like what?' he said.
What does Atticus think that Heck Tate's doing?
Max: Protecting Jem.
T: By? By sup- right, yeah, I'm writing him . . . (meaning not clear)
Nigel: He thinks that Jem killed, eh, Ewell.
T: Atticus thinks that, ah, Jem killed Bob Ewell. And he thinks that Heck's going to write a phoney report to protect Jem. Uh.
'I'm sorry if I spoke sharply . . . Bob Ewell fell on his knife and I can prove it. . . . he stumbled on a root under the tree. Look, I can show you.' That's the way he says it. *Mr. Tate reached in his side pocket and withdrew a long switch blade knife. As he did so Doctor Reynolds came to the door . . . 'That the knife that killed him, Heck?' 'No Sir, still in him. Looked like a kitchen knife from the handle.'*
T: Now, how many knives have we got, ah, now?
Max: Two.
T: OK, two. What are they?
Max: Switch blade and one stuck in Bob Ewell.
Nigel: Switch blade. The other one stuck in . . . Ewell.
T: Right. Now, it's crucial you know that there were two knives, OK?

Max: What happened? Boo isn't saying anything.
T: Because he's a recluse and he, he, he's totally frightened by other people. So he sits there.
Max: He was made totally frightened. (Said with emphasis on 'made'.)
T: Yeah. And he still is.

[Section of the text is omitted. Discussion develops about why the sheriff is suggesting that Bob Ewell killed himself, rather than being murdered.]

Max: But the sheriff is saying that, ah, Bob Ewell killed himself.
T: And I think . . . what I want you to know is that Heck Tate is saying something but he wants Atticus Finch to understand a completely different meaning. And why he slammed his foot down is because he had to say out loud who he was talking about: 'I'm not talkin' about Jem.' So, who he's talking about protecting?
Nigel: Boo Radley.

[Text is omitted.]

T: OK, back to it! Back to it! Back to it! Back to it! Back to it! Shshshshsh. Because the meaning of the title now becomes clear.
Mr. Tate stamped off the porch . . . 'Scout,' he said, 'Mr. Ewell fell on his knife. Can you possibly understand?'
I think he's sayin', can you understand why I'm telling this lie?
Atticus looked like he needed cheering up . . . Well, it'd be sort of like shooting a mockingbird, wouldn't it?
T: Now, what was the mockingbird?
Max: That bird that like sang . . . (overlaps)
Nan: Sings only to . . . (overlaps)
Nigel: Sings to people (overlaps)
Max: Made life pleasant.
T: Right.
Nigel: Just used to sing all day.
T: So, the mockingbird . . . who is like the mockingbird?
Kim: Boo Radley.
Max: Boo.
T: 'Cos he'd done no wrong. He's killed this kind of criminal. He's a completely harmless person.

[Text is omitted.]

T: *Atticus put his face in my hair and rubbed it. When he got up and walked across the porch into the shadows his youthful step had returned. Before he went inside the house he stopped in front of Boo Radley. 'Thank you for my children Arthur,' he said.*
T: That's a beautiful moment that.

[Text is omitted.]

T: *Boo's hand hovered over Jem's head.*
So he doesn't want to touch him, because touching would be a real commit-

ment and he doesn't . . . he's lived the whole of his life without touching any-
body. It's just grotesque what they've done to this guy.
Boo's hand hovered over Jem's head. . . . Mr. Arthur, bend your arm down here, like that.
That's right. Sir. I slipped my hand into the crook of his arm.
So, she says, I'm not going to hold his hand and drag him along. I'm going to
walk like a lady. So she makes him hold his hand like that (gestures) so she can
slip her hand in his arm and they're walking down the street like good friends.
She's so sweet for an eight year old. She's so beautiful, little Scout.
Mr Arthur bend your arm down here like that . . . I never saw him again. (Lengthy
pause in the reading.)

[Text is omitted.]

T: OK, so she understands that Boo, um, had such an empty life that he made
the children that he could see up the street his loved ones.

[Text is omitted.]

The street lights were fuzzy . . . He would be there all night and he would be there when
Jem waked up in the morning.
That's it.
Nigel: (sighs)
T: One of the things that moves me incredibly about that book is how unfair the
world is. Scout and Jem, their Daddy really, really loves 'em. And so they're kind
of set in the world. And you think about it, the other people that are around.
You think about, you think about, ah, Tom Robinson, what's he got going for
him? You think about the children in ah, . . . excuse me (students are restless
and some are chatting) . . . you think about the children in, ah, Bob Ewell's
family, what have they got going for them? It just, and . . . and kind of, there's
one other person who is really badly persecuted in that book. Boo Radley. What
an incredible life. What a job his family has done on him. (pause) They made
him frightened to live.

[Text is omitted.]

T: OK I got nothin' more. You got anything to say?
Nigel: It was a good book.
Teacher: You like that.
Students: Yeah.
Nigel: At the start, you know, it was boring.
Max: Sir, what does poignant mean? (he is reading this word on the back cover
of the book)
T: Well, gee . . . when things are . . . when poignant things affect, um, me I'm
really moved by them because of the specialness of the moment.
Max: That's what this book was, poignant.
T: Because there were many moments in it that were very special.

Some resources in which the regulative register is marked in teacher talk
include:

> I **want** you to ah, look at the part [[where Atticus was sitting in the swing]][7]
> And Nan I **really want** you to know what the next word is, because this requires
> some clever attention.
> Right, now it**'s crucial** [[you know [[that there were two knives]]]] OK
> And I think . . . [[what I **want** you to know]] is [[that Heck Tate is saying some-
> thing . . .]]

In these instances the teacher uses interpersonal metaphor (Halliday
1994: 354–67). When he says *I want you to know . . .* the congruent meaning, involving high modality would be *you must look or know*. Teachers often
use such interpersonal metaphor, and students normally have little trouble recognizing the sense of strong direction involved. A similar sense of
interpersonal metaphor is also involved in the clause where the teacher
says *it's crucial [[you know [[that there were two knives]]]]*. Here again a sense
of high modality, and hence of strong obligation, is apparent in the relational process and its attribute *it's crucial . . .* The students' reading behaviour is being regulated towards the adoption of certain understandings
about the details of the novel. In Bernstein's terms the reading of the
novel is strongly framed (Bernstein 1975: 88).

In building the shared reader position, there is a progress from shared
comprehension of events, to shared interpretation of behaviours of characters, to shared judgement on the significance of events, and finally to
shared judgement on the moral significance of the book. While in principle several of these are recursive, there is a deliberate progression in the
movement from shared comprehension towards eventual adoption of
moral judgement about the book. The progression marks a movement in
terms of abstraction, in the shift from the immediate recreation of event
to eventual making of moral judgement. Focusing mainly on the resource
of transitivity (transitivity processes are indicated in bold), but making
some reference to other linguistic resources, we can track the progress in
a series of clauses:

A) Shared comprehension of events realized in:

(i) Material processes to reconstruct activities in the novel (shown in bold), and
specific reference to characters:
Atticus **was sitting** on the swing
and Mister Tate **was sitting** in the chair next to him.

(ii) Mental processes of cognition to build reflection on why characters do as
they do, and hence build explanation of actions, as in the folowing, where again
specific reference is used:

what **does** Atticus **think** that Heck Tate's doing?
he **thinks** that Jim killed Ewell.

B) Shared interpretation of behaviours of characters, realized in:

(i) processes of attribution or processes of affect;
(ii) associated lexical items that realize attitude (shown in italics);
(iii) intensity (underlined);
(iv) specific reference:
he's a **recluse** (process of attribution)
and he's <u>totally</u> *frightened* by other people (process of affect)
he was made <u>totally</u> *frightened* (causative process of attribution)
he's a <u>completely</u> *harmless* person (process of attribution)
she's <u>so</u> *sweet* for an eight year old (process of attribution)
she's <u>so</u> *beautiful* little Scout (process of attribution)

C) Shared judgement on significance of events, also realized in

a relational process of attribution, but where the item realizing the Carrier role
(*that*) and the general nominal group realizing the Attribute help build general
statement, not statement on a particular person:

that's a beautiful moment, that

D) Shared judgement on the moral significance of the book, realized in:

(i) an identifying process that builds a general statement:
one of the things [[that moves me incredibly about that book]] is
[[how unfair the world is]]
(ii) exclamations, using general nominal groups to help build general evaluative statement ('an incredible life'; 'a job'):
what an incredible life
what a job [[his family has done on him]]
(iii) mental processes of cognition (in bold) to help create reflection upon the
moral significance of events, as in:
you **know** one of the good things about living in the 1990s? These days I **reckon**
Nathan Radley would be in a court room explaining why he could make someone like Boo suffer so badly.
(iv) processes of attribution to build statements on the value of the book, where
attitude is realized in the lexical choices for Attribute (shown in italics)
it was a *good* book
that's what this book was, *poignant.*

Most of the talk expressing attitude, is teacher talk. One student, Max,
twice offers contributions which reinforce teacher statements. The role
the teacher takes is important. He is teaching the students to make judgements by predisposing them towards adopting certain attitudes and
ethical positions. He models how to express these attitudes and ethical
positions, and this is a first step towards preparing the students to offer
attitudes and ethical positions of their own. In this, the teacher's

behaviour accords with that suggested by Hunter (1994), who argues that, contrary to much received wisdom about developing self expression in students, English teachers take up a 'pastoral' role towards their students, essentially supervising them as they adopt ethically acceptable positions.

To return to the model of the pedagogic device outlined in Figure 6.1, we can see that in Bernstein's terms the teacher is relaying the recognition rules of the instructional discourse very explicitly; it is upon these that the realization rules are elaborated. These realization rules position students morally with respect to the criteria by which the novel is to be judged.

It is notable that the teacher's behaviour is different from that apparently adopted by teachers in other subjects. The opening genres in curriculum macrogenres in science (Christie 1998) and in geography (Christie 1996), for example, typically introduce aspects of a technical language, subsequently revisited, enlarged upon and often added to, in the course of the macrogenre. The introduction and subsequent use of such a technical language is part of teaching and learning how to deploy that language in adopting methods of reasoning, and engaging in processes of defining and answering questions that are a characteristic feature of the school subjects which they construct. An important measure of the logogenetic growth in successful science and geography macrogenres will be the way students acquire the technical language and deploy it with increasing independence.

No comparable use of a technical language is found in an English literary classroom of the kind sampled here, although as noted, there is a shift logogenetically by the end of the macrogenre, such that the students' language is marked by capacity to offer abstractions about life, but this requires no technical language.[8] English literary studies it seems, are primarily concerned with development of ethical positions, where these are arrived at by generalizing about life. Theorists about English teaching have sometimes made a virtue of this. Britton and Squires (1975: xviii), for example wrote of the content of English that

> it proves impossible to mark out an area less than the sum total of the planned
> and unplanned experiences through language by means of which a child gains
> control of himself [sic] and of his relations with the surrounding world.

Where the subject is so ill-defined, it becomes impossible to give it substance for teaching purposes. In Bernstein's terms, English literary studies of the kind examined here are weakly classified (Bernstein 1975: 88–9), for such studies are not clearly 'insulated' from others, or even from the more general concerns of daily living.

English literary studies in the tradition discussed do not address how the literary text constructs its meanings. To do so would involve the adoption of a technical language; in this case a metalanguage for considering literary as well as other texts. This would enable students to consider and discuss such matters as: how texts are organized as text types or genres;

the textual features that appear to characterize the text types; the social functions served by such text types; the kinds of sociohistorical and/or sociopolitical contexts that shaped such texts types; and the particular subject positions constructed in them. Rothery and Christie (1995), Macken-Horarik (1995), Rothery and Stenglin (1997) and Misson (1998) all offer discussions of possible approaches to aspects of English teaching involving pedagogically helpful use of a metalanguage. Rothery and Christie and Rothery and Stenglin offer analyses of narrative structures, considering among other things the role of narrative in building subjectivity, with particular consequences for teaching the writing of narrative. Macken-Horarik draws on the work of a junior secondary English teacher, and examines a unit of work devoted to romance narratives in fiction and film taught to a Year 9 class of girls. Guided viewing and reading of narratives involved development of a metalanguage to analyse how the narratives were put together, and to critique the values and subject positions constructed in the narratives. Misson, drawing from different theoretical paradigms, offers a discussion of the ways contemporary theories of narrative can inform the teaching of reading of narratives.

In the classroom text under discussion, no attempt is made to develop students who can theorize, for example, about how the characters are constructed, or about the kinds of reader positions intended by the writer. An effort is made to develop some kind of heightened sensibility about life, where, as Cranny-Francis (1996) has suggested, the ideological stance adopted owes much to Leavis, and his hostility to theoretical knowledge. Yet this is surely a matter of concern in subject English – the very subject in which very strident claims are often made about its role in developing students' ability to express independent points of view.

Curriculum Activity: reflection on issues

The Curriculum Activity genre consisted of eleven lessons, most of which will not be considered. The most significant activity, lasting several lessons, involved talking and writing about *issues* in the novel, to use the teacher's term. We will consider two lessons (actually a double period), where some talk led to a writing task. To facilitate talk initially, the teacher arranged the students facing each other. The opening part of the extract is devoted to preparing the students for their tasks, while the latter part is devoted to the students talking about issues.

A. Preparing the students

The regulative register is foregrounded in the opening teacher talk:

> T: OK. Alright, shhh, alright. The lesson's about to, this is the, . . . the learning part of the lesson's about to begin. Here we go. Your attention please. Look this way. OK, thanks Nigel. (addressed because he is inattentive) OK, we've got two, ah,

things to, ah, do in today's, ah, lesson. The first one is, ah, is to work through the things in this sheet. (displays it) And can you see the things, the headings marked one through to seven?

Max: Huh?

T: Um, for this lesson, we're going to have a talk about, ah, those. And I've got you in a group like this to, ah, talk in a particular way.

[Text is omitted]

The, um, second thing is that, ah, in the second part of the lesson, the second part of the double, I'm going to show you how I want you to write about them. Ah, I've got prepared, ah, (shows students the overheads) some overhead sheets, and, ah I'll put them on the overhead projector when we move upstairs for period two. Right, so, that's where we're heading. Ah, so, in the end it's going to be some writing, by the end of the double I'll show you some writing that I expect you to do between now and Thursday. Ah, can I . . . have a look at the top of this then, please. (reads from the handout) 'The purpose of this section is for you to show yourself thinking about the issues raised in *To Kill A Mockingbird*.'

[Text is omitted]

T: Most often in English, the assessor looks for, and this is true of me: sensitivity to the complexities of certain situations. Sensitivity to the complexities of certain situations. In other words, an all one way view is probably, ah, not going to do the trick in English. Um, I want people to say on the one hand such and such, on the other hand such and such. If you can see how things are a bit complicated, um, that's good. In, . . . most often in English the assessor looks for a genuine response. That is, one in which it is clear the writer is true to his or her own feelings about the book and writes a response with conviction. So, if your own real feeling is that I am not sure about any of these, um, questions, when you write it, don't pretend. (Pause) When writing is pretend, gee it looks bad. Um, people will try and sound as if, sound like will try and sound as if, sound like the teacher, when it's not really their own, um, ideas or their own . . . voice.

[Text is omitted]

T: You've got to practise your opinion, or say out what your opinion is or say to the, um, person next to you, I'm not sure of my opinion, um, so that before people have a chance to speak to the whole group they've just got to say what they think it is to the person next to them.

B. Talking about issues.

Later, one student Kay, is asked to answer a question on the teacher's sheet, namely 'Explain why the lynch mob disperses peacefully'.[9]

Kay: Well, Tom Robinson's in the jail and Atticus is sitting out the front in a chair reading the paper. Then, the lynch mob turns up and they're there to get Tom Robinson to hang him right there and then so, because they don't like him and because they don't believe he's right and they think he's lying. And

Scout and her two little friends, whoever they are, turned up, and, then isn't there? . . . and Scout starts talking to the lynch mob as if they're completely rational and it's just an everyday conversation and they realise what they're doing is wrong and then they just leave.

T: Right. OK, ah, take, ah, that's perfect, ah, take thirty seconds to explain to the person next to you why it is that they do it. (Students talk among themselves, but this is difficult to record.)

T: (pause, as he looks around the group to select a student) Thanks Kristina.

Kristina: OK, um, I'm not sure, but it might have had something to do with the fact that Scout was just, as Kay said, was talking to them rationally and made them think for a moment, exactly what they were doing. And so they just had doubts about it or something along those lines anyway. And that's it.

T: Anybody want to add anything to that? (Pause) OK, fine.

SOME RESOURCES IN WHICH THE TWO REGISTERS ARE REALIZED IN THE CURRICULUM ACTIVITY: THINKING ABOUT ISSUES

A. Opening: setting pedagogical purposes and directions realized in:

(i) clusters of textual theme choices to point directions and build continuity (OK) plus some imperatives (*look this way*)

(ii) behavioural and verbal processes to establish desired behaviours plus, interpersonally, first person plural *we* to establish solidarity in a jointly undertaken task and second person plural *you* to direct student behaviour:

we're going to have a talk about those (questions) (behavioural)

I'm going to show you (verbal process) how I want you

to write about them (behavioural process)

(ii) identifying processes to establish tasks: the purpose of this section is for [[you to show [[yourself thinking about the issues [[raised in *To Kill a Mockingbird.*]]]]]]

[[(a genuine response)]] is one [[in which it is clear the writer is true to his or her own feelings about the book [[and writes a response with conviction]]]]

(iii) behavioural process to establish teacher expectation: the assessor looks for sensitivity to the complexities of the situation

(iv) frequent use of interpersonal metaphor to establish what students must do, and where the congruent meaning is 'you must':

I want people to say . . .

I want Kay to set the scene . . .

I want everybody to ah, turn to their partners and say what they think

(v) some congruent expression of teacher requirements for desired behaviour, using high modality:

you've got to practise your opinion . . .

(vi) frequent attitudinal expression in various lexical choices (shown in bold):

in English the assessor looks for a genuine response

when writing is pretend, gee it looks bad

The teacher's language for regulaton is forceful, and strong claims are made about the functions of the English classroom and the obligation to express *genuine response*. It is in the teacher talk that we can see most clearly the criteria for evaluation. As was earlier indicated, it is the evaluation criteria that are crucial to the pedagogic device, for, writes Bernstein (1996: 50) 'evaluation condenses the meaning of the whole device'. The evaluation criteria here are strongly framed, despite the call for a unique voice in the students. The purpose is to develop certain moral positionings.

If we turn to the language in the subequent discourse where Kay outlines the scene and Kristina *says what she thinks*, we can note:

B. 'Setting the scene'

'Setting the scene', is realized in a recount (Rothery 1984) so called because it involves a series of clauses using various processes (mainly but not exclusively material) to build events (in bold) and a range of mainly additive, temporal and, to some extent, causal conjunctive relations (in italics) to link events as in their time sequence:

Well, Tom Robinson's in the jail
and Atticus **is sitting** out the front in a chair
reading the paper.
Then, the lynch mob turns up
and they're there
to get Tom Robinson
to hang him right there and then so . . .
because they **don't like** him
and because they **don't believe**
he's right
and they **think**
he**'s lying**.
And Scout and her two little friends, whoever they are, turned up,
and, then isn't there? . . .
and Scout **starts talking** to the lynch mob
as if they're completely rational
and it's just an everyday conversation
and they **realise**
[[what they're doing]] **is** wrong
and then they just **leave**.

C. 'Saying what one thinks', as undertaken by Kristina is most marked in instances of modality to build opinion:

I'm not sure
but it **might** have had something to do with the fact [[that Scout was just, as Kim said, was talking to them rationally and [[made them think for a moment exactly [[what they were doing]]]]]]

Students differed in their oral responses to questions, but what has been examined is reasonably representative. The usual response of the students was to offer a recount of the events in the novel, involving simple reconstruction. No interpretation of the events was offered, and hence there was no moral positioning involved.

This observation need not surprise. Reading a novel involves learning to interpret it in a manner, at least initially, consistent with its themes and ideologies. Development of an independent – perhaps a resistant – reader position will depend in part upon understanding the position against which an independent and/or resistant position is to be defined. But the ideology of the teacher suggests a view that personal, and hence presumably independent, responses or interpretations are sought. This matter is of concern, not because the teacher is unusual (anecdotal evidence suggests he is very orthodox in his commitment to the development of personal responses to literature) but because the ideology confuses teacher and student. English studies, like other studies in the curriculum, seek to develop pedagogic subjects who take up particular values and adopt particular perspectives upon human activity. These are neither as far reaching nor as capable of independent expression as the commitment to individual self-expression would have teacher or student believe. In the specific instance of the novel *To Kill a Mockingbird,* there is a quite finite range of interpretations that the novel would allow, or that the teacher would tolerate. It will be better when English teachers are encouraged to abandon the commitment to an ideology of self-expression that is at best confusing, and at worst, dishonest. Abandonment of the ideology will cause English teachers to turn away from personal response, and direct attention to the ways the literary piece is constructed, and hence to the ways students might learn to read, interpret, and, where appropriate, challenge its values.

The absence of a strong sense of interpretation in the girls' talk was partly a feature of the fact that they were functioning in the oral mode. With the movement to the written mode there was a shift, so that events were given a moral significance.

WRITING ABOUT ISSUES

We will look at Max's written answer to the question 'Explain why the lynch mob disperses'. Max's success in writing as he does is a measure that he is appropriately apprenticed into taking up the moral position upon the events of the novel.

The Lynch Mob

When the lynch mob arrived at the jail they were hell bent on killing or at least causing Tom Robinson serious injury. Their deep set prejudice had led them to believe that any black man accused of causing 'white folk' harm did not deserve

a trial to prove whether or not he was innocent and came looking for Tom
Robinson in order to deal out their own form of justice.

But an innocent little girl made them see reason. Not knowing why the mob
had come to the jail Scout began innocently chatting with a man she recognized in the crowd, Mr Walter Cunningham, who she assumed was a reasonable
human being. Mr Cunningham does not acknowledge Scout but when he
finally acknowledges Scout he has come to see reason.

Mr Cunningham sees reason because Scout unknowingly has made him see it
by treating Mr Cunningham as a reasonable human being and by doing so has
made Mr Cunningham and the men actually think and thus see through their
prejudice and realise that any reasonable person would not deny anyone the
chance to prove their innocence.

Thus Scout not only made Mr Cunningham see reason but the rest of the
mob as well so when Mr Cunningham said 'let's clear' the mob dispersed and a
little girl's innocence had saved a man's life.

Max does not retell the events. Rather, he creates a moral tale. In Bernstein's
terms, he has acquired the instructional rules, as well as the evaluation
criteria. There are several uses of abstraction. Often the abstractions depend
on instances of grammatical metaphor (Halliday 1994: 342–67; Martin 1992:
406–17): instances, that is, in which the congruent realization of a meaning is
transferred or made metaphorical, where this is often a condition of the shift
from speech to writing. (See Rose, Chapter 8 of this volume for a discussion
of grammatical metaphor in writing.) Some examples of grammatical
metaphor and their more congruent realizations in Max's text include:

metaphorical	congruent
they were hell bent on killing or at least causing Tom Robinson serious injury	they were determined to kill Tom Robinson or at least injure him seriously
their deep set prejudice had led them to believe that any black man [[accused of causing white folk harm]] did not deserve a trial	they were prejudiced against blacks and they therefore believed that any black man [[accused of harming white folk]] did not deserve a trial
(they) came looking for Tom Robinson in order to deal out their own form of justice	they came looking for Tom Robinson in order to punish him in their own way

Expressions such as *serious injury, their deep set prejudice* or *their own form of
justice* represent abstractions about the characters in the book and their
motivation. (Grammatical metaphor is not accounted for only in instances
in which a nominal group is created, a point not developed here.) Other
abstractions, not dependent on grammatical metaphor, include *a reasonable human being* or *a little girl's innocence,* or *the chance [[to prove their inno-*

cence]]. All the expressions reviewed make use of nominal groups, in which a great deal of experiential information is compressed. Phenomena of various kinds are created, around which Max can build his text's claims about the moral significance of the events.

Students feel the force of the moral imperative at work on them, and sometimes challenge it. In a later lesson a student, Peter, refused to have a view about an issue. The teacher, willing to discuss this, nonetheless advised Peter he was *complacent*, because he refused to care about important issues. Another student, Janet, then expressed a view held apparently by several others: *So we're supposed to spend 24 hours a day awake worrying about everything. Worrying about everything in the world, carrrying everything of the world on our shoulders, when we may have our own problems we need to deal with?* Later, she again challenged the teacher by saying that he had implied they must think about issues all the time, and she said, *Sometimes we need to block them out.* Later still, challenged by another student, the teacher said that English *asks you to be articulate,* and that an English student should have *a genuine response and at the same time be aware of the complexities of the situation.* Elsewhere he said that students should be *sensitive.* This was also challenged by a student (Kathleen), who said *But a genuine response might not be sensitive, you know what I mean? 'Cos you should have your own feelings and not be told to put sensitivity into them.*

It says much for the teacher that he showed himself open to the challenges. But he did not change his mind about the need for *sensitivity.* This is not surprising, since the pedagogic discourse in which the teacher was participating did not allow him to change his position on this, above all other points.

The Curriculum Closure: construction of judgement

In the final lessons, the students prepared for the task of writing essays about the novel. Three possible essay topics were given, and advice was provided about the need to structure the essay well, to provide evidence in support of argument, and the need for accuracy in paragraphing and spelling. One essay, judged successful (written by Catherine), will be shown. It is an instance of an essay type commonly found in subject English. Rothery (1994) terms it an interpretation genre, one of several responses genres she identified in secondary English essays. While following much of what she says of the elements of structure, I have called it a judgement genre, since its most marked feature, and surely its primary purpose, is that the student make judgements about life through literature.

The question provided and the essay are set out below. The elements of schematic structure are inserted. Instances of grammatical metaphor are marked in bold and four incidents in the book, identified in the Preview of Incidents, are numbered, the better to trace where each of these is taken up in greater detail in the body of the essay.

Question: "To Kill a Mockingbird" is a book about growing up. It shows children learning some important lessons about life. Do you agree?

Text Evaluation
Life is about growing up, learning new things, meeting different people, and
the book 'To Kill a Mockingbird' is about all of these. Many situations throughout the book show the children's reactions and emotions. Jem and Scout are
the main characters in the story and being children, **they view everything with a
fresh and unprejudiced outlook. They are guided by the steady hand of their
father** – Atticus Finch, the local lawyer and distinguished member of the town's
society. **He helps them deal with life's blows,** the good times and the bad.

Preview of incidents
Throughout the entire novel the children change and grow even when they
least expect to. The scenes that show this the best are (i) the scenes right from
when Scout notices Jem's mood swings, (ii) to watching the court case unravel,
(iii) to Scout reading the local newspapers and coming to the realisation of the
case, (iv) to her standing on the Radley porch.

Incident 1
One of the scenes where Scout notices Jem's strange behaviour was when Mr
Radley fills up the notch in the tree, where a mysterious stranger (Boo) had
been leaving special gifts for the children. Horrified, Jem asks Mr Radley if it
really was him who had filled up the tree with cement. The following is an
extraction from "To Kill a Mockingbird"- Page no. 68:

'Yes', he said. 'I filled it up.'
'Why'd you do it, sir?'
'Tree's dying. You plug 'em up with cement when they're sick.
You ought to know that Jem.'

Jem was still unsure as to why he did it and so
consulted Atticus (page 69):

'Is that tree dyin'?'
'Why no, son I don't think so. Look at the leaves,
they're all green and full, no brown patches anywhere.'
'It ain't even sick?'
'That tree's as healthy as you are, Jem. Why?'

Jem then understood that Mr Radley had probably
filled it up to stop Boo leaving things for them.
Scout noticed this and observed (extract from page 69 Chapter 7):

'He stood there until nightfall, and I waited for him. When we went in the
house I saw that he had been crying; his face was dirty in the right places, but I
thought it odd that I had not heard him.'

Incident 2
As the court case unravels it is apparent to the children that there is a lot of
prejudice and injustice amongst the people of Maycomb County. It is especially
noticeable against Tom Robinson and the Black community **because of the
accusation that Tom Robinson raped a white girl,** and when it comes down to a

black man's word against a white man's, no matter how bad the white person is and what people think of him, they'd win every time.

Incident 3

Jem gets very distraught by all of this as he finally comes to terms with it, in his own time, whereas Scout doesn't grasp the whole concept, until after reading Mr Underwood (the local editor of the Maycomb Tribune) write his opinion on Atticus Finch (from chapter 25, Page 245):

'Then Mr Underwood's meaning became clear: Atticus had used every tool available to free men to save Tom Robinson, but in the secret courts of men's hearts Atticus had no case. Tom was a dead man the minute Mayella Ewell opened her mouth and screamed.'

Incident 4

After Boo Radley rescues the children from Mayella Ewell's vengeful father, Bob Ewell, Scout meets him with tears in her eyes for the first time and the last time. She walks him home, and then, standing on the Radley porch, she recalls her father saying: 'You never really know a person until you stand in their shoes and walk around in them', and she then experiences empathy with Boo.

An extract in the last chapter on page 282 is very beautiful and poig(n)ant because Scout realises that Boo had given them so much and they had given nothing in return.

'Neighbours bring food with death and flowers with sickness and little things in between. Boo was our neighbour. He gave us two soap dolls, a broken watch and chain, a pair of good-luck pennies, and our lives. But neighbours give in return. We never put back into the tree what we took out of it: we had given him nothing and that made me sad.'

Later as Scout walks home she feels very old and sad and thinks that there is not much else she could possibly need to learn about – except maybe algebra.

Restatement of Text Evaluation

As previously shown **Scout and Jem's life is full (of) exuberant and detailed events**. They experience together sadness, knowledge, surprise, concern, and even wisdom.

Children take in all that's going on around them from all different sides, trying to soak it all up in one go, and then getting muddled a bit, but it is books like Harper Lee's 'To Kill a Mockingbird' that make both adults and children alike get a little closer to understanding one another.

Yet, it is agreeable that the novel 'To Kill a Mockingbird' is all about children growing up as that is what children do best. They try new things, figure stuff out, cope with their own struggles and the rest of the world's, while at the same time just try to have some adventure and little fun.

No linguistic analysis will be offered, in the interests of space. Suffice it to note that in the Text Evaluation the writer establishes a broad generalization about life and some information about the principal characters in the book.

Life is about growing up, learning new things, meeting different people, and the book "To Kill a Mockingbird" is about all of these.

Jem and Scout are identified as the *main characters*, and the role of their father in guiding them is also established.

The Preview of Text Incidents indicates four significant incidents, used to develop evidence later for the claims about children and growing up. The final element, the Restatement of the Evaluation, returns to the issues identified in the Text Evaluation, and finishes with the judgement on life:

> *Yet, it is agreeable that the novel 'To Kill a Mockingbird' is all about children growing up as that is what children do best. They try new things, figure stuff out, cope with their own struggles and the rest of the world's, while at the same time just try to have some adventure and little fun.*

This essay was not unlike some others collected from the students. Capacity to write such an essay is evidence that the student was successfully apprenticed to the ideal pedagogic subject position. We can see how the regulative register has disappeared from the written text, and only the instructional register remains. The writer has adopted the desired pedagogic subject position: that of one able to make generalizations about life, where these are informed by a concern for social justice, a disapproval of racial prejudice, and some sensitivity towards the children in the novel.

The logogenesis in the curriculum macrogenre

Much earlier, it was suggested that the macrogenre was marked by a logogenetic growth. The latter growth, it was suggested, was apparent in a developing capacity on the part of the students to offer moral judgement and generalization about life, where this was abstracted from the novel. The teacher's role was to model the making of such judgements, making clear the evaluation criteria by which the students would be judged.

Figure 6.3 shows the logogenesis in the classroom text. Linguistically, there is a series of moves, from reconstruction of event, to interpretation of characters' motives, to judgement on character, to judgement on significance of event, to judgement on the significance of the book, to judgement on life. For each of these linguistic moves, the figure uses extracts from the classroom text, shown in the various boxes. The first five extracts, ranging from 'Reconstruction of event' to 'Judgement on the significance of the book', are drawn from the opening genre, and most are produced by the teacher. Such expressions occur recursively throughout the text, and they are not uniquely a feature of the opening genre: they have a role in the Curriculum Activity, where the goal is reflection on issues. But the 'Judgement about life' comes in the culminating genre, and the generalizations about life that are offered are written by a student: *life is about growing up, learning new things, meeting different people* and *(growing up) is what children do best.*

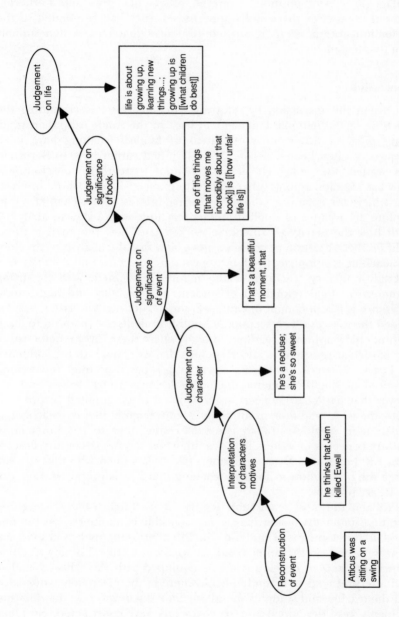

Figure 6.3 How grammar works: from Reconstruction to Interpretation to Abstraction about life

Judgement on life

life is about growing up, learning new things...; growing up is [[what children do best]]

Judgement on significance of book

one of the things [[that moves me incredibly about that book]] is [[how unfair life is]]

Judgement on significance of event

that's a beautiful moment, that

Judgement on character

he's a recluse; she's so sweet

Interpretation of characters motives

he thinks that Jem killed Ewell

Reconstruction of event

Atticus was sitting on a swing

Overall, we can see that the pedagogic device has done its work. Particular evaluation criteria have been made available throughout the classroom text. As we have seen, some students resisted adoption of the ideal pedagogic subject position. However, others like Max and Catherine showed themselves successfully apprenticed: they had responded to the evaluation criteria, shaping written responses that represented suitably moral statements.

Conclusion

We began this discussion by referring to controversies surrounding the teaching of the national language, at least in the Anglo-Australian tradition, much of this century. All areas of English teaching have been subjects of often heated debate. We also noted earlier how, so Bernstein has argued, the pedagogic device functions to regulate consciousness. This has led him, among other things, to pursue issues of whose interests are achieved in such regulation. A principal interest in this chapter was to explore an instance of English literary teaching, with a view to analysing both how the pedagogic discourse worked, and how the analysis threw light on the regulation of consciousness. Now that the analysis of the literary teaching is complete, it will be appropriate to return to these matters.

English literary teaching in the manner examined, with its strong commitment to development of students of sensibility and high moral positions, is not uncommon. Cranny-Francis (1996), cited earlier, has discussed the ways in which secondary English students are required to learn institutionally approved readings of texts, where these involve demonstrating particular sensibilities and responses that owe much to the influence of Leavis. Relatedly, Rothery (1991, 1994) has examined the writing required of English students, including literary critical essays, and has shown that particular subject positions need to be adopted in order to write these. A tradition in thinking about English literary teaching is apparent in Anglo-Australian contexts, owing most to the nineteenth-century concerns of writers like Arnold, whose twentieth-century descendant F.R. Leavis was. Despite numbers of scholars today who wish to challenge the orientation to English teaching that Leavis proposed, much of his legacy remains.

Probably the most remarkable feature of the English literary teaching tradition under discussion here is its ostensible commitment on the one hand, to development of students who can express themselves in independent ways, and on the other hand, its apparent eschewal of any teaching principles likely to develop students equipped with the skills to analyse and interpret texts independently. Nowhere in the macrogenre discussed did the teacher and students spend any time discussing how the different incidents were developed and/or characters were constructed. No metalanguage was needed to study the novel, because no theories to do with text construction were invoked. Yet a number of questions were worth asking, provided some principles for answering these were pursued. What linguistic resources were drawn upon by Harper Lee to create the world of her novel, and what particular values and positions was it necessary to accept if one were to understand and endorse what she wrote? How likely was it, for example, that a child like Scout should actually prevent a mob of angry men from lynching a black man they thought guilty of rape? What was it about the ways this incident was told that persuaded the reader to believe in it – if indeed the reader did? These and other questions might take the students into development of more critical capacities in considering literary texts than were in fact displayed.

As it was, in the classroom text considered, the student Catherine constructed her final essay skilfully, creating a pedagogic subject position for herself that accorded with the evaluation criteria. Whether the opinions she expressed were her 'own' we can never tell with any certainty, although the rather banal note on which she concluded her essay suggested she was striving for an effect to please the teacher (*(growing up) is what children do best*). She had accepted the evaluation criteria, and had learned to express opinions in a manner endorsed in much mainstream English teaching. However, the processes by which she arrived at them remained largely implicit, and hence not readily subject to scrutiny. Where this is so, the student is to that extent dispossessed, able it would seem faithfully to produce acceptable positions, yet not conscious that such positions are themselves constructs, and as such, open to review and perhaps to challenge.

Other subjects, such as science and geography referred to earlier, when well taught, are more overt about the technical language they use and about the models of experience and phenomena they construct. They are to that extent always more open to potential challenge, if only because they lay their meaning making on the line. A school study that leaves issues of how it constructs its meanings and hence its pedagogic subject positions so diffuse and ill defined, always privileges those most enabled by life experience and their associated coding orientations to interpret the implicit meanings involved. (Williams this volume Chapter 4, pursues a related point.)

The pedagogic device serves to regulate consciousness, so Bernstein claims, and he notes it is 'a condition for the production, reproduction and transformation of culture' (1996: 52). Surely it can be no accident that the national language – that resource in which so much is constructed that is fundamental to the maintenance and transformation of culture – is often so poorly served pedagogically. The interests of the state are involved in pedagogic practices that leave the national language not well understood, for where people are not aware of how language works to construct the various positions available to them, they are less likely to challenge those positions. Small wonder then, that English language and literary teaching remain the subject of significant debate. At some level, generally not well understood in English-speaking cultures, battles rage for control of the English curriculum, for it is involved in the regulation of consciousness.

The national English curriculum will probably always be a volatile site for argument and challenge (see Misson 1996 for a related discussion). We earlier noted that Bernstein suggests the state, through its official recontextualizing field, is seeking to weaken the more local pedagogic recontextualizing field, and we can conclude that the adoption of national curriculum statements, including English statements, are an important measure of this attempt. Yet he also suggests that the pedagogic device that lies behind the pedagogic endeavour generally is not determinist (Bernstein, 1996, 52), so that the endeavour is never wholly within the control of the state. There are at least two reasons why the pedagogic device is not determinist, the one internal, the other external. Of the internal reason, Bernstein notes that in that the device works to control the unthinkable, it always makes possible the unthinkable as well. As for the external reason, Bernstein notes that 'the distribution of power which speaks through the device creates potential sites of challenge and opposition' (Bernstein 1996: 52).

Notes

1 The research reported in this chapter was funded by the Australian Research Council.
2 The 1988 report, covering 5 to 11 years was subsumed into the report, dated 1989, dealing with 5 to 16 years. A further draft proposed curriculum was produced in 1994, and in 1995 the School Curriculum and Assessment Authority produced a document 'English in the National Curriculum'. Some of the issues raised in this series of revized versions are discussed in Protherough and King (eds) 1995.
3 Cox (1994; 30) notes that Marenbon, a member of the right wing Centre for Policy Studies, declared that by age 16, 'children should have read Bacon, Dryden, Pope, Milton and Dr Johnson'.
4 Bernstein argues that the pedagogic device operates in relationships other than those in schools, but this discussion is confined to schooling.
5 In the following discussion some critique of teaching practices is offered. However, I intend no criticism of the teacher. I am very grateful to both teacher and students for allowing me to do the research reported.
6 All names used in the classroom text are pseudonyms.
7 The notations [[ ]] indicate an embedded clause.
8 Ethics within a university study no doubt has a technical language, and this is one indication of how different it is from ethics in the school English classroom.
9 A lynch mob comes to the jail to kill Tom Robinson, but Scout causes the mob to withdraw without harming him.

References

Arnold, M. (1869) *Culture and Anarchy: An Essay in Political and Social Criticism.* London: Nelson.
Belsey, C. (1980) *Critical Practice.* London: New York.
Bernstein, B. (1975) *Class, Codes and Control, Vol. 3: Towards a Theory of Educational*

Transmissions. London: Routledge & Kegan Paul.

Bernstein, B. (1990), *Class, Codes and Control, vol. 4: The Structuring of Pedagogic Discourse.* London: Routledge.

Bernstein, B. (1996) *Pedagogy, Symbolic Control and Identity: Theory, Research, Critique.* London: Taylor & Francis.

Britton, J. and Squires, J. (1975) 'Foreword'. In J. Dixon, *Growth through English* (3rd edn) London: NATE and Oxford University Press, vii–xviii.

Butt, D., Fahey, R., Spinks, S. and Yallop, C. (1995) *Using Functional Grammar: An Explorer's Guide.* Sydney: National Centre for English Language Teaching & Research.

Cameron, D. and Bourne, J. (1998), 'No common ground: Kingman, grammar and the nation', *Language and Education*, 2 (3), 147–60.

Carter, R. (1993), 'Keywords: discourses about language and literacy'. In F. Christie (ed.), *Literacy: International Literacy Special. Education Australia*, 19–20: 8–10.

Carter, R. (1996) 'Politics and knowledge about language: the LINC project'. In R. Hasan and G. Williams (eds), *Literacy in Society.* London: Longman, 1–28.

Christie, F. (1989) 'Curriculum genres in early childhood education: a case study in writing development'. Unpublished PhD thesis, University of Sydney.

Christie, F. (1991) 'First and second order registers in education'. In E. Ventola (ed.), *Functional and Systemic Linguistics: Approaches and Uses.* Berlin: Walter de Gruyter, 235–56.

Christie, F. (1995) 'Pedagogic discourse in the primary school', *Linguistics and Education*, 3 (7), 221–42.

Christie, F. (1996) *The Pedagogic Discourse of Secondary School Social Sciences: Geography.* Melbourne: University of Melbourne Press.

Christie, F. (1997) 'Curriculum genres as forms of initiation into a culture'. In F. Christie and J.R. Martin (eds), *Genres and Institutions: Social Processes in the Workplace and School.* London: Cassell, 134–60.

Christie, F. (1998) 'Science and apprenticeship: the pedagogic discourse', in J.R. Martin and R. Veel (eds), *Reading Science: Critical and Functional Perspectives on Discourses of Science.* London, Routledge.

Christie, F., Devlin, B., Freebody, P., Luke, A., Martin, J., Threadgold, T., and Walton, C. (1991) *Teaching English Literacy: A Project of National Significance on the Preservice Preparation of Teachers to Teach English Literacy.* Canberra: Department of Employment, Education and Training/Darwin: Northern Territories University.

Christie, F. and Martin, J.R. (eds) (1997) *Genres and Institutions: Social Processes in the Workplace and School.* London: Cassell.

Cox, B. (1994) 'The national curriculum in English'. In S. Brindley (ed.), *Teaching English.* London: Routledge, 25–30.

Cox National Curriculum English Working Group (1989) *English for Ages 5 to 16: Proposals of the Secretary of State for Education and Science and the Secretary of State for Wales.* London: Department of Education and Science and the Welsh Office.

Cranny-Francis, A. (1996) 'Technology and/or weapon: the discipline of reading in the secondary classroom'. In R. Hasan and G. Williams (eds), *Literacy in Society.* London: Longman, 172–90.

Eggins, S. and Martin, J.R. (1997) 'Genres and registers of discourse'. In T. van Dijk (ed.), *Discourse as Structure and Process.* London: Sage, 230–56.

Eggins, S. and Slade, D. (1997) *Analysing Casual Conversation.* London: Cassell.

Gerot, L. and Wignell, P. (1994) *Making Sense of Functional Grammar.* Sydney: Antipodean Educational Enterprises.

Halliday, M.A.K. (1979) 'Modes of meaning and modes of saying'. In D.J. Allerton, E. Carney and D. Holdcroft (eds), *Function and Context in Linguistic Analysis: Essays Offered to William Haas.* Cambridge: Cambridge University Press, 57–79.

Halliday, M.A.K. (1981) 'Types of structure'. In M.A.K. Halliday and J.R. Martin (eds), *Readings in Systemic Linguistics*. London: Batsford, 29–41.

Halliday, M.A.K. (1982) 'How is a text like a clause?' In S. Allen (ed.), *Text Processing: Text Analysis and Generation, Text Typology and Attribution* (Proceedings of Nobel Symposium 51). Stockholm: Almqvist & Wiksell, 209–247.

Halliday, M.A.K. (1994) *An Introduction to Functional Grammar* (2nd edn). London: Arnold.

Halliday, M.A.K. and Martin, J.R. (1993) *Writing Science: Literacy and Discursive Power*. London: Falmer Press.

Hunter, I. (1994) 'Four anxieties about English', *Interpretations*, 27 (3) 1–19.

Kingman Report (1988) 'Report of the Committee of Inquiry into the Teaching of English Language'. Committee chaired by Sir John Kingman. London: HMSO.

Leavis, F.R. (1975) *The Living Principle: 'English' as a Discipline of Thought*. London: Chatto & Windus.

Lock, G. (1996) *Functional English Grammar: An Introduction for Second Language Teachers*. Cambridge: Cambridge University Press.

Macken-Horarik, M. (1995) 'Modelling the limitations, demands, possibilities of English, *Interpretations*, 28 (3), 33–61.

Martin, J.R. (1992) *English Text: System and Structure*. The Hague: Benjamins.

Martin, J.R., Matthiessen, C. and Painter, C. (1997) *Working with Functional Grammar*. London: Arnold.

Martin, J.R. and Veel, R. (1998) *Reading Science: Critical and Functional Perpectives of Discourses of Science*. London: Routledge.

Matthiessen, C . (1988) 'Representational issues in systemic functional grammar'. In J.D. Benson and W.S. Greaves (eds), *Systemic Functional Approaches to Discourse: Selected Papers from the Twelfth International Systemic Workshop*. Norwood, NJ: Ablex, 136–75.

Matthiessen, C. (1992) 'Interpreting the textual metafunction'. In M. Davies and L. Ravelli (eds), *Advances in Systemic: Linguistics. Recent Theory and Practice*. London: Pinter, 37–81.

Misson, R. (1996) 'Complex mundanity: four assertions about English', *Interpretations*, 29(3), 14–28.

Misson, R. (1998) 'Telling tales out of school'. In F. Christie and R. Misson (eds), *Literacy and Schooling*. London: Routledge.

Protherough, R. and King, P. (1995) *The Challenge of English in the National Curriculum*. London: Routledge.

Rothery, J. (1984) 'The development of genres: primary to junior secondary school'. In F. Christie (ed.), *Deakin B.Ed. Study Guide: Children Writing*. Geelong: Deakin University, 67–114.

Rothery, J. (1991) 'Developing critical literacy through systemic functional linguistics: an analysis of the 'hidden' curriculum for writing in junior secondary English in New South Wales'. Paper given at the Second Australian Systemic Functional Linguistics Conference, University of Queensland, 11–13 January.

Rothery, J. (1994) *Exploring Literacy in School English*. Sydney: Disadvantaged Schools Program and NSW Department of School Education.

Rothery, J. and Christie, F. (1995) 'The craft of writing narrative', *Interpretations*, 28 (3), 77–96.

Rothery, J. and Stenglin, M. (1997) 'Entertaining and instructing: exploring experience through story'. In F. Christie and J.R. Martin (eds), *Genre and Institutions*. London: Cassell, 231–63.

Thompson, G. (1996) *Introducing Functional Grammar*. London: Arnold.

Ventola, E. (1987) *The Structure of Social Interaction*. London: Pinter.

West, A. (1994) 'The centrality of literature'. In S. Brindley (ed.), *Teaching English*. London: Routledge in association with the Open University, 124–132.

7   Language, knowledge and authority in school mathematics

Robert Veel

For the academic linguist and educational sociologist, the language of mathematics fascinates. It is a language unlike any other: an amalgam of symbols and images with spoken and written English, which constructs forms of knowledge – ways of modelling the world – which are unlike any other and which have seemingly endless applications. In the mathematics classroom, language is used to construct knowledge and regulate access to that knowledge in ways totally different from those used in other pedagogical contexts.

For language educators, those with the job of sharing knowledge about language with teachers and students, the language of mathematics terrifies. Its very uniqueness means that one cannot bring in understandings about language from other fields of activity. There are no essays to write in mathematics, no great chunks of written prose in textbooks. Moreover, the whole field of mathematics education is so strongly insulated from other fields that the language educator often suffers from 'impostor syndrome', feeling out-of-place in the company of those who control the arcane and mysterious language of mathematics.

Like the language itself, *research* on the language of mathematics is itself very different from research on other areas of language education. Most descriptions of mathematical language are to be found in journals of mathematics education, not in journals of language education. To the mathematician, the research on mathematical language in language education journals frequently appears to be woefully inadequate in its understanding of mathematical knowledge. To the linguist, the research in mathematics journals seems horribly simplistic in the role it assigns to language in learning. The result of all this is that language educators and mathematicians rarely talk to one another.

This chapter takes steps towards synthesizing these two areas of concern: that the nature of mathematical knowledge be well understood and that the role of language in constructing and exchanging this knowledge be fully appreciated. The educational sociology developed by Basil Bernstein and his colleagues over the last thirty or so years (Bernstein 1977, 1990, 1996) and the systemic-functional linguistics (SFL) developed by Michael Halliday and his colleagues over a similar period (Eggins 1994; Halliday 1977, 1994; Halliday and Hasan 1985; Martin 1992; Mattheissen 1996) provide useful models for attempting this synthesis. Bernstein's sociology has as one of its central concerns the role of language in constructing knowledge through pedagogical discourse. Hallidayan linguistics is particularly sensitive to the dialectical relationship between forms of language and types of social context. Bernstein's sociology and Halliday's linguistics have, of course, been used together to synthesize the linguistic and sociological concerns of a number of other sites of pedagogical activity, including the primary school classroom (see Williams, Chapter 4, and Christie, Chapter 5 this volume), early schooling (Williams 1995) and mother/child interaction (Hasan 1996).

The first part of the chapter identifies and describes some of the distinctive features of language in the mathematics classroom, using descriptions from SFL. The texts and descriptions are taken from research conducted between 1992 and 1996 in socio-economically disadvantaged secondary schools in the inner suburbs of Sydney. The second part reflects on the nature of mathematical discourse as it is recontextualized in secondary schools using some of the insights of Bernstein's sociology.

Linguistic perspectives on mathematical discourse

There is much that can be, and has been, said about the linguistic forms to be found in mathematical texts and it is not intended to try and report on all aspects of mathematical language here. It is possible, however, to enumerate a number of linguistic features which make the kind of language used in mathematics classrooms distinctive. It should be noted that the discussion below is of limited scope and in no way should be considered a complete account of the language of mathematics. The discussion is limited in at least two ways. First, it is concerned mainly with how the language of mathematics is different from the language used to explore and construct other bodies of knowledge in the school context. Thus the meaning of 'distinctive' linguistic features is limited here to those linguistic features which make the language of mathematics different from the language of other school disciplines. There has been considerable research within SFL of the specific language features of a range of schools subjects which can be contrasted with the language of school mathematics. These include English (Cranny-Francis 1996; Martin 1996; Rothery 1994, 1996), geography (van Leeuwen and Humphrey 1996), history (Veel and Coffin 1996) and science (Martin 1993; Veel 1997, 1998). There are many other possible ways of describing the 'salience' or 'distinctiveness' of mathematical language in schools – how it is different from the language of university and research mathematics (i.e. the pressures put on language through pedagogical recontextualization), how it is different from 'everyday' language in non-pedagogical contexts (i.e. the pressures of institutional recontextualization), how it is different from child language (i.e. ontological pressures), gender, etc. Second, the discussion of mathematical text is restricted to the use of spoken and written language in mathematical 'texts'. It has been convincingly argued (Kress and van Leeuwen 1996, Lemke 1998, McInnes and Murison 1992, O'Halloran 1996) that mathematical texts are 'multimodal', consisting of semiotically rich configurations of images, diagrams and physical activity as well as language. The meaning potential of multimodal mathematical text is thus far greater than that of any single element viewed in isolation, although Hasan (1996) has argued convincingly for the pre-eminent role of language in the great majority of multimodal texts, especially those used in schooling. Figure 7.1 illustrates a multimodal text in the written medium. Thus the claims being made here about mathematical language are necessarily only part of the overall picture, albeit an essential part.

The distinctive linguistic features to be discussed here are:

● The predominance of teacher spoken language
● The predominance of distinctive patterns of spoken language interaction
● The technical fields of knowledge construed through spoken and written language
● The hierarchical ordering of mathematical concepts through language
● The gap between student use of mathematical language and teacher/ textbook use of mathematical language

The predominance of teacher spoken language

Compared to other subject areas in the secondary school, mathematics relies extraordinarily on spoken language as the channel of communication for construing uncommonsense mathematical knowledge.[1] Whereas most other subject areas rely on an extensive canon of written prose (to be found in textbooks, encyclopedias and school libraries) to provide an impression of the stability and permanence of knowledge, this is noticeably absent in mathematics. Textbooks tend to be pastiches of repetitive activities and fragments of knowledge, and encyclopedia-style reference works are not present in the school context.

In a great number of mathematics classrooms there is a distinctive division of 'semiotic labour' between the spoken and the written modes. The written mode, through the use of the blackboard or (occasionally) the overhead projector, is mainly used for *symbolic* and *visual* construals of mathematical knowledge. The teacher's spoken language, on the other hand, provides a commentary on the visual and symbolic language being used on the blackboard. This commentary is often a vital aspect of the teaching situation, for it allows teachers to explain the meaning of the highly elaborated code of the symbolic and visual construals and to make links between students' (usually more 'everyday') construals of knowledge

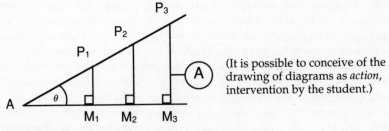

(It is possible to conceive of the drawing of diagrams as *action*, intervention by the student.)

Cosine Ratio

Since the triangles AP_1M_1, AP_2M_2 and AP_3M_3 are similar.

These ratios are equal.

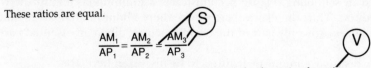

$$\frac{AM_1}{AP_1} = \frac{AM_2}{AP_2} = \frac{AM_3}{AP_3}$$

This meanshat for the acute angleθ in a right triangle of any size the ratio

$$\frac{\text{adjacent side}}{\text{hypotenuse}}$$

always has the same value.

This ratio is called the cosine ratio of angle θ.

In any right triangle the ratio

$$\frac{\text{adjacent side}}{\text{hypotenuse}}$$

for any acute angle is called the cosine ratio of that angle.

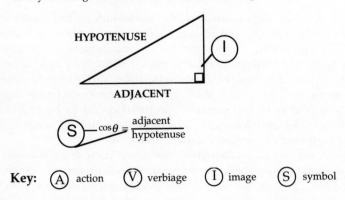

Key: (A) action   (V) verbiage   (I) image   (S) symbol

Figure 7.1 Multimodal semiosis in written mathematical text (from McInnes and Murison 1992: 12)

and those officially recognized in the pedagogic field. It is spoken language which provides the link between the symbolic and visual representations for students, and is therefore a powerful agent in the learning process. Text 1 exemplifies the 'bridging' role played by spoken language in mathematics classrooms. The class is one of senior students (16 to 17), studying circle geometry and the teacher is explaining the meaning of radians as a unit of measurement.

Text 1

> If we look at any circle, normally we take the unit circle to keep it simple. Any circle will do, if we draw in two radii, then we have the section of circumference between those two radii that is an arc length, and we have the angle subtended by that arc length at the centre of the circle, so we have that length we call it s, a section of the arc and the angle β at the centre of the circle. When we talk about a radian and we want to define what it means we want a radian to be a relationship between the length on the circumference, an arc length and the angle at the centre. Alright, so instead of talking about degrees and how much of a rotation we make, we're talking about this angle in terms of, if this is the angle how big will the arc length be, and for the unit circle we want it to be to correspond one to one, we want to say if this is one radian, then arc, that arc length is three. On any other circle, you take the arc length divided by what the radius is, if we're taking the radius to be one we don't have to worry about that, so it's a ratio between the arc length and the radius. Now, in our case, (sound of chalk) . . . one radian (sound of chalk) . . . subtends an arc (sound of chalk) . . . of length one unit (sound of chalk) . . . on the unit circle.

This reliance on the spoken mode has important social and linguistic consequences. It privileges particular forms of interaction in mathematics classrooms and it encourages 'strongly framed' teaching sequences. Over time, it has probably limited the kinds of knowledge written texts can construe and, therefore, what learners can achieve without access to a living, talking teacher. Text 2 illustrates what happens when a publisher attempts to provide through written language what a teacher will normally do in spoken language. The shift from the spoken to the written mode turns what is usually a fairly straightforward technique in algebra into an almost impenetrable theoretical piece. The text comes from a book which was designed for independent learning and aimed at adults who have little formal education in mathematics!

Text 2

Be an expert
Study this definition

An axiom is a general statement which is accepted as true without proof.

Axiom 1: If equal quantities are added to equal quantities, the sums are equal.

This is called the addition *axiom.*

The addition axiom is used in solving an equation such as:

$$x - 3 = 7$$

To solve this equation we must first find a value of x that will make the equation a true statement when substituted for the unknown quantity 'x'. Let us deal with the left hand member in such a way that all numerical terms are removed, leaving only the letter x. If we add $+3$ to -3, the sum is o (zero). But, to maintain our mathematical balance, we must also add $+3$ to the right member.

$$x - 3 = 7$$
$$+3 = +3$$
$$x = 10$$

By adding an equal value to both sides of the equation, we have changed it to an *equivalent* equation which is simpler in form and, in this problem, gives us the root.

In order to be certain, we must check the value which we found, by substituting it into the original equation.

$$x - 3 = 7$$
$$10 - 3 = 7$$
$$7 = 7$$

(Herrick *et al.* 1962: 126)

The predominance of distinctive patterns of spoken language interaction

When one examines the spoken language of mathematics classrooms a second distinctive feature emerges. In those parts of the lesson where the spoken language consists of teacher-student dialogue, the interaction tends to be of a highly ritualized form, relying heavily on Input-Response-Evaluation (IRE) exchanges of the type first identified by Sinclair and Coulthard (1975). Extended sequences of IRE exchanges render the spoken interaction into a kind of catechism in which mathematical facts, previously introduced by the teacher, are elicited from students and then evaluated. The following extract from Text 3 (below) illustrates a typical IRE exchange:

Input:	T:	If I have something multiplied together, what do I do to get rid of it?
Response:	Ps:	Divide.
Evaluation:	T:	Divide.

As researchers note, the question asked by the teacher is not a 'genuine' one, in the sense that the teacher is not seeking information which she does not already know.[2] Thus the student's role is typically one of a catechistic parrot, rather than a genuine 'knower'.

Extending this analysis beyond IRE sequences, Martin (1992: 31–91), in his examination of 'negotiation' in spoken interaction, distinguishes between 'primary' knowers and actors (encoded in the analysis as K1 or A1) and 'secondary' knowers and actors (encoded as K2, A2). Drawing on research by Ventola (1987), Martin further distinguishes other kinds of conversational moves in terms of whether they are 'delayed'(d), 'follow-up'(f), 'confirmation'(cf), reconfirmation (rcf) or 'clarification (cl). In Martin's analysis, the IRE sequence is coded in the following way:

dK1:	T:	If I have something multiplied together, what do I do to get rid of it?
K2:	Ps:	Divide.
K1:	T:	Divide.

Thus for Martin it is in the 'evaluation' move of the IRE that the teacher declares herself to be the primary knower – the one with the answers. Even though students do provide information, the teacher's evaluation move relegates them to the role of 'secondary knowers'. Martin's analysis allows us to move beyond individual IRE sequences and see how conversational roles are ascribed in extended pieces of interaction. Text 3 is an excerpt from an extended piece of classroom interaction, coded using Martin's analysis.

Text 3 (from a Year 11 mathematics lesson)

Move	Analysis	Text	
1.	**dK1**	T:	What do I mean by opposite operations?
2.	**cf**	P:	Pardon?
3.	**rcf**	T:	What do I mean by opposite operations?
4.	**K2**	P:	It's opposite.
5.	**K1**	T:	Yeah,
6.	**dK1**		so if I have plus what do I do?
7.	**K2**	Ps:	Minus.
8.	**K1**	T:	Okay,
9.	**K1**		that's what I mean by opposite operations.
10.	**K2**	P:	So you're going to have to take . . .
11.	**dK1**	T:	If I have something multiplied together, what do I do to get rid of it?
12.	**K2**	Ps:	Divide.
13.	**K1**	T:	Divide. All right,
14.	**K1**		so that's what I mean by opposite operations.
15.	**K2**	P:	Are you going to put S equals a certain number and D equals a certain number?
16.	**K1**	T:	No, I'm not going to substitute yet.
17.	**K1**		What I'm going to do is . . .
18.	**dK1**		All right, Jim you tell me what the subject of that formula is?
19.	**cf**	P:	Subject?
20.	**rcf**	T:	Mmmm.

21.	**dK1**		What's the subject? Which pronumeral is the subject?
22.	**K2**	P:	*S*
23.	**K1**	T:	*S*

In this extract we see that the teacher maintains the primary knower (K1) role in 14 of the 23 moves. Students maintain the secondary knower (K2) role in 8 of the 23 moves. Whenever the students do ask 'genuine questions' (i.e where their K2 move is not preceded by a dK1 move by the teacher), the teacher either ignores the question (move 10) or very quickly ends the exchange and moves on to another (moves 15–17).

The long-term result of the unvaried use of interaction patterns such as that in Text 3 is that students are rarely given the opportunity to occupy the role of the 'knowers' or 'producers' of mathematical knowledge. They do not get the chance to construct extended and grammatically complex text (such as Text 1) in which generalized mathematical ideas are combined with measurable quantities in order to spin a rich web of mathematical knowledge. Not only does this interaction pattern accentuate the power difference between teacher and student, it creates serious problems for many students when they are placed in situations, such as written exams, where they *do* have to produce mathematical text independently. Unfortunately for students, it is precisely in these situations, and not in spoken classroom interaction, that we tend to assess them.

How have these catechistic kinds of spoken interaction in mathematics come about? In part they are a result of general traditions of classroom teaching, a vestige of more overtly authoritarian relationships between teachers and students. In part they arise from the heavy reliance on the spoken mode for construing knowledge. Careful control must be maintained over the spoken interaction in order for the desired kinds of meanings to be construed, for there can be no recourse to canonical written texts. In part they are due to the 'strongly classified' nature of mathematical knowledge itself (see below), where facts and ideas are seen as discrete units of knowledge.

The technical fields of knowledge construed through spoken and written language

As in many areas of technical knowledge, language is used in mathematics to construe systematically organized, technical bodies of knowledge. Many people will readily recognize a distinctive **technical lexis** in mathematics, but there are also a number of other, mainly grammatical, devices through which knowledge is construed. These include **grammatical metaphor**, **relational clauses** and a very particular use of the resources of the **nominal group**. We will examine each of these briefly.

Technical lexis

As Halliday (1977: 195–6) notes, technical lexis in mathematics consists both of items that have uniquely technical meaning and the re-use of non-technical items as technical lexis. Items with a uniquely technical meaning are usually latinate (*parallel, denominator, bisect, quadrilateral*). Because of their unique technical meaning these items cause little confusion for students (although they may still be difficult to learn). The re-use of non-technical items as technical lexis occurs particularly in items which describe mathematical processes (*find, simplify, integrate, get, reduce, power, average*) and require students to distinguish between the meaning of these items in mathematical fields of activity and their meaning in non-mathematical fields.[3] Most mathematics teachers are aware of the potential difficulties presented by technical lexis and both introduce and reinforce this lexis with great care.

GRAMMATICAL METAPHOR

Grammatical metaphor refers to the re-configuration of meanings in text, where more 'congruent' linguistic representations of the world (events represented through verbs/verb groups; sequences and logical relationships represented through conjunctions; qualities through adjectives) are recast for the purposes of creating new knowledge, placing objects and events in relationships to one another that are not necessarily congruent with our everyday experience of the world (events and qualities represented as nouns; logical relationships as verbs). The use of grammatical metaphor in science to create chains of causality and technical categories has been explored in considerable detail by Halliday (Halliday 1993b, 1998) and the reader is referred to Halliday's work for further discussion of the formal properties and functions of grammatical metaphor.

Grammatical metaphor is certainly a prominent linguistic feature of mathematical text, as it is for scientific discourse. The following example illustrates grammatical metaphor in mathematics:

> Which of the following is the best *estimate* for the *weight* of a hen's egg?
>
> (New South Wales Board of Studies, 1990: 3)

In this example two 'virtual entities' are created through grammatical metaphor: *estimate* (the result of the process of estimating) and *weight* (a measure of how much something weighs). Both terms are grammatically metaphorical because they have more congruent forms in the verbs 'to estimate' and 'to weigh'. The usefulness of grammatical metaphor for mathematical discourse comes not simply from the creation of two previously non-existent entities, but because, once created, words such as 'estimate' and 'weight' can then be put into new relationships with one another, and with other elements, through the grammar of the clause. Hence we are able to construe a nominal group (see below) 'the best estimate for the weight of a hen's egg' which is itself part of a larger structure, the clause '*Which of the following is the best estimate for the weight of a hen's egg?*'

Although grammatical metaphor is a feature of many formally organized bodies of knowledge, there are some particular functions of grammatical metaphor which are emphasized in mathematics.[4] One of these is the creation of **quantifiable entities** for the purposes of calculation. Once an event or a quality has been turned into a 'thing', a noun, it can generally be counted. Consider, for example, the idea of 'change' in mathematics. Represented congruently, as a verb (to change), there are limited resources for describing change in a mathematically salient fashion:

> *it changes a lot*
> *it changes often*
> *it changes every two hours*

Once we have re-construed the event as a *thing* (the change), it becomes possible to quantify the amount of change:

> *25% change*
> *50% change*
> *70% change*

Moreover, the newly created entity can be combined with other entities (actual or virtual) to realize new meanings:

> *rate of change*
> *increasing rate of change*
> *different rate of change between men and women*
> *the change differential according to gender*

Some areas of mathematics, such as calculus, would be literally unthinkable without grammatical metaphor.

Another characteristic use of grammatical metaphor in mathematics is **the reification of mathematical activities as topic areas, or concepts**. Thus the activity of 'multiplying' becomes the concept of 'multiplication'; 'adding up' becomes 'addition'. There is a substantial difference in meaning between the congruent representation of an activity and the reified naming of the concept or topic. It is generally thought, for example, that a student is able to multiply numbers without necessarily understanding the generalized concept of multiplication, and that when a student understands the concept of multiplication as well as the operation there is a qualitative change in the student's learning. Not surprisingly, this use of grammatical metaphor is particularly prevalent in mathematics education, where there is a need to distinguish between 'operational facility' and 'conceptual understanding'.

RELATIONAL CLAUSES

There is a tendency in mathematical language to exploit the meaning potential of relational clause types in English (see Halliday 1994; Chapter 5 for a discussion of clause types). Relational clauses are also a feature of scientific language, as described by Martin (1993), Wignell (1998) and Halliday (1993a). Here are some analysed examples of relational clauses from mathematics:

Relational: Attributive (non-reversible: *x* is a type of *y*; *x* belongs to group *y*)

A square	*is*	*a quadrilateral.*
Carrier	**Process: Relational: Attributive**	**Attribute**

Three and four	*are*	*factors of twelve.*
Carrier	**Process: Relational: Attributive**	**Attribute**

Relational: Identifying (reversible: *x* is equal to *y*; *x* stands for *y*)

A prime number	*is*	*a number which can only be divided by one and itself.*
Token/Identifier	**Process: Relational: Identifying**	**Value/Identified**

The mean, or average, score	*is*	*the sum of the scores divided by the number of scores.*
Token/Identifier	**Process: Relational: Identifying**	**Value/Identified**

In mathematics the function of **attributive clauses** appears to be very similar to that in science: to classify objects and events according to the technical taxonomies of the field. In doing so these clauses render explicit to students the organization of uncommonsense knowledge in mathematics and play an important role in apprenticing students into mathematical knowledge. In school textbooks, clauses such as those above are frequently placed in a box, or shown in large or coloured fonts. This visual prominence further underlines their significance.

Identifying clauses appear to function in a number of ways. Most obviously, they are used to introduce a technical term and to negotiate between technical and less-technical construals of knowledge, providing a bridge between 'what students (are assumed to) know' and 'what is to be learned'. In a clause such as 'The mean, or average, score is the sum of the scores divided by the number of scores', the Token, *the mean, or* *average, score,* is the more technical term being introduced. In order to function in the learning context it must be assumed that the less technical Value, *the sum of the scores divided by the number of scores,* can be readily understood by students.

A second and vital function of identifying clauses is that they provide a nexus between linguistic and symbolic representation in mathematics. In an identifying clause the Process (often the verb *to be*) **is the linguistic equivalent of the equals sign** in algebraic representation. The identifying clause 'The mean, or average, score is the sum of the scores divided by the number of scores', for example, parallels the algebraic formula: $\bar{x} = \Sigma \frac{x}{n}$. In discussing and preparing students for algebraic representation teachers will often systematically manipulate spoken language until an identifying clause is reached. This provides the stepping-off point for continued work in the symbolic mode. Text 1, discussed earlier, contains just such a build-up to a relational identifying clause (shown in bold):

> Alright, so instead of talking about degrees and how much of a rotation we make, we're talking about this angle in terms of, if this is the angle how big will the arc length be, and for the unit circle we want it to be to correspond one to one, we want to say if this is one radian then arc that arc length is three. On any other circle, you take the arc length divided by what the radius is, if we're taking the radius to be one we don't have to worry about that, so **it's a ratio between the arc length and the radius**.

A third, and less laudable, role for identifying processes in mathematics is that **they allow for the construction of multiple-choice questions**. In order to construct a multiple-choice question it is necessary to construe mathematical knowledge as a relationship of equivalence. The following multiple-choice questions, which come from the 1990 New South Wales *Year 10 General Mathematics Reference Test,* all construe knowledge as equivalence relationships. Identifying processes were used for at least 70 per cent of the multiple-choice questions in this test. The question 'stems' only are shown, and the Relational Identifying Processes are shown in italics.

> On this scale, what *is* the length of the pencil?
> Written as a fraction, 0.03 *is equivalent to:*
> Which of the following *is* the best estimate for the weight of a hen's egg?
> The shape of this nesting box *could be described as:*
> The greatest increase in population *was:*
> When cut out and folded along the dotted lines, which shape *will not form* a cube?

The predominance of multiple-choice questions in public examinations has rightly been criticized by educators because they present mathematical understanding as atomistic fragments of knowledge, emphasizing the correctness of the response rather than the process used to achieve the response. From a linguistic viewpoint we can also see how multiple choice questions put pressure on language to represent knowledge as equivalence relationships (x is equal to y). As well as using Relational Identifying Processes the formation of multiple-choice questions also requires the frequent use of grammatical metaphor and complex nominal groups (see below) in order to construe knowledge as 'correspondences between things'. The following example, examined earlier, shows this:

Which of the following	*is*	the best	estimate *metaphorical entity*	for the	weight *metaphorical entity*	of a hen's egg?
			Nominal Group			
Token			**Value**			

A question such as this is a long way removed from testing the *practical skill* of estimation, as examiners might claim it does. Rather, it is asking students to identify a linguistically construed relationship of equivalence. The question necessarily tests students' language skills as much as it does their mathematical understanding.

NOMINAL GROUP

In any uncommonsense discourse the resources of the Nominal Group are used to elaborate the meaning of a single entity by describing qualities of the entity, showing how it relates to other entities or by qualifying or restricting the range of meaning of the entity. A range of grammatical resources function to realize these meanings in the nominal group (Halliday 1994: 180–96). Although mathematical language exploits the full potential of the nominal group, three resources, **Pre-numerative**, **Classifiers** and **Qualifiers** play a particularly prominent role. The following example shows these three resources at work:

the volume of	*a*	*rectangular*	*prism*	*with sides 8, 10 and 12cm*
Pre-numerative	**Deictic**	**Classifier**	**Thing**	**Qualifier**

In mathematics **Pre-numerative**, phrases which precede the Deictic element of the Nominal group, function to select an abstract, but quantifiable, mathematical attribute with which to describe the main entity, the 'Thing' (The Deictic functions to indicate if the Thing is specific – *the, this, that* etc – or non-specific – *any, some, a,* etc.). Very often the Pre-numerative has the effect of endowing an everyday entity with a *mathematical attribute* (e.g *The length of* a pencil). This attribute is often a kind of measurement (length, area, volume, temperature etc.) or a technical term for a numerical relationship (e.g. *the first derivative* of the expression). There is often a close link between a Pre-numerative and a previously-introduced mathematical formula. Thus when a student reads the instruction 'Find the area of a circle of diameter 12cm', the Pre-numerative *area of* needs to be linked to the formula $a = \pi r^2$ in order for the student to proceed.

Classifiers are used in mathematics (as they are in other disciplines) to realize taxonomic relations of type/sub-type between entities (i.e. the relationship between the Classifier and the Thing in the nominal group). Here are some examples:

| *Rectangular* | *prism* | (general category: Prism, sub-type: rectangular) |
| **Classifier** | **Thing** | |

| *Prime* | *number* | (general category: number, sub-type: prime). |
| **Classifier** | **Thing** | |

Classifiers are particularly evident in the areas of number and geometry, where elaborate multi-layered systems of classification exist.

Qualifiers function to restrict the range of meaning of the nominal group. Very frequently in mathematics qualifiers provide numerical specifications. Thus the Qualifier renders the Thing a **specifiable entity**, a most important feature in mathematics.

Table 7.1 summarizes the chief functions of the Nominal Group in mathematics.

Table 7.1 Resources of the Nominal Group in mathematics

Element	Example	Function
Pre-numerative	*the volume of*	Selects a quantifiable mathematical attribute with which to describe the Thing
	a	
Classifier	*rectangular*	Sub-classifies Thing into a taxonomically ordered grouping
Thing	*prism*	Entity which is being described
Qualifier	*with sides 8, 10 and 12cm*	Restricts the range of meaning of the Thing; provides specifiable attributes of the Thing

THE HIERARCHICAL ORDERING OF MATHEMATICAL CONCEPTS THROUGH LANGUAGE

A striking feature of mathematical language is the way it builds up hierarchies of technicality, with the construal of technicality at one level dependent upon the construal of technicality at a previous level. Each successive level of technicality takes the language user one step further away from any 'congruent' or 'everyday' construal of meaning. Equally striking is the *rapidity* with which this process occurs in mathematics education. Students are very quickly apprenticed into the technicality of mathematics, and this initial technicality is used as the basis for further levels of technicality. Any everyday or congruent representations very quickly give way to interlocking sets of technical knowledge.[5] As a new level of technicality is introduced, subordinate and more congruent levels of technicality are disposed of. The following hierarchy shows this:

First level	length = how long something is width = how far across something is height = how far off the ground something is
Second level	area = length x breadth
Third level	volume = area x height

At the first level of technicality, the technical term is equated to a relatively everyday construal through a relational clause (*x is equivalent to y*). At the second level, the technical terms generated at the previous level (*length, width*) are combined to construe a new technical term, and the everyday construals (*how long something is, how far across something is*) are disposed of. At the third level, technical terms generated at the first and second levels (*height, area*) are combined to construe a new technical term, and technical terms construed at the second level (*length, breadth*) are disposed of. The technical term *volume* is thus at least two steps away from an everyday construal, and is very difficult to conceive of in everyday terms. This hierarchy (length–area–volume) is a relatively simple example. At more advanced levels of mathematics, many more hierarchical layers of technicality are added and any notion of an 'everyday' construal is literally unthinkable. Consider, for example, the many levels of technicality that have been built up to construe the following statement:

> If p is positive at point P on a curve, then the tangent is positive at that point and its function is said to be an *increasing function* at P.
>
> (Jones and Couchman 1981: 232)

THE GAP BETWEEN STUDENT AND TEACHER/TEXTBOOK USE OF MATHEMATICAL
LANGUAGE

Given the considerable technicality of mathematical language and the
rapidity with which it is built up, it is not surprising to find that there are
significant differences between teachers/textbooks and students in the way
they employ language in the classroom. Text 4, in which senior secondary
students discuss the solution to a relatively simple perimeter problem with
one another, will be used to contrast student language both with the 'official' language of teachers, as exemplified by Text 1, and with the written
language of multiple choice questions, such as those discussed above.

Text 4

F = Female M = Male
Segments where students are reading from question are shown in italics.

M1:   You read the next one. Now.
F: All right. *A five-metre length of fencing timber costs $8.00 and fence posts cost
       $5.00 each. If 9 metres of timber are needed to fence a triangular paddock and a
       fence post is needed for each metre of fence, explain whether the fence timber or the
       fence post will cost more and why?*
M1:   Yeah. This is a current problem. *A five-metre length of fencing timber costs $8.*
F: I think we could best read it to ourselves.
M1:   Yeah. Yeah. Go.
       (Period of silence)
M1:   Is it worth it trying to link this up? (Mmmm) Three there, three there
       and three there.
F: Yeah. Two more.
M2:   *A five-metre length of fencing timber costs $8.*
F: Mmmm. One of these costs $8 and the other one. One post costs $5.
M1:   No. You've gotta work out the triangle, how many posts you need.
F.   Yeah . . . wouldn't you wanna find . . . 9 posts.
M1:   Yeah, you need how many posts.
F: Wouldn't you want the perimeter, 'cause you're putting on a fence and –
M1:   Yeah.
M2:   All right. Ugh. First the um the per perimeter of the ah fence is 9
       lengths. Right.
F: Yeah.*
M1:   Mmmm.*
M2:   Is given. And . . .
M1:   Each length's . . .
M2:   But they don't give you (Mmm) the length of the triangle. It says 9
       lengths. What is lengths?
M1:   Each length is 5 metres.
M2:   Each length is 5 metres. Okay, fair enough.
M1:   So the perimeter is 45.
M2:   Uh. Okay, so if there's 9 lengths, right . . .
F: Yeah.*

M1:   Yeah.*
M1:   So the perimeter is 45. Okay.
M2:   9 lengths.
M1:   Equals 45.
M2:   1, 2, 3, 4, 5, 6, 7, 8, 9.
M1:   So you've got 45, divide that by 3.
M2:   So you've got 1,2,3 . . .
F: Triangle. You've got three on each side.
M2:   Okay, so you've got 9 lengths of ummm . . .
F: 5 metres.
M2:   9 lengths of 5 metres.
F: Which is where you get 45.
M2:   So 9 times 5 which is $45. The cost of the . . .
F: Metres.
M1:   No. 45 metres. The cost is $8.
F: Yeah the cost is $8 . . . You get 45 metres.
M1:   Yeah.
F: And if fencing posts, one post is one metre . . .
M2:   So the cost of um of 45 metres would be 5 times 45, right.
M1:   Yeah.
M2:   So the cost of um of 45 metres would be 5 times 45, right.
M1:   Yeah.
M2:   Which is $225. That is for the . . . That's it.
F: The timber.
M2:   Just the timber. Okay.
M1:   Yeah.*
F: Yeah.*
M2:   Ah, the post would needed would be 9 plus 1 because there would be
       more posts and it would be . . . no wait, see how many posts around . . .
       1, 2 3, 4, 5, 6, 7 . . .
F: No.
M2:   See first you would draw a triangle (laughs) to see how many posts, see,
       see how many posts . . .
F: No, no. Because it says that one post is one metre long.
M1:   Yeah one post, one post is . . .
M2:   Oh now.
F: Yeah, you see. Read it Noel.
M2:   One post right one . . .
F: . . . is one metre..
M1:   Is that the fence
F: The thing is that a fence post is needed . . .
M2:   For each metre of fence . . . Okay . . . for each metre of fence.
F.   You've got 45 fence?
M1:   No.
F: Or you've got 45 thing, er, 45 post . . .
M2:   But if it's an enclosed area, right, the number of um posts would be the
       same . . .
M1:   Yeah 'cause it says post.
M2:   as the number of metres, right?
M1:   Yep.*

F: Yeah.*
M2:   So that should be 45 posts.
M1:   Posts. Yeah
M2:   Okay, and since each post cost . . .
F: . . . cost $5
M2:   . . . costs $5 . . .
F: Times by 5.
M2:   It would be the same 225 bucks.
F: . . . and so . . . $5 . . .
M2:   Oops, sorry.
M1:   Wrong.
M2:   It's wrong, wrong, wrong, wrong. 5 metres cost $8.
F: Couldn't trust you.
M2:   Five-metre lengths fencing costs $8.
M1: $8. That's that'd be 45 times $8 . . .
F: Yeah . . . .Yeah
M2:   So the cost of the fencing . . .
M1:   . . . fencing
F: Timber.
M2:   Would be 8 times 45, not 5 times 45.
M1:   Exactly..
F: Mmm
M2:   So would be . . . what . . . 300, er, 360 . . .
M1:   360, yeah.
F: 360.
M2:   So 45.
M1:   Thanks for supporting me on that.
M2:   That' all right.
F: What are you trying to say?
M1:   47, 45 posts.
M2:   So the posts would cost *$225
F: *$225. So it's cheaper *by using the post.

Because it allows for students to take on a range of roles in constructing and manipulating knowledge, it is easy to see why many teachers are keen to introduce group discussion into mathematics classrooms. Compared to the catechistic nature of teacher–student interaction, such as that in Text 3, student–student interaction provides the possibility for students to take on the role of 'primary knower' (K1) and 'primary actor' more frequently. Moreover, in student–student interaction these roles can be moved around more easily and students who are less willing and/or able to take on these roles can be coaxed into doing so. There is clear evidence in Text 4, for example, that initially hesitant students, such as M1, progressively contribute more and more to the group discussion as it unfolds. This is far less likely to occur with teacher–student interaction where there are twenty or more students in the classroom.

The chief issue which arises from Text 4 comes not from differences in interaction patterns, however, but from differences in the linguistic quality of the utterances. Compared to teacher talk and to textbooks, the students' talk is far more like everyday spoken language. It does not exploit the meaning potential of grammatical resources such as the Nominal Group and Relational Process to construe technical knowledge to nearly as great an extent as the teacher talk or the test questions. Table 7.2 compares the student interaction with the teacher talk of Text 1 and the written mathematical language of multiple choice questions.

Table 7.2 Comparison of three grammatical features of student talk, teacher talk and exam questions

	Student group interaction (Text 4)	Teacher talk (Text 1)	Multiple-choice test questions†
Lexical density (i.e. average number of 'content words' per clause)	1.66	4.36	4.54
Ratio of relational processes to non-relational processes	1:1.05	1.13:1	2.5:1
Ratio of long Nominal Groups to short Nominal Groups*	1:2.86	1:1.06	1.22:1

† The first 10 multiple-choice questions from the *1990 Year 10 General Mathematics Reference Test*
* A short Nominal Group is one consisting of Deictic/Numerative + Thing or less

In terms of *lexical density*, the average number of content words, or lexical items, per clause (Halliday and Hasan 1985: 61–72), there is roughly one-third the number of lexical items per clause in the student talk as in either the teacher talk or the Reference Test questions. Although the *topic* of the students talk is mathematical, the quality of their talk insofar as it is measurable by lexical density is about the same as everyday conversation (Halliday 1985: 65). The greater lexical density of the other texts allows for the 'packing-in' of meanings into grammatical relationships in a way that is qualitatively different from everyday talk, and thus assists the construal of technical mathematical meanings. This is further confirmed by the comparison of **Nominal Group** structure and **Process type** across the text. In terms of the nominal group, we can see that there is a far greater proportion of short nominal groups in the student text, meaning that this text does not exploit the potential of the nominal group to select attributes, sub-classify and qualify nearly so much as the teacher talk or the test questions (clearly this differing exploitation of the Nominal Group is what gives rise to the differing lexical densities of the three texts). In terms of process type, the test questions appear to concern themselves far more with construing relationships between entities (equivalence, group membership, attributes etc.) than with describing events. In the teacher talk and the student talk, on the other hand, there is a fairly even balance between representing 'going-on' (actions, thoughts, speech) and representing relationships. Figure 7.2 sets out the differences between the three texts in graph form.

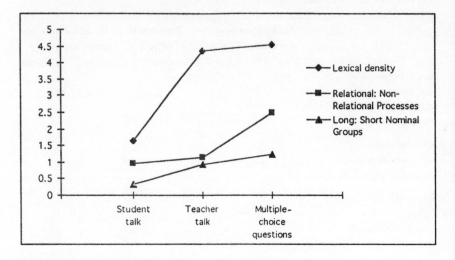

Figure 7.2 Trends in lexicogrammatical features across texts

In using SFL to analyse the language of mathematics in this chapter I have tried to provide explicit visible evidence with which to identify and explore a number of important issues in mathematics education. As the analysis shows, there are some clear, if not surprising, differences between expert and learner use of language in mathematics classrooms. It stands to reason that if students are to become competent at independently construing mathematical meanings, then increased control over the language of mathematics is one of the ways they can achieve this. Moreover, the linguistic analysis makes clear what could be the areas of focus for any potential language-based intervention in mathematics classrooms, and renders visible what might count as criteria of the success (or otherwise) of these interventions. However, the analysis also leaves open several important sociological questions. What is the nature of mathematical knowledge? Are the power relationships between experts and learners, so obvious in the language, a product of the nature of knowledge itself or of the way it is transmitted in the classroom, or both? If one is to 'democratize' mathematics education what kinds of issues have to be considered? To seek answers to these questions we need to apply sociological understandings to our linguistic analyses. The second part of this chapter attempts to do this.

Sociological perspectives on the language of mathematics

For many years now considerable attention has been paid to the way knowledge is construed in the mathematics classroom, and how that knowledge is perceived by students (Dossey 1992). In particular educators are concerned with the isolated, atomistic nature of mathematical knowledge as it is recontextualized in classrooms, and the perception by many students that mathematics comprises nothing more than a 'necessary set of rules and procedures to be learned by rote' (Crawford *et al.* 1994: 331). In a direct reaction to these perceptions, many maths educators stress the interconnectedness of mathematical knowledge:

> We believe that the notion of connected representations of knowledge will continue to provide a useful way to think about understanding mathematics, for several reasons. Firstly, it provides a level of analysis that makes contact with the theoretical cognitive issues and practical educational issues . . . Second, it generates a coherent theoretical framework for connecting a variety of issues in mathematics teaching and learning, both past and present. . . . Third, it suggests interpretations of students' learning that help to explain their successes and failures, both in and out of school.
>
> (Hiebert and Carpenter 1992: 67)

It is this interconnectedness, Hiebert and Carpenter go on to say (74–7), which constitutes 'mathematical understanding'. In summarizing research in the area they claim the following benefits from 'learning and teaching with understanding':

> Understanding is generative . . . Understanding promotes remembering . . . Understanding reduces the amount that must be remembered . . . Understanding enhances transfer . . . Understanding influences beliefs.

Although mathematics educators recognize that classroom construals and student perceptions of mathematics are significant issues, most research in the area lacks a clearly articulated sociological theory with which to link the structure of educational institutions, the power relations within these structures, the discursive ordering of knowledge in classroom mathematics, and student perceptions. Instead of looking to language and institutional culture for explanations, mathematics teachers are exhorted to foster a 'constructivist' approach which encourages students to make psychologically 'internal' connections between information (Cobb *et al.* 1992). In taking such a view, mathematics educators are denying themselves the insights offered by a sociological perspective.

Thus far, our linguistic exploration of the language of mathematics has revealed the way very distinctive kinds of technical meanings are

construed through mathematical language and has described the kinds of
spoken language interaction which typify many mathematics classrooms.
Of course, these two aspects of mathematics education are not unrelated.
Many researchers have noted that there is a relationship between the
kinds of linguistic interaction in which people engage and the kinds of
meanings which can be realized by speakers. Such a relationship is fundamental to a range of socio-semiotic theories of meaning, including those
of text and context in SFL (Halliday and Hasan 1985), semantic variation
(Hasan 1996), speech genre (Bahktin 1986; Martin 1992) and semiotic
mediation in higher mental functions (Vygotsky 1978, Volosinov 1983). A
socio-semiotic approach requires us to examine closely the relationship
between forms of expression and forms of knowledge. What is the relationship between the *kinds of interaction* between students and teachers
that go on in the mathematics classroom and the *forms of consciousness*
about mathematics that students develop as a result of their mathematics
education?

In educational contexts this question begs to be reformulated as a sociological one: that of *differentiated access to meaning potential.* What role do
language and classroom interaction play in providing some students with
access to the technical meaning potential of mathematics while simultaneously denying access to others? Moreover, if we are considering intervention in mathematics education, we need to ask if the use of language
currently found in mathematics classrooms is optimal for all students, and,
if not, what the alternatives might be. It is in answering these questions
that Bernstein's educational sociology is particularly useful.

Seen in Bernstein's terms, mathematics is a discipline whose discursive
construction through language seems to be unusually closely aligned to
the regulative discourse of the classroom and the macro-regulative
discourse of the ordering of space and time in the school. Although
Bernstein warns that 'it is very important to see that these discourses do
not always move in a complementary relation to each other' (1996: 28), it
appears that in school mathematics they do. There is a kind of synchronic-
ity – a conspiracy if you like – between classification, instructional
discourse, regulative discourse and language that is noticeably stronger
than in other subject areas. This is evident both in what Bernstein calls the
classification of knowledge in mathematics and the **framing** of pedagogic
transmission of that knowledge.

Classification

Bernstein interprets the connectedness (or conversely, the separation) of
knowledge as in terms of **classification**. For Bernstein (1996: 20–1, 24)
classification is fundamentally about power:

> Dominant power relations establish boundaries, that is relationships between
> boundaries, relationships between categories . . . the crucial space that creates

the specialization of the category is not internal to that discourse but is the space between that discourse and another. In other words A can only be A if it can effectively insulate itself from B . . . In the case of strong classification each category has its unique identity, its unique voice, its own specialised rules of internal relations . . . .The arbitrary nature of these power relations is disguised, hidden by the principle of classification, for the principle of classification comes to have the force of the natural order and the identities that it constructs are taken as real, as authentic, as integral, as the source of integrity.

If there is a very strong classification between inside and outside then the knowledge here is given a special quality of otherness. If there is a strong classification between inside and outside then there is a hierarchy of knowledge classification between the so-called common sense and the so-called uncommonsense.

It is clear from both the differences between teacher and student language and in the way that mathematical language differs sharply from 'commonsense' forms of interaction that mathematics realizes a strongly classified discipline. Moreover, the calls from mathematics educators for greater interconnectedness of knowledge can be seen as calls for a weakening of classification. Since mathematics educators often claim that knowledge in 'real' mathematics (i.e university research mathematics) is much more interconnected than in school mathematics, it would appear that the institution of schooling plays a major role in reshaping mathematical knowledge as strongly classified. Using Bernstein's insights we can posit that it is the need to make mathematical knowledge teachable and learnable within the power, space and time structures of the school and the need to make mathematical knowledge assessable through public examination, much more than individual teaching 'style', that makes school mathematics the way it is. Appeals to teachers to modify their 'traditional' teaching styles are, therefore, likely to meet with only modest success, since the teacher is not the only agent in the recontextualization process.

The implications of strong classification for mathematics education are many; however I shall illustrate them here with just one example. A classic issue of classification and recognition comes in the area of 'word problems' in mathematics. The status of word problems in relation to commonsense and uncommonsense knowledge is often somewhat ambiguous in mathematics syllabuses. In most teaching sequences word problems are added on to the end of the study of a topic. Teachers are told that word problems are challenging, help students to relate mathematics to the 'real world' and, above all, will be relevant to the way students will need to use mathematical knowledge outside of school. Yet word problems are nearly always contrived by teachers in order to fit within the parameters of the discipline. It is the uncommonsense, strongly classified discursive order in school mathematics which guides the selection and expression of word problems, not everyday, commonsense experience of the world. Knowledge for outside is only permitted as long as it fits into the 'specialised rules of internal relations' of school mathematics. A highly predictable 'canon' of word problems thus emerges. The study of Pythagoras' theorem, for example, will always be accompanied by word problems about ladders being placed against walls or the use of compass bearings to work out how far someone has travelled; the study of perimeter will be accompanied by problems about fencing and marking the limits of a sports field; the study of area will be accompanied by problems about laying carpet or grass in a back garden, etc.

While most word problems can be effectively negotiated by most students while they remain within the strongly classified ordering of knowledge in the classroom, difficulties arise when word problems appear in random order, detached from an explicitly enunciated topic area in examinations. Many teachers with whom I have worked in Australia report that particular groups of students (generally people who are marginalized from the mainstream Anglo social milieu) have difficulty in recognizing the mathematical content of word problems which have been separated in space and time from their *uncommonsense* context – i.e. from the teaching of a particular topic in the classroom. These students are at particular risk in examinations and other assessment tasks, where space, time and language have removed the knowledge from the strongly classified context in which it was first introduced. This occurs for at least two reasons. First, many of these students simply do not recognize the so-called *commonsense* context construed by the problem – because mowing the lawn, travelling around the country, calculating income tax, etc. are not part of their everyday experience and secondly because sitting in an exam room reading word problems is *not* a commonsense context.

The misrecognition of the status of word problems is exacerbated by two official educational discourses, the first revolving around Piagetian notions of the concrete and abstract and the second around notions of the perceived advantages for less able students in doing 'real world' mathematics. It is frequently claimed that word problems will be easier because they represent concrete experience and that 'formal' mathematical knowledge is, by biological imperative, more difficult for students. By presenting situations which are assumed to be within students' everyday experience, the argument goes, students will be able to 'construct' 'internal' mathematical representations, rather than relying on 'external' 'imposed' forms of knowledge. Problems arise not from the viability or otherwise of this view, but from the mistaken assumption that the word problems that are produced in classroom mathematics actually constitute everyday forms of knowledge, and the denial of the role of language and symbols in semiotically mediating experience. It is assumed that the move from reading an 'everyday' problem to expressing an 'everyday' solution is one that does not require engagement with formal mathematical knowledge and will thus be easier for 'weaker' students.

The impact of economic rationalism on curriculum planners has also resulted in a privileging of word problems in mathematics. The assumption here is that being able to do things with mathematics: calculate wages, overtime, taxes, interest rates, hire-purchase payments and exchange rates, and read graphs and tables, etc. is an economically more 'useful' kind of knowledge than 'pure mathematics' (the understanding of principles, axioms, formulae, etc).

The tendency of mathematics to be strongly classified has implications for the kinds of language-based intervention which one might attempt. As Martin (this volume Chapter 5) argues, reform is not simply a matter of weakening classification: this may simply act to render the discipline unteachable or to further disempower students by denying them access to highly valued forms of knowledge which are still being taught elsewhere. A more effective response would be to design teaching programmes which attempt to move backwards and forwards between strong and weak classification. Martin explains how some intervention programmes in Australia have attempted to do just this. Certainly, one very clear implication is to recognize that word problems, or any other kind of 'real world' maths that is introduced to the classroom is, by virtue of the fact that it is recontextualized as school learning, just as uncommonsense and esoteric as other more theoretical kinds of knowledge, and needs to be dealt with with the same explicitness as other kinds of knowledge. Simply leaving it to students to 'construct' 'internal' representations would seem an inadequate response, especially for marginalized students.

Framing

The patterns of spoken interaction described in the first part of this chapter make it clear that, as well as being strongly classified, the transmission, or framing, of mathematical knowledge is also tightly controlled in many classrooms. Framing, as Bernstein (1996: 27–8) sees it is all about control:

> the form of control which regulates and legitimizes communication in pedagogic relations, the control of communication in local, interactional pedagogic relations [here teacher/pupil and pupil/pupil]. Framing refers to the nature of the control over:
>
> ● the selection of the communication;
> ● its sequencing (what comes first, what comes second)
> ● its pacing (the rate of expected acquisition)
> ● the criteria, and
> ● the control over the social base which makes this transmission possible
>
> . . . We can distinguish analytically two systems of rules regulating the framing. And these rules can vary independently of each other . . . These are rules of social order and rules of discursive order. We shall call the rules of the social order regulative discourse and the rules of discursive order instructional discourse. And we shall then write this as follows:

framing = <u>instructional discourse</u>
                regulative discourse

In other words, the instructional discourse is always embedded in the regulative discourse, and the regulative discourse is the dominant discourse.

SELECTION AND SEQUENCING

In examining mathematics syllabuses it becomes clear that the strongly classified nature of the knowledge necessitates a high degree of control over the selection and sequencing of content. Only with careful control of selection and sequencing can the knowledge be rendered teachable. Of course, this degree of control serves only to further strengthen the classification of mathematical knowledge – strong classification and strong framing thus feed off one another. Examples of carefully controlled selection and sequencing can be found in just about all areas of mathematics syllabuses. In all junior secondary school syllabuses in Australia, for instance, basic co-ordinate geometry is taught. Students are taught about ordered pairs {x, y} and how to plot these pairs on the number plane. At this point the uncommonsense content is often cloaked in the guise of relevance and fun, with activities such as map reading, locating places with latitude and longitude, finding grid references on a street directory and looking for hidden treasure on an island. A bit later on, map reading and treasure hunts give way to plotting basic functions on the number plane (straight lines, circles and possibly even parabolas). What is the purpose of this selection and this sequence? Not to make students better map-readers or treasure hunters, but to provide students with the requisite skills for the study of polynomials and calculus in the senior years. The rules of the discursive order within a strongly classified discipline thus shape selection and sequencing of learning experiences offered up to students, no matter how everyday or relevant they are dressed up to be.

PACING AND CONTROL OVER THE SOCIAL BASE

In the area of pacing and control over the social base it is clear that there is a close relationship in mathematics between the social order of the school, the regulative discourse, and forms of the mathematical knowledge itself. This is shown most clearly in catechistic teacher–student interactions. Consider the following transcription from a Year 7 classroom:

Text 5

T: Okay, class. Books out. There's five questions going on the board. You have one minute.
P: Okay, Sir.
      (Sounds of chalk on board)
P: How come you've got a . . .

T: Would you like it?
Ps.   Yeah.
T: We might do a little bit more of that later on.
P: Oh, great.
P.   When? Today?
T: No, not today.
P: Sir, what about our test results?
T: Test results. There's a couple of people still to do them in other classes so
      I can't give them back just yet.
      (Class noise)
T: Come on, mate.
P: Sir, when are we going to get our test results back?
      (Class noise)
T: No I want these answers in the books.
P: About the sheets, Sir?
T: No, I'll tell you all about the sheets later.
          . . .
T: Troy. Are you finished?
P: Yeah.
T: Okay, Troy, the first one.
P: (undecipherable) 0.8.
T: 0.8. Correct. Second one, Craig.
P: I haven't even started.
T: Quick, do it in your head. 6.6 divided by 3.
P: 2.2.
T: Why is it 2.2?
P: (undecipherable)
T: Don't look at other people's answers. Helen?
P: 2.2.
T: 2.2. Yes. Craig. 6 divided by 3 is 2. 6 divided by 3 is 2. 2.2. Third answer . . .
      Girl. Kelly?
P: I don't have that one yet, but I done the last one.
T: Do it in your head then, number 3.

Like the interaction examined earlier in Text 3, the teacher in this
transcript consistently occupies the role of primary knower, posing and
then evaluating questions. The difference here is that much of the IRE
interaction is not about knowledge, but about the control of the *physical
activity* of students in the classroom:

T: Troy. Are you finished?
P: Yeah.
T: Okay.

This control of *physical activity* is seamlessly integrated with control over
the knowledge:

T: Second one, Craig.
P: I haven't even started.

T: Quick do it in your head. 6.6 divided by 3.
P: 2.2.
T: Why is it 2.2?
P: (undecipherable)
T: Don't look at other people's answers. Helen?
P: 2.2.
T: 2.2. Yes.

Thus the regulation of physical behaviour and the construal of mathematical knowledge are virtually indistinguishable from one another in the
pedagogic discourse. In such a context, it is not really surprising that
many students may see mathematics as 'a necessary set of rules and procedures to be learned by rote'. In the light of Text 4 it can be seen that the
IRE exchanges in the Year 11 class, illustrated in Text 2, while being
overtly about the exchange of information, are also, by virtue of their
highly ritualized form, about the control of physical behaviour. The basis
for the forms of knowledge that are construed in mathematics would
appear to lie just as much in the social order of classroom life as they do
in the discursive order of the discipline.

When it comes to the question of appropriate intervention, there are
once again no clear cut, simplistic solutions. An obvious response to the
strong framing evidenced by Texts 2 and 4 would be to seek communicative alternatives to the IRE style of teacher-student exchange. This seems
to be what is motivating the strong push towards group-based work in
mathematics education. Cobb *et al.* (1991: 7) advocate the following role
for the teacher:

> The teacher's role in initiating and guiding mathematical negotiations is a
> highly complex activity that includes highlighting conflicts between alternative
> interpretations or solutions, helping students develop productive small-group
> collaborative relationships, facilitating mathematical dialogue between stu-
> dents, implicitly legitimizing selected aspects of contributions to discussion in
> light of their potential fruitfulness for further mathematical constructions,
> redescribing students' explanations in more sophisticated terms that are
> nonetheless comprehensible to students, and guiding the development of
> taken-to-be-shared interpretations when particular representational systems are
> established.

While Cobb *et al.* offer a well-meaning alternative to the oppressive
regime of the strongly classified, strongly framed pedagogy of many mathematics classrooms, their vision of the mathematics classroom is largely
asociological and predicated on a number of assumptions about students'
linguistic and social habits. Where for example do 'alternative interpretations or solutions' come from if students do not have the linguistic skills to
generate them? An analysis of student–student interaction, such as Text 4,
suggests that even talented senior students in socio-economically disadvantaged schools cannot readily use language to present clearly articulated

alternative interpretations or solutions, even though they are prepared to debate isolated *answers* among one another. What counts as 'productive small-group collaborative relationships' and which social groups are more likely to fall easily into this kind of compliant behaviour? Will all students be equally able to read the hidden message in the 'implicitly legitimizing [of] selected aspects of contributions to discussion in light of their potential fruitfulness for further mathematical constructions'? Which students will pick up on the teacher's 'more sophisticated terms' when she 'redescribes students' explanations'? The continued poor performance of socio-economically disadvantaged students in classrooms where the response has been simply to weaken framing suggests that not all students stand to gain equally from a simplistic interpretation of the constructivist vision.

Perhaps a more responsible approach (and probably one which would be approved of by constructivists) would be the careful scaffolding of knowledge through a process of guided interaction. The implications of this in terms of framing are discussed by Martin (this volume Chapter 5). Christie (1998) has put forward a clear case for different kinds of interaction, including IRE exchanges, at different points in the teaching/learning process.

Conclusion: the role of a sociologically informed educational linguistics in mathematics education

My purpose in writing this chapter has not been to offer easy solutions to issues in mathematics education, nor has it been to offer details of language-based intervention in mathematics classrooms.[6] Rather I have sought to make clear what it is that a socio-semiotic model of language, such as SFL, and an elaborate theory of the sociology of education, such as Bernstein's, can offer mathematics educators. Neither socio-linguistics nor sociology appear to have made a particularly strong impact on mathematics education in the past, both because of the strongly classified nature of mathematics education (like the discipline itself) and the privileging of psychological models of learning in mathematics, such as that of constructivism. It is important to note that socio-linguistic and sociological contributions do not necessarily entail a rejection of psychological models, although they may challenge some of the assumptions of psychological models, or at least bring to the foreground issues which do not receive great emphasis in psychological models.

As I see it, socio-linguistic and sociological models can make the following contributions:

1. Make explicit the kinds of language which are employed to construe the technical meanings of mathematics. This description goes well beyond the identification of technical lexis and phrases and includes grammatical structures, discourse analysis and the identification of spoken and written genres.

2. Allow us to understand clearly differences in linguistic behaviour among different language users and in different social contexts within the mathematics classroom.

3. Provide clear direction for language-based intervention in mathematics; a clear but not atomistic focus for language-based activities; and clear criteria for effective language use which can be shared by teachers and students.

4. Allow for a detailed analysis and critique of current linguistic practices in mathematics education, especially in teacher language, interaction patterns, written resources and public examinations.

5. Provide a way of linking broader sociological factors, such as power, space and time relationships in the school, to the way in which mathematical knowledge is construed in the classroom and perceived by students.

6. Expand the critical tools available to mathematics educators to analyse the kinds of intervention they seek to encourage in the classroom. In particular those that can effectively complement psychological models.

In helping us to understand these areas of concern, socio-linguistic and sociological models constitute a worthwhile tool for investigation and intervention in mathematics education.

Notes

1 'Uncommonsense', following Bernstein (1977, 1990), is being used here to distinguish educational knowledge from 'commonsense', or 'everyday' knowledge. The latter is accumulated through our experience of the physical world on a day-to-day basis, whereas the former is usually acquired through formal education, which reformulates knowledge from its 'primary context' (mainly through language) according to the principles and relations of the pedagogic context.

2 Although some researchers have decided that IRE exchanges are undesirable because they are not 'genuine' and have exhorted teachers to avoid them, others, notably Christie (1998), have argued for their functional status in certain stages of classroom discourse.

3 One mathematics teacher told me the story of a student who, having being presented with an equation and told to 'find x', drew an arrow pointing to the symbol x and wrote 'here it is'!

4 Christie, Martin and Rose all discuss grammatical metaphor in this volume.

5 Halliday identifies 'interlocking definitions' as an aspect of *scientific* language, but curiously he uses mathematical terms (radius, centre, circle, circumference, diameter) as an example (Halliday 1993b).

6 Though this has certainly been done using SFL (Veel 1994).

References

Bahktin, M. (1986) *Speech Genres and Other Late Essays*, C. Emerson and M. Holquist (eds). Austin: University of Texas Press.

Bernstein, B. (1977) *Class, Codes and Control: Vol. 3*. London: Routledge & Kegan Paul.

Bernstein, B. (1990) *The Structuring of Pedagogical Discourse*. London: Routledge.

Bernstein, B, (1996) *Pedagogy, Symbolic Control and Identity*. London: Taylor and Francis.

Christie, F. (1998) 'Science and apprenticeship: the pedagogic discourse'. In J. Martin and R. Veel (eds), *Reading Science: Functional and Critical Perspectives on Science Discourses*. London: Routledge.

Cobb, P., Wood, T., Yackell, E., Nicholls, J., Wheatley, G., Trigatti, B. and Perlwitz, M. (1991) 'Assessment of a problem-centred second-grade mathematics project', *Journal for Research in Mathematics Education* 22 (1), 3–29.

Cobb, P., Yackell, E. and Wood, T. (1992) 'A constructivist alternative to the representational view of the mind in mathematics education'. *Journal for Research in Mathematics Education*, 23, 2–33.

Cranny-Francis, A. (1996) 'Technology and/or weapon: the discipline of reading in the secondary English classroom'. In R. Hasan and G. Williams (eds), *Literacy in Society*. London: Longman.

Crawford, K., Gordon S., Nicholas J. and Prosser, M. (1994) 'Conceptions of mathematics and how it is learned: the perspectives of students entering university', *Learning and Instruction*, 4, 331–45.

Dossey, J. (1992) 'The nature of mathematics: its role and influence'. In D.A. Grouws (ed.), *Handbook of Research on Mathematics Teaching and Learning*. New York: Macmillan/National Council of Teachers of Mathematics.

Eggins, S. (1994) *An Introduction to Systemic Functional Linguistics*. London: Pinter.

Halliday, M.A.K. (1977) *Language as Social Semiotic*. London: Edward Arnold.

Halliday, M.A.K. (1993a) 'On the language of physical science'. In M.A.K. Halliday and J. Martin, *Writing Science*. London: Falmer, 54–68.

Halliday, M.A.K. (1993b) 'Some grammatical problems in scientific English'. In M.A.K. Halliday and J. Martin, *Writing Science*. London: Falmer, 69–85.

Halliday, M.A.K. (1994) *An Introduction to Functional Grammar*. London: Edward Arnold.

Halliday, M.A.K. (1998) 'Things and relations: regrammaticizing experience as technical knowledge'. In J. Martin and R. Veel (eds), *Reading Science: Functional and Critical Perspectives on the Discourses of Science*. London: Routledge, 185–235.

Halliday, M.A.K. and R. Hasan (1985) *Language, Context and Text: Aspects of Language in a Social-semiotic Perspective*. Geelong, Vic: Deakin University Press.

Halliday, M.A.K. and J. Martin (1993) *Writing Science*. London: Falmer.

Hasan, R. (1996) 'Speech genre, semiotic mediation and the development of higher mental functions, in C. Cloran, D. Butt and G. Williams (eds), *Ways of Saying, Ways of Meaning*. London: Cassell, pp. 152–90.

Herrick, M., Hendrick, V. and Adams, H. (1962) *Essential Skills in Algebra*. New York: Harcourt, Brace & World.

Hiebert, J. and Carpenter, P. (1992) 'Learning and teaching with understanding'. In D.A. Grouws (ed.), *Handbook of Research on Mathematics Teaching and Learning*. New York: Macmillan/National Council of Teachers of Mathematics.

Jones, S. and Couchman, K. (1981) *3 Unit Mathematics: Book 1*. Melbourne: Shakespeare Head Press.

Kress, G. and Van Leeuwen, T. (1996) *Reading Images: The Grammar of Visual Design*. London: Routledge.

Lemke, J. (1998) 'Multiplying meaning'. In J. Martin and R. Veel (eds), *Reading Science:*

Functional and Critical Perspectives on the Discourses of Science. London: Routledge.

McInnes, D. and Murison B. (1992) 'A model for understanding the literacy demands of mathematics'. Unpublished research report, Disadvantaged Schools Program, Metropolitan East Region, NSW Department of School Education.

Martin, J. (1992) *English Text: System and Structure.* Amsterdam: Benjamins.

Martin, J. (1993) 'Literacy in science: learning to handle the text as technology'. In M.A.K. Halliday and J. Martin, *Writing Science.* London: Falmer.

Martin J. (1996) 'Evaluating disruption: symbolizing theme in junior secondary narrative'. In R. Hasan and G. Williams (eds), *Literacy in Society.* London: Longman.

Matthiessen, C. (1996) *Lexicogrammatical Cartography: English Systems.* Tokyo: International Language Science Publishers.

New South Wales Board of Studies (1990) 'School Certificate reference test, Year 10, Mathematics General'. Sydney: NSW Board of Studies.

O'Halloran, K.L. (1996) 'The discourses of secondary school mathematics'. Unpublished PhD thesis, Murdoch University, Western Australia.

Rothery, J. (1994) *Exploring Literacy in School English.* Sydney: Disadvantaged Schools Programme, Department of School Education, Metropolitan East Region.

Rothery, J. (1996) 'Making changes: developing an educational linguistics'. In R. Hasan and G. Williams (eds), *Literacy in Society.* London: Longman.

Sinclair, J. McH. and Coulthard, R.M. (1975) *Towards an Analysis of Discourse: The English Used by Teachers and Pupils.* London: Oxford University Press.

van Leeuwen, T. and Humphrey, S. (1996) 'On learning to look through a geographer's eyes'. In R. Hasan and G. Williams (eds), *Literacy in Society.* London: Longman.

Veel, R. (1994) 'The language of mathematics. Training notes for a professional development course'. Centre for Continuing Education, University of Sydney.

Veel, R. (1997) 'Learning how to mean: scientifically speaking'. In F. Christie and J. Martin (eds), *Genres and Institutions: Social Processes in the Workplace and School.* London: Cassell.

Veel, R. (1998) 'The greening of school science: ecogenesis in secondary classrooms'. In J. Martin and R. Veel (eds), *Reading Science: Functional and Critical Perspectives on the Discourses of Science.* London: Routledge.

Veel, R. and Coffin, C. (1996) 'Learning how to think like an historian'. In R. Hasan and G. Williams (eds), *Literacy in Society.* London: Longman.

Ventola, E. (1987) *The Structure of Social Interaction: A Systemic Approach to the Semiotics of Service Encounters.* London: Pinter.

Volosinov, N. (1983) *Marxism and the Philosophy of Language* (trans. L. Matejka and I. Titunik). Cambridge, MA: Harvard University Press.

Vygotsky, L. (1978) *Mind in Society: The Development of Higher Psychological Processes.* M. Cole, V. John-Steiner, S. Scribner and E. Souberman (eds). Cambridge, MA: Harvard University Press.

Wignell, P. (1998) 'Technicality and abstraction in social science'. In J. Martin and R. Veel (eds), *Reading Science: Functional and Critical Perspectives on the Discourses of Science.* London: Routledge, 297–326.

Williams, G. (1995) 'Joint book-reading and literacy pedagogy: a socio-semantic examination'. Unpublished PhD dissertation, School of English, Linguistics and Media, Macquarie University, Australia.

8 Culture, competence and schooling: approaches to literacy teaching in indigenous school education

David Rose

My goal in this contribution is to offer some practical, theoretically grounded strategies to teachers of indigenous children, that will assist them in developing effective English literacy programmes. I begin by outlining some expectations for English literacy teaching from indigenous Australian communities,[1] discuss problems with current approaches to language education in meeting these expectations, illustrate some features of indigenous varieties of English that are pedagogically significant, and finally propose a methodology that has proven successful in helping indigenous children overcome difficulties with English literacy. In contrast to more conventional discussions of indigenous education, the focus is less on characteristics of indigenous learners, and more on approaches to teaching practice that they experience. The discussion is framed with particular reference to Bernstein's (1996) analysis of contemporary western pedagogic practices, which tend to alternatively foreground either 'competences' that are presumed to be innate to learners, or textual 'performances' that may be explicitly taught to learners to enable their educational success. I will argue that the ideological struggle over competence versus performance (or 'process vs product', 'difference vs deficit', etc.) has inhibited the development of effective English literacy methodologies for indigenous children, and that systematic understandings from both perspectives are required to design and implement appropriate language pedagogies. While the discussion focuses on the Australian experience it is relevant for literacy programmes in other regions where indigenous children are students in state or community schools.

The last twenty-five years have been a period of particularly disruptive changes for indigenous communities in their social and economic environments. These changes have had major consequences for their children's educational needs: in the values and practices of their communities on the one hand, and in the skills needed for educational success on the other. Indigenous peoples no longer live the way many did a generation ago, through either remote location or segregationist government policies, in isolation from national and global economies, mass media and politics. For communities to succeed economically and politically, and to control the cultural changes they are undergoing, they now need access to the best possible opportunities for secondary and further education. Unfortunately for the majority, such opportunities have been too slow in coming. High school completion rates for indigenous students in Australia are still well below national averages, there is still little secondary provision for students in remote communities, and many indigenous access and annexe programmes at secondary and tertiary levels still need to provide remedial literacy classes for their students. Educational outcomes are reflected most starkly in indigenous unemployment rates which are often several times the national average, even within indigenous communities whose services are often staffed and administered by trained non-indigenous employees.

Literacy in educational English is at the heart of many of these problems. The teaching profession has struggled to develop more appropriate and effective language pedagogies for indigenous students, trying out new approaches and taking students' cultural differences into account, but improvements in outcomes remain disappointingly slow, as both indigenous and non-indigenous leaders in the profession acknowledge. A recent parliamentary report found that the average literacy ability of indigenous children in remote communities in the Northern Territory (NT) was eight years behind their non-indigenous peers (Public Accounts Committee, NT 1996). A few examples of what indigenous leaders see as the needs for English literacy, and the problems schools have in delivering it, follow. For example, Chris Japangardi Poulson (1988: 68), an indigenous teacher in the central desert community of Yuendumu argues that,

> English is important, it is the language of the world outside the community. We need Aboriginal teachers, managers, storekeepers, lawyers and doctors – in every area of life we need to have Aboriginal people in there doing the jobs for themselves and for any of these jobs they need English. School which does not give priority to teaching English is failing to train leaders for the future. At the moment not enough English is taught in school and because of this there are many Aboriginal people who cannot get work of any kind.

The literacy approach taken in many remote communities such as Yuendumu has focused on teaching reading and writing first in vernacular spoken languages. Such curricula are generally known as 'bilingual'. *Anangu*[2] people of the Pitjantjatjara and Yankuntjatjara communities in South Australia have had such a school curriculum since 1940. Political leader Yami Lester (1993: 171) is critical of its results and concerned about the future.

> When I look at Bilingual education on the Anangu Pitjantjatjara Lands, I think: There must be something wrong here. . . . our people are left behind, still only talking Pitjantjatjara and Yankuntjatjara. I started changing my ideas about bilingual education. . . . I'm just worried about Anangu learning English because reading and writing is important. If they read and write and speak English they can work in offices, they can go to college or university. They can

learn to be accountants, mechanics, electricians, plumbers, builders. If we don't get a good education for them, we're always going to have white advisers in the communities.

While much of the demand for English literacy has focused on vocational and professional goals for educational achievement, these are by no means its only purposes. Martin Nakata from Torres Strait argues (1996: 19) for the political value of high-level literacy, and suspects the political motives behind not providing it.

> One of the premises for the teaching of English [is] the primary principle of its incorporation into our lives as a political tool. If this could be the premise then the teaching of it might have to gear up, with a sense of urgency, to the task of equipping Islanders with English skills to fully participate in their own history. I suspect, in fact I know, that the teaching of English is geared down, ... and the arguments for teaching traditional languages are in the ascendancy because linguists and anthropologists tell us we won't have an identity without it. ... I think that the understanding of the historical call for English might help proponents of bilingualism to really think about all the possibilities in trying to meet Islanders' need for English, or at the very least, to not override the urgency of effective English teaching.

For Nakata there is no question that a much higher proportion of his people are able to achieve high-level English literacy than currently do, and in a remarkable paper he details the history of their successes to prove it. He sees the fault as lying with a state education system that once openly denied indigenous people more than rudimentary schooling, but today impedes their access to English literacy by prioritizing a 'cultural agenda' that is advocated and legitimated in non-indigenous academic professions.

Models of language pedagogy in indigenous education

The Pitjantjatjara experience parallels what Nakata describes for the Torres Strait. During the 1980s for example, when I worked on community-based cultural training and rehabilitation programmes for Pitjantjatjara teenagers, up to 80 per cent of children from 12 to 20 were engaged in chronic continuous petrol sniffing, resulting in death or neurological damage for a great many. To the community leaders who directed our work there seemed to be some connection between this disaster and problems with the education their children were receiving in the state-run community schools (Rose and Tjungutu Uwankaraku 1985). However, the schools generally denied responsibility for being the cause of or providing the solution to the substance abuse problem. The schools insisted that families alone were responsible for the behaviour of their children. This seemed paradoxical to us, since the schools' vernacular literacy curriculum was embedded in the principle of school responsibility

for culture and language 'maintenance', initiated by progressive missionaries in the 1940s (Duguid 1972), and continued under the influence of
contemporary linguists and educational theorists (Rose 1992). In talking
to members of the schools' staff at that time, we were often puzzled at the
apparent disjunction between what many understood the schools to be
doing and the reality of the outcomes, the lives of children outside the
schools, and the perceptions and goals of their families. Neither the
community members nor the school staff were fully aware of the extent to
which school philosophy, curricula and methods were driven by ideological struggles at the highest levels of the Western education system, and
how little autonomy the local schools had to fashion appropriate teaching
methods for Anangu children that could ensure their community goals.
While the school staff were led to believe their vernacular curriculum was
meeting community needs, it was, in Bernstein's terms, a 'recontextualised discourse'. This discourse was not recontextualized directly from
the community into the school however; it had been mediated through a
hierarchy of linguists, educational researchers, teacher trainers and curriculum producers – 'recontextualizing agents' whose work was framed
within highly contested theories of language and learning.

These ideological struggles over pedagogy were not local only to
Australia. They had emerged from movements in the socio-economic
structure of the western middle class, which had major effects on educational philosophy in British, North American and Australian schools
(Kalantzis and Cope 1993), and consequently on indigenous education.
The cultural protectionism associated with vernacular literacy programmes was one of three contemporary approaches to pedagogy that
Bernstein (1996) describes as 'competence models'. During the 1970s,
proponents of competence models had successfully opposed themselves
to traditional 'performance models' in Australian primary schooling; subsequently they had come to dominate literacy teaching theory in indigenous education. Other researchers, such as Delpit (1988), have referred
to the antagonism of competence towards performance more narrowly as
'the skills/process debate'. Bernstein identifies two other types of competence model: progessivism, associated with contemporary 'child-centred'
writing methodologies in primary schools such as 'whole language' or
'process writing'; and radicalism, associated with 'critical' or 'self-directed'
theories of education that feature particularly in indigenous teacher and
adult education programmes. Each presupposes an innate set of competences within the learner – cognitive, linguistic, cultural or emancipatory –
that can ostensibly be actualized through appropriate pedagogic practices
and contexts.

Briefly, performance models emphasize acquisition of 'the specialized
skills necessary to [produce] a specific output, text or product' (Bernstein
1996: 58). They are oriented towards goals in vocational and professional
training and are sequenced and paced to enable successful learners to
meet these goals. Performance models are associated with what Bernstein

has called 'visible pedagogies', in which the expected textual performances, the procedures for producing them, and the criteria for assessing
them are made visible to learners. Providing this information to learners is
an explicit role of teachers in these modes. Partly on this basis, visible pedagogies are opposed as 'teacher-centred', authoritarian and repressive by
proponents of competence models, where 'the emphasis is upon the realization of competences that acquirers already possess, or are thought to
possess' (Bernstein 1996: 58). Competence models tend to be associated
with 'invisible pedagogies', in which educational goals are construed as
internal to the learner, so their acquisition may not be externally observable. Sequencing and pacing may be flattened to ensure that all learners
have equal opportunity to actualize competences. Competence models
claim to be 'learner-centred' and demand that teachers' roles as instructional authorities should be constrained to managing the contexts for
learners' self-actualization. Consequently teachers' roles as regulative
authorities in the classroom tend also to be realized implicitly; authority is
present but it may be less visible, especially to learners from non-middle
class groups such as indigenous children. In these modes,

> the discursive rules (the rules of order of instruction) are known only to the
> transmitter, and in this sense a pedagogic practice of this type is invisible to the
> acquirer, essentially because the acquirer appears to fill the pedagogic space
> rather than the transmitter (Bernstein 1990: 70).

Features of competence and performance models are summarized in
Table 8.1.

Table 8.1 Features of pedagogic models

Pedagogic model	Emphasis	Pedagogic practice	Modes
performance	acquiring skills for text production	visible	e.g. vocational, professional
competence	actualizing innate competences	invisible	progressivist, 'bilingual', radical

Although the origins of competence pedagogies lie in Western intellectual
movements of the 1960s and 1970s (e.g. Chomsky, Piaget, Labov, Freire),
they have been legitimated in indigenous Australian education by portraying them as therapeutic for communities and individuals' (potential)
crises of personal identity, cultural maintenance or ideological domination. Conversely performance models are portrayed as personally intrusive, culturally polluting or ideologically hegemonic. Unfortunately, as
Japangardi Poulson, Lester and Nakata point out, English literacy out-

comes for indigenous students, over the past twenty years of competence pedagogies, have been disappointing. It is notable on the other hand, that these indigenous leaders acquired their own English skills in the pre-1970 tradition of performance-oriented literacy methods. As these outcomes suggest, the literacy methods of competence theories, whether 'vernacular', 'progressive' or 'critical', have no more inherent legitimacy in indigenous education than traditional Western approaches to literacy. Rather, competence theories are recontextualized and legitimated in indigenous education by portraying a unique set of characteristics for indigenous students – psychological, cultural or ideological – for which competence practices are then argued to be uniquely appropriate. They are not designed to enable the kinds of educational achievement required for vocational and professional training.

While indigenous communities are concerned to transmit their traditional cultures and languages to their children, most see the crucial role of primary schooling as providing the English literacy skills needed for educational success. Japangardi Poulson (1988: 68) stresses this:

> School should teach English and the job of looking after Aboriginal culture is best left to the families. Aboriginal culture belongs to Aboriginal families as it always has and it is not the business of the school to protect it or look after it.

Delpit (1988: 283) illustrates the same point for Native American and African-American parents, quoting one parent who demands that 'My kids know how to be Black – you all teach them how to be successful in the white man's world'. In other words the dichotomy drawn by competence theorists between cultural competence and performance in school does not serve the interests of marginalized minorities. As Delpit (1988) puts it,

> those who are most skillful at educating Black and poor children do not allow themselves to be placed in 'skills' or 'process' boxes. They understand the need for both approaches, the need to help students to establish their own voices, but to coach those voices to produce notes that will be heard clearly in the larger society.

In this view, learners' existing 'competences' are recognized as starting points for exploring new ways of meaning, that will eventually enable discursive 'performances' that are successful in formal education contexts. To inform such an approach, teachers need to understand the learning sequence from both sides; they need to know something of the cultural and linguistic competences that learners bring to the learning task, as well as the nature of the new tasks they need to learn.

Cultural contexts and school discourse

The English literacy tasks associated with school education are framed within specific kinds of cultural contexts by the indigenous leaders we have quoted. These include the vocational and professional contexts that are crucial to any modern community, as well as broader contexts of political participation. For these leaders the goal of school is to apprentice indigenous learners into the discourses associated with these cultural contexts, discourses that they recognize are only accessible through the medium of written English. (For perspectives on cultural positioning of discourses, see for example Kress 1985; Fairclough 1989; Gee 1990.) However these discourses are highly specialized, not only horizontally by the type of profession they are associated with, but also vertically by socioeconomic class. Western education systems have evolved in this context to deliver outcomes that are specialized both horizontally and vertically, most generally as professional, vocational or manual (Rose *et al.* 1992; Rose 1997). Only about 10 to 20 per cent of students are enabled to continue to professional tertiary education, a larger proportion are able to enter vocational training, while the majority who are least successful may only be able to find manual work on leaving school, or no work at all.

In other words, schooling also fails to prepare large sectors of nonindigenous communities for the professional cultural contexts that indigenous parents want their children to become competent in. It restricts access to these vocational and professional contexts by providing unequal degrees of access to the discourses in which they are framed (Martin 1990). These discourses are associated with what Bernstein has called 'elaborated codes', which he argues have evolved in stratified industrial cultures, and are realized, for example, in the abstract written discourses of the sciences and bureaucratic administration. Halliday (1985, 1993), and Martin (1993) demonstrate how the grammatical realizations of these discourses differ qualitatively from everyday spoken discourse, employing in particular the resources of grammatical metaphor (e.g. nominalization of processes and causal relations between them). Halliday and Martin demonstrate how these grammatical resources have evolved in written modes, to enable elements of meaning to be textually 're-packaged', to organize the flow of information in written text.[3] These modes of meaning have evolved to enable written discourse, but they also exclude speakers who are unfamiliar with them, an effect sometimes exploited to deliberately prevent participation in technocratic decision-making (Lemke 1990).

Bernstein describes elaborated codes as constituting the 'cultural/ pedagogic relay' of modern stratified mass societies and traces their origin to the institutionalizing of theological discourse in medieval universities and monastic schools. However he draws a distinction between an *elaborated code* and *elaborated orientations*. He argues that abstract orders of meaning can be features of societies with either complex or simple divisions of labour, that both elaborated codes and elaborated orientations 'are the media for thinking the 'unthinkable', the 'impossible', because the meanings they give rise to go beyond local space, time, context and embed and relate the latter to a transcendental space, time, context' (1990: 182). Elaborated orientations are realized, for example, in the cosmologies of small-scale societies, but their 'code of cultural transmission, *the relay itself*, is not an elaborated code' (1990: 251). While the grammatical patterns of their realization as spoken texts are no different from those of everyday spoken discourse, the elaborated orientations to meaning that these texts encode are realized by layers of interlocking semantic features whose significance is revealed in stages of members' ceremonial apprenticeship (Rose 1991, 1993). In Anangu cosmology for example, a mythic hero's rescue and distribution of domestic fire to the people is linked, through narrative and ceremony, to the elders' distribution of 'cultural fire' (i.e. secret/sacred knowledge) to new initiates, encoding an abstract principle of social order embedded in the powerful transforming experience of initiation.4 Access to elaborated orientations to meaning is as crucial for social control in indigenous as in Western societies; but while access in the former is distributed according to age and ceremonial participation, in stratified societies it is distributed according to socio-economic class, through access to the abstract resources of written text. In indigenous cultures, apprenticeship into elaborated ways of meaning begins at around puberty in the education surrounding initiation. In Western schooling this is the time when successful learners begin to acquire the elaborated *code* of middle-class culture, that is, in the early years of secondary school.

Schooling provides access for the minority to elaborated codes by means of a set of discursive practices that are specialized to school education – discourses that Bernstein describes as 'recontextualized' from their fields of production. So in order to master vocational and professional discourses, learners must first master the recontextualized discourses of schooling. These discourses are realized in types of written texts and classroom interactions that become progressively more complex and abstract from early primary to senior secondary school. The sequence ensures that those learners who do not acquire them in primary years will not have access to their more complex, abstract forms in later years, and so will not be able to go on to higher education. School discourses, from early primary on, have evolved to apprentice children into decontextualized ways of meaning (Wertsch 1990; Olson 1994) thus enabling them to develop an orientation to meaning that is abstracted from familiar local contexts. School discourse is, in other words, a discourse about other discourses whose contexts lie beyond the walls of the classroom (Christie 1993). It involves learning to do more than interact discursively with elders and peers, but to interact with them around the construction of texts. The subject matter of these texts, spoken and written, lies beyond the immediate contexts of classroom interactions; the subject matter of the interactions is the discursive construction of the texts – the meanings they represent and the realizations of these meanings as wordings, i.e. as their language features.

Children from literate middle-class families are already prepared to engage in these decontextualized forms of discourse before they arrive at school, and as they progress through the sequence, their discursive experiences of home and school may be mutually reinforced. This preparation for engagement with decontextualized meanings pervades their home experience from their earliest years in the form of spoken interactions and joint book readings with parents modelling elaborated orientations to spoken and written texts (Painter 1986, this volume Chapter 3; Williams, this volume Chapter 4; Cloran, this volume Chapter 2). These modes of child-parent interaction around texts have certainly evolved very recently within the Western middle class, in tandem with the evolution of schooling, maximizing the probabilities for maintenance or advancement of families' class positioning. From this perspective an invisible school pedagogy is advantageous to those sectors of a stratified society whose economic base is discursive rather than material. The outcomes of these pedagogies suggest that they have evolved to enable success for middle-class learners and to simultaneously ensure failure for others, despite the apparently liberal progressive ideologies in which they are framed.

Indigenous students in particular are excluded by invisible pedagogies from accessing school discourses. The discursive experience that most young indigenous children bring to school does not include the same orientation to decontextualized meanings that middle-class Western families inculcate. Whether their home languages include traditional languages or varieties of English, young indigenous children's discursive experience is predominantly grounded in familiar local contexts of spoken interaction (Gray 1986, 1990). This does not mean that decontextualized meanings are not a feature of adult discourse in indigenous communities, as I have exemplified for religious texts, but that children learn to engage with them through a learning sequence that differs from that of the Western middle class. They are not prepared by their family experience, before they come to school, to engage with the particular elaborated orientations to discourse that are crucial for 'doing school'. What this does mean is that when indigenous children come to school, in order to engage successfully with the decontextualizing forms of school discourse, they will tend to need explicit instruction in their purposes, texts and forms of interaction. That this currently does not happen sufficiently is attested by the difficulties experienced by indigenous children from the earliest years of schooling (Malin 1994), and their unacceptably high drop-out rate in middle secondary school.

What is required is an approach to language pedagogy that makes the realizations of decontextualized discourses visible to indigenous children. These realizations include both the language features of the written texts they are engaging with, and the patterns of teacher-learner interaction around these language features. In other words, teachers need to design learning activities that will enable children to develop an elaborated orientation to discourse; they need to be clear about how the procedures of each learning activity will enable children to meet these goals, and they need to make these procedures visible to the children. In order to do this teachers need to be able to analyse both the cultural and linguistic competences that children bring to a learning task, and the cultural and linguistic features of the texts and interactions they will learn to engage with. To illustrate the competences that indigenous children bring with them to school, I will present a few texts spoken and written by learners in varieties of English. The analysis is also intended to introduce the reader to a functional perspective on language features that can be applied in English language and literacy teaching (e.g. Martin and Rothery 1993). These texts were produced by older learners, but they are little different from the English texts produced by indigenous children at any stage of primary schooling. The texts exemplify the failure of much current practice to enable effective English literacy development. This will be followed by a discussion of current literacy methodologies in indigenous schooling, concluding with a description of a literacy approach, developed by Gray (1986, 1987, 1990), that has proven successful for indigenous children.

Some features of 'Aboriginal English': spoken and written

Various types of 'Aboriginal English' are spoken in all indigenous communities in Australia, whether the variety is classified by linguists as a 'creole', a 'pidgin' or a 'non-standard English'. In each of these varieties the lexical 'content' words tend to be mainly English, but grammatical structures may be hybrids of English and indigenous grammar structures, and English grammatical items such as prepositions, reference items, relational verbs, and auxiliary verbs of tense and modality may be absent or transformed. Despite these structural differences, there is no question that the meaning potential of these indigenous varieties is just as functional for spoken communication as are other dialects of English spoken by other speech communities. Our question here concerns the relation between these spoken dialects and the written mode of English that children need to engage with to succeed in schooling. From this perspective the thirty-year-old debate between 'deficit' and 'difference' views of dialect (e.g. Labov 1969) that still plagues indigenous education (e.g. Harkins 1994) is irrelevant. This debate fails to address the problem that no matter what spoken dialect children bring to school, it still remains only a starting point for engaging with school discourse. Furthermore 'difference' arguments gloss over the fact that if the variety children speak differs significantly from the variety spoken and written by their teachers, they will have an additional learning load that teachers need additional resources to help with.

To illustrate the kinds of resources that teachers need, we can begin by exemplifying a few linguistic differences, both between indigenous and 'standard' dialects and between spoken and written modes of English, first with a spoken example (Text 1), and then with two written examples (Texts 2, 3). Text 1 is a story told (with some prompting by a teacher) by a young man (W) educated in Northern Territory 'bilingual' community schools and at a secondary college for indigenous students. W's spoken and written English skills were evaluated by his community adult educator as higher than many of his peers in Anangu communities in South Australia. The story is about an Anangu family that was found by their kinsmen in the late 1980s, still living in the desert twenty-five years after all their neighbours had been removed to a distant government settlement. Each line in W's story is numbered for analysis. The teacher's prompts are indicated by 'Tch' and italics.

Text 1

1   This at Kiwirrkurra.
2   They saw two bush mens coming, for the water.
3   They thought a *kutatji* (wild man).
4   They followed track in the morning
5   and they found all the family was there.
Tch *What did those bush people think?*
6   They was thinking,
7   and them old ones say 'Oh, we our own country.'
Tch *Did they tell the story about what happened?*
8   They thinks 'a lotta people roun' here',
9   like only they left, just mother and father.
Tch *Are they alright now, still there?*
10   Yeah, they still there.
11   They've got homeland.

There is no doubt, as competence theorists would argue, that this text is a successful instance of communication. The speaker is able to represent a sequence of events to his English-speaking listener and, with prompting, provide an evaluation (6–9) and coda (10–11) to the story. However the text also provides us with information about W's current English competence that could inform the literacy teaching he expects from his community adult education programme. This information includes first, a set of consistent grammatical differences from general spoken English. For example, there is no verb in the relational clause in line 1 'This (was) at Kiwirrkurra', nor in 3, 7, 8, 9 and 10, because relational clauses in Australian (and many other) languages need not include a verb, and this feature is carried over into W's approximation of English relational clauses. In line 3 ('they thought a *kutatji*'), thinking is treated like perceiving – 'they saw/heard a *kutatji*' – because thinking and perceiving are construed similarly in Australian languages (Rose 1996), whereas English makes clear grammatical distinctions between them, e.g. 'they thought it was a *kutatji*' (Halliday 1994). We can also readily identify absent or changed reference items, such as:

- pronominal reference: in line 2, 'they' refers exophorically to the people of Kiwirrkurra, whose identity would first be introduced explicitly in a typical English narrative (Martin 1992); and in 7, the non-standard 'them old ones';

- possessive reference: in 4 'they followed (the bush men's) track'
- demonstrative reference: in 9, 'just (a/the) mother and father', and in 11 'They've got (a) homeland'; and the double plural in 2, 'two bush mens'. There are also tense differences, such as 'say' for said in 7, and 'thinks' for thought in 8.

These elements of grammar and discourse structure are potential points of focus for English teaching. However, above the level of grammar we also need to look at the whole text, how it is organized, and what kinds of meanings are expected and given at each stage. The story begins with setting the location, just as in any English recount, but very soon ends with finding the family in line 5. The teacher however prompts for an evaluation, 'What did they think?'. W recognizes what is expected, although he responds to the request for a mental reaction with a verbal one, 'them old ones say "Oh, we our own country"'. The teacher then asks for this to be elaborated, and W struggles with his repertoire of the English grammar of mental and verbal projection to respond in 8 and 9, to describe what the old people said they were thinking. The sentence begins in 8 as a quoted thought 'They thinks "a lotta people round here"', but winds up in 9 as a reported one, 'like only they left, just mother and father', as W struggles with person, place and time references and conjunctions in English projections. The meaning apparently intended is 'They told us that they'd thought, "There used to be a lot of people around here, but now only we are left, just a mother and father"'. Mental projections in Australian languages may also either be quoted or reported, but their grammar differs from English projections in precisely those features that are problematic for this speaker. Finally the teacher probes for a comment or coda, which W supplies in 10 and 11, returning the narrative to the present and closing the story.

The short recount of lines 1 to 5 closely resembles much of the English writing that indigenous children do in primary and early secondary school, particularly where English is a second language, i.e. a simple narrative sequence with little elaboration of lexis, time sequencing, reactions, dialogue, complications or evaluations. Gray (1986) reported that English texts written by indigenous children in Northern Territory schools *all* belong to the type 'recount', i.e. simple transcriptions from a text type familiar in children's oral experience. This recount is an example of what W can achieve alone without support, and he appears to consider it a sufficient text. However, when the teacher demands more interpersonally oriented content, by means of specifically focused prompt questions, W recognizes what is expected and responds appropriately. He is able to do so because such evaluative meanings are a feature of narrative in Australian languages, as much as English narratives. What he has difficulty with is the complex English grammar in which to express such meanings.

Clearly these grammatical features have not been a significant or effective focus of W's English language education to date. Some of his teachers may have recognized problems of limited English vocabulary, so-called 'errors' of grammatical structure, and so on. But it is probable, given the withdrawal from teacher training in Australia of both grammar and direct approaches to intervention in literacy learning, that they have not had the resources to help him to extend his repertoire significantly. Minimal interventions allowed in progressivist writing methods, such as 'How would you make the story longer?', or 'What could you do to make it more interesting?', are unlikely to elicit language resources very different from what has already been presented in a short recount, but rather more of the same. Such questions do not sufficiently specify the kinds of information expected, because they don't reflect the grammatical features that encode the desired information. In contrast, the teacher's focus questions in Text 1 do specify that mental or verbal projections are expected to express evaluations, 'What did they think?', 'Did they tell?'. In a teaching cycle, W's responses could then have formed the basis for practising some of the grammatical structures he has difficulty with, looking for examples in other texts, using comparison between contrasting examples to show how they work, and by the teacher modelling their use in context. The important lesson here, however, is that there is a gap between what a learner can do independently, and what s/he can achieve with support and focused prompting by a teacher, the interactional learning space that Vygotsky (1978) called a 'zone of proximal development'. Armed with sufficient knowledge about language, and with appropriate strategies to focus and extend learners' attention to specific meanings, teachers can guide their students to produce more effective texts than they can on their own.

To illustrate this further, the following are two texts written by indigenous children with minimal intervention. Both texts are responses produced by 14-year-old secondary school students to an autobiographical writing task.

Text 2 My Home is Fregon

1   I like to played football
2   and I like to ride on my motor bike
3   and I like to go to Fregon school and training
4   and I like played wass my brother
5   and I go to Ernabella to I to stay wass my little brother
6   and on the weekend liked to play game
7   and I likes to played B-grade for Fregon
8   and played wass my little brother for walk to

Text 2 was evaluated by the secondary programme as 'low achievement'. The writer (V) is from an Anangu community in South Australia, where his primary schooling consisted of a combination of vernacular literacy and English. The text consists of a series of comments, responding to a task such as 'Write about your community', and prompts such as 'What do you like about it?' So each activity but two are written as mental projections of the same type 'I like to . . . ', a type of wording common to both Australian languages and English (Rose 1996). However language resources in the text do not reflect V's competence either in his indigenous language or his dialect of English. He uses a far more limited repertoire of English lexis and grammar than he speaks, including only four verbs besides 'like', seven common nouns, and a single resource for linking clauses, the conjunction 'and'. He uses only two tenses and, like W, cannot manipulate time reference in English projections, e.g. 'I likes to played B-grade'.

On the other hand, it is interesting to see a range of time and place phrases, all with prepositions. V has clearly been taught the functions of English prepositions, and also that time phrases can come first in a sentence, as in line 6, 'on the weekend . . . '. He understands the semantic necessity for prepositions in English to the extent that he makes the effort to invent spelling for one ('wass my little brother'), to express the distinction between location 'on', and accompaniment 'with' (Halliday 1994). What he can't do unassisted is to use resources such as time phrases for sequencing a narrative, an essential resource in written English (Rothery 1990), nor is he able to interpret the task as requiring a narrative response. It is likely that V is a poor reader of English. Although he has control over the core of the English graphic system, and can spell common words accurately, he has not acquired sufficient skills to be able to recognize many common language features, nor how to appropriate them to extend his own writing.

Text 3 was evaluated as 'satisfactory'. The writer (Y) is from a Northern Territory community where English literacy has been the focus of the school curriculum. Y is able to respond to the task with a sequenced story, and uses a larger range of English language features to do so. Among these are not only time and place phrases for sequencing events, but also subordinate clauses 'When we got there . . . ', 'When we parked the Toyota . . . ', 'When we watched video . . . ' (Halliday 1994). These marked 'themes' of sentences are in italic below.

Text 3 In few years' time

1   *In the holiday* I went with Lisa to Alice Springs.
2   *When we got there* we went to the disco
3   Lisa and I were sitting on the car
4   because we were too scared to get out
5   lots of drunks were standing outside the disco.
6   *After that* we saw Justin and his uncle
7   they came on a bus.
8   *When we parked the Toyota,* Lisa and I we were still sitting on the Toyota.
9   *After that* a drunk woman came
10 and said to us 'have you seen my boyfriend'
11 and we said 'no we haven't seen your boyfriend and we don't know who is it.'
12 *After that* we went back to home.

13   *When we got there* we were watching video about cartoon.
14   *When we watched video* we went to sleep.

Y has attempted to respond to the task with a narrative of personal experience, but has difficulty employing the English resources she knows to construct a successful written narrative. The temporal themes are used, not to mark discrete stages of the text, but rather each event, possibly because Y has been taught to use 'when' and 'after', instead of stringing a sequence together with 'and': it is crossed out in 3, and only used in 10 and 11 for the dialogue sequence. There is an Orientation stage from 1–5, but a potential Complication is not clearly signalled ('After that a drunk woman came'), and there is no effective Resolution other than 'After that we went back to home'. If the writer had been able to deploy resources such as marked themes for staging of the text, and mental reactions for evaluating the Complication, the story might have been more successful. We could also note that, although it is more elaborate than Text 2, there is still a very limited range of lexis used in Text 3, and little expansion of nominal groups to elaborate descriptions.

Despite their limited written English resources, W, V and Y all display a potential conscious orientation to patterns of language, and the ability to extend their English repertoire when their attention is drawn to specific features. The features they attend to include text stages, such as evaluation or comment, and grammatical features such as mental projections, temporal clauses and prepositional phrases. This capacity to attend to language patterns constitutes the central resource for literacy learning that teachers need to take advantage of and extend. But teachers can only do so effectively if they themselves possess a systematic knowledge of the language patterns they are teaching. Clearly, some teachers of V and Y have been aware of certain features of written English that their students need to learn, and have explicitly shown how to use them. These range from elements of the graphic system such as spelling and punctuation, to grammatical items such as prepositions, conjunctions and temporal themes. However the features these young writers have acquired are isolated, both from their potential functions in constructing meaningful texts, and from the whole system of English grammar resources they are part of.

These children are already approaching middle high school age, and their writing skills are representative of those of many of their indigenous peers. If they are to have a chance of going further in their education, they need to rapidly extend their command of written English text. The question is how this could be achieved, given that they have already spent up to eight years immersed in school. The difficulties such children have with writing development can no longer be blamed on cultural differences or unfamiliarity with 'Western' teaching methods, since these have been a significant part of their cultural experience throughout childhood. Rather, to understand the problem and identify effective approaches, we need to look squarely at the nature of the literacy methodologies they

have been experiencing all this time. These methodologies usually
include progressivist approaches to writing and in many schools include
writing in local vernacular languages. Both models share similar assumptions about the nature of linguistic and cultural competence.

Vernacular literacy

The issue of vernacular literacy is a complicated one. These programmes
are legitimated in indigenous education along three general lines. The primary rationale is maintenance or revival of community languages, which is
a concern for many communities. However, since English literacy is also
their goal for schools, teaching vernacular literacy before English is ratio-
nalized along two lines: first that learning literacy in children's first language facilitates transfer of this skill to written English, and second that
there is essentially no difference in meaning potential between indigenous
languages and written English, so teaching written English in the primary
years is an unnecessary imposition. In its extreme form this argument por-
trays English teaching from early primary school as 'assimilationist' (e.g.
Harkins 1994). What it ignores is the fact that many indigenous communities that maintain strong cultural and linguistic traditions have had all-Eng-
lish teaching in their schools for three or more generations. English
literacy should make available to children opportunities for learning new
cultural contexts that will enable them to control the changes to come in
their lives. Teaching English literacy in school does not exclude them from
learning in the traditional cultural contexts of their communities; to por-
tray it as assimilationism is a misrepresentation. Assimilationism was practised in the colonial era by forcibly denying communities the opportunity
to teach their traditions to their children, by severely punishing the use of
traditional languages and ceremonial practices, by locking children up in
dormitories away from their families, or by removing children from their
families and placing them in institutions or foster care.

   For these reasons the need and value of schools to support community
language maintenance varies considerably across regions. In most rural
and urban communities in Australia, traditional languages are no longer
spoken – a consequence of dispersal, enforced settlement and assimilationist policies of state and mission authorities. Many of these communities are now interested in re-learning traditional languages from written
records of missionaries, ethnologists and linguists, together with advice
from the few surviving speakers where available. In regions colonized this
century, such as the pastoral areas of outback Australia, traditional languages may still be widely spoken but communities are concerned that
children are not learning them, since their cultural contexts of use have
been disrupted and varieties of English have become linguae francae.
There is a potential role in these and other communities for schools to
support traditional language learning, for example by providing curriculum time and resources for community elders to instruct children

within appropriate cultural contexts, particularly in contexts outside the classroom (Nganyintja and Rose 1991). Such activities can also be linked to context-based English literacy learning programmes, such as the 'concentrated language encounters' developed by Gray (1986, 1987, 1990).

However, vernacular literacy programmes as they are currently taught in community schools do not originate from the cultural contexts of children's natural language learning. Their curricula are recontextualized from academic descriptions of indigenous languages and are largely taught within conventional classroom contexts, typically by non-indigenous teachers assisted by indigenous teacher aides, with community contexts as occasional adjuncts. While it is often claimed that vernacular literacy 'empowers' indigenous teachers, the necessity for professional English literacy ensures that control of curriculum, school management and most classrooms remains in non-indigenous hands. Furthermore, the value of these programmes for culture and language maintenance remains questionable, as the long-term social outcomes in the Pitjantjatjara communities suggest. Researching their linguistic outcomes, Martin (1990: 16) found that,

> currently, writing in the vernacular does not complement speaking; it's simply a rather ineffective watered down version of it – a poor relation . . . This kind of writing program does not appear to be what Aboriginal people want or need to make their languages and cultures strong.

In practice, because of the prohibitive costs of linguistic description, curriculum development and teaching by non-local professionals, it is usually those languages which are most widely spoken and least likely to be lost that are exploited for vernacular literacy programmes. Vernacular programmes tend to exploit languages spoken in reserve communities settled since the 1930s, although descriptions of local creoles and 'Aboriginal English' are also written into curricula. Indigenous communities call these varieties '[cattle] station' or 'broken' English, and associate them with a passing colonial era. But descriptive linguists (who codify the language features in doctoral theses) argue that they should not just be recognized and valued in schools, but that they must be 'conserved' through vernacular literacy curricula. Rhydwen (1993) characterizes these recontextualizing practices as a form of neo-colonialism. Muhlhauser (1995: 252) demonstrates that,

> the idea that pidgins and creoles of the area (Australia and the South Pacific) should be reduced to writing originated with outsiders; it neither reflects the socio-economic realities of the main user groups, nor necessarily their aspirations.

The second claim, that English literacy is facilitated by first learning an orthography devised for local spoken languages, appears to have some merit, but is not borne out by the experience of indigenous children. The

claim is typically legitimated from studies of second-language learning
where the first language already has a written mode, and arises from a
naive perception of the nature of written language as little more than
grapho-phonic correspondences with speech. This results in what Martin
(1990: 17) calls 'the transcription model of literacy currently being
implemented in the vernacular'. The most damning evidence against the
transferability claim is from the longest running vernacular literacy programme in indigenous Australian schools, the programme in the Pitjantjatjara communities. This programme was finally abandoned in 1991 after
a ten-year campaign by the communities to win policy control over the
schools, precisely because, like the two generations before them, their
children were not acquiring even a primary school level of English literacy
(Rose 1992). As a result middle secondary schooling is offered to only 10
to 15 per cent of Anangu children, and senior secondary to only a small
handful. Rather than 'vernacular literacy first', a more effective sequence
may be to teach oral English from the first years of school, as a step
towards English literacy. Such a programme could be one component of a
truly bilingual curriculum, grounded in the cultural contexts of both community languages and English.

While descriptive linguists demand that schools model language curriculum on their descriptions of community languages, few can offer
teachers much in the way of practical classroom strategies. A recent example is Harkins (1994: 195). Following a conventional formal linguistic
account of characteristic words, phrases and sentences of 'Aboriginal English', teachers are offered no more than,

> teaching or drilling aimed at getting them to speak English in a non-Aboriginal
> way will probably fail, since *that is not their goal*. They will probably want to
> develop a *passive* but quite deep understanding of English constructions, styles
> and registers that *they may never choose to use themselves*. (emphasis added)

Although opposed to 'teaching [*sic*] or drilling', descriptive linguists such
as Harkins can offer little positive advice to teachers to enable even a
'passive understanding' of English. In practice, since they are based on
formalist linguistic orthographies and grammars, drilling in sound-letter
correspondences and syntactic structures is one of the few teaching strategies available to vernacular literacy programmes (Brian Gray personal
communication 1997).

This failure of formal descriptive linguistics to inform practical classroom English literacy strategies is compounded by a widespread set of
assumptions about 'Aboriginal learning styles' that originate in ethnologi-
cal research of the 1970s, framed within competence assumptions. Most
influential in Australia has been Harris (1980) who, on the basis of a
series of observations of hunting, ceremonial and other practices, claimed
that 'observation', 'imitation' and 'trial-and-error' are the predominant
learning modes in indigenous cultures, and that verbal interaction

between children and adults 'is largely unnecessary to Yolngu learning situations'. However, even Harris' examples of 'trial-and-error' include verbal instructions, and he concedes that 'Yolngu will instruct others verbally when in new situations'. Indeed close observation of how children learn cultural procedures over time, and how families guide the linguistic development of young children, reveals that verbal interaction is as crucial to learning as it has been shown to be in Western families (Halliday 1975; Wells 1981; Bruner 1986; Painter 1985, 1986). In my own experience of learning and long-term observations of children learning indigenous languages, efforts at communication are continually scaffolded by adult speakers, carefully adjusting the complexity of their speech to extend learner's competence, rephrasing learners' wordings to model the grammatical features of adult discourse, explaining meanings, and giving positive feedback at each new step in acquisition. In the contexts of apprenticeship into ceremonial Law,[5] I have also experienced and observed how young men are continually guided and instructed in the rules of performance of ceremonial practices and texts, and in the abstract orders of meaning they realize, by senior men and our classificatory older brothers. Similar observations are made by Gray (1990) of interaction in ceremonial contexts as well as classroom interaction between indigenous children and teachers. These teaching practices closely parallel Bernstein's description of visible pedagogies. They are focused on enabling learners to meet the criteria of successful performance; the teachers' authority is an explicit component of the interactive context.[6]

Progressivist writing methodologies

These observations of explicit teaching practice also contrast with some other popular characterizations of indigenous 'learning styles', such as 'the initiative often lies with the learner' and 'most learning activities are ends in themselves and not necessarily means to future ends' (Hughes 1984: 22). Such statements could be applied to a range of contexts in any culture, but as I have illustrated, there are as many examples of indigenous learning situations where the initiative lies with teachers and the activities are merely components of a long-term learning process. However statements such as these happen to mesh with the other pervasive influence on indigenous education practice – the set of 'child-centred' writing methodologies known as progressivism. Whether or not vernacular literacy is part of the school curriculum, progressivist methods dominate language teaching in indigenous schools, as much as they have dominated 'mainstream' Australian primary teaching for the past twenty years.

Like vernacular literacy, progressivist theories value what they see as children's pre-existing linguistic competences over any new information a teacher is likely to present. These are in Bernstein's analysis invisible pedagogies. As Gray (1987: 10) describes them, the teacher challenges the child to look into his/her own language resources. The challenge assumes the child will look back into what Harste, Woodward and Burke (1984) call his/her 'linguistic data bank', which the child has internalised from his prior experience, to find for himself the language resources required to complete the task.

Most contemporary writing methodologies in Australian schools still construe grammar in traditional formal terms, as sets of rules for 'correct' utterances, so 'no writer can worry about spelling and grammar and things like that while first trying to get his ideas down' (Harste *et al.* 1984: 227). This contrasts with the functional perspective on grammar as a resource that enables speakers to interact, represent their experience and organize text in various ways. (See Martin and Rothery 1993 for comparisons of these linguistic paradigms.) In the formalist view of language, meaning is located in individual words, as in a dictionary, so that 'linguistic data' consists of collections of words, and is expanded by vocabulary extension exercises. Grammar is construed in this view as the 'mechanics of language', as arbitrary and non-meaningful as the rules of spelling. In general the progressivist orientation in contemporary writing methodologies either proscribes, or places strong limits on, intervention by the teacher in learners' creative processes, except to help correct spelling and grammar 'errors' afterwards, in the 'editing' phase.

'Editing' is the only point in these methodologies where there is much opportunity to explicitly teach the language features of written English, but it is not possible to teach more than a few isolated features, without intervening in the learner's authorial 'ownership' of the text. Higher level features such as appropriate genre, text staging, sequencing of events, elaboration of descriptions, thoughts, feelings and dialogue, time and person reference and so on, are left up to learners to discover for themselves. While some methodologies may encourage provision of 'model texts' for learners, teachers' interventions in writing activities using such models is virtually non-existent. In effect the text model is provided and learners are left to their own resources to draw from it. For middle-class English-speaking children, discovering these resources on their own is possible to some extent; they acquire the literate resources of school discourse from their home experience of interacting and reading, but indigenous children, whose home language(s) may differ from school English, are seriously disadvantaged by progressivist assumptions about pre-existing linguistic competences.

While vernacular literacy and progressivist methods are intended to get children started with writing, they scarcely begin to address the difficulties indigenous children experience in engaging with the discourses of schooling. To the recontextualizing agents who propound these competence models, school discourses tend to be transparent. Their class positioning enabled them to acquire school discourses tacitly, without requiring explicit instruction, and the pedagogies they advance continue to treat these discourses as transparent, thus reproducing the cycle of exclusion. What is needed is a pedagogy that makes the forms of school discourses visible to indigenous learners, so that they have an equal opportunity to acquire them, a pedagogy that takes their discursive experience as a starting point and enables them to develop an elaborated orientation to written text.

A visible English literacy pedagogy for indigenous children

A language pedagogy designed to apprentice learners into new cultural contexts needs to be able to take these contexts as its starting point, and enable learners to recognize and appropriate new features of language that realize new contexts. In other words, the approach to learning language needs to move from its contexts of use, via the meanings that are features of these contexts, on to the wordings that realize these meanings. Such an approach contrasts with traditional 'rule'-based language teaching methods, that take the structures of wordings as their starting point, but significantly extends communicative approaches to language teaching by making explicit the meanings and wordings that realize communicative contexts. To inform such an approach, teachers need access to a model of language that can systematically relate wordings to meanings to the cultural contexts they realize, such as Halliday's (1994) functional description of English grammar, and Halliday and Hasan's (1976) and Martin's (1994) functional descriptions of English text. (For a practical, accessible outline of functional grammar see Gerot and Wignell 1994.) On the other hand, teachers also need access to strategies that will enable indigenous learners to make connections for themselves between new cultural contexts and the language features that realize them.

In this regard, Brian Gray's work with indigenous children in Alice Springs has influenced many teachers in the field. Gray (1985, 1986, 1990) advocated developing the content of language activities within academically task-focused interactive contexts, which he called 'concentrated language encounters'. Concentrated encounters provide for a negotiated approach to 'joint construction of meaning', influenced by the work of Bruner (1986) on 'scaffolding' and Vygotsky's social psychology of learning. This approach employs interaction in direct joint experiences, such as bringing horses and indigenous experts into the school, or hatching chickens in the classroom, that lead to jointly constructing texts such as specialized procedures or scientific explanations. However they can also be constructed around the joint exploration of written texts by teacher and learners. Gray's work also contributed to the evolution of the 'genre' approach to writing development (Martin et al. 1987; Christie et al. 1990–92; Hyon 1996), which has begun to infiltrate literacy teaching in indigenous education. These literacy pedagogies are 'visible' in Bernstein's terms since they are explicitly goal-oriented towards a sociocultural performance that lies beyond the learner's current individual competence. However they are not 'teacher-centred'. Rather the framing of authority shunts from teachers to learners at various stages of a learning sequence (Martin, this volume Chapter 5), parallelling the interaction of learners and elders in indigenous learning activities.

Building teacher–learner interaction around the deconstruction and reconstruction of meanings in written text is particularly important, for there is a point beyond which spoken interaction alone cannot teach written resources, the point at which reading has to take over. But as with spoken interaction, reading activities also need to be guided by teachers, focusing learners' attention on the language features they need to acquire. Progressive methods such as 'lap reading' and 'shared book experience', as these are currently employed in many classrooms, do not provide this focused guidance to the extent that many learners, especially indigenous children, require. On the other hand, the kinds of deconstruction and reconstruction of text in Gray's concentrated encounters, and also in the 'research' and 'text modelling' phases of the 'genre writing cycle', are designed to focus attention on significant features of written texts. A key area for teaching writing to indigenous learners is to enable them to participate meaningfully in these kinds of text deconstruction activities. Too many indigenous learners, like the writers of Texts 2 and 3, are inexperienced or poor readers of English; they do not have enough experience of reading to be able to identify, decode or appropriate unfamiliar wordings to extend their own repertoire. What is needed for these learners are strategies that can integrate learning to read school English with learning to write it, strategies in which written texts themselves constitute the language context to be explored together by teachers and learners.

Gray and his colleagues at the Schools and Community Centre of Canberra University have developed just such an approach for children experiencing difficulties with English literacy, using fluent and successful reading as the starting point for acquiring resources that are then applied in learning to write (Gray *et al.* 1995, forthcoming). The strategies they have developed are designed to take maximal advantage of learners' capacity to attend to language patterns, and are carefully planned and implemented to maximize the potential of teacher-learner interactions. Their goal is to enable children to shift the focus of their attention from the local context of interaction to the abstract context of the discursive task, and from ineffective literacy strategies, such as decoding words letter-by-letter, to fluent strategies such as automatic visual processing of written language features. An underlying principle is to take as much pressure as possible off learners to independently perform complex language tasks, by giving them sufficient support to achieve their potential in shared activities. An essential element of each learning activity is to explain and demonstrate task procedures to learners, so that they can focus on learning the skills involved, and not be placed under additional pressure to interpret an invisible structure and goal for each activity. Because the learning activity tasks are finite and proceduralized, they also have the advantage of being relatively easily learned and implemented by teachers.

The approach developed by Gray, Cowey and Graetz depends on teachers being able to analyse and select texts across the curriculum that are accessible to their students, including a finite set of language features beyond what they can currently read and write independently, but not more than they can learn without overload. In the first stage of the approach, 'text orientation', teacher and students jointly explore the selected text on several levels using a variety of strategies. These strategies represent an expansion of the 'research' and 'text modelling' phases in the genre approach (Martin this volume Chapter 5), providing a higher level of support for learners to recognize and appropriate features of model texts. In the process of joint reading, the teacher draws students' attention – through explanation, discussion and focused questioning – to the text-building functions of specific meanings, that students can then locate in the wordings of the text and make connections for themselves between meanings and written language features. The first level explored is the context that the text evokes: the field of experience it represents, the social relationships it enacts, and the discursive modes (oral and written) in which these can be presented. This is the point at which literacy learning may be thoroughly integrated with other curriculum activities (Kalantzis and Cope 1990). The next level to explore concerns the written resources that realize these dimensions of context. The focus on these features begins with text staging, and resources for linking clauses in a sequence. Within sentences it includes grammatical resources for elaborating events and descriptions, such as expanding clauses, circumstantial elements, and expanding nominal groups. Finally at word rank, it focuses on lexical items that represent specific kinds of processes, things or qualities, in order to extend learners' vocabulary. This is the point at which much current grammar teaching begins and ends, with vocabulary exercises such as spelling lists. However the approach here integrates vocabulary extension with the grammar and discourse contexts in which individual words work. Learning to recognize and use new lexis is part of a whole process of learning to recognize and use the lexicogrammatical patterns in which they occur. And the same approach applies in focusing learners' attention on meanings which they can identify as the written wordings that realize them.

Most importantly, Gray maintains that learners need to be able to read a text fluently before they can efficiently move on to deconstructing its language resources to appropriate for their own writing. Children who are poor readers frequently use a limited set of grapho-phonic strategies for decoding written text. They are often under too much processing stress (reading words letter-by-letter) to attend to higher level meanings; it is essential for them to attain fluency in reading a text before moving on to the next stage. By means of text orientation strategies, learners are supported to read the text fluently using their limited grapho-phonic skills together with their ability to predict meanings in context that familiarity with the text facilitates. Once they are able to read the text fluently it becomes possible to focus on both its lexicogrammatical features, and on learning the spelling patterns of words in the text. A key to the latter is shifting the learner from processing words in terms of letter–sound relationships, to processing them in terms of visual patterns, which is what efficient readers do automatically (Temple *et al.* 1993).

The next phase in the approach Gray calls 'reconstructed writing', in which the language resources of the selected text are appropriated by learners in order to construct their own texts. These resources include its field, stages, event sequence, grammar and lexis. This takes the pressure off learners to find or invent new resources for an original text. Instead they are guided, as much as they need, to practise writing a text from an existing model. The teacher is able to guide learners by means of discussion focused on specific text features, because they already have a basis of shared knowledge of the meanings in the original text and the wordings that realize them. Each of the text deconstruction and reconstruction strategies can continue to be used as learners move towards producing more original texts, both jointly with teachers and peers, and independently. They are designed to extend learners' conscious orientation to the features of texts they are reading and writing, enabling them to make choices themselves in how to use them to their own ends. The text patterns that were appropriated by the learners in their reconstructed writing form the basis for them to write other texts with new fields of their own choosing. Eventually the overall principle of text deconstruction and reconstruction is taken over by the learners and used independently to extend their own repertoire, as experienced writers do intuitively (Kress 1985).

The activities involved in reconstructed writing reflect learning activities that indigenous children regularly experience in their families and communities. The goal is to produce an approximate reproduction of a cultural product that is part of the community's repertoire. In this case the product to be reproduced is a text, and the interactive mode of its production resembles the ways that indigenous children are supported to produce oral texts by their elders and peers. Text deconstruction and reconstruction exploit the fact that written texts are both semiotic processes as well as products whose features can be pointed out and examined as models to approximate. The learner can use the adult product as a template for her own approximation, and the teacher can point out its features and take turns with the learner to demonstrate how it is produced. This is precisely how young indigenous people learn to produce both the material and semiotic products of their cultures, in joint activities with their elders who accompany the activity with commentary on the production process, drawing attention to the procedure, significant steps in it, and features of the product. In all societies such interactive learning activities are the foundation on which children learn to engage in the social construction of their cultures.

Conclusion

Indigenous communities have given a clear responsibility to educators to improve English literacy outcomes for their children. These improvements are well within reach, but they require certain changes in philosophy and practice. On the one hand, we need to modify ideas arising in Western middle-class culture, about the innate cultural and linguistic competences of learners, while embracing teaching methods that focus on how learners acquire competence through social interaction. On the other hand, we need to understand the features of written English that learners need to manipulate to perform successfully in school education, and to find effective teaching resources that will enable them to do so. In my own experience as a teacher and student of indigenous communities, one such effective resource is the writing methodology developed in the genre approach, employing Halliday's functional grammar of English. Even more promising for indigenous students struggling with written English, are the kinds of strategies developed by Gray, Cowey and Graetz. If these rich resources were available to teachers working with indigenous learners, it would go a long way towards fulfilling our responsibilities to their communities.

Notes

1 Indigenous peoples in the Australian context include Aboriginal peoples of the mainland states and Tasmania, and Torres Strait Islanders who identify as a separate people.

2 *Anangu* or *Yanangu* in Australian Western Desert languages means 'person', and is now used by people of that region to denote themselves in particular and indigenous people in general, as *Yolngu* is used in the tropical north of the Northern Territory.

3 Grammatical metaphor is one of the major difficulties for indigenous learners of written English in secondary and tertiary education, and one that is rarely addressed systematically in literacy teaching. Practical descriptions of the functions of grammatical metaphor are provided by Martin (1990) in the context of literacy needs in indigenous communities, and by Halliday and Martin (1993) in the contexts of the natural and social sciences.

4 This is comparable to the realization of elaborated orientations in Western religious discourses and practices, e.g. the Gospels and Holy Communion.

5 The term 'Law' refers to the system of sacred texts and ceremonial practices that govern communal land ownership and social relations in traditional Aboriginal Australia (see Strehlow 1947, Myers 1986).

6 However these examples of indigenous teaching modes demonstrate that visible pedagogies need not be 'stratifying practices of transmission' as Bernstein (1990: 71) suggests, since their outcomes are 'shared competences'. On the other hand the outcomes of invisible pedagogies clearly can be stratified, since this has been the consequence over the past twenty years of their hegemony in Australian schools.

References

Bernstein, B. (1990) *Class, Codes and Control Vl 4: The Structuring of Pedagogic Discourse*. London: Routledge.

Bernstein, B. (1996) *Pedagogy, Symbolic Control and Identity: Theory, Research, Critique*. London: Taylor & Francis.

Bruner, J. (1986) *Actual Minds, Possible Worlds*. Cambridge, MA: Harvard University Press.

Christie, F. (ed.) (1990) *Literacy for a Changing World*. Melbourne: Australian Council for Educational Research.

Christie, F. (1993) 'Curriculum genres: planning for effective teaching'. In B. Cope and M. Kalantzis (eds), *The Powers of Literacy: A Genre Approach to Teaching Writing*. London: Falmer, 154–78.

Christie, F., Gray, B., Gray, P., Macken, M., Martin, J. and Rothery, J. (1990–92) *Language: A Resource for Meaning*. Including *Procedures*, Books 1-4 and Teacher Manual; *Reports*, Books 1-4 and Teacher Manual. Sydney: Harcourt Brace Jovanovich.

Cope, B. and Kalantzis, M. (eds) (1993) *The Powers of Literacy: A Genre Approach to Teaching Writing*. London: Falmer.

Delpit, L. (1988) 'The silenced dialogue: power and pedagogy in educating other people's children', *Harvard Educational Review*, 58(3), 280–98.

Duguid, C. (1972) *Doctor and the Aborigines*. Sydney: Angus & Robertson.

Fairclough, N. (1989) *Language and Power*. London: Longman.

Gee, J. (1990) *Social Linguistics and Literacies: Ideology in Discourses*. London: Falmer.

Gerot, L. and Wignell, P. (1994) *Making Sense of Functional Grammar*. Sydney: Antipodean Educational Services.

Gray, B. (1985) 'Helping children to become language learners in the classroom'. In M. Christie (ed.), *Aboriginal Perspectives on Experience and Learning: The Role of Language in Aboriginal Education*. Geelong: Deakin University, 87–104.

Gray, B. (1986) 'Aboriginal education: some implications of genre for literacy development'. In C. Painter, and J.R. Martin (eds), *Writing to Mean: Teaching Genres Across the Curriculum*. Applied Linguistics Association of Australia, Occasional Papers no.6, 188–209.

Gray, B. (1987) 'How natural is "natural" language teaching?: employing wholistic methodology in the classroom', *Australian Journal of Early Childhood*, 12(4), 3–19.

Gray, B. (1990) 'Natural language learning in Aboriginal classrooms: reflections on teaching and learning style for empowerment in English'. In C. Walton and W. Eggington (eds), *Language: Maintenance, Power and Education in Australian Aboriginal Contexts*. Darwin: NTU Press, 105–39.

Gray, B., Cowey, W. and Graetz, M. (1995) 'Systemic functional linguistics: classroom practice and curriculum planning'. Paper presented at the Australian Systemic Functional Linguistics Conference, University of Melbourne, 22–29 September.

Gray, B., Cowey, W. and Graetz, M. (forthcoming) *Supporting Children with Literacy Difficulties* (A series of teaching resources for parents and teachers). Canberra: Schools and Community Centre, University of Canberra.

Halliday, M.A.K. (1975) *Learning how to Mean: Explorations in the Development of Language*. London: Edward Arnold.

Halliday, M.A.K. (1985) *Spoken and Written Language*. Geelong: Deakin University Press.

Halliday, M.A.K. (1993) 'On the language of physical science'. In M.A.K. Halliday and J.R. Martin, *Writing Science: Literacy and Discursive Power*. London: Falmer, 54–64.

Halliday, M.A.K. (1994) *An Introduction to Functional Grammar*. London: Edward Arnold.

Halliday, M.A.K. and Hasan, R. (1976) *Cohesion in English*. London: Longman.

Halliday, M.A.K. and Martin, J.R. (1993) *Writing Science: Literacy and Discursive Power*. London: Falmer.

Harkins, J. (1994) *Bridging Two Worlds: Aboriginal English and Crosscultural Understanding*. Brisbane: University of Queensland Press

Harris, S. (1980) *Culture and Learning*. Darwin: Northern Territory Department of Education

Harste, J., Woodward, V. and Burke, C. (1984) *Language Stories and Literacy Lessons*. Concord, NH: Heineman.

Hughes, P. (1984) 'A call for an aboriginal pedagogy', *Australian Teacher*, 9, 20–2.

Hyon, S. (1996) 'Genre in three traditions: implications for ESL', *TESOL Quarterly*, 30(4), 693–722

Japangardi Poulson, C. (1988) 'The school curriculum I would like for my children', *Curriculum Perspectives*, 8(2), 68–9.

Kalantzis, M. and Cope, B. (1990) 'Literacy in the social sciences'. In F. Christie (ed.), *Literacy for a Changing World*. Melbourne: Australian Council for Educational Research, 118–42.

Kalantzis, M. and Cope, B. (1993) 'Histories of pedagogy, cultures of schooling'. In B. Cope and M. Kalantzis (eds), *The Powers of Literacy: A Genre Approach to Teaching Writing*. London: Falmer, 38–62.

Kress, G. (1985) *Linguistic Processes in Sociocultural Practice*. Geelong: Deakin University Press.

Labov, W. (1969) 'The logic of non-standard English'. In *Georgetown Monographs on Language and Linguistics*, 22. Washington: Georgetown University Press. (reproduced in *Language and Social Context*, ed. by P.P. Giglioni. Harmondsworth: Penguin, 1972).

Lemke, J. (1990) 'Technical discourse and technocratic ideology'. In M.A.K. Halliday, J. Gibbons and H. Nicholas (eds), *Learning, Keeping and Using Language: Selected Papers from the 8th World Congress of Applied Linguistics*, 2. Amsterdam: Benjamins, 435-60

Lester, Y. (1993) *Yami: The Autobiography of Yami Lester*. Alice Springs: Institute for Aboriginal Development.

Malin, M. (1994) 'Why is life so hard for Aboriginal students in urban classrooms'. *Aboriginal Child at School*, 22(2), 141–54.

Martin, J.R. (1990) 'Language and control: fighting with words'. In C. Walton and W. Eggington (eds), *Language: Maintenance, Power and Education in Australian Aboriginal Contexts*, Darwin: NTU Press, 12–43.

Martin, J.R. (1992) *English Text*. Amsterdam: Benjamins.

Martin, J.R. (1993) 'Life as a Noun: arresting the universe in science and the humanities'. In M.A.K. Halliday and J.R. Martin, *Writing Science: Literacy and Discursive Power*. London: Falmer, 221–67.

Martin, J.R., Christie, F. and Rothery, J. (1987) 'Social processes in education: a reply to Sawyer and Watson (and others)'. In I. Reid (ed.), *The Place of Genre in Learning: Current Debates*. Geelong: Typereader Publications.

Martin, J.R. and Rothery, J. (1993) 'Grammar: making meaning in writing'. In B. Cope and M. Kalantzis (eds), *The Powers of Literacy: A Genre Approach to Teaching Writing*. London: Falmer, 137–53.

Muhhauser, P. (1995) 'Attitudes to literacy in the pidgins and creoles of the Pacific

244 DAVID ROSE

area', *English World-Wide: A Journal of Varieties of English*, 16(2), 251–71.

Myers, F. (1986) *Pintupi Country, Pintupi Self.* Canberra: Australian Institute of Aboriginal Studies.

Nakata, M. (1996) 'History, cultural diversity and language teaching'. Plenary paper presented at the ACTA-ATESOL 7th TESOL in Teacher Education Conference, Darwin.

Nganyintja and Rose, D. (1991) 'Tawarra: a proposal for secondary education on the Anangu Pitjantjatjara Lands'. Mimeo.

Olson, D.R. (1994) *The World on Paper: The Conceptual and Cognitive Implications of Reading and Writing.* Cambridge: Cambridge University Press

Painter, C. (1985) *Learning the Mother Tongue.* Geelong, Vic.: Deakin University Press.

Painter, C. (1986) 'The role of interaction in learning to speak and learning to write'. In C. Painter and J.R. Martin (eds), *Writing to Mean: Teaching Genres Across the Curriculum.* Applied Linguistics Association of Australia, Occasional Papers no 6. 62–97.

Painter, C. and Martin, J.R. (eds) (1986) *Writing to Mean: Teaching Genres Across the Curriculum.* Applied Linguistics Association of Australia, Occasional Papers no 6.

Public Accounts Committee, NT (1996) 'Report on the provision of school education services for remote Aboriginal communities'. Tabled in the Northern Territory Legislative Assembly, 21 August.

Rhydwen, M. (1993) 'Writing on the backs of the blacks: literacy, creole and language change in the Northern Territory of Australia'. Unpublished PhD thesis, University of Sydney.

Rose, D. (1990) "'First-language enrichment programs" or "intensive exposure to the second language"'. Unpublished MSc thesis, University of Sydney.

Rose, D. (1991) 'Kipara: the origin of fire'. Unpublished BA (Hons) thesis, University of Technology, Sydney.

Rose, D. (1992) 'Protection, self-determination and language learning in Aboriginal early childhood education: review of Aboriginal language education policy statements', *Education Australia*, Spring.

Rose, D. (1993) 'On becoming: the grammar of causality in Pitjantjatjara and English', *Cultural Dynamics* VI (1-2) Leiden: E.J. Brill, 42–83.

Rose, D. (1996) 'Pitjantjatjara processes: an Australian grammar of experience'. In R. Hasan, D. Butt and C. Cloran (eds), *Functional Descriptions: Language Form and Linguistic Theory.* Amsterdam: Benjamins, 287–322.

Rose, D. (1997) 'Science, technology and technical literacies'. In F. Christie and J.R. Martin (eds), *Genres and Institutions: Social Practices in the Workplace and School.* London: Cassell, 40–72.

Rose, D. (1998) 'The Western Desert Code: a cryptogrammar of Pitjantjatjara'. PhD thesis, University of Sydney.

Rose, D. and Tjungutu Uwankaraku (1985) 'Amata: social crisis and substance abuse'. Report for the Minister of Health, South Australia.

Rose, D., Korner, H. and McInnes, D. (1992) *Write it Right: Scientific Literacy in Industry.* NSW Department of Education, Metropolitan East Disadvantaged Schools Programme, Sydney.

Rothery, J. (1990) 'Story writing in primary school: assessing narrative type genres'. Unpublished PhD thesis, University of Sydney.

Strehlow, C. (1947) *Aranda Traditions.* Melbourne: Melbourne University Press

Temple, C., Nathan, R., Temple, F. and Burris, N. (1993) *The Beginnings of Writing.* Boston: Allyn & Bacon.

Vygotsky, L. (1978) *Mind in Society: The Development of Higher Psychological Process.* (M. Cole, S. Scribner, V. John-Steiner and E. Souderman, eds). Cambridge, MA: Harvard University Press.

Walton, C. and Eggleton, W. (eds), *Language: Maintenance, Power and Education in Australian Aboriginal Contexts.* Darwin: NTU Press.

Wells, G. (1981) *Learning through Interaction: The Study of Language Development.* Cambridge: Cambridge University Press.

Wertsch, J.V. (1990) 'The voice of rationality in a sociocultural appoach to mind'. In C. Mole (ed.), *Vygotsky and Education: Instructional Implications and Applications of Sociohistorical Psychology.* Cambridge: Cambridge University Press.

9   Official knowledge and pedagogic identities

Basil Bernstein

I want to share with you, on this occasion what is really no more than a sketch, no more than an embryonic outline, rather than a completed painting ready to be signed and framed. Unfortunately, within this sketch, the figures, their interactions, and their tensions may not all be recognized by you. However, despite the possible difficulty of recognizing their relevance to you today, it may be that some of the figures, interactions and tensions will be recognized by you but in the future. Now this may be both a presumptuous and dangerous prediction. I can only hope you will not think it presumptuous. I am afraid I have always lived somewhat dangerously, at least in academic terms, so I cannot apologize for that.

'Official Knowledge' in the title refers to the educational knowledge which the state constructs and distributes in educational institutions. I am going to be concerned with changes in the bias and focus of this official knowledge brought about by contemporary curricula reform currently ongoing in most societies. I shall propose that the bias and focus which inhere in different modalities of reform construct different pedagogic identities. From this perspective, curricula reform emerges out of a struggle between groups to make their bias (and focus) state policy and practice. Thus the bias and focus of this official discourse are expected to construct in teachers and students a particular moral disposition, motivation and aspiration, embedded in particular performances and practices. I shall develop a simple model of the official arena in which this struggle takes place. The model will generate four positions. These positions differ in their bias and focus, and so differ in the pedagogic identities they are projecting. I will apply this model particularly to the UK but also hint of its application to other societies. I will then use the same model to consider resources for the construction of *local* identities under today's conditions of cultural, economic and technological change. Finally I will look briefly at the relation between the official pedagogic identities of the state and the local identities available in communities and groups.

Pedagogic identity

I want first to indicate how I am using the term pedagogic identity (see notes). From the point of view of this chapter a pedagogic identity is the result of embedding a career in a collective base. The career of a student is a knowledge career, a moral career and a locational career. The collective base of that career is provided by the principles of social order (or the orderings of the social, if of a postmodern persuasion) expected to be relayed in schools and institutionalized by the state. The local social base of that career is provided by the orderings of the local context.

It is commonplace today to say that over the last fifty years there have been major changes in the collective base of European societies, and major changes in the principles of social order. There have also been major changes in the contexts in which careers are enacted, whether these contexts be international, national, domestic, economic, educational or leisure. Curricula reform today arises out of the requirement to engage with this contemporary cultural, economic and technological change. The four positions I shall discuss in the official arena represent, through their different biases and foci, different approaches to regulating and managing change, moral, cultural and economic. And these different approaches to the management of change are expected to become the lived experience of teachers and students, through the shaping of their pedagogic identity (Figure 9.1).

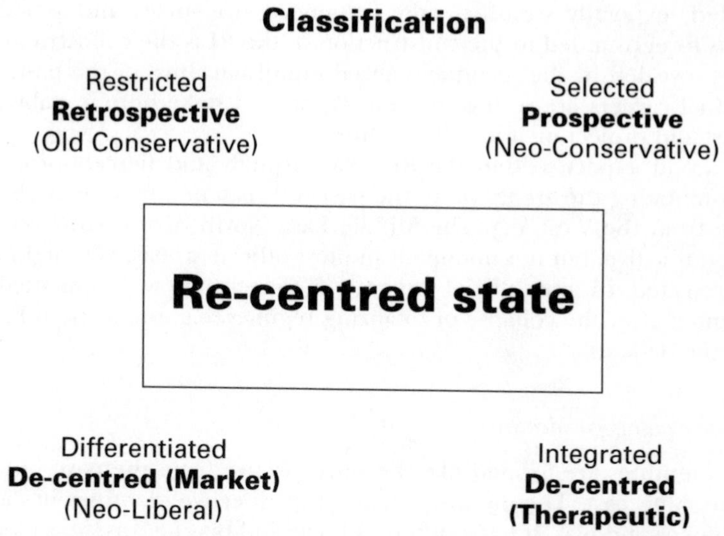

Classification

Restricted	Selected
Retrospective	**Prospective**
(Old Conservative)	(Neo-Conservative)

Re-centred state

Differentiated	Integrated
De-centred (Market)	**De-centred**
(Neo-Liberal)	**(Therapeutic)**

In any one case there can be opposition and collaborations between these positions in the arena of reform, alternatively, some positions may be illegitimate and excluded from the arena.

Figure 9.1 Modelling pedagogic identities

I am proposing then an official arena of four positions for the projecting of pedagogic identities, through the process of educational reform. Any one educational reform can then be regarded as the outcome of the struggle to project and institutionalize particular identities.

Two of these identities I shall discuss are generated by resources managed by the state: centring resources. Two identities are generated from local resources where the institutions concerned have some autonomy over their resources: de-centred resources. I shall consider first the identities constructed from centring resources. These resources are drawn from some central, often considered national discourse. De-centred resources are drawn from local contexts or local discourses and focus upon the present, whereas centred resources focus upon the past.

Retrospective pedagogic identities (RI)

What are the resources which construct retrospective identities? Retrospective identities (RI) are shaped by national, religious, cultural, grand narratives of the past. These narratives are appropriately recontextualized to stabilize that past in the future. An important feature of the resources that construct RI is that the discourse does not enter into an exchange relation with the economy. The bias, focus and management here leads to a tight control over discursive *inputs* to education, that is its contents, *not* over its *outputs*. RIs are formed by hierarchically ordered, strongly bounded, explicitly stratified and sequenced discourses and practices. What is foregrounded in the construction of the RI is the collective social base as revealed by the recontextualized grand narrative of the past. The individual careers are of less interest. What is at stake here is stabilizing the past and projecting it into the future.

We would expect to find the RI today strongly and fiercely projected and dominating the arena where the past is threatened by secular change issuing from the West, e.g. The Middle East, North Africa. However, the position is active, but not dominant in most official arenas. We might find RIs projected in the official arenas of societies now fragmented or segmented after the collapse of totalizing regimes, e.g. the Russian Federation, the Balkans.

Prospective pedagogic identities

These identities are formed like the retrospective from the past, but it is not the same past. The discursive base of prospective identities has a different focus and bias. It has a different focus and bias because this identity is constructed *to deal with cultural, economic and technological change.* Prospective identities are shaped by *selective* recontextualizing of features of the past to defend or raise economic performance. For example in the case of Thatcherism features of the past were selected which would legitimate, which would motivate, and which would create what were considered to be appropriate attitudes, dispositions and performances relevant to a market culture and reduced state welfare. A new collective social base was formed by fusing nation, family, individual responsibility and individual enterprise. Thus prospective identities are formed by recontextualizing *selected* features from the past to stabilize the future through *engaging with contemporary change*. Here, unlike retrospective identities where only the collective base is foregrounded, with prospective identities it is careers (that is dispositions and economic performance) which are foregrounded and *embedded in an especially selected past*. The management of prospective identities, because of the emphasis upon performances which have an exchange value, requires the state to control both *inputs* to education and *outputs*. (I am grateful to Joseph Solomon, University of Patras, for this concise formulation.)

We can consider Blair's New Labour entry into the official pedagogic arena as launching a new prospective identity, an identity drawing on resources of a different past. An amalgam of notions of community (really communities) and local responsibilities to motivate and restore belonging in the cultural sphere, and a new participatory responsibility in the economic sphere. Thus the underlying collective of New Labour appears to be a recontextualizing of the concept of the organic society. In this new potential official arena, the retrospective identity would be projected by 'old Labour'. The positions remain but the players change. Blair's New Labour, as with the New Right, would control both inputs and outputs of education but in the service of a different prospective identity.

De-centred pedagogic identities

I now want to turn to the resources for the construction of the two de-centred identities. These are the identities where the relevant institutions have some autonomy over their resources. In the case of the Therapeutic identity the autonomy of the institution is necessary to produce the features of this identity; an integrated modality of knowing and a participating, co-operative modality of social relation. In the case of the de-centred Market, autonomy is necessary so that the institution and its units can vary their resources in order to produce a competitive output. Whereas the centring resources of retrospective and prospective identities recontextualizes the past, although different pasts, de-centring resources construct the present although different 'presents'.

I call the identity 'therapeutic' because this identity is produced by complex theories of personal, cognitive and social development, often labelled progressive. These theories are the means of a control invisible to the student. This identity is orientated to autonomous, non-specialized, flexible thinking, and socially to team work as an active participant. It is very costly to produce and the output is not easily measured: the position projecting this identity is a very weak position in all contemporary arenas so the social group which sponsors it has little power.

De-centred market (DCM)

I now want to turn to the resources which construct the de-centred market identity. I think there will be difficulty in recognizing this as this identity is not as yet an identity projected from a position in your official arena. Imagine an educational institution which has considerable autonomy over the use of its budget, the organization of its discourse, how it uses its staff, the number and type of staff, the courses it constructs, provided: (1) it can attract students who have choice of institution, (2) it can meet external performance criteria, and (3) it can optimize its position in relation to similar institutions. The basic unit of the institution, a department or a group, will also have autonomy over its discourse and practice, and may vary this in order to optimize its own position in the market; that is to optimize its position with respect to the exchange value of its products, namely students. Thus the pedagogic practice will be contingent on the market in which the identity is to be enacted. The management system here is explicitly hierarchical: small, non-elected committees, few in number, which will distribute resources to local units, according to their efficiency and their procedures of accountability. Management ideally reveals itself to distribute rewards and punishments. Managements monitor the effectiveness of the local units, groups or departments in satisfying and creating local markets. The transmission here arises to produce an identity whose product has an exchange value in a market. The focus is upon those inputs which optimize this exchange value. We have here a culture and context to facilitate the survival of the fittest as judged by market demands. The focus is on the short term rather than the long term, on the extrinsic rather than the intrinsic, upon the exploration of vocational applications rather than upon exploration of knowledge. The transmission here views knowledge as money. And like money it should flow easily to where demand calls. There must be no impediments to this flow. Personal commitment and particular dedication of staff and students are regarded as resistances, as oppositions to the free circulation of knowledge. And so personal commitments, inner dedications, not only are not encouraged, but are regarded as equivalent to monopolies in the market, and like such monopolies should be dissolved. The de-centred market (DCM) position constructs an outwardly responsive identity rather than one driven by inner dedication. Contract replaces covenant.

The resources which construct DCM identities may also create a new stratification both of knowledge and identities. If we consider the university sector the outlines of this stratification are already perhaps becoming clear. Elite universities can maintain their position by buying in research leaders, and as a consequence will have *less* need to change their discourse or its organization to maintain their power and position. This does not mean that such universities will not change their discursive organization in the light of new technological knowledge and market potential, only that the *organizational* structure will still be essentially retrospective.

Despite tensions from the change of focus to applied research (Mace 1995) the identities formed in élite institutions are likely to be formed by introjection of knowledge. That is, the identity finds its core in its place in an organization of knowledge and practice. It is inwardly driven, although perhaps today more riven than driven. In the case of non-élite institutions, these do not have the resources (economic or symbolic) to attract high-ranking scholars as a means of maintaining their powers of attraction, so we can expect here that the discursive organization itself will be the means to maintain or improve competitive position. In these non-élite institutions the unit of discourse is likely to be a unit which with other units can create varying packages according to the contingencies of local markets. As these market contingencies change, or are expected to change, then 'new' permutations of units can be constructed. Here the identity of staff and students are likely to be formed less through mechanisms of introjection but far more through mechanisms of *projection*. That is, the identity is a reflection of external contingencies. The maintenance of this identity depends upon the facility of *projecting* discursive organization/practices themselves driven by external contingencies. The resources which produce DCM Market identities, organizational and discursive, have complex and profound consequences.

De-centred therapeutic identities (DCT)

Finally I want briefly to consider the de-centred therapeutic position. I shall spend little time because it is not a strong player in any arena. The transmission here which produces this identity is against specialized categories of discourse and against stratification of groups. The transmission prefers weak boundaries, integration prefers to talk of regions of knowledge, areas of experience. The management style is soft, hierarchies are veiled, power is disguised by communication networks and inter-personal relations. Whereas the DCM position projects contingent, differentiated competitive identities, the de-centred therapeutic (DCT) position ideally projects stable, integrated identities with adaptable co-operative practices.

Application of the model

If we now briefly consider the curricular reforms of the late 1980s and early 1990s in England and Wales, we can give some interpretations according to Figure 9.1. In general, contemporary educational reforms aim to achieve control over both inputs and outputs of education, and this can be done effectively by tight and public evaluation over inputs. This requires standardization of knowledge inputs if comparisons are to be made, and local autonomy (both of customers and suppliers) if institutions are to be competitively optimum. How did this work out in the official arena of the late 1980s out of which emerged the radical educational reforms?

Clearly there was a complementary relation between the prospective (neo-conservative) position and the de-centred market (the neo-liberal position) with respect to integrating a de-centralized centralized device of management (evaluation and enterprise), embedded in a curriculum emphasizing national enterprise (cultural, economic and political). However, this complementary relation was not without tension. Ideally the neo-liberal position would be against a centralized national curriculum. However, if we look at the contents and organization of the educational reform this would appear to have emanated from the *retrospective* position, as it consisted (with an occasional new subject) to be the segmented, serial array of subjects (on the whole departmentally organized), typical of the past, and included a focus upon 'basic skills'. There clearly have been vocational insertions in the curriculum stemming from the prospective position (see Figure 9.1). The de-centred therapeutic identity projected from the professionals of the pedagogic recontextualizing field, and despite having some support among civil servants of the Department of Education, itself was not a strong player and its proposals were severely restricted. The complex profiling forms of assessment of students were reduced to simple tests. Although thematic connection between the segments of the national array of separate subjects were written into the reform these were rarely effective in practice (Whitty *et al.* 1991, 1994).

If we now look at the outcome of the play of positions in the official arena with respect to the radical educational reforms it appears that the de-centred market position has transformed the managerial structure of educational institutions, from primary school to university, and it has created an enterprise competitive culture. While it has had little or no effect upon the curriculum, it introduced new discourses of management and economy in the training of heads of schools and so in the concept of leadership. Although the de-centred market position had little effect on the institutional discourse of the school which was firmly sited in the retrospective position (1), it can be said to have radically transformed the *regulative* discourse of *the institution as this affected its conditions of survival.* The de-centred market (DCM) oriented identities towards satisfying external competitive demands, whereas the segmental, serial ordering of the subjects of the curriculum orientated the identities towards the intrinsic value of the discourse. This tension between the intrinsic and the extrinsic is not, of course, new. What is new is the official institutionalizing of the DCM and the legitimizing of the identity it projects. We have a new pathological position at work in education: the pedagogic schizoid position.

Modelling local identities

The analysis so far has been entirely concerned with the development of modelling resources, positions and identities in the struggle for dominance within the official arena of educational policy and reform. But these identity projections from the official arena are by no means exempt from the effects of identity constructions external to the official arena to which we now turn.

Much has been written about 'postmodernism', 'late modernism', 'globalizing capitalism', 'disembedding expert systems' and I have no wish to rehearse the literature here (Giddens 1990, 1991; Harvey 1989; O'Neil 1995; Touraine 1996). However, it does seem clear that, in the old speak, 'ascribed' identities, those identities which had a biological referent, (age, gender and age relation) have been considerably weakened. These cultural punctuations and specializations of time (age, gender, age relation) are today weak resources for the construction of identities with a stable collective base. To some extent these previously ascribed identities are now potentially achievable by individual practice, contemporary resources and technologies. At the same time there has been a *contraction in the range of that life space which is socially significant.* At one extreme the young through style resources can project themselves as older, while individuals are now excluded from the labour market in their fifties and sometimes earlier. Time punctuations have shifted. Further, in the old speak, 'achieved' identities of class and occupation have also become weaker resources for stable, unambiguous identities. However, this should *not* be taken to mean that because of changes in oppositional working-class solidarities, consequent upon changes in technology, economy and state regulation, that unequal distributive consequences of class have weakened. So far then the punctuations of time and space have shifted. It is also the case that geographical movements of population, appropriated by the internationalizing of labour, have created new sets of cultural pressures on generations and gender. The weakening of stable, unambiguous collective resources for the construction of identities consequent upon this new period of reorganizing capitalism has brought about a disturbance and disembedding of identities and facilitated new identity constructions.

It should be noted here that the identity constructions to be discussed do not necessarily replace or displace the 'old' established formations of social identity. Simply the positions and oppositions in the identity field we will discuss take on a new valency under contemporary conditions of change.

I want to use the same model for the construction of official pedagogic identities to model the emerging local identity field and its arenas of opposition. Basically I distinguished 'de-centred', 'retrospective' and 'prospective' positions, resources and projections. 'De-centred' were constructed on the basis of local resources oriented to the present; 'retrospective' were constructed on the basis of grand past narratives, national, religious, cultural; 'prospective' were constructed from past narratives to create a re-centring of the identity to provide for a new social base and to open a new future.

I shall now apply this model to the emerging identity field and its arenas of opposition (see Figure 9.2). I will first discuss de-centred identities, then centring retrospective and finally re-centring prospective.

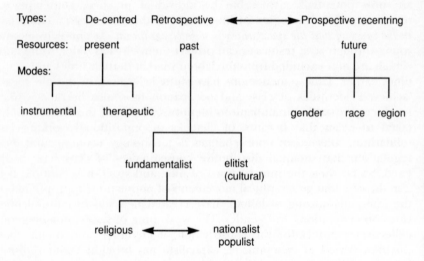

Figure 9.2 The contemporary identity field

De-centred identities

I shall distinguish here an instrumental identity (in the previous model 'de-centred market') and a therapeutic identity. These are constructed from differently localized and oppositional resources. In one case the resources are market, and in the other they are sense-making resources to create internal coherence.

INSTRUMENTAL

These identities are constructed out of market signifiers. The identity arises out of a *projection* on to consumables. This projection relays to self and others the spatial and temporal attributes of the identity; that is, its what, where, who and progression. Such constructions are stable only in their procedure of construction, *not* in their temporal realizations which are contingent. For these identities, boundaries are permeable, and the past is no necessary guide to the present, let alone the future. The economic base of these identities orients their politics: anti-centralist.

THERAPEUTIC

These identities are also constructed from local resources but these are *internal*, unlike instrumental which are external. If instrumental identities are produced by projection, then the therapeutic is produced by introjection. Here the concept of self is crucial and the self is regarded as a personal project. It is an internally regulated construction and relatively independent of external consumer signifiers. It is a truly symbolic construction. The identity takes the form of an open narrative which constructs a personal time. It shares some features with the oppositional instrumental. As with the instrumental, for the therapeutic, boundaries are permeable and the past is no necessary guide to the present or the future. If the instrumental is dependent upon the segmentations of the shopping mall, then the therapeutic is dependent upon internal sense-making procedures of the external segmentation. Both of these constructions are differently fragile. In the case of the instrumental, the identity depends upon economic resources, and when those are not available then a shift to other possible resources in the field is likely. In the case of the therapeutic, the dependency here is upon internal sense-making procedures, and if those fail then a shift to other resources is likely. Tentatively, instrumental may shift to retrospective (nationalist) and therapeutic to prospective, but these shifts may depend in turn upon age and context.

Retrospective identities

These identities use as resources narratives of the past which provide exemplars, criteria, belonging and coherence. In these respects retrospective identities are opposed to de-centred identities. For both of these modes reject past narratives as the source for criteria, belonging and coherence for the present and future. And for both of these de-centred modes boundaries are permeable. In the same way as we distinguished two opposing modes of de-centred identities, we shall distinguish two basic opposing modes of retrospective identity: fundamentalist and élitist.

FUNDAMENTALIST

As the diagram illustrates there are a number of subsets of this position but they all share a fundamentalist religious or nationalist, or combination, resource. This provides for an unambiguous, stable, intellectually impervious, collective identity. This consumes the self in all its manifestations and gives it a site outside of current and future instabilities, beyond current ambiguities of judgement, relation and conduct. In some contexts it produces a strong insulation between the sacred and profane, such that it is possible to enter the profane world without either being appropriated or colonized by it. Islamic fundamentalism enables the appropriation of Western technologies without cultural penetration. Nearer home, Orthodox Jews in the 1920s, and even earlier, occupied small shops and business slots in the economy and retained their identity through strict Orthodox practice. In the 1960s and onwards many British Asian Muslims occupied a similar economic and cultural context. The problem here for such retrospective identities is their reproduction in the next generation, and here we might expect a shift to prospective or even therapeutic positions. Age may well influence the expression of the retrospective identity through differential selection of resources. It may well be that the young are attracted to the current revival of charismatic Christianity with its emphasis upon the subjective, the emotional, upon intense interactive participation and upon oppositions to institutional orthodoxies. On a more anecdotal level I have been impressed with the revival of student fraternity rituals in Portugal, Norway and Germany. Finally we can consider nationalism and populism as subsets of retrospective fundamentalism, drawing on mythological resources of origin, belonging, progression and destiny (rise of the extreme right). Any weakening of the collective resource on which the fundamentalist identity draws and which minutely regulates conduct, belief and participation, as is likely in inter-generation reproduction, may entail a shift to re-centring identities on the part of the young (see later discussion).

ELITIST

This is a retrospective identity entirely opposed to fundamentalist, indeed to all other possibilities in the field. It is constructed on the resource of high culture: an élitist appropriation. This narrative of the past is as consuming of the self as fundamentalist, and provides exemplars, canons and criteria, and develops aesthetic sensibilities. It is an amalgam of knowledge, sensitivities, manners, education and upbringing. However, it can be appropriated by education and social networks without the intervention of upbringing. It shares with fundamentalist identities strong classifications and internal hierarchies, but unlike fundamentalist, it refuses to engage in the market. Whereas fundamentalist identities (other than those resting on national or populist resources), allow for conversion and often actually encourage conversion, this is much less the case for élitist identities as these require a very long and arduous apprenticeship into the aesthetic mode – a mode which needs to be maintained without the intense solidarities in which fundamentalist identities are embedded. Perhaps narcissistic formations underlie and maintain élitist identities, whereas fundamentalist identities are maintained by strong super-ego formations and communalized selves.

Prospective

These identities are essentially future oriented in contrast to the past of retrospective and the present of de-centred identities. They rest, as with retrospective identities, upon narratives but these narrative resources ground the identity not in the past but in the *future*. These are narratives of becoming, but a new becoming not of an individual but of a social category, e.g. race, gender, or region. The narrative resources of de-centred identities announce distance from a collective, social base for these are individualized constructions. But the narratives constructing the new becoming of prospective identities create a new basis for social relations, for solidarities and for oppositions. In this respect prospective identities involve a *re-centring*. Prospective identities are often launched by social movements, for example gender, race and region. They are in their take-off stage evangelist and confrontational, and, as we shall see later, have strong schismatic tendencies. Prospective identities share with fundamentalist the consummation of the self, in that the manifestations involve the whole self in the new becoming. De-socialization procedures are necessary to erase the previous identity. New group supports facilitate this process, protect vulnerabilities, and orient re-centring. Prospective identities, as with fundamentalist, engage in economic and political activity to provide for the development of their potential. In the USA Islamic movements have created a new basis for black identity, for a revitalized politics, and a new entrepreneuralism. Here is an example of a prospective identity arising out of a recontextualizing of a retrospective narrative.

I have mentioned earlier that there is a strong schismatic tendency in the social base of the resources and relations which construct prospective identities. These resources are narratives of becoming other than the projections and impositions of others; a becoming which is so to speak a recovery of something not yet spoken of, a new fusion. But there may be more than one path to this new future. The identities of becoming are prone to heresy, to pollution, to waywardness, and require close supervision, delicate monitoring before recognition of authenticity and licensing. The group basis of prospective identities contains gatekeepers and licensers. It may well be that it is more accurate to conceive of each social category (gender, race, region) as giving rise to its own arena of positions, struggling to dominate the narrative resource for the construction of authentic becoming.

Implicit in the emerging identity field, and especially in its arenas, is perhaps the beginning of a change in the moral imagination. One of the momentous outcomes of the Enlightenment was the announcement of universal rights but this was at the cost of the anonymity of the subject. All were entitled and guaranteed rights, but the very universalism de-contextualized the subject. Today we can query whether we are experiencing a *shrinking* of the moral imagination. Empathy and sympathy can only be offered and received by those who are so licensed to offer and receive.

It may well be that the emerging identity field and its arenas facilitate the shrinking of the moral imagination, but, unlike the de-contextualized subject of the Enlightenment, the subject is now no longer anonymous but eloquent in a new contextualizing.

A caricature may help here. I am two and a half inches under the average height, losing ground with every dietary improvement, and subject to the projections and impositions of others which have produced a spoiled identity. To discover with others in my social category the possibility of a new becoming, a narrative resource (to interpret my past otherness, to discover authentic voice, to create a new language of participation and discovery) is developed on the basis of valid scholarship and research. Valid scholarship and research can only be valid if carried out by a licensed member of the social category. Only we can know us or are allowed the possibility of knowing us. Exemplars are found (perhaps Napoleon, Chaplin). A prospective identity has been constructed, criteria of membership, belief and practice developed, economic and political aims formulated; a new social category has been established. However, some years later a junior member of the group produces a more radical agenda, with new membership criteria on the basis of a new narrative resource. New membership criteria in the new narrative sets membership at three and half inches below average height. Most of my group are excluded and now seen as part of otherness. We have the first schism and a new shrinking of the moral imagination.

Conclusion

What appears to be happening at the end of the twentieth century is a weakening of, and a change of place of, the sacred. In the beginning of this century the sacred was centrally located and informed the collective social base of society through the inter-relation of state, religion and education. Today this collective base has been considerably weakened (more in some societies than others) as a resource for a centralized sacred. The sacred now reveals itself in dispersed sites, movements and discourses. It is less fragmentation of the sacred but more its segmentation and specialization.

From this perspective the diversity of local identities we have discussed (with the exception of the instrumental) may be less an index of cultural fragmentation as in some postmodern stories, but more a general cultural resurgence of the rituals of inwardness in new social forms. In the first section of this paper we noted the growing pathology in educational institutions which we referred to as a pedagogic schizoid position. We are in the process of producing for the first time a virtually secular, market-driven official pedagogic discourse, practice and context, but at the same time, there is a revival of forms of the sacred external to it.

There appears to be a reversal of the Durkheimian sites of the sacred and the profane, and a rusting of the bars of Weber's iron cage of dismal prophecy. There are new sources of tension, change and possibility in the relation between the official pedagogic identities and their contexts of transmission and acquisition, and the local identities of the emerging field. But this is not to say that all new local identities now becoming available are to be welcomed, sponsored or legitimated.

Notes

1. Attempts are being made to modify the 'A' level examination taken at 17/18 years to vocational subjects with academic subjects on equal footing.

Official knowledge
The term 'official knowledge' is derived from Bernstein (1986), where I distinguished the Official Recontextualizing Field, a state-constructed field of agents concerned to produce official pedagogic discourse. On official pedagogic practice, see Bernstein (1990), also on Official Knowledge, Apple (1993).

Re-centred state
This refers to new forms of centralized regulation whereby the State de-centralizes and through (a) central setting of criteria and (b) the central assessment of outputs of agencies, financially (and otherwise), rewards success and punishes failures: 'choice', selection control and reproduction.

Pedagogy
I should offer here a definition of pedagogy.

Pedagogy is a sustained process whereby somebody(s) acquires new forms or develops existing forms of conduct, knowledge, practice and criteria, from somebody(s) or something deemed to be an appropriate provider and evaluator. Appropriate either from the point of view of the acquirer or by some other body(s) or both.

We can distinguish between: institutional pedagogy and segmental (informal) pedagogy.

Institutional pedagogy is carried out in official sites (state religious, communal), usually with accredited providers, and where acquirers are concentrated voluntarily or involuntarily as a group or social category.

Segmental pedagogy is carried out usually in the face-to-face relations of everyday experience and practice by informal providers. This pedagogy may be tacitly or explicitly transmitted *and* the provider may not be aware a transmission has taken place. Unlike institutional pedagogy, the pedagogic process may be no longer than the context or segment in which it is enacted. Segmental, that is, *unrelated* competences result from such pedagogic action. For example, a child learning to dress, tie shoe-laces, or count change in a supermarket, are competences acquired through segmental pedagogies which may vary in their explicitness and in their code of realization. Learning to be a patient – waiting room behaviour, doctor/patient conduct and report – are examples of a tacit mode of a segmental pedagogy where the provider(s) *may* be unaware that they are providers. What is of

interest is the interactional consequences of the relation between institutional and
segmental pedagogies.

Identity

In the code theory, 'identity' and its realizations are constructed by variations in
classification and framing relations. From this perspective classificatory relations
establish 'voice'. 'Voice' is regarded somewhat like a cultural larynx which sets the
limits on what can be legitimately put together (communicated). Framing relations regulate the acquisition of this 'voice' and create the 'message' (what is made
manifest, what can be realized). The dynamics of the framing relations *initiated* by
the acquirer can initiate change in the expected message and so in the governing
'voice'. Thus identity in the code theory is the outcome of the 'voice message' relations. With respect to the definition of pedagogic identity – the embedding of a
career in principles of social order – acquisition would be regulated by the classification and framing relations ($\pm C^{ie}/\pm F^{ie}$) of the pedagogic practice.

Local identity: social location

It is difficult to give the social location of the social identities as these vary with
age, gender, social class, occupational field, and economic or symbolic control.
Further, as we have indicated in the text, these identities are not necessarily stable
positions and shifts can be expected depending upon the possibility of maintaining the discursive or in some cases on the economic base of the identity. In Bernstein 1996 Chapter 3 there are some tentative hypotheses. The present discussion
is a development of that chapter.

Moral imagination

This imagination is differently and more dangerously threatened by collective
stereotyping stemming from fundamentalist retrospective positions. Thus what is
at stake today is both the shrinking of the moral imagination (prospective
positions) and the eroding of this imagination (fundamentalist retrospective positions).

Sources

The model of the four positions and the projected identities in the official arena
had its origins in a response (Bernstein 1995) to a paper by Tyler (1995). I have
drawn on the research of Ball (1990), Dale (1994), Grace (1995), and Whitty *et al.*
(1991, 1994) on the origins, dynamics, and consequences of the radical educational
reforms of the late 1980s and 1990s initiated by the Conservative Government. I have
enjoyed and benefited from discussions and disputes with Wexler on the resurgence
of the sacred (Wexler 1995, 1996, Bernstein 1995).

References

Apple, M.W. (1993) *Official Knowledge: Education in a Conservative Age*. London:
    Routledge.
Ball, S.J. (1990) *Politics and Policy Making in Education*. London: Routledge.
Bernstein, B. (1986) 'On pedagogic discourse'. In J.G. Richardson (ed.), *Handbook
    of Theory and Research for the Sociology of Education*. New York: Greenwood.
Bernstein, B. (1990) *Class, Codes and Controls, Vol. 4: The Structuring of Pedagogic
    Discourse*. London, Routledge.

Bernstein, B. (1995) 'Response'. In A.R. Sadovnik (ed.), *Knowledge and Pedagogy: The Sociology of Basil Bernstein*. Norwood, NJ: Ablex.

Bernstein, B. (1996) *Pedagogy, Symbolic Control and Identity: Theory, Research and Critique*. London: Taylor & Francis.

Dale, R. (1994) 'Marketing the educational market and the polarisation of schools'. In D. Kallos and S. Lindblad (eds), *New Policy Contexts for Education: Sweden and the United Kingdom*. Pedagogiska institutionen Umea University, *Pedagogiska rapporter*, 42, 35–66.

Durkheim, E. (1915) *The Elementary Forms of the Religious Life*, trans. J.S. Swan, London: Allen & Unwin.

Giddens, A. (1990) *The Consequence of Modernity*. Cambridge: Polity Press.

Giddens, A. (1991) *Modernity and Self-Identity*. Cambridge: Polity Press.

Grace, G.R. (1995) *School Leadership: Beyond Education Management: An Essay in Policy and Scholarship*. London: Falmer.

Harvey, D. (1989) *The Condition of Post Modernity: An Inquiry into the Origins of Cultural Change*. Oxford: Blackwell.

Mace, J. (1995) 'Funding matters', *Journal of Education Policy*, 10(1), 57–64.

Moore, R. and Hickox, M. (1995) 'Vocationalism and educational change', *Curriculum Journal*, 5(3), 281–93.

O'Neil, J. (1995) *The Poverty of Postmodernism*. London: Routledge.

Touraine, R. (1996) *Critique of Modernity*. Oxford: Blackwell.

Sadovnik, A.R. (ed.) *Knowledge and Pedagogy: The Sociology of Basil Bernstein*. Norwood, NJ: Ablex.

Tyler, W. (1995) 'De-coding school reform: Bernstein market-oriented pedagogy and postmodern power'. In A.R. Sadovnik (ed.), *Knowledge and Pedagogy: The Sociology of Basil Bernstein*. Norwood, NJ: Ablex. See also Bernstein's response, 407–12.

Wexler, P. (1995) 'Bernstein: a Jewish misreading'. In A.R. Sadovnik (ed.), *Knowledge and Pedagogy: The Sociology of Basil Bernstein*. Norwood, NJ: Ablex. See also Bernstein's response, 396–9.

Wexler, P. (1996) *Holy Sparks: Social Theory, Education and Religion*. New York: St Martin's Press.

Wexler, P. (1996) *Critique of Social Psychology* (2nd edn). New York: Peter Lang.

Whitty, G. (1991) 'The new right and the national curriculum.' In R. Moore and J. Ozga (eds), *Curriculum Policy*. Oxford: Pergamon/Open University Press.

Whitty, G., Rowe, G. and Aggleton, P. (1994) 'Subjects and themes in the secondary school', *Research Papers in Education Policy and Practice*, 9(2) 159–179.

10   Pedagogic identities and educational reform in the
     1990s: the cultural dynamics of national curricula

William Tyler

In a paper, 'Decoding school reform' that appeared in a volume dedicated
to the work of Basil Bernstein (Tyler 1995), I argued that Bernstein's
formulations of pedagogic discourse appeared to be central to an
understanding of the marketization of schooling, an issue which has dominated sociological debate on school reform in the 1990s (Marginson 1992;
Ball 1993; Kenway (ed). 1995; Dehli 1996). While these devolved and
market-oriented reforms share the de-centring features of postmodernity, it
appeared that, in an ironic reversal, they seemed to be governed by the very
recontextualizing logic which, as Bernstein has argued (1990: 165–218) is a
distinctive feature of pedagogic discourse itself.

   In a comment on this paper, Bernstein (1995: 410–12) further outlined
an approach which positioned these marketized reforms within a wider
typology of the 'various strategies for dealing with contemporary cultural
and economic changes as they destabilise solidarities, careers and the formation of identity' (1995: 410). This typology of pedagogic identities was
subsequently developed into a more elaborate statement in his 'Peda-
gogizing knowledge' paper (1996: 54–81), discussed in detail below, and
constitutes the main thematic of Bernstein's chapter in the present
volume ('Official knowledge and pedagogic identities'). The present
paper explores the theoretical basis of this scheme, its relationship to
Bernstein's previous typologies of educational knowledge (especially the
'Classification and framing' paper, 1975) and insights into Bernstein's
neo-Durkheimian approach into the dynamics of contemporary cultural
politics.

   While the de-centring of the pedagogic field by the logic of market
forces may represent one dominant postmodernizing tendency of educational systems, this is by no means the whole picture. Marketized reforms
appear to be matched by a simultaneous drive towards homogenization,
standardization and 'hypercodification' of the pedagogic process. In the
contemporary cultural politics of education, conformity to state-imposed
regulations and expectations, rather than localized diversity, has become
ruling concerns in many areas of school life – in the practices of mass standardized testing as well as in the creation of the conditions for marketized
choice to take effect, as in the enforced publication of examination

results. The revived popularity of school uniforms (Meadmore and Symes 1997) exposes another form of localized governmentality arising from national preferences for greater homogeneity and centralized regulation of educational practices. It is symptomatic of this impulse to standardize that in the 1996 elections in the USA, whose localized systems have historically followed a relatively permissive dress code, dress codes became a major electoral issue. The paradoxes of educational reform (Whitty 1992) are not untypical of the general tendencies in the cultural dynamic of postmodernity (Dunn 1991; Baudrillard 1993; Gane, 1995). The drive towards accountability and transparency of teaching and learning can therefore no longer be confined to the constraints of economic efficiency under some corporate model based on market rationality.

Bernstein's theory of pedagogic discourse and pedagogic identities has yet to be formulated in a way that satisfactorily explains the nature of the contradictory and paradoxical tendencies in the cultural politics of education. Nor have these tendencies been systematically expounded in terms of the underlying theory of educational transmissions, the coding principles of collection and integration which derive both from Durkheim's early writings on mechanical and organic solidarity as well as his later work on the problems of symbolic representation (Bernstein 1996: 127).

This paper addresses these issues through:

1. A brief review of national curriculum movements, with a focus on the Australian experience.
2. A survey of the left-critical interpretations which conventionally draw on political-economic frameworks.
3. A 'postmodernist' reworking of these interpretations, derived from Bernstein's theory of pedagogic discourse and his typology of pedagogic identities.
4. A development of Bernstein's theory of educational coding schema (integrated/collection codes) which positions the national curriculum movement and other reforms within a more general model of cultural dynamics of postmodernity.

The national curriculum movement: the Australian experience

The contradictory tendency to the deregulative impulse is perhaps represented most dramatically in the attempts to standardize, control and evaluate through the device of the 'national curriculum'. This has been expressed as something of an international trend, which has taken the form of various national curriculum 'movements' with distinctive local features and manifestations. The trend towards a homogenous curriculum backed up by national systems of standardized testing and monitoring represents, at least superficially, an attempt in the English-speaking democracies, particularly in the United Kingdom, to achieve a similar level of harmonization of educational policies and practices as have those which have already been established in the systems of many continental countries and Japan.

In a pragmatic sense, the various national manifestations of this trend have been driven by administrative and practical necessities, particularly arising from the disruption to schooling experienced by the increasing numbers of pupils whose families are geographically mobile. At another, more constitutional level, the pattern of the innovation and adoption suggests that a national curriculum has proven more attractive in those nations which lack a unified, or even regionally centralized, set of curricular guidelines. Thus the national curriculum option has not proven as attractive in Australia and Canada, where state and provincial education departments have historically had a much more centrally regulated and bureaucratized teaching environment than the United Kingdom, whose state system, as Green (1990) has argued, 'suffers from a pattern of underdevelopment' born of the Victorian legacy of voluntarism, localism and class division.

At an ideological level, however, these differences are subsumed as governments, whether social democratic or conservative in complexion, have in the past twenty years moved their attention successively from inputs and policies to the assessment of outputs, notably through mass standardized testing at a number of age levels of core or basic subjects, followed up by the development of national and local systems of reporting. Although resisted in systems with strong traditions of local autonomy and professional organization, the call for national testing and reporting under the name of accountability, transparency and efficiency has considerable political appeal and has taken the national curriculum movement into the wider national political arena. The Australian case is of interest in that it shares many of the features of that of the UK but exhibits as well considerable variations from this rather extreme model.

Although Australian public education has been characterized by very centralized and bureaucratic state systems which have primary constitutional responsibility, the move towards a national curriculum has rapidly advanced over the past ten years. The point of departure for this movement in Australia can be dated fairly clearly from the intervention of John Dawkins, Commonwealth Minister for Employment, Education and Training who, in 1988, sent out a proposal – *Strengthening Australian Schools*. This document set out a number of national priorities: a common curriculum framework, a common approach to assessment, strategies for improving teacher training, for raising the retention rate, for addressing equity issues in gender, ethnicity and Aboriginality, and for maximizing the efficiency of state systems. This was taken up by the Australian Education Council (AEC) which issued the Hobart Declaration on Schooling (*Common and Agreed National Goals for Schooling*, 1989) whose recommendations dominated the national scene into the 1990s. A Curriculum Corporation of Australia was set up which took on the broad headings of the Dawkins paper, including the rather quaint, if not nostalgic, goal of 'developing an appropriate handwriting style for Australian schools'.

These objectives were matched in 1991 with the development of joint Statements and Profiles for Australian schools under the AEC Curriculum and Assessment Committee (CURASS) for eight broad learning areas. These were completed in 1993 (published early in 1994) and referred to the States and Territories. There they met considerable resistance from the conservative (Liberal/National Party) governments, particularly in the area of science education. Nevertheless, each State and Territory followed through its commitment to ensuring that its curriculum content at each level through to Year 12 is consistent with the national Statements and Profiles and is currently re-writing its curriculum objectives, statements and profiles within this framework. All States and Territories have also, since the early 1990s, implemented a form of universal standardized testing in the core subjects at around Years 4 and 6, with systems of reporting.

The Statements and Profiles have exercised a particularly decisive influence on the terms of reference and funding of all professional development and training initiatives since their publication. The conservative Coalition (Howard) Government which assumed office in 1996 has pledged itself to the further implementation of these methods. This initiative was given considerable political impetus by the Federal Minister for Schools and Vocational Training, Dr David Kemp, following the release of an Australian Council of Educational Research Report (1996). Extensive publicity was given to the finding taken from longitudinal studies that almost a third of Year 9 students have not achieved basic literacy skills and that standards had not improved since the mid-1970s (Keeves and Bourke 1976). The mass testing initiative was confirmed in March 1997 in a commitment by the same Minister to put in place a national system of literacy testing (National Literacy Survey) for all students in Years 3 and 5. These would create a set of benchmarked standards by which deficiencies in the various State and Territory systems could be pinpointed.

One might ask, other than for some obvious and fairly secondary considerations of economy and efficiency, why there needs to be a national framework for education in Australia? Such an initiative, unlike those in other fields such as disabilities and equal opportunities legislation, is not driven by international treaty and convention obligations. The secular drift to federal control is not by any means inevitable. One might expect that this trend would be rejected, rather than embraced, by State and Territory governments who are not known for willingness to surrender control unless there are substantial funding returns. The individual State systems have historically operated quite effectively under State-centralized system syllabuses for well over a century. What is there then about the present *Zeitgeist* which may be impelling these trends towards uniformity, just at the time that devolution, community empowerment and market responsiveness are the dominant forms of the restructuring movement of the 1990s?

The national curriculum and testing movement in Australia, as in other English-speaking nations over the past two decades, presents a challenge to the features of the new or emerging age of fragmentation, difference and deregulation. In contrast to the deregulative logic of the market, we have new and explicit forms of homogenization, integration and centralized monitoring and surveillance. Instead of the normalization which was claimed to be wrought through the invisible pressures and seductions of the market, we have the dull visible regimes of national statements, profiles, periodic assessments, inspections, annual audits and reports. Instead of a market-driven aesthetic which positions educational systems in the wider polysemic spaces of global capitalism, we have the bloodless moral and technical rhetoric of national educational goals with a distinct national or local appeal.

Sociological responses to the national curriculum movements

The trend towards national curricula appears to support a radical political-economic critique of the contradictions of the New Right. Often this is seen as an attempt to fill the moral vacuum at the heart of revolutionary market liberalism with rather reactionary traditionalism which takes the form of national mythmaking. In some cases this nostalgia for a vanished national past may appear to provide little more than the legitimating framework for a new and dangerous form of state surveillance. It may be argued, however, that this one-dimensional critique from a basis in political economy points in the wrong direction, towards contradiction, cleavage and crisis within a national framework, rather than to an emergent global environment characterized by homology, stability and semiotic closure. The circuits of symbolic exchange at this level may be too multidimensional, intractable and indeterminate to contain the superficial incongruities of the currency of even a typically Thatcherite or New Right formation.

This tension between deregulation on the one hand and new forms of centralization on the other is the heart of the 'paradox' of contemporary educational reform noted earlier. This problem has been considered in some detail by the left-critical sociologists of education such as Whitty (1992) for the UK, Lingard *et al.* (1993) for Australia, and Apple (1993, 1996) for the USA. An approach to the paradoxes of reform from the perspective of a radical political economy raises a number of contingent and important questions. What is the driving force behind the new national curricula? Is it political economy (Fordist or post-Fordist), the imperative of reproducing class structures through cultural domination, the emerging postmodern forms of social solidarity, or could it be just a new twist to the longstanding alliance between state and ruling class?

Left-critical analysts appear to respond in a manner appropriate to their national contexts. In the Australian case, the developments over the national curriculum are seen by Bartlett (1993) as being defined by a 'code' of corporate federalism having 'metapolicy status' (Yeatman 1990). This code is 'an amalgam of neocorporatism, economic rationalism, modified human capital theory and corporate managerialism' (1993: 294). In Australia, it seems, the economic and the managerial aspects seem to dominate sociological debates about national curricula. In the case of the United States, Apple's (1993, 1996) critique is based largely in the struggles in the market place over ideas and policies, in the culture wars of authoritarian populism versus liberal activism. Although Apple exhibits a curious ambivalence towards the potential of a common core curriculum to generate equality of educational outcomes (understandable in a nation where resources and standards vary so widely by state and region), he rejects the dominant-cultural consensus and mass testing of a national curriculum as another agent of entrenched divisions along the well-documented lines of class, race and gender. Apple cites the experience of the United Kingdom, where, in the form of the National Curriculum (identified by capitals henceforth), this centralizing and authoritarian movement has had its most socially divisive effects. One of the more authoritative reviews of this experience is that of Whitty (1992), in a critical survey of the sociological debate over the National Curriculum in the UK, which followed its introduction through the Conservative (Thatcher) Government's 1988 Education Act. Whitty's analysis in fact may be taken as typical of the left-critical response in its most sophisticated form.

Although the left-critical response takes the contradictions and complexities of the reform movements as its main problematic, it is ultimately rather restrictive and unsatisfactory. On the one hand, Whitty is dismissive of the reductionist political economy of the 'correspondence principle' of Bowles and Gintis (1976), which tends to ignore the state as a creative and autonomous force, and to favour the exigencies of schooling as socialization into the hierarchical division of labour of the capitalist enterprise. He is equally critical of the version of postmodernity which celebrates 'difference' and 'heterogeneity' at the expense of the enduring patterns of 'distinction' and 'hierarchy' which are reproduced by market-oriented policies. While the National Curriculum may appear to be contradictory to these pluralizing policies, and may even have the appearances of what Dale (1989/90) and Green (1990) see as a form of 'conservative modernisation', Whitty argues that they may be actually complementary to the deregulative policies which characterize the other sections of the 1988 Act.

The National Curriculum, in the analysis of Whitty and of others such as Gamble (1983) and Dale (1989/90), is seen to celebrate a peculiar form of nostalgia for an imagined national past. This apparently provides an interim strategy which legitimates a strong state through the repressive apparatuses of law and order, while at the same time it facilitates the free play of market forces in the delivery of an increased range of cultural goods and services. The National Curriculum is therefore seen by the left as a kind of defensive or protective device which, in Dale's words, 'frees individuals for economic purposes while controlling them for social ones'. Because existing social inequalities in class, gender and race stratify access to these new cultural and educational goods, Whitty questions whether the reforms indicate a move beyond modernity towards a more pluralized, deregulated field of consumer choice. At most, he claims, these reforms suggest an 'education system of post-modern capitalism, a development of modernity rather than something distinctively post-modern' (1992: 303).

While these often finely wrought analyses acknowledge the complexities of the National Curriculum, they expose at the same time the aridity of a tradition which reduces the whole complex field of contemporary peda-gogic identities to something of a neo-conservative strategy for ensuring a weak state, a strong right-wing hegemony and an expanding area of privatization. While this analysis may define strategically necessary posi-tions (e.g. for mobilizing teacher unions and associations), its theoretical base resonates with the economic reductionism of much Marxist writing on education. Feminist critics of marketization (Kenway *et al.* 1993; Kenway and Epstein 1996; Hey 1996) stress the limitations of the conven-tional left treatment of cultural issues. Kenway and Epstein (1996: 303) point to the 'bigger material social, economic and cultural shifts associ-ated with postmodernity', particularly through the new technologies and 'hybrid and postmodern market forms which have the capacity to recast education in dramatically new ways'. Hey (1996: 352) is also critical of neo-Marxist and post-Fordist arguments for their complicity in the repro-duction of hegemonic masculinity: 'in seeking to return us to a different version of Nirvana – when men were Marxists, when schooling was equated with comprehensivisation and comprehensivisation with securing better chances for working class white boys'. In a similar vein, Dehli (1996: 354) argues that the leftist dualism of a 'good' strong state set against an 'evil' market makes it 'difficult to consider how gendered power, knowledge and subjectivity may be differently constituted in dis-courses and practices that transcend the ideologically-constructed state–market divide'. Clearly the counter-hegemonic account of the left omits a great deal in their apparent fixation with the political and economic agenda of the New Right.

The lack of sociological imagination of the left may stem from the ambivalence that many left commentators feel towards the modernist project of equality of opportunity which a national curriculum so seduc-tively simulates. It is interesting to note that Green, another writer in the same tradition, views the UK National Curriculum positively as a 'gen-uinely modernising measure' (1990: 315–16). The same ambivalence, as noted above, is expressed by Apple (1993) who claims that he is 'not opposed in principle to a national curriculum', nor 'to the idea of activity and testing'. He recognizes as well at least some of the positive egalitarian and stimulating effects ascribed to a national curriculum in the US by lib-erals such as Smith *et al.* (1990). Troyna and Vincent also point out that the National Curriculum was enthusiastically welcomed by many support-ers of multicultural education, although 'the framing and content of the NC largely ignore issues of race and gender' (1995: 153).

Despite the egalitarian appeal of a national curriculum, the negative reaction of left-sociological commentators has been overwhelming. This revulsion appears to derive in part from the political and ideological origins of the national curriculum movements (although this is denied by Apple 1993). Primarily, however, the objection is to the undemocratic, centralized methods of selection of content, of what constitutes knowledge and the reinforcement of dominant definitions of knowledge and belief in national testing. To the left critics such as Troyna and Vincent, the 'what' cannot be divorced from the 'how much' (1995: 153). Their quote from Connell (1993: 18) that: 'There is an inescapable link between distribution and content', though indisputable, reveals a tendency to marginalize the modalities of knowledge transmission and the autonomies of discursive positioning on the formation of desire, subjectivities and identities. For a less reductionist account of these paradoxes of reform we turn to consider the neo-Durkheimian analysis of Bernstein.

Pedagogic discourse, symbolic control and educational reform

Bernstein is unequivocally opposed to a content-dominated approach to the class-reproductive effects of the curriculum and even describes the theories of Bourdieu (1977, 1984), frequently cited in support of the class reproductive thesis by these critics, as 'more concerned with the *relation* to pedagogic communication, rather than with the relations *within* pedagogic communication' (1990: 167). While Bernstein too sees the distinction between distribution and content as quite superficial, his approach is formulated in completely different terms. Here it is the discursive forms and media of cultural transmission rather than the influence, direct and indirect, of powerful interests, which determine and shape the content of the curriculum. Bernstein (1990: 166) ultimately rejects these left critical theories because they

> appear to be more concerned with an analysis of what is reproduced in, and by, education than with an analysis of the medium of reproduction, the nature of the specialised discourse. It is as if the specialised discourse of education is only a voice through which others speak (class, gender, religion, race, region). It is as if pedagogic discourse is itself no more than a relay for power relations external to itself.

Bernstein's analysis points to the structural autonomy of pedagogic discourse as a field of reproductive practices. His approach, like that of many poststructuralist writers, is non-reductionist, integrative and oriented to the relations of discourse rather than to the distributive arrangements of political economy. While in no way aligned with the concern with systems of communication and signification of many postmodernists like Baudrillard (1988, 1993) who proclaim the 'death of the social', Bernstein's project points away from the primordial, willing subject of resistance theories to the interconnectedness of symbolic forms as they position actors in the regionalized and de-centred modalities of specific discourses. Though he would agree with Apple that these communicative processes have important class reproductive consequences, Bernstein sees neo-Marxist theories of class relations as inadequate or contradictory in explaining the direction of contemporary educational reforms. Bernstein concludes that class-based models are 'singularly weak' in their 'contribution to our understanding of the social grammar of this regulation' (1995: 389).

Bernstein's approach suggests that the apparent paradoxes and contradictions of homogenizing national curricula and marketized reform may therefore be explained more satisfactorily in terms of the deeper and less accessible mediations of pedagogic discourse, rather than in the convenient language of their short-term 'complementarity' in the projects of the New Right. However, the tensions between class and control, whose inner logic is increasingly remote from the contingencies of class analysis, has created particular problems for Bernstein's extension of this analysis of social reproduction.

These tensions have been most evident in the contradictions inherent in his construct of the 'market-oriented pedagogy', that version of pedagogic discourse which is expressed in the curriculum trends towards greater vocational relevance, the commercialization of their support services, and the insertion of a wider range of curriculum choice in marketized modes. This pedagogy is seen by Bernstein (1990: 87) as a 'new pedagogic Janus' which preserves visibility of outcomes but is realized through the weaker frames of an invisible pedagogy, through personalized and implicit forms of control and flexible pacing.

In the 1995 article cited above, I argued that Bernstein's initial reading of these trends which underpinned the 'restructuring' of Western educational systems in the past two decades, appeared to undervalue the potential of his more general theory of cultural transmissions. Indeed pedagogic discourse itself holds considerable promise for interpreting these trends as part of a wider cultural transformation in which education politics are embedded. Bernstein's ultimate grounding of his theory in class reproductive theory, while not reductionist in the sense of the left critique reviewed above, appeared to place conceptual restrictions on the potential of the theory to reposition educational reforms in terms of wider cultural transformation. The inner communicative logic of pedagogic discourse still needed to be 'writ large' if it were to encompass those reforms in which it was embedded. By treating these market modalities as class-embedded processes, rather than aspects of an emergent code of power embedded in a system of signs, Bernstein's original formulation of a market-oriented pedagogy seems insufficiently developed to cope with the other and often contradictory elements to be found in the restructuring movements.

These new labour-market-oriented reforms, such as the introduction of vocational and training schemes into the early years of the secondary school, rather than being devices which reproduce cheap and docile labour (what Bernstein termed 'imaginary apprenticeships'), could also be viewed as examples of what Baudrillard (1981, 1983) has termed 'simulacra' – scenic productions based on a virtualizing and self-referential system of signs. In the postmodern simulacrum as Baudrillard defines it, social reality becomes 'entirely impregnated by an aesthetic which is inseparable from its own structure' and 'confused with its own image' (1983: 150). Such formations which invert the relations of sign and signified, cannot be contained easily within the classical interpretations of state, class or party. Ironically, the New Right agendas which were driving these reforms, although imposed from outside the educational system, appeared to be driven by the same recontextualizing logic and modalities which Bernstein recognizes as the distinctive feature of the pedagogic discourse (1990: 165–218).

Pedagogic discourse and pedagogic identities

In a detailed comment on my 'Decoding school reform' paper, Bernstein (1995: 407–12) recognized the limitations of and contradictions of his original formulation of the market-oriented pedagogy. While not accepting the whole paradigmatic shift to the radical semiurgy implied in my reading of educational reform, he proposed a typology of identities for the 'new pedagogic arena' presented by contemporary cultural and social conditions. He suggested that 'these new positions (and the possible relations between them) are various strategies for dealing with contemporary cultural and economic changes as they destabilise solidarities, careers, and the formation of identity' (Bernstein, 1995: 410). These positions were subsequently developed into a fuller typology (1996: 76–80), and are repeated in Bernstein's contribution to this volume.

There are four basic 'new identity constructions' in this typology:

1. the retrospective, which are 'shaped by national, religious, or cultural grand narratives recontextualised to stabilise the past in the future', now emerging in the old Soviet Union and the Balkans;
2. the prospective (recentring) which 'are a recontextualising of a past collective base to legitimate, motivate and create appropriate attitudes towards current change' as seen in the new conservatism;
3. the de-centred market (instrumental), 'constructed out of market signifiers', and which, unlike the retrospective identity, exhibits permeable temporal boundaries (1996: 77);
4. the de-centred therapeutic, a 'truly symbolic construction', to which 'the concept of the self is crucial'. This identity 'takes the form of an open narrative which constructs internal linearity' (1996: 77). It has thus a much more stable temporal projection than does the market form.

Bernstein sees the last two in a kind of opposition where the de-centred therapeutic differs from the de-centred market in identity in substituting 'the general for the local, integration for differentiation, weak for strong knowledge boundaries – hence regions of knowledge, arenas of experience' (1995: 411). While the identities produced by the de-centred market pedagogy are 'specialized but contingent', de-centred therapeutic pedagogies produce 'integrated identities with adaptable practices' (1995: 411). Each of these would appear to have a separate function within a marketized culture.

In the reforms in the United Kingdom, particularly those surrounding the National Curriculum, Bernstein discerns elements of all of these identities, with the possible exception of the de-centred therapeutic identity which 'is projected weakly, if at all'. He opposes the discourse of secondary schooling where there is the 'overwhelming projection of retrospective identities' of the national past to the discourse of management and enterprise, where the prospective identities are projected in a market-oriented form. Because of the opposition of these two 'apparently different positions', Bernstein questions my suggestion that these developments may be reflecting the emergence of a new code which lies beneath the surface of fragmentation. Instead of the new code, he suggests that 'it is relevant to talk about a new arena of pedagogics for launching identities'. In his most recent paper (Chapter 9 in the present volume), there is a suggestion that the four positions may be underpinned by a tension between two tendencies – one governed by de-centring (market and therapeutic identities) and one by 're-centring', which is prospective in character but may involve (as with Islamic movements in the United States), a recontextualizing of a retrospective narrative.

Despite these perceptive insights, the general properties of this new arena, and in particular the generative communicative logic of the interplay between movements towards de-centring and re-centring, have not been described in Bernstein's recent writings. We appear to be left still with the surface features of modalities, identities, arenas and positions, of vaguely specified tendencies and trends. If contemporary educational politics are little more that a 'new arena of pedagogics for launching identities', then a neo-Durkheimian, not to say post-structuralist, understanding of contemporary pedagogics (as represented in Bernstein's recent writings) would appear to hang in the balance. The possibility that some more general principle of integration or structuring may lie beneath this array of pedagogic positions certainly deserves a fuller exploration.

Such an exercise would appear to be doubly imperative, since, as has been argued above, Bernstein's anatomy of pedagogic discourse provides unique insights into the constitutive properties of postmodern power itself. By analogy with Bernstein's earlier writings on regulation and communication, we might begin by asking which interchanges between these four positions are more likely to generate restriction and closure and which are more likely to generate elaboration and openness. Is a coding theory of knowledge to be jettisoned in this new era, or is the whole arena of discourse so fragmented that such a project is impossible?

Can a further extension of Bernstein's theory, derived from a more comprehensive analytical framework which captures those communicative possibilities, elude the logic of both the earlier 'Classification and Framing' paper and the pedagogic identities typology? Furthermore, could such a framework still be resonant with a Durkheimian framework of mechanical/organic solidarity which has inspired so much of Bernstein's project? Any response to these questions, if successful, promises to illuminate some of the dilemmas and 'contradictions' of the way in which the new positions are realized in the pedagogic formations of postmodern reformism.

Such a model would need to elucidate:

1. a strategy in which these new identity positions may be described in terms of their knowledge coding properties (i.e. classification and framing);
2. the generative processes, particularly those which underlie the 'contradictions' (e.g. towards de-centring and re-centring positions), whose dynamic may be stated in reformulations of the earlier terminology of classification and framing.

These questions will be approached through an analysis which tends to relocate the communicative logic of Bernstein's notion of 'symbolic control' into a framework which accords a greater autonomy to semiotic processes. Since 'symbolic control' is grounded ultimately in a system of hierarchical social relations, however disguised or transmuted, the preferred framework is one which leads from the symbolic processes of social reproduction to the highly mediated processes of pure exchange. These processes not only generate the virtual or imaginary subjects of pedagogic discourse (Bernstein 1990: 184), but also much of the national imaginary which sustains such projects as a national curriculum.

While Bernstein's writings on pedagogic discourse appear to offer a radically different framework for repositioning the cultural politics of the curriculum, their links with the market place and the inner logic of the coding of knowledge have yet to be made clear. In this culturally mediated framework, it would not be possible, on the one hand, to reduce the 'shopping mall high school' (Powell et al. 1985) to its correspondences with the political economy of the shopping mall itself. Any correspondences here would reside not so much in social and economic relations between schools and their economic environments but in the patterns of symbolic exchange which they each mediate and reproduce. As Bernstein himself has observed, while the market identity is 'dependent on the segmentation of the shopping mall, then the therapeutic is dependent upon the internal making sense of the external segmentation' (1996: 78). It is the nature of this interdependency which remains to be explored.

In the following analysis, I shall attempt to demonstrate that the constitution and effects of a national curriculum movement might be developed
in such an integrative framework. Not only does such an analysis allow for
the free play of the rich interdependencies and autonomies within the elements of pedagogic discourse, it may also hold implications for exploring
the relevance of the Durkheimian tradition in an age of postmodernity.
Within the terms of the analyses of postmodernity, it may therefore be
rather limiting to read a national curriculum movement merely as a vehi-
cle of cultural and political domination or of more efficient strategies of
flexible accumulation. Though it may achieve these effects, its generative
principles may be less susceptible to such a reductive reading. The
approach taken in this paper goes well beyond the immediate politics of
the curriculum by placing the analysis of the national curriculum movements within a much wider project which lies at the heart of Bernstein's
sociology of cultural transmissions, his theories of symbolic control and
his more recent writings on pedagogic discourse and pedagogic identities.

Educational reform and the social semiotics of postmodernity

In contrast with the political–economic analysis of cultural changes, 'postmodernists' (for want of a better term) such as Kroker and Cook (1984) and
Baudrillard (1988, 1993), see contemporary power in terms of a circulatory
system of signs rather than a distributive system of hierarchical relations. The
radical autonomy of the sign challenges the whole tradition of classical social
theory from Hobbes to Weber. It challenges the more sophisticated analyses
of class reproduction through education as formulated by the left-critical
analysis of Whitty, Apple or Bourdieu. This conception of power is particularly
appropriate for an age of globalized, virtualized electronic culture. Its logic is
grounded in paradoxes, reversals and regressions of the semiotic processes of
'postculture' (Crook *et al.* 1992) rather than in the thematics of domination
and resistance which characterize mainstream sociologies of reproduction.

Bernstein has frequently acknowledged his debt to the classical traditions of
sociology, both conflictual and functionalist (Bernstein, 1971, 1975, 1990). It
is significant, however, that the semiotic processes he describes in Volume 4 of
Class, Codes and Control, particularly in the papers 'Symbolic Control and
Social Practices' and 'The Social Construction of Pedagogic Discourse', seem
to fit a circulatory rather than distributional conception of power. Indeed it
would appear that in these papers the reproduction of class through education tends to be subordinated to the coding and modalities of knowledge.

In an age of regionalized grammars of communication, of commodified
knowledge, of global circuits of communication, it would appear, however, that
the classical conceptions of the 'social' (in terms of class, race and gender) no
longer provide foundational perspectives for his understanding of the reproduction of contemporary culture. In Bernstein's recent writings on symbolic
control, we seem to be passing through a stage of organized subjects where
education no longer depends on a knowing subject. Today, 'Knowledge, after

nearly a thousand years, is divorced from inwardness and is literally dehumanised' (1990: 155). Knowledge becomes another form of capital – 'Indeed knowledge is not just like money: it *is* money' (1990: 155). As we move towards the 'reorganized' capitalism of the twentieth century, the field of symbolic control reconstitutes the very grounds of inwardness itself and becomes important in the constitution of identities, as 'the boundaries between the field of symbolic control and the cultural field may well become blurred' (1990: 159).

In this emerging field, where semiotic processes are indistinguishable from the social fields in which they are played out, pedagogic discourse, as defined in the recent writings of Bernstein, occupies a central, if unrecognized, role in framing the 'postmodern'. Bernstein's treatment of pedagogic discourse, in producing virtual or imaginary objects, mirrors the de-subjectifying and socially corrosive forms of postmodernity and has the same potential for transforming meaning into imploded systems of signs and knowledge into digitalized and commodified forms of information. The syntagmatics of this discourse are characterized by Bernstein as recontextualizing practices which could also be seen as exemplary of the age of the culture of postmodernity, marked as this age is by a technologized media which realizes regionalized strategies of cultural reproduction. Here the local, the social and the socially 'real' are typically excluded or marginalized in the circuits of symbolic exchange in favour of their sign values governed by a self-constitutive – and as some would argue, ultimately Fascist (Kroker and Cook 1984: 29) – kind of power.

In this section we will consider: (a) whether educational reforms, including the national curriculum movements, can be adequately described in terms of Bernstein's earlier 'classification and framing' coding theory; (b) whether an alternative framework, built around the affinities between his typology of pedagogic identities and the postmodern semiotics of exchange, may provide some insights into the processes of educational reform; and (c) whether Bernstein's typology of pedagogic identities may be repositioned into this framework in order to throw some light on the 'paradox' of recent educational reforms. If the sociological analysis of political economy cannot deliver a convincing explanation of this conundrum, can Bernsteinian analysis, rooted in the Durkheimian tradition of the relative autonomy of cultural processes, do any better?

Coding pedagogic identities: classifications and frames

First, how might the national curriculum movements be explained in Bernstein's writings on pedagogic discourse and pedagogic identities? Although Bernstein has not written a great deal on this explicitly, a point of departure might be to explore the possibilities of the typology of pedagogic identities described above (Bernstein 1995: 410–11, 1996: 75–80). At the end of the previous section, we queried whether these four new positions (retrospective, prospective, de-centred market and de-centred therapeutic) were, as Bernstein claims, merely a range of separate or opposed strategies for 'launching identities'. If they are only a loose 'collection' of opposing and contradictory positions, then there is little more that could be said about their deeper communicative properties. Although Bernstein has appeared to confront the problems of his treatment of the market pedagogy which I raised in my 'Decoding School Reform' paper, the deeper problematic of the generative logic of these contradictory modalities (that is their underlying cultural dynamic), has not really been addressed. Such an exercise would be approached by first positioning Bernstein's four pedagogic types by the strength of their knowledge boundaries and associational properties.

The first stage of this experiment is suggested by Bernstein in his own description of the classification and framing properties of these new positions (1995: 411). Following the terminology of his well-known paper on these features of cultural forms (1975), the de-centred therapeutic position might first be readily described as weakly classified and framed, since it exhibits low specialization and localized, adaptable practices. At the other extreme there is the retrospective identity, with strong subject boundaries and inflexible and generalized identities, which may, by inference, be described as having both strong classification and framing properties. Occupying an intermediate position, we have the de-centred market pedagogy, similar to the 'visible market pedagogy' which Bernstein typifies in an earlier paper (1990: 87) as a 'pedagogic Janus' with its strong knowledge boundaries but contingent and personalized practices. Such a positioning would be consistent too with that of my 1995 paper, which draws on the coding description of vocational courses of Dickenson Erben (1983). This leaves us with the prospective identity, externally-oriented, managerial ideology. This type – with its acute adherence to role and mission statements, strategic planning and restructuring schedules – may be fairly accurately described as exhibiting strong framing. However, with its interventionist, innovative and often irreverent disregard for traditional disciplinary boundaries and academic identities, it may be plausibly described also as 'weakly classified' (Figure 10.1).

Classification

		Strong	Weak
Framing	Weak	De-centred market	De-centred therapeutic
	Strong	Retrospective	Prospective

Figure 10.1 A typology of pedagogic identities (based on Bernstein, 1995)

However, at the level of practice where these identities are realized, Bernstein's own coding descriptions of specific educational reforms appear to elude such a simplistic and relatively static positioning. The National Curriculum of the UK, for example, 'with its strong subject base and history and English celebrating national epics, points to an over-whelming projection of retrospective identities' (Bernstein 1995: 411). This suggests a pattern of strong classification and framing or collection code (Figure 10.1). However, the production of a national curriculum is to a large extent a de-centred market exercise and is often built on a close relationship with industrial, academic and business interests. These de-centred market identities are as well very often commodified versions of the imagined communities of nation, place and tradition. In the UK the homogenizing functions of Her Majesty's Inspectorate (HMI) have, after all, been effectively debureaucratized and deregulated through contracting out to teams of consulting agencies. Bernstein does in fact recognize this 'impurity' in his more recent comments on hybrid coding properties of the National Curriculum:

> State monitoring of this curriculum through national testing and the structures of public examinations support this collection code. Framing, on the other hand, in respect of evaluation has weakened as a consequence of the growing significance of course-work assessment and the opportunities for students to repeat their course work if their grade is not as they wish. Schools may well exploit this weak framing over evaluation as a means of monitoring their performance. (1996: 75)

A coding analysis of pedagogic positions therefore reveals the continuities of the various pedagogic types with Bernstein's earlier formulation of the theory of classification and framing of knowledge, while raising another important question about the logic of the pedagogic realizations which these various positions may generate in a complex formation like the National Curriculum. If, in Saussurean terms, Bernstein's pedagogic identities are the 'langue' of reform, we still need some greater insight into their contradictory realizations in the 'parole' of policy and practice. It is at the level of policy that these contradictions emerge. What is behind Bernstein's claim, for example, that the state has 'embedded a retrospective pedagogic culture into a prospective management culture' (1996: 75)? On analysis, all of the 'restructuring' movements of the 1990s appear to be as 'paradoxical', unstable and contradictory when examined individually as when they are juxtaposed one against the other. A national history curriculum, for example, appears as an unstable, kaleidescopic and anomalous pattern of many points of closure and openness. The rather static and homogeneous categories of the coding principles may not be able to produce an adequate account of these internal contradictions.

What seem to be generated in the case of national curricula, as with so many other formations of the 'restructuring' movements of the 1990s, are *simultaneous* communication flows *across* the boundaries of collection and integration. These seem to be more obviously and naturally grouped along the twin axes of spatiality (centredness/de-centredness and temporality (prospectivity/retrospectivity) than of the coding oppositions of the earlier classification and framing typology, or even of their 'hybrid' variants like the market-oriented pedagogy. Elements of mechanical solidarity, in other words, seem to coexist with elements of organic solidarity in complex formations which defy conventional sociological analysis and critique.

The tensions between extremes of pluralization and of homogenizaton which characterize the ensemble of the educational reforms of the 1990s, thus seem also to be repeated within each of these movements themselves. It is this very dynamism and instability of the cluster of recent reforms, both within and between their various formations, which makes them so difficult to interpret. Their hybrid mix of communitarian rhetoric, elitist appeals to 'excellence' and economistic demands for greater 'accountability' seems to render them intractable to conventional sociological analysis. Is it any wonder that teachers and administrators continually wonder whether the next political demand will, on the one hand, project them back to an era of autarchic schools and diffused power – or on the other hand, flip them towards an overdetermined world of Orwellian surveillance?

What we need to work towards then is a revision of the Bernsteinian model of educational transmissions, situated within the Durkheimian tradition of solidarity types but which also: (a) allows for complex interchanges among the four main positions of Bernstein's pedagogic identities and (b) provides some insights into the cultural and communicative dynamics which generate the paradoxical and anomalous properties of contemporary educational reform.

Postmodernity, symbolic exchange and the division of labour

Bernstein's major sociological contribution has been to show us the enduring relevance of Durkheim's typology of mechanical and organic solidarity of the *Division of Labour* (1893) to the descriptions of a modern curriculum and its socially reproductive effects. However, given the volatile system of interdependencies which characterize the postmodern formations of educational reform movements, might it not be profitable to explore the communicative syntax by which the more dynamic field of restructuring reform is being played out? In this enterprise we would be attempting not merely to recover the positions of Durkheim's famous typology as Bernstein appears to have done in his recent typology of educational identities. Rather we need to explore the cultural dynamic of the transactions *between* elements of both mechanical and of organic solidarity as they co-exist in the complex simultaneities of contemporary policy formations. Here we will be making a case for the relevance of another and often-neglected branch of the Durkheimian tradition, that of Talcott Parsons and his followers.

A theoretical strategy for detaching the interpretation of these positions might be to pursue the suggestion of Kroker and Cook (1984: 239) that Parsons, particularly in his later writings (1969), offers a neglected framework for re-orienting classical and modernist conceptions of a perspectival power (grounded on class, gender, the state) to a postmodern and disembodied formulation (grounded in symbols, knowledge, communication structures). These authors claim:

> For Parsons, the secret of the 'power network' is that power circulates now (always immanent to but never localised in) through the societal community (or, inversely 'the disciplinary society') like a language, and much like those other languages that are disenchanted symbols – money, intelligence, health, influence and value-commitments. Power has its own grammatical-syntactical structure, its own specific codes (authority) and its own 'symbols of effectiveness'. Thus, those who would search for the historical originary of power will be disappointed; for power operates now, not in the name of representation, but always as a *symbol of effectiveness*. In a description that is remarkably convergent with Foucault's insight into the relational character of power relationships, Parsons also posits that the power network is a circulatory medium, and one that is relational and combinatorial in character. (emphasis in original)

Drawing such correspondences between Foucault and Parsons may seem bizarre and grating, given the greatly differing ontological and epistemological assumptions of each of these figures in the sociological pantheon. How can one compare Parsons' macro-realist and value-based analytics of society as an equilibrating system with the micro-political, de-centred and discourse-oriented formulations of Foucault? While we may allow Foucault's post-structuralist accounts into the broad canon of 'postmodern' thought, how can the same claim be made for Parsons'?

Kroker and Cook nevertheless claim that, in his later writings, Parsons (1969) moved away from representational theories of systemic functions, and concentrated instead on the mediational properties of the symbolic flows by which order is constituted. This radical revision of his project yielded a view of function as constituted through its symbolic processes through which control, information and communication media are in a dynamic inter-relationship. Just as Durkheim in his later period moved away from the mechanistic, functional imperatives of order to the problems of symbolic representation, so it appears that Parsons too shifted his focus to the problematic of communication and generalized symbolic media for an understanding of relational properties of power, meaning and control.

According to Kroker and Cook, this re-orientation brings Parsons' later project much more in line with Baudrillard's theory of the 'simulacra and simulations' (1981, 1983) where free-floating signs circulate as self-constituting codes of pure semiotic exchange. In this sense then, it is possible to see Parsons' fascination with the logic of symbolic exchange in its virtualized and non-representational forms and patterns, and consistent in this reading with Baudrillard's proclamation of the 'end of the social' through its implosion into the mass media (1988: 207–19). This point is particularly relevant in view of the affinities between the analysis of pedagogic forms as a particularly important form of virtualization and the constitution of postmodern power. While Bernstein is certainly not a Parsonian (nor a functionalist in the American sense), one nevertheless may take up this insight by Kroker and Cook by considering these four pedagogic positions as nodes in a circulatory medium of symbolic exchange within the Parsonian four function framework or 'paradigm'.

This insight suggests a matching of each of Bernstein's positions (Figure 10.1) against the analytical subsystem of Parsons' functional paradigm of systems of action (Parsons 1953, Rocher 1974). Parsons, it will be recalled, identified the four functions of any system in terms of (1) adaptation (associated with economy), (2) goal attainment (polity), (3) integration (societal community) and (4) latency or pattern maintenance (socialization). While the first two relate to the external relations of the system, the latter two have internal reference only. He also makes a further distinction between the instrumental functions (adaptation and latency) and the 'consummatory' (goal attainment and integration). In his later writings, Parsons (1969: 311–473) develops a theory of the interchanges between each of these functional subsystems and all the others – adaptation communicates through money, goal attainment through power, integration through influence and latency through commitments.

Without doing too much violence to Bernstein's typology, it appears possible to align market pedagogies with the function of adaptation, prospective pedagogic identities with goal attainment (management), therapeutic positions with integration and retrospective identities with latency or pattern management (Figure 10.2). This repositioning appears to generate a considerable gain in insight into the possible mediational and combinatorial properties of the interchanges among Bernstein's four contemporary pedagogic identities. Not only do the four positions appear to acquire a good deal of depth, generality and resonance within this established functional paradigm, but their configuration is slightly, though significantly different from the structuralist one of Figure 10.1.

	Instrumental	Consummatory
External	De-centred market *(Adaption)*	Prospective *(Goal Attainment)*
Internal	*Retrospective (Pattern Maintenance)*	*De-centred therapeutic (Integration)*

Figure 10.2 Bernstein's pedagogic identities repositioned in parsons' functional paradigm of systems of action

It appears that the polarities of Bernstein's collection/integration code type (i.e. from strong classification and frames to weak classification and frames) are now realized, in Parsonian terms, as a horizontal link rather than as a central, integrating diagonal (or emergent, centralizing axis) as suggested by Figure 10.1. The pattern of oppositions of Figure 10.2 therefore moves the centre of gravity of Bernstein's typology of pedagogic positions away from the axes of classification and framing and suggests alternative models and combinatorial possibilities. In this Parsonian framework, it would appear that Bernstein's collection/integration code typology falls within the inter-changes between 'implication' (integration) and 'significance' (latency). While Bernstein's knowledge codes successfully map the internal patterning of knowledge systems, they are not (in Parsonian terms at least), devised to include the external subsystems of economy and polity as constitutive com-ponents of their communication flow, preferring to leave these to the struc-turalist problematic of 'relative autonomy'. Is it possible that Bernstein has tended to marginalize these other communication possibilities from a more comprehensive and dynamic model of communication processes? If this is so, what other communicative possibilities are suggested by this repositioning?

Bernstein's focus on the internal systems of exchange is an enormous source of theoretical strength, particularly in light of the reductionist tendencies of left political economy critiques. However, this discursive orientation may also bring with it a neglect of the radical possibilities of an integrative theory of communication which could embrace the more dynamic aspects of symbolic processes. The full development of the theory of codes would seem, therefore, to depend on a confrontation with the complexities and dynamics of postmodern cultural politics, as illustrated in the surface contradictions of the constitution of a national curriculum.

From symbolic exchange to simulation: a neo-Durkheimian model

Some of the more interesting developments of Parsons' later writings are found in the work of his followers, particularly in the Festschrift, *Explorations in General Theory in Social Science* (Loubser *et al.* 1976, Vols 1 and 2). Baum's contribution to the project (1976: 522–57) is set out in the form of a model of generalized media in action, which demonstrates the importance of the diagonal interchanges which flow across rather than around the subsystems of the four-function paradigm. Baum claims that 'Compared with the vertical (G-function) and horizontal (A-function) interchanges, the diago-nals have a special 'integrative status', because controlling flows of output and input here have to cross the double cleavage of both the instrumental-consummatory and the external-internal boundaries'.

Baum then goes on to identify the kinds of information flow which are generated by interchanges across these subsystems. The flows between latency and goal attainment are characterized in terms of 'stabilisation through generalisation', while those across the adaptation/integration divide are characterized in terms of 'complexification through specification' (1976: 548). The relationships which govern these cross-paradigm interchanges are in principle equilibrating: 'The effects and functions performed for the system are precisely opposite, viz. complexification in A-I and stabilisation in L-G'. It is significant, in terms of continuities with Bernstein's theories, that Baum discerns in this pattern of interchange a restatement of the tensions in modernity in Durkheim's early writings. As Baum observes, this formulation establishes a 'tie between stabilisation and Parsons' analysis of Durkheim's mechanical solidarity on the one hand and between complexification and organic solidarity on the other' (1976: 549).

In conditions of high turbulence, the tensions between these two opposing tendencies will become quite intense and the overall state of the system of exchange quite 'unstable'. It is not surprising perhaps that this analysis seems to resonate with those of postmodernists who, like Baudrillard, are working in the Durkheimian tradition of social pathology. Under the extreme conditions of moral ambiguity, and the proliferating technical and legal innovations which accompany the excesses of consumerism, the contradictions at the heart of the functional model of regulation take on an unexpected centrality and importance. Gane (1995: 109–23) captures the Durkheimian roots of Baudrillard's sense of the cultural dynamic of postmodernity in terms of a similar condition of endless paradox and anomaly: 'It is as if the complex contrary movement combines both of Durkheim's drives beyond all thresholds *at the same time:* greater totalitarian control (and fatalism) especially of the individual over him/herself on the one side, and deregulation beyond all norms (anomie) into the system itself (anomaly)' (118). This opposition has also been well discussed in the contradictory movement of the division of labour in postmodernity. Here we note too a stabilizing trend towards 'de-differentiation' on the one hand (Lash 1990), combined with a complexifying trend to 'hyperdifferentiation' (Crook *et al.* 1992: 68–74) on the other.

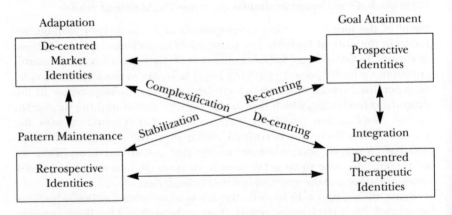

Figure 10.3 Process of pedagogic communication in postmodernity: a generalized model (based on Bernstein, 1997 and Baum, 1976, after Parsons, 1969)

This patterning suggests that 'complexification' appears to be deeply implicated in the spatializing, de-centring dynamics of organic solidarity, while
'stabilization' appears to be grounded in the temporal (past *vs.* future),
though in a simulated or highly mediated form. The cultural media of the
interchanges involved in complexification (through specialization) therefore are now positioned in paradigmatic terms, while those of stabilization
(through generalization) may appear as the syntagmatic axis.

This deeper resolution also appears entirely consistent, as it turns out,
with Bernstein's own formulation of the field of pedagogic discourse of
reproduction (Figure 5.6, 1990: 197), where the flows of 'organisation/
space/specialised contexts and agencies' are contrasted with those of
'communication/time/selection/transmission/evaluation). Figure 10.3
positions Bernstein's typology of contemporary pedagogic identities into
this more dynamic field of cross-paradigm interchanges. Here we see
emerging the two axes of the fundamental Durkheimian opposition
between mechanical and organic solidarity, only this time they shift from
an evolutionary framework towards a more dynamic and generalized
system of simultaneous oppositions. While, in Figure 10.1, the defining
axis flowed from the strongly classified and framed retrospective position
(mechanical solidarity) to the weakly classified and framed de-centred
therapeutic (organic solidarity), here there are two axes: one of organic
solidarity which joins both de-centred pedagogies, and the other of
mechanical solidarity which links the prospective and the retrospective
positions. This latter axis would appear to capture a counter tendency
towards stabilization through what Bernstein has called 're-centring'
which, as we have seen, involves an interplay between these two positions.

What are the connections between the contradictions at the heart of
this functional model and the semiotic reversals and paradoxes of postmodernity? Can the Durkheimian order of symbolic representation be
transformed into the semiological problematic of simulation? The conceptual framework of functionalism – whether Durkheimian or Parsonian
– does not appear to help very much here. This is because these are largely
concerned with the regulative functions of symbolic exchange, in its broad-
est sense, rather than with the underlying modalities of communication. It
is all very well to speak of 'paradox' and 'anomaly' but much more difficult
to explicate these conditions in terms of precise descriptions of the forms
by which these are generated. The logic of the Durkheimian problematic
as set out in Figure 10.3 suggests that the cultural processes must be trans-
lated into modalities of communication before the generative dynamics of
the postmodern simulacrum can be properly described.

It is in this connection that Bernstein's theory of educational and
cultural transmissions, as set out in the third volume of *Class, Codes and
Control*, appears to hold out most promise, since the thematic of the
papers was to translate the Durkheimian types of solidarity into the coding
of communicative processes in late modernity. Can Bernstein's reshaping
of the Durkheimian types to the knowledge forms of late modernity there-

fore throw any light on the deeper logic whereby a functional model of
the processes of symbolic exchange mutate towards the ironic and fatal
regressions of postmodernity?

Bernstein's theory of educational transmissions explores the interplay
between mechanical and organic types of solidarity within his own typology of codes of 'collection' and 'integration'. This typology was most
definitively set out in the 'Classification and Framing' paper (1975).
While these knowledge or curriculum codes parallel a transition from
mechanical to organic solidarity, each nevertheless contains elements of
both Durkheimian types. Bernstein (1975: 110) sees this interplay in the
form of a 'paradox' at the heart of the regulative principles found in conditions of advanced organic solidarity:

> Yet the covert structure of mechanical solidarity of collection codes creates
> through its specialized outputs *organic* solidarity. On the other hand, the overt
> structure of organic solidarity of integrated codes creates through its less spe-
> cialized outputs *mechanical solidarity*. And it will do this to the extent to which its
> ideology is explicit, elaborated, and closed *and* effectively and *implicitly* transmit-
> ted through its low insulations. (emphasis in original)

Bernstein's point is that, in the conditions of high differentiation which
typify late modernity, we often observe the 'deep ideological closure of
mechanical solidarity' as an emergent feature of integrated codes. This
can create, through an internal communicative structure of elaboration,
an external effect of restriction and closure. This novel insight into the
Durkheimian paradoxes of modalities of symbolic control, when positioned in the Parsonian paradigm, suggests a precise mechanism whereby
the cultural dynamics of contemporary educational reform may be
expressed.

The contradictions of educational reform may then appear as nothing
more than a specific aspect of a more general communicative process in
which some form of this paradox is constitutive and even normal. In the
'excessive' conditions of postmodernity, we might only expect this phenomenon to become more general and less tractable, to the point of generating indeterminate and unstable processes which feed off their
'hyper-differentiating' dynamic. As an aside, we may point to the postmodern phenomenon of 'political correctness' as a kind of confirmatory
example of the way in which everyday life can become suffused with the
semiotic closures of the language games which generate volatile and
polarizing effects, political and social. At the heart of these tensions of regulation, the unexpected reappearance of mechanical solidarity, albeit in a
transmuted and highly mediated form, therefore provides an important
theoretical link between the Durkheimian typology of solidarity to the
semiotic anomalies of postmodernity.

Under the critically destabilizing conditions of postmodernity, therefore, the 'retrospective' aspects of a national curriculum, for example,

may be seen to provide a form of closure typical of mechanical solidarity through the condensed symbolic system of an imagined (or virtualized) community of the nation. While the 'overt' weak insulations of official culture may exhibit the features of openness in the recognition of a widening spectrum of 'difference' (e.g. in the negotiation of therapeutic and multicultural strategies), they are, at a deeper level, regulated by the aesthetic of a national imaginary whose logic is grounded in the ideological closures of mechanical solidarity. The simulacrum of a nostalgic past thus provides the syncretic, de-differentiating framework for this process, as well as for its attendant repressive apparatus of testing, surveillance and discursive shaming for those schools or teachers who do not (or cannot) comply. The de-centring tendencies towards fragmentation and deregulation, which are often seen as the dominant principle of postmodernity (Lyotard 1984; Giroux 1991), are thereby stabilized and refocused. The cultural dynamics of the interchanges among the positions of pedagogic discourse are now constituted by and through the simulacrum of the nation state, projected in terms of a spatialized and (ultimately) dehistoricized past, open to perpetual reconstruction and remodelling, like an exhibit in a theme park.

The overall control of this project becomes a highly centralized state function which confers a huge ideological power to frame the 'official knowledge' which had previously been the domain of the specialized practitioners (Apple 1993; Bernstein 1997). Conversely, the corporatized, marketized regime of the 'self-managing' school amplifies the complexification of the routine regulative and financial functions that were so recently the domain of central bureaucracies. Though this is hardly an original empirical observation of contemporary trends in educational policy, the logic of this involution can only be discovered through an analysis of the cultural dynamic which is realized through the semiotic processes of postmodernity.

The case study of the national curricula movements does, however, suggest more general insights into the modalities of postmodern power. Might the paradoxes of symbolic exchange of late modernity as anatomized by Bernstein be central to the generation of the 'fatal strategies' of postmodernity? Might the roots of semiurgy be found in the ironies of such a neo-Durkheimian formulation? Clearly there is a great deal more to be done by way of exploring these processes, perhaps with the assistance of the recent insights of chaos and catastrophe theories (Brown 1995). These explorations might build on Thompson's (1976) application of catastrophe theory to the shift from collection to integrated codes, or on Tyler's (1984) use of information theory and canonical analysis to the classification and framing of organizational structures. These models might also draw on Baudrillard's (1993) metaphoric use of the terminology of chaos theory ('fractals' 'strange attractors') to describe eliptical processes of postmodernity. Bernstein's analysis of the paradoxes of late modernity and the processes of pedagogic discourse provide at least a well-developed base for exploring these cultural dynamics and for charting the conditions whereby the symbolic core of mechanical solidarity is transmuted into a semiotically-sustained order of aestheticized representation. The ironies which underpin this transformation cannot be overstated, even if they are not now well understood. Without a theory of these dynamics, however, it would seem that sociological analysis is condemned to reproduce their effects.

Conclusion

It has been argued here that centralizing and homogenizing movements like a national curriculum cannot be dismissed as transitional to a new era of unrestrained market forces, nor are they merely a temporary tactic of élites to neutralize previous 'excesses' of teacher autonomy. Rather, they appear in this analysis to be constitutive of the dynamics of the cultural field in which the restructuring reforms of the 1990s occurred. These dynamics are typical of the cultural and communicative processes of postmodernity. This is a formula for perpetual contradiction, involution and paradox, rather than for either the equilibrated resolution of moral or regulative crises of functionalist theory or for an emancipation built on the resistant and counter-hegemonic practices of left critical theories.

This logic seems also to describe the cultural processes through which many educational reforms have progressed during the past decade. Through explicating the relatively stable set of contemporary cultural positions as set out in Bernstein's typology of pedagogic identities, this analysis has exposed a rather unstable set of oppositions, forming and reforming in patterns of constant interplay and tension, whose underlying dimensions are consistent with Durkheim's original types of solidarity. The complexity of this field of communicative processes, in which these formations are embedded, indicates just how misleading it may be to read these patterns at a surface rather than at a generative or relational level. These deceptive, intricate and complex formations deserve much more detailed study in their own right, since they represent deeper structural insights into the ways in which social reproduction may be ultimately effected. While this analysis privileges the modality of curriculum over content and the dynamics of regulation over an ill-defined process of class hegemony, it may seem to support a formalist, even a conservative position. However, it is only by appreciating the relational and mediational constitution of postmodern formations like the national curricula that their logic can be understood and their effects resisted. This framework, drawn from the Durkheimian tradition which Bernstein has creatively reshaped, confronts these movements in their own terms of their internal symbolic processes.

This methodology also has the advantage of deconstructing their semiotic processes whose effects are rendered all the more subtle and insidious by being situated within the normalizing devices of a culture which is already highly dependent on the recontextualizing principle of pedagogic discourse. In light of the similarities between pedagogic discourse and the flows of postmodern power, it seems that the current political mood to re-constitute schools as factories, shopping malls or welfare agencies may conceal an unrecognized version of the distinctive discourse of education itself. Educational institutions, by this ellipsis, would appear to be particularly vulnerable to the intrusions by the invisible device by which they have themselves been discursively constituted. These ironic possibilities appear to be beyond the scope of conventional critical analyses, which appear to be locked into repeating the same representational illusions and perspectives which drive the cultural logic of educational 'restructuring' itself. Bernstein's reading of pedagogic discourse alone provides the conceptual tools for avoiding this representational fallacy. It holds, by implication, the potential to generate deeper insights into the constitution of the dynamics of the symbolic processes in which educational politics themselves are embedded.

By making explicit the principles of symbolic exchange, and ultimately of simulation, which connect the rather loosely-formulated typology of pedagogic identities, it would appear that we may now have the basis for a powerful, flexible and integrated framework for generating descriptions of other realizations of pedagogic discourse. Along the way we have rediscovered the enduring relevance of both streams of the Durkheimian tradition (functionalist, structuralist/poststructuralist and socio-semiotic) which have flowed together in Bernstein's project. While Bernstein's early functionalist interest in social solidarity and the division of labour provided its original formulations of closure and openness, the later structuralist concern with the symbolic constitution of order has informed his structuralist and post-structuralist writings on the coding of symbolic control and of cultural transmissions.

I have attempted to demonstrate here how the differing perspectives of the 'two Durkheims', as mediated by Bernstein's theories of codes, discourse and identities, may be reconciled with readings of the dynamics of postmodern culture. Here, in the contemporary educational reform movements like a national curriculum, the original types of solidarity may be seen as intertwined in the play of signifiers whose logic repeats the Durkheimian model of regulation in an endless loop of anomaly and paradox. While this framework owes a good deal to Baudrillard's reading of Durkheim and to Kroker and Cook's rather unorthodox reading of Parsons, it points to the continuing vitality of the Durkheimian tradition and provides a fruitful model for the deeper exploration of the contradictions of national curricula and related movements, as they are constituted by and in the involuted cultural dynamics of postmodernity.

References

Apple, M. (1993) 'The politics of official knowledge: does a national curriculum make sense?' *Teachers College Record*, 95(2), 222–41.
Apple, M. (1996) *Cultural Politics and Education*. New York: Teachers College Press.
Australian Council for Educational Research (1996) *Literacy: The Longitudinal Surveys of the Australian Youth Program*. Public Statement. Melbourne: ACER.
Australian Education Council (State, Territory and Commonwealth Ministers of Education) (1989) *The Hobart Declaration on Schooling*. Canberra: Australian

Government Publishing Service.

Australian Education Council, Curriculum and Assessment Committee (CURASS) (1994) *A Statement on English for Australian Schools.* Carlton, Vic.: Curriculum Corporation.

Ball, S.J. (1993) 'Education markets, choice and social class: the market as a class strategy in the UK and the USA'. *British Journal of Sociology of Education,* 14(1), 3–19.

Bartlett, L. (1993) '"Nothing but the facts, sir": curriculum reform as a function of corporate federalism'. In B. Lingard, J. Knight and P. Porter (eds), *Schooling Reform in Hard Times.* London: Falmer.

Baudrillard, J. (1981, 1983) *Simulacres et Simulations.* Paris: Editions Galilee. Trans. P. Beitchmann, *Simulations,* New York: Semiotexte.

Baudrillard, J. (1988) *Selected Writings* (ed. and introduced by M. Poster). Stanford: Stanford University Press.

Baudrillard, J. (1993) *The Transparency of Evil: Essays on Extreme Phenomena,* trans. J. Benedict. London: Verso.

Baum, R.C. (1976), 'Communication and media', in J.J. Loubser, R.C. Baum, A. Effrat and V.M. Lidz (eds), *Explorations in General Theory in Social Science: Essays in Honor of Talcott Parsons, Vol. 2,* New York: Free Press.

Bernstein, B. (1971) *Class, Codes and Control, Vol. 1: Theoretical Studies Towards a Sociology of Language.* London: Routledge and Kegan Paul.

Bernstein, B. (1975) *Class, Codes and Control, Vol. 3: Towards a Theory of Educational Transmissions* (2nd edn). London: Routledge and Kegan Paul.

Bernstein, B. (1990) *Class, Codes and Control, Vol. 4: The Structuring of Pedagogic Discourse.* London: Routledge.

Bernstein, B. (1995) 'A response'. In A. Sadovnik (ed.), *Knowledge and Pedagogy: The Sociology of Basil Bernstein.* Norwood, NJ: Ablex.

Bernstein, B. (1996) *Pedagogy, Symbolic Control and Identity: Theory, Research, Critique.* London: Taylor & Francis.

Bernstein, B. (1999) 'Official knowledge and pedagogic identities'. In this volume.

Bourdieu, P. (1984) *Distinction: A Social Critique of Taste,* trans. R. Nice London: Routledge and Kegan Paul.

Bourdieu, P. and Passeron, J.-C. (1977) *Reproduction in Education, Society and Culture,* trans. R. Nice. Beverly Hills: Sage.

Bowles, S. and Gintis, H. (1976) *Schooling in Capitalist America.* London: Routledge and Kegan Paul.

Brown, C. (1995) *Chaos and Catastrophe Theories.* London: Sage.

Connell, R.W. (1993) *Schools and Social Justice.* Philadelphia: Temple University Press.

Crook, S., Waters, M. and Pakulski, J. (1992) *Postmodernisation: Change in Advanced Society.* London: Sage.

Dale, R. (1989/90) 'The Thatcherite project in education', *Critical Social Policy,* 9(3), 4–19.

Dawkins, J. (1988) *Strengthening Australia's Schools: A Consideration of the Focus and Content of Schooling.* Canberra: Australian Government Publishing Service.

Dehli, K. (1996) 'Between "market" and "state"? Engendering education change in the 1990s', *Discourse,* 17(3), 363–76.

Dickenson, H. and Erben, M. (1983) 'The "technicisation" of morality and culture'. In D. Gleeson (ed.), *Youth Training and the Search for Work.* London: Routledge and Kegan Paul.

Dunn, R. (1991), 'Postmodernism: populism, mass culture and avant-garde', *Theory, Culture and Society,* 8, 111–35.

Durkheim, E. (1893, 1964) *The Division of Labour in Society,* trans. with an introduction by George Simpson. New York: Macmillan.

Gamble, A. (1983) 'Thatcherism and conservative politics'. In S. Hall and M. Jacques (eds), *The Politics of Thatcherism.* London: Lawrence and Wishart.

Gane, M. (1995) 'Radical theory: Baudrillard and vulnerability', *Theory, Culture and*

Society, 12, 109–23.

Giroux, H. (ed.) (1991) *Postmodernism, Feminism, and Cultural Politics: Redrawing Educational Boundaries*. Albany: SUNY Press.

Green, A. (1990) *Education and State Formation*. London: Macmillan.

Hey, V. (1996) "'A game of two halves'": a critique of some complicities between hegemonic and counter-hegemonic discourses concerning marketisation and education', *Discourse*, 17(3), 351–62.

Keeves, J.P. and Bourke, S.F. (1976) *Literacy and Numeracy in Australian Schools: A First Report*. Australian Studies in School Performance, Vol. I. ERDC, Report No. 8. Canberra: Australian Government Publishing Service.

Kenway, J. (ed.) (1995) *Marketing Education: Some Critical Issues*. Victoria: University of Deakin Press.

Kenway, J., Bigum, C. and Fitzclarence, L. (1993) 'Marketing education in the post-modern age', *Journal of Education Policy*, 8(2), 105–23.

Kenway, J. and Epstein, D. (1996) 'Introduction: the marketisation of school education: feminist studies and perspectives', *Discourse* (Special Issue on Feminist Perspectives on the Marketisation of Education), 17(3), 301–14.

Kroker, A. and Cook, D. (1984) *The Postmodern Scene: Excremental Culture and Hyper-Aesthetics*. New York: St. Martin's Press.

Lash, S. (1990) *The Sociology of Postmodernism*. London: Routledg.

Lingard, B., Knight, J. and Porter, P. (eds) (1993) *Schooling Reform in Hard Times*. London: Falmer.

Loubser, J.J., Baum, R.C., Effrat, A., Lidz, V.M. (eds) (1976) 'Explorations in the general theory of social action: essays in honour of Talcott Parsons' (2 vols). New York: Free Press.

Lyotard, J. F. (1984) *The Postmodern Condition*. Minneapolis: University of Mineapolis Press.

Marginson, S. (1992) 'The market in schooling: issues in theory and policy'. Paper for the Australian College of Education Seminar, Canberra.

Meadmore, D. and Symes, C. (1997) 'Keeping up appearances: uniform policy for school diversity?' *British Journal of Educational Studies*, 45(2), 174–86.

Parsons, T. (1953) 'Some comments on the state of general theory of action', *American Sociological Review*, 18(6), 618–31.

Parsons, T. (1969) *Politics and Political Structure*. New York: Free Press.

Powell, A.G., Farrar, E. and Cohen, D.K. (1985) *The Shopping Mall High School: Winners and Losers in the Educational Marketplace*. Boston: Houghton Mifflin.

Rocher, G. (1974) *Talcott Parsons and American Sociology*. London: Nelson.

Smith, M.S., O'Day, J. and Cohen, D.K. (1990) 'National curriculum, American style: what might it look like?' *American Educator*, 14 (Winter), 10–17, 40–7.

Thompson, M. (1976) 'Class, caste, the curriculum cycle and the cusp catastrophe', *Studies in Higher Education*, 1(1), 31–45.

Troyna, B. and Vincent, C. (1995) 'The discourses of social justice in education', *Discourse*, 16(2), 149–66.

Tyler, W. (1984) Organisations, factors and codes: a methodological enquiry into Bernstein's theory of educational transmissions. Unpublished PhD thesis, University of Kent at Canterbury. Published in *Collected Original Research in Education (CORE)* (1989), 13(2), Fiche 3, G4.

Tyler, W. (1995) 'Decoding school reform: Bernstein's market-oriented pedagogy and postmodern power'. In A. Sadovnik (ed.), *Knowledge and Pedagogy: The Sociology of Basil Bernstein*. Norwood, NJ: Ablex.

Whitty, G. (1992) 'Education, economy and national culture'. In R. Bocock and K. Thompson (eds), *Social and Cultural Forms of Modernity*. Cambridge: Polity Press/Open University Press.

Yeatman, A. (1990) *Bureaucrats, Technocrats, Femocrats: Essays on the Contemporary Australian State*. Sydney: Allen and Unwin.

Index

Figure numbers are shown in italics at the end of entries.